First and Second Chronicles

INTERPRETATION
A Bible Commentary for Teaching and Preaching

INTERPRETATION
A BIBLE COMMENTARY FOR TEACHING AND PREACHING

James Luther Mays, *Editor*
Patrick D. Miller, *Old Testament Editor*
Paul J. Achtemeier, *New Testament Editor*

STEVEN S. TUELL

First and Second Chronicles

INTERPRETATION

A Bible Commentary
for Teaching and Preaching

John Knox Press
LOUISVILLE

Scripture quotations from the New Revised Standard Version of the Bible are copyright © 1989 by the Division of Christian Education of the National Council of the Churches of Christ in the U.S.A. and are used by permission.

Comments on Psalms adapted from "Praising God" and "Responding to God," by Steven Tuell, in *Adult Bible Studies Teacher,* June–August 1996, are © 1996 by Cokesbury. Adapted by permission.

Library of Congress Cataloging-in-Publication Data

A catalog record for this book is available from the Library of Congress.
ISBN 0-8042-3110-9

© copyright Steven S. Tuell 2001
This book is printed on acid-free paper that meets the American National Standards Institute Z39.48 standard. ♾
01 02 03 04 05 06 07 08 09 10 — 10 9 8 7 6 5 4 3 2 1
Printed in the United States of America
John Knox Press
Louisville, Kentucky

SERIES PREFACE

This series of commentaries offers an interpretation of the books of the Bible. It is designed to meet the need of students, teachers, ministers, and priests for a contemporary expository commentary. These volumes will not replace the historical critical commentary or homiletical aids to preaching. The purpose of this series is rather to provide a third kind of resource, a commentary which presents the integrated result of historical and theological work with the biblical text.

An interpretation in the full sense of the term involves a text, an interpreter, and someone for whom the interpretation is made. Here, the text is what stands written in the Bible in its full identity as literature from the time of "the prophets and apostles," the literature which is read to inform, inspire, and guide the life of faith. The interpreters are scholars who seek to create an interpretation which is both faithful to the text and useful to the church. The series is written for those who teach, preach, and study the Bible in the community of faith.

The comment generally takes the form of expository essays. It is planned and written in the light of the needs and questions which arise in the use of the Bible as Holy Scripture. The insights and results of contemporary scholarly research are used for the sake of the exposition. The commentators write as exegetes and theologians. The task which they undertake is both to deal with what the texts say and to discern their meaning for faith and life. The exposition is the unified work of one interpreter.

The text on which the comment is based is the Revised Standard Version of the Bible and, since its appearance, the New Revised Standard Version. The general availability of these translations makes the printing of a text in the commentary unnecessary. The commentators have also had other current versions in view as they worked and refer to their readings where it is helpful. The text is divided into sections appropriate to the particular book; comment deals with passages as a whole, rather than proceeding word by word, or verse by verse.

Writers have planned their volumes in light of the requirements set by the exposition of the book assigned to them. Biblical books differ in character, content, and arrangement. They also differ in the way they have been and are used in the liturgy, thought, and devotion of the church. The distinctiveness and use of particular books have been taken into account in decisions about the approach, emphasis, and use of

v

space in the commentaries. The goal has been to allow writers to develop the format which provides for the best presentation of their interpretation.

The result, writers and editors hope, is a commentary which both explains and applies, an interpretation which deals with both the meaning and the significance of biblical texts. Each commentary reflects, of course, the writer's own approach and perception of the church and world. It could and should not be otherwise. Every interpretation of any kind is individual in that sense; it is one reading of the text. But all who work at the interpretation of Scripture in the church need the help and stimulation of a colleague's reading and understanding of the text. If these volumes serve and encourage interpretation in that way, their preparation and publication will realize their purpose.

The Editors

ACKNOWLEDGMENTS

Professors James Luther Mays and Patrick Miller gave me the opportunity to write for this fine series, and provided guidance and help throughout the project. I am grateful for their time and expertise. I thank Dr. John Trotti and the staff of the William Smith Morton Library of Union Theological Seminary and Presbyterian School of Christian Education in Richmond, Virginia, for the use of a study room in the building to carry out my early, intensive research, and for access to the many resources of this phenomenal library.

Randolph-Macon College gave me sabbatical leave to complete this book, as well as access to printing and copying resources. Thanks are owed to the Randolph-Macon Honors Council, especially to Rob Licht and Jennifer West, for inviting me to reflect on my sabbatical work with the students in the honors program; to Professor Joe Beatty, who invited me to present my work on Chronicles to interested Randolph-Macon faculty as a part of the Philosophy Department's Faculty Research Exchange; and to my department chair, Professor Betty Jean Seymour, for her unfailing support and encouragement.

Several churches gave me the opportunity to preach or teach from Chronicles, so that I could tell if my exegesis translated into exposition. Special thanks are owed to the congregations and pastors of these churches: Central United Methodist Church in Florence, South Carolina, and pastors Jim Pietila and Gerry Lord; Cherry Hill United Methodist Church in South Boston, Virginia, and pastor Robert Lewis; Woodlake United Methodist Church in Midlothian, Virginia, and pastor Dennis Perry; the congregation at the Stonewall Jackson Arts and Crafts Jubilee in Weston, West Virginia, and Kenneth Parker, who is responsible for the music and the worship services at this wonderful folk festival; my home church, Duncan Memorial United Methodist in Ashland, Virginia, and my good friends and pastors, Larry Buxton and Dwight Zavitz. I am especially indebted to Larry, to Dwight, and to my friend Dr. Frank Reding, who read portions of the work in progress and offered their prayers and advice.

My family has supported me with their love and prayers, and with exceptional patience. My deepest thanks, love, and appreciation go to my sons, Sean, Anthony, and Mark. I dedicate this book to Wendy, my beloved wife and friend, who patiently proofread this volume, and whose love enriches everything that I do.

CONTENTS

1 CHRONICLES

2 CHRONICLES

INTERPRETATION

Introduction

The Content and Character of Chronicles

Chronicles is not a popular book. Despite its length (sixty-four chapters in all) and its breathtaking scope, spanning all of Israel's story from the creation of the world to the reconstruction following the Babylonian exile, few sermons or Bible studies touch on Chronicles. Indeed, not a single reading from Chronicles is found in the common lectionary. Perhaps this is not so surprising. To many readers, Chronicles seems little more than a dull rewrite of Samuel and Kings, biased in favor of David and his descendants. What benefit can be found in working over such barren ground?

This negative assessment is reflected in the title given to Chronicles in the Greek translation of the Hebrew Bible, the Septuagint (commonly abbreviated as LXX). There, Chronicles is called *Paraleipomena*, meaning "things left out" or even "left over." This title expresses a still common impression of Chronicles—that it is a kind of appendix to Scripture, a work of mediocre value both historically and theologically that offers little to the ordinary layperson or pastor. Compared to the rich banquet available in books such as Isaiah, Genesis, or the Psalms, Chronicles may indeed look like "leftovers"!

A very different assessment is to be found in other ancient sources. The Mishnah, an important collection of Jewish law and tradition, lists Chronicles as one of the books to be read by the high priest on the night before Yom Kippur, so that he will keep awake (Yoma 1:6)—showing that the rabbis considered Chronicles not only important reading, but stimulating reading as well! In fact, the great Christian scholar Jerome, translator of the Bible into Latin, said that we find in Chronicles "the meaning of the whole of sacred history."

An outline of Chronicles confirms that Jerome's proposal concerning this book's content and character was correct. Chronicles opens with a series of genealogical lists (1 Chr. 1—9), which present us with the entire sweep of God's dealings with humanity. These lists literally begin at the beginning: the first word in the book is "Adam," the name of the first human. The latest names in the genealogies appear to be contemporaries of the scribes responsible for giving us this text in its final form. In 1 Chronicles 3:17–24, the text of our Hebrew Bible (also called the Masoretic Text, or MT) traces the line of David's descendants through

1

seven generations—from Jeconiah (also called Jehoiachin; he went into exile in Babylon in 597 B.C.) to Anani, who was probably born in 445 B.C.—around the time that Nehemiah began his mission. Anani was probably still alive when the Chronicler's History (as 1 and 2 Chronicles, Ezra, and Nehemiah together are often called; for the relationship of these books to one another, see below) was completed around 400 B.C. Intriguingly, the LXX translation of 1 Chronicles 3:17–24 divides the names in these verses into *eleven* generations, which would take us up to around 250 B.C.: within striking distance of the second century B.C., when the LXX text of Chronicles was prepared. The individual or group that produced the book of Chronicles (usually referred to, for convenience' sake, as the Chronicler) attempts to present a record from the dawn of time to the "present day." Later generations of scribes and translators continued with this intention.

The interest in David's line as the connection between Israel's past and the Chronicler's present continues throughout the book. In Chronicles, the first person who is said to reign in Israel is David (1 Chr. 3:4). The Chronicler's history of the monarchy begins with Saul's death in battle at Mount Gilboa (1 Chr. 10:1–14), thus passing over Saul with scarcely a mention. David is the subject of the remainder of 1 Chronicles (11—29). Then, 2 Chronicles 1—9 details the reign of Solomon. The remainder of the book (2 Chr. 10—36) traces the Davidic monarchy of the southern kingdom of Judah, from the division of the kingdoms following Solomon's death down to the destruction of Jerusalem by Babylon. In sharp contrast to the parallel history in Samuel–Kings, Chronicles pays little attention to the northern kingdom of Israel. The Chronicler's interest is focused on David and his line.

But more broadly, the Chronicler is interested in the whole sweep of God's plan and purpose for Israel, and in Scripture as the means by which that plan and purpose are revealed. David and his line are important for the vital role they play in the texts the Chronicler studies and interprets, but his primary interest is in the *text*, not in kingship for its own sake.

The Place of Chronicles in the Hebrew Bible

Chronicles was originally a single book. The division of the book into 1 and 2 Chronicles was first made by the Greek translators of the LXX, and is of course followed in Christian Bibles. However, it was not until the fifteenth century A.D. that Hebrew Bibles began presenting Chronicles in two parts. This commentary will treat Chronicles as a single book, with a single, sustained story line.

In Christian Bibles, 1 and 2 Chronicles are placed after 1 and 2

Kings and before Ezra and Nehemiah. This arrangement, based upon the pattern of the LXX, has the effect of placing all the so-called "historical" books together. But the books are arranged quite differently in the Hebrew Bible. In Jewish tradition, the Bible is divided into three parts: first the *Torah*, or Law (also called the Five Books of Moses, or the Pentateuch); then the *Nebi'im*, or Prophets; and finally the *Kethuvim*, or Writings. In the Hebrew Bible, the books of Joshua, Judges, 1 and 2 Samuel, and 1 and 2 Kings are found in the Prophets. Together, these historical books serve as an introduction to Isaiah, Jeremiah, Ezekiel, and twelve shorter books called simply the Book of the Twelve, or the Minor Prophets.

On the other hand, both Chronicles and Ezra–Nehemiah (also a single book in the Hebrew) are found at the end of the canon, in the Writings. A few ancient texts place Chronicles at the beginning of the Writings, just before Psalms—a placement perhaps suggested by the tremendous importance of the temple and its worship in both books. Most texts, however, following the authoritative ruling of rabbis from the great Jewish scholarly community in Babylon, place Chronicles at the end of the Writings, after Ezra–Nehemiah. This makes Chronicles the last book of the Hebrew Bible.

For first-century Christian and Jewish communities, Scripture was understood to extend from Genesis to Chronicles (Braun 1998, 342). This is shown in the Gospels, when Jesus condemns the shedding of innocent blood "from the blood of righteous Abel to the blood of Zechariah son of Barachiah, whom you murdered between the sanctuary and the altar" (Matt. 23:35//Luke 11:51). The story of Abel, the victim of the first murder, is of course found in Genesis 4:1–16; the account of Zechariah's murder is found in 2 Chronicles 24:20–22. Chronicles, then, was regarded as the last book of Scripture—an appropriate placement for a work that attempts to distill and summarize the entire history of God's dealings with God's people.

Chronicles and the Deuteronomistic History

Chronicles is dependent in large measure on the earlier history of Israel found in Joshua, Judges, 1 and 2 Samuel and 1 and 2 Kings—often called the Deuteronomistic History because of its close relationship, in style and theme, with the book of Deuteronomy. While it is perhaps possible that both the Chronicler and the Deuteronomistic Historian made independent use of some other source since lost to us, this appears unlikely. The parallels between Chronicles and the Deuteronomistic History are so close that it is possible to arrange Chronicles and Samuel–Kings in parallel columns, rather like the three

3

Synoptic Gospels in the New Testament. The best and simplest explanation for this "synoptic" feature is, in the case of Chronicles as in the case of the Gospels, the literary dependence of the one text upon the other.

Consider, too, that some elements in the Chronicles account can only be understood with reference to Samuel–Kings. For example, 1 Chronicles 10:11–12 (which parallels 1 Sam. 31:11–13) concerns the people of Jabesh-gilead who cared for Saul's corpse. The Chronicles version, however, is incomplete. Chronicles jumps into the account of Saul's death without preamble. The author assumes that the reader knows not only who Saul is, but why the people of Jabesh-gilead took such risks to show respect to his corpse (see 1 Sam. 11:1–13). The point of the story is that this loyalty to Saul prompts David to bless the people of Jabesh-gilead, and call upon them to support his kingship as they had supported Saul's (2 Sam. 2:4b–7; see Klein 1992, 996). However, this conclusion to the story is not found in Chronicles. The best explanation, surely, is that the Chronicles account is based on Samuel–Kings.

At one time, a great deal of exegetical weight was given to subtle and not-so-subtle distinctions between the language of Chronicles and that of Samuel–Kings. Discoveries among the so-called Dead Sea Scrolls from Qumran, however, now show that many such differences owe themselves to a different Hebrew text of Samuel–Kings used by the Chronicler, rather than to changes the Chronicler made to the text of those books that we have. The Hebrew text upon which our Old Testament is based, the MT, was probably passed down in Babylon. Scholars have long realized that the MT of 1 and 2 Samuel is poorly preserved, containing numerous scribal errors. The LXX translators in Egypt appear to have had access to a better Hebrew text of Samuel than the MT. Now, the Dead Sea materials have given us access to fragments of another "local text" of Samuel (witnessed particularly in a fragmentary text called 4QSam^a), preserved and passed down in Palestine. This Palestinian text type appears to be related to the oldest and best LXX texts. Quite probably, it was this Palestinian text type that was used as a source by the Chronicler. We need to be cautious, then, about reading too much into apparent divergences in wording between Samuel–Kings and Chronicles, until we are certain that the divergences involve a deliberate shift in meaning, and not a textual variant.

The Chronicler uses the material from Samuel–Kings very selectively. For example, in Chronicles' depiction of David's reign virtually the entire Court History (2 Sam. 11—1 Kgs. 2), with its sordid accounts of such scandals as Bathsheba's seduction, Uriah's murder, and Absalom's rebellion, is skipped. Often, this has been taken to mean that the

4

Chronicler is trying to clean up his presentation of David, including only positive and complimentary material. Notice, however, that the Chronicler also ignores the positive statements about David's childhood and coming to power in 1 Samuel 16—30, and includes derogatory information: David's census (1 Chr. 21:1–27//2 Sam. 24:1–25), and the rejection of his request to build the temple, on the grounds that he has "shed so much blood" (1 Chr. 22:8). Far from attempting to ignore David's story in Samuel and Kings, or to replace it with a whitewashed account, the Chronicler assumes that the reader is familiar with that earlier history. The Chronicler does not try to cover up the crimes and peccadilloes of David's family. He is simply not interested in them.

As we will see, what *does* interest the Chronicler is the temple and its worship. David as the founder of the temple's liturgy, and Solomon as the temple's builder, are therefore of primary importance. Later kings are praised or blamed for their actions regarding the temple: hence, the special attention given to Hezekiah (2 Chr. 29—32) and Josiah (2 Chr. 34—35). The Davidic kings are important for their roles in establishing and preserving the temple, but it is the temple and its liturgy that primarily concern the Chronicler.

The Chronicler's Use of Other Scriptures

Although the Chronicler's most obvious, and most used, source is the books of Samuel and Kings, Chronicles draws extensively from the whole of Hebrew Scripture. The Chronicler's genealogies draw upon Genesis, Exodus, and Numbers (from the Law), as well as Joshua (from the Prophets) and Ruth (from the Writings). Scripture quotes abound in Chronicles. For example, Psalm 105:1–15 is quoted in 1 Chronicles 16:8–22, together with Psalm 96 (compare 1 Chr. 16:23–33) and the first and last verses of Psalm 106 (compare 1 Chr. 16:34–36). Consider, too, the Chronicler's allusions to or quotes from prophetic books such as Jeremiah (compare 2 Chr. 36:21 with Jer. 17:21–27; 25:11–12; 29:10) and Zechariah (2 Chr. 16:9 quotes from Zech. 4:10).

Not only does Chronicles quote and allude to earlier biblical texts, the Chronicler also thinks biblically, using the whole story of Israel to structure his account. For example, three of the great festivals that punctuate the Chronicler's history refer back to progressively earlier stages in Israel's tradition (Blenkinsopp 1998, 54). In the first of these accounts, regarding the Passover celebrated by King Hezekiah, we read: "There was great joy in Jerusalem, for since the time of Solomon son of King David of Israel there had been nothing like this in Jerusalem" (2 Chr. 30:26). Later, in 35:18, the celebration of the Passover following Josiah's reforms prompts the writer to look still further back: "No passover like it had been kept in Israel since the days of the prophet Samuel." Finally, to describe the Festival of Booths celebrated following the reading of Ezra's law, the Chronicler must look all the way back to the time of Joshua for a comparable feast (Neh. 8:17; the connection between Ezra–Nehemiah and Chronicles will be discussed below). In this way, each stage of Israel's history is understood in terms of more and more ancient tradition. The present builds upon the foundation laid in Israel's past. Note, too, that in all three accounts explicit reference is made to Scripture: specifically, to the law of Moses, which provided the proper directions for these celebrations (2 Chr. 30:16; 35:6, 12; Neh. 8:14).

In short, the Chronicler draws upon the entire range of Hebrew Scripture to relate the story of God's dealings with God's people. Indeed, what we might call an emerging Bible piety is the hallmark of Chronicles. In the Chronicler's devotional world, God's will is revealed through meditation upon texts. In Chronicles, as we will see, prophets write books, and kings are guided by the word of God in Mosaic Torah. In Ezra–Nehemiah, it is through inspired interpreters of texts, such as the scribe Ezra, that God's will is made known.

The Literary Genre of Chronicles

Over the last century, assessments of the Chronicler's History *as* history have ranged broadly. Some scholars have viewed the Chronicler's additions to the source material from Samuel–Kings as pure fabrication. Others have held that the Chronicler did have access to genuine historical sources either not available to, or not used by, the Deuteronomist, and that the Chronicler is a reliable witness to history.

Evidence is not lacking for either extreme. The exaggerated numbers in Chronicles would seem to argue against the accuracy of its reporting. For example, in 2 Chronicles 14:8, Asa is said to stand off an invasion of one million Ethiopians with an army of 580,000! Attempts have been made to shore up the accuracy of such numbers by the claim that the Hebrew word *'eleph*, usually translated as "thousand," refers to a military unit from a tribal subsection, rather than a literal thousand. However, such exaggerated numbers are not restricted to military contexts. Consider 1 Chronicles 22:14, where David is said to have amassed one hundred thousand talents of gold and one million talents of silver for the Jerusalem temple.

Of course, contemporary ideals of accuracy and objectivity in historical research were not the standards of history in the ancient world. Early Greek historical writings from the fifth century B.C. onward show features similar to Chronicles, including genealogies, speeches from wise advisors, and exaggerated numbers. From this, one could conclude

6

that Chronicles is a history, conforming to ancient standards of histori-ography (Hoglund 1997, 19–29). Further, the Chronicler plainly had access to sources that provided accurate historical information. For example, the material regarding Hezekiah's reign unique to Chronicles has proven historically accurate, so far as it can be tested. Second Chronicles 32:30 records that Hezekiah built "an outlet of the waters of Gihon." A tunnel 1,550 feet long, which enables access to the waters of the Gihon spring from within Jerusalem itself, is still accessible today. An inscription found in this tunnel, the famous Siloam Inscription, can be reliably dated to the eighth century, supporting the Chronicler's ascription of the tunnel to Hezekiah (so most recently Hendel 1996, 233–37). Similarly, the description of Hezekiah's economic buildup in preparation for Sennacherib's invasion is supported by archaeological investigation, particularly by the distribution of clay jars impressed with Hezekiah's royal seal, which show "that Hezekiah established store-houses throughout the kingdom of Judah" (Vaughn 1999, 172).

Still, the Chronicler's History shows in various places such cheer-ful disregard for chronology that it is difficult to think of this work as a history in any sense. Consider the use of names contemporaneous with Solomon, taken from 1 Kings 4:31, to fill out the genealogy of Judah's son Zerah (1 Chr. 2:6), or the treatment of Ezra and Nehemiah as con-temporaries (Neh. 8:9; 12:26). Where the Chronicler's sources were faithful witnesses to historical events, Chronicles is historically reliable. However, Chronicles is not itself a history.

The most distinctive feature of Chronicles is the large degree to which it reproduces other biblical texts, particularly the narrative in Samuel–Kings. A type of literature discovered among the so-called Dead Sea Scrolls of Qumran appears very similar to Chronicles in com-position. This genre, sometimes called "rewritten Bible," involves "a narrative that follows Scripture but includes a substantial amount of supplements and interpretive developments" (Geza Vermes, quoted by Alexander 1988, 99). Examples from Qumran include the Book of Jubilees and the Genesis Apocryphon. However, the best-known exam-ple of the rewritten Bible genre is the famous work by the Jewish his-torian Josephus, *The Antiquities of the Jews*, which retells the history of the people of Israel from the Hebrew Bible. Arguably, the Chronicler was the inventor of the rewritten Bible. In Chronicles, as in other exam-ples of this genre, the original text is followed closely and faithfully. However, it is also expanded with additional material, and revised in ways that aim to unify the tradition on a biblical foundation.   7

Simply put, Chronicles is a Bible study—an extended meditation on the Hebrew Scriptures, which seeks to draw from the texts meaning and direction for the community in the Chronicler's own time. The Chronicler, then, is engaged in the same enterprise that we pursue when we come to Scripture, as teachers, as preachers, or simply as pilgrims in search of guidance and strength.

The Date and Composition of Chronicles

Although this commentary will primarily concern itself with Chronicles in its biblical context, the historical context of this work cannot be ignored. Understanding the composition history of Chronicles will help us to understand the theological focus of this work, and guide us through some of its more puzzling features.

The Relationship between Chronicles and Ezra–Nehemiah

Since 1832, when Leopold Zunz first proposed that Chronicles and Ezra–Nehemiah together constitute a connected Chronicler's History, most scholars have held that these works were produced by the same author or group of authors. But in recent years the common authorship of Chronicles and Ezra–Nehemiah has been called into question, due to major differences alleged in the language and theology of Ezra–Nehemiah and Chronicles (so especially Japhet 1993, 4–5). Although contemporary investigations have shown the linguistic arguments to be inconclusive either way (see Throntveit 1982, 215), the alleged theological differences between Chronicles and Ezra–Nehemiah remain persuasive to many scholars. Perhaps the four most important of these theological distinctions are as follows: (1) the emphasis on David and the Davidic covenant in Chronicles is lacking in Ezra–Nehemiah; (2) the Exodus traditions prominent in Ezra–Nehemiah are lacking in Chronicles; (3) Ezra–Nehemiah's rejection of foreign marriages is difficult to reconcile with Chronicles' tolerance of Solomon's Egyptian wife; and (4) immediate retribution from God for wrongdoing, which Throntveit calls the "theological lodestone" of Chronicles, is absent in Ezra–Nehemiah (Throntveit 1992, 9).

Some of these distinctions can be explained by the different eras described in these two texts. It is little wonder that kingship should figure prominently in Chronicles, which describes the time of the monarchy. Nor is it any wonder that Exodus themes are stressed in Ezra–Nehemiah, which describes the return from exile and the early Judean restoration—a time filled with typological parallels to the exodus from Egypt and the journey to the promised land. Other distinctions could be explained by the use of source material, particularly the autobiographies of Ezra and Nehemiah, which do not follow the Chronicler's theological ideals (Blenkinsopp 1988, 49). Still, the differences between Chronicles and Ezra–Nehemiah have been sufficient to persuade many scholars that these are two separate works.

8

Perhaps the most significant bit of evidence *for* a close relationship between Chronicles and Ezra–Nehemiah is the book of 1 Esdras, from the LXX. The Greek text of 1 Esdras parallels 2 Chronicles 35:1 through Ezra 10:44, then concludes with Nehemiah 8:1–13, ending abruptly in the middle of a verse. 1 Esdras, then, may be a fragment of an original Chronicler's History (Cross 1975, 191). Opponents of a unified Chronicler's History argue instead that 1 Esdras is a compilation from Chronicles and Ezra–Nehemiah, and can be read as a coherent work in its own right (see Williamson 1996, 213–15; van der Kooij 1991, 45–47). Still, 1 Esdras draws our attention to the natural flow from 2 Chronicles 36 into the opening chapters of Ezra.

When read in isolation from Ezra–Nehemiah, the book of Chronicles ends abruptly. Jerusalem is destroyed, its survivors are taken into exile in Babylon, and the duration of the exile is set "until the establishment of the kingdom of Persia" (2 Chr. 36:20), a period also described as Jeremiah's seventy years (2 Chr. 36:21; see Jer. 25:11–12; 29:10). Nothing is said of why Persia will be important. Nor are we told what becomes of the exiles or, more importantly, of the fate of the temple. The exiles are invited by Cyrus to "go up" to Jerusalem and rebuild the temple (2 Chr. 36:22–23), but the reader is left not knowing if anyone actually went!

Given the focus upon the temple that runs through the entire text of Chronicles, the rebuilding of the temple and the renewal of its liturgy described in the opening chapters of Ezra seem a natural continuation of the Chronicler's narrative. This renewal of right worship is followed by the celebration of Passover (Ezra 6:19–22): a pattern familiar to the student of Chronicles, where cult renewals carried out by Hezekiah (2 Chr. 30) and Josiah (2 Chr. 35:1–19) also culminate in Passover celebrations (see Gelston 1996, 54). The reading of the law during the Festival of Booths (Neh. 8) also fits this pattern, suggesting once again a unified Chronicler's History.

At the very least, the existence of 1 Esdras reveals that Chronicles and Ezra–Nehemiah were read together. A literary connection between these two works is evident as well in the closing verses of Chronicles (2 Chr. 36:22–23) and the opening verses of Ezra (1:1–3a), which are virtually identical. In those texts of the Hebrew Bible that end with Ezra–Nehemiah followed by Chronicles, these words stand like brackets around the two books, suggesting that they are intended to be read together, whether they share a common compositional history or not.

The assumption of this commentary is that Chronicles and Ezra–Nehemiah should be read together as a single, intentional narrative. Although the commentary itself is concerned solely with Chronicles, this judgment has great bearing on the dating of Chronicles, as well as, more importantly, on the theme and purpose of Chronicles.

Dating the Chronicler's History

The external evidence demonstrates that Chronicles had been written and widely circulated by the second century B.C. The LXX book Paraleipomena (the Greek version of Chronicles) is cited by Eupolemus (around 150 B.C.). Ben Sirach (from around 190 B.C.) presupposes Chronicles' view of David appointing the temple singers (Sir. 47:8–10). Finally, Daniel (around 164 B.C.) is probably dependent on Chronicles for its ideas about the exile of Jehoiakim (compare Dan. 1:1–2 with 2 Chr. 36:5–7). The internal evidence for the dating of Chronicles enables us to move the probable date of composition back to the late fifth century B.C. The genealogical lists that open Chronicles, as we have seen, go from Adam to Anani, a descendant of David who was born around 445 B.C. If we include Ezra–Nehemiah as a part of the Chronicler's History, the last name mentioned would be the high priest Jaddua (probably Jaddua II), who was born around 420 B.C. (Neh. 12:11) and so may have been a contemporary of Anani.

This date is in agreement with other evidence from the book of Chronicles alone. The explicit reference to the Persians in 2 Chronicles 36:20 makes it clear that Chronicles dates from the Persian period. The quotes from the Torah (likely brought into its final form early in the Persian period) and from the postexilic prophet Zechariah (2 Chr. 16:9//Zech. 4:10) also point to this time. Finally, the late form of Hebrew in which Chronicles is written, and such anachronisms as 1 Chronicles 29:7 (where contributions to David's temple fund are paid in darics, coinage of the Persian period in the reign of Darius) and 2 Chronicles 3:3 (where Solomon's temple is said to have been built according to "the old standard" of measurement—that is, before Persian standards were implemented) confirm a Persian period date.

However, the emphasis on David and on temple-building in Chronicles is difficult to reconcile with a date as late as 400 B.C. By that time, the second temple was finished and functioning, and the Davidic line no longer played any significant role in government. An original date early in the Persian period, when the rebuilding of the temple and the dignity of David's line were still issues of vital concern, would more likely explain these concerns in Chronicles (Freedman 1961, 439–40). Perhaps the best way to make sense of all the evidence is to propose that the Chronicler's History was not composed all at one time, but rather was written in stages (following the proposal of Cross 1975, 194–98).

The Composition of the Chronicler's History

If 1 Esdras is a fragment of an earlier edition of the Chronicler's History, that earlier edition was significantly different from the text before us. In that edition, the memoirs of Nehemiah were not included—indeed, Nehemiah was not mentioned at all (compare Neh. 8:9 with 1 Esd. 9:49–50). On the other hand, that edition did include a wisdom tale praising Zerubbabel, the governor of Judah at the time of the temple's rebuilding (1 Esd. 3—4)—a story not found in the version of the Chronicler's History that we have.

The emphasis upon the temple and the Davidic line in Chronicles, together with the high regard for Zerubbabel in 1 Esdras, suggests that the earliest form of the Chronicler's History may have been written soon after the founding of the second temple under Zerubbabel, in around 520 B.C. The book of Haggai, which dates to that time, also holds an exalted view of Zerubbabel, who is called the Lord's signet ring (Hag. 2:23). However, Haggai's contemporary Zechariah found it necessary to defend Zerubbabel against his detractors: though Zerubbabel had no kingly might or power, he had nonetheless been empowered by God's spirit to rebuild the temple (Zech. 4:6). Those scoffers who "despised the day of small things" (Zech. 4:10) would realize their error, and join in the general rejoicing, when they saw Zerubbabel finish the task that he had begun.

All of this suggests that the Chronicler's History was originally intended, like the prophecies of Haggai and Zechariah, to legitimate both the second temple and the Davidic descendant charged with its rebuilding. This original text would have included an earlier version of 1 Chronicles 10:1—2 Chronicles 34:33, plus the Hebrew original for 1 Esdras 1:1—5:65 (the equivalent of our 2 Chr. 35:1—Ezra 3:13, with some differences in organization), and would have been completed around 520 B.C. Later, when the temple was completed and Ezra had returned with the Law (around 450 B.C.), the history would have been expanded up through the end of our present book of Ezra, plus the account of the Law's reading and the celebration of the Festival of Booths in our Nehemiah 8 (the likely extent of the original Hebrew text from which the Greek 1 Esdras was translated). Particularly given the interest in Scripture evidenced by the Chronicler, the reading of the law by Ezra in Nehemiah 8 would have provided a fitting climax for this second edition of the Chronicler's History. It would have been at this stage that the more exclusivist ideas associated with Ezra, such as the abhorrence of foreign marriages, entered the text, without being reflected in the earlier material.

Later still, likely around 400 B.C., the addition of the genealogies at

11

the beginning and the memoirs of Nehemiah at the end would have brought the Chronicler's History to a close. The inclusion of Nehemiah's memoirs would have made sense to the Chronicler's community on several grounds. First, continuing the Chronicler's emphasis on the temple, Nehemiah reformed and purified the temple, insuring the continuity of the Levitical singers and gatekeepers established by David (Neh. 11:23; 12:24, 36, 45–46; 13:10–13) and expelling Tobiah the Ammonite from the temple precincts (Neh. 13:4–9). Second, Nehemiah's enforcement of sabbath regulations (Neh. 13:15–22) is in keeping with the Chronicler's concern for the Torah (and for sabbath in particular; see especially 2 Chr. 36:21). Third, Nehemiah's work on Jerusalem's fortifications parallels the work by Judah's kings, recorded already by the Chronicler. Finally, the inclusion of Nehemiah's memoirs would have brought the history up to the Chronicler's own time, just as the inclusion of the genealogical prologue summed up the scope of sacred history, from Adam to the present day.

In the final form of the text, Nehemiah's memoirs have been woven into the Ezra story, with casual disregard for chronology (so, in Neh. 8, both are present for the reading of the Law). Similarly, in the earlier edition of the Chronicler's History, correspondence regarding the rebuilding of Jerusalem from the time of Artaxerxes I (465–424 B.C.) was used to set the stage for Zerubbabel's return (1 Esd. 2:16–30; 4:42–57; compare Ezra 4:7–24). Note, too, that in the final form of the History, the account of Zerubbabel's wisdom (1 Esd. 3—4) has vanished, and his role has been downplayed—doubtless because, after the high hopes evidenced in Haggai, Zechariah, and 1 Esdras, Zerubbabel had proven to be a disappointment.

As the canon was brought into its final form, Chronicles was separated from Ezra–Nehemiah and moved to the end of the Writings. There, the genealogies which open Chronicles, beginning with Adam, provided a neat reference back to Genesis, the first book of the Law. Genesis and Chronicles thus bracketed the entire Hebrew Bible, with Chronicles standing as a fitting summary of the whole of Scripture. In order to maintain the original connection between Chronicles and Ezra–Nehemiah, a copy of the opening words of Ezra was placed at the end of Chronicles, bringing about the form of the book that we have before us.

The Theological Perspective of Chronicles

12

The doctrine of immediate retribution is often held to be the heart of the Chronicler's theology. However, Chronicles is far more subtly nuanced than is generally recognized. The rebellion of the northern kingdom, for example, is described as a fulfillment of the prophecy of Ahijah the Shilonite, which blamed Solomon for the breakup of David's united kingdom (2 Chr. 9:29; 10:15; see 1 Kgs. 11:29–39). Yet, it was not Solomon, but Rehoboam who was faced with the collapse. The good king Abijah, about whom the Chronicler has nothing but good to say, died after reigning only three years (2 Chr. 13:2), while the consequences of Jehoshaphat's ill-considered alliance with Israel reverberated through the next three generations (2 Chr. 21—23). Indeed, the exile itself appears as the end result of all Judah's faithlessness, not just the immediate result of Zedekiah's sin (2 Chr. 36:14–16; so Johnstone 1998, 122–23). In short, it is simply not the case that Chronicles adheres, rigidly and mechanistically, to a doctrine of immediate retribution.

A better approach to the Chronicler's theology would be through his attitude toward Scripture. In the text of Chronicles, "the word of the Lord" refers always either to prophetic revelation (for example, 1 Chr. 11:3; 2 Chr. 36:21) or to the word of Scripture, specifically the law of Moses (1 Chr. 15:15; 2 Chr. 34:21; 35:6). Indeed, this may be an artificial distinction, since in the Chronicler's view prophets write books (for example, Samuel, Nathan, and Gad in 1 Chr. 29:29; Iddo in 2 Chr. 13:22; Isaiah in 2 Chr. 26:22), and so may be seen as composers of Scripture. Significantly, the plan for the temple and its worship is also revealed to David as a written text (1 Chr. 28:19). The purpose of life is to seek God, in the words of Scripture and in the worship of the temple. Only those who seek God can find God's will and purpose for their lives, and living accordingly, experience blessing. To ignore God's word is to ignore God, and cut oneself off from blessing. This idea is expressed by David to Solomon in David's second farewell speech, in what could be called the "golden text" of Chronicles: "If you seek him, he will be found by you; but if you forsake him, he will abandon you forever" (1 Chr. 28:9; see also 2 Chr. 15:2).

We have already identified an emerging Bible piety as the hallmark of Chronicles. The Chronicler comes to the texts of Scripture as we do, for direction and inspiration. In Chronicles, the word of the Lord comes increasingly not from inspired individuals, but from the codified tradition of Israel in Scripture.

With this shift from ecstatic revelation to Bible piety comes another shift: the Chronicler begins to draw us out of the fabulous world of "Bible times," and into a world much like our own. In the Chronicler's History, God's presence and activity are manifest in the events of ordinary life. Contrast, for instance, the stone-and-mortar reality of Solomon's temple building, or Nehemiah's wall-building, with the mythopoeic expressions of God's activity in Exodus, or even in Second

13

Isaiah's new exodus. This pattern extends on into texts later than Chronicles. So Ecclesiastes and Job wrestle with a world of apparent randomness, in which God's place and presence are unclear. In Esther, God is not mentioned at all—not because God is absent, but because, rather than breaking into the order of things, God is present behind the scenes. The emergence of apocalypse, which might seem to run counter to this view, is indeed the exception that proves the rule. The powerful mythic and symbolic language of apocalypses such as Daniel derives precisely from the projection of the radically interventionist God into the distant heavens, and onto the future. In this present age, for the apocalyptist, God does not act directly, as God once did and one day will again.

The Chronicler, then, stands at an important cusp in the history of Israelite religion. More and more in the Second Temple period, a time which would ultimately see the emergence both of Judaism and Christianity, God would be assumed to be working in the realm of ordinary life, not via extraordinary revelation. More and more, texts and their interpretation would take precedence over ecstatic experience as the means of discerning God's will. The Chronicler, with his emphasis upon Scripture, points the way to that future. As Jerome claimed concerning Chronicles, here we find "the meaning of the whole of sacred history." This commentary will take Jerome's ancient insight as an organizing principle and theme.

1 Chronicles

The Genealogies

The Chronicler's history begins with a complex series of genealogies and lists, drawn from numerous sources. Some of these sources we can identify and locate, especially in the Torah and the Deuteronomistic History; others are unknown to us. To further complicate the picture, the various lists are not always consistent with one another. In large measure, the Chronicler has presented this material to us as is, with few if any internal modifications to make each piece fit.

It may help a Christian reader, tempted to despair at this welter of ancient ancestors and family gossip, to recall that the New Testament begins in much the same way (Matt. 1:1–17)! Indeed, the purposes of Matthew's genealogy and the Chronicler's are in many ways similar. Like the Chronicler, Matthew wants to establish from the start a connection between the ancient wellsprings of Israel's faith and the experience of his own community. Each, too, has a particular interest in the line of David as the sign of God's faithfulness to Israel.

In both genealogies, there are surprises. For Matthew, the line that leads to Jesus passes through Tamar's deception of Judah (Matt. 1:3; see Gen. 38:1–30) and David's acts of adultery and murder (Matt. 1:6; see 2 Sam. 11:1–27; note that Matthew refers to Bathsheba as "the wife of Uriah"). Similarly, the Chronicler notes that David's family tree has strange branches—leading, through Abraham's son Ishmael, to the Arabs (bitter enemies of Judah in the latest portion of the Chronicler's history; see Neh. 2:19; 4:7; 6:1–6), and through Jacob's son Esau, to the Edomites (who, after the fall of Jerusalem, took advantage of Judah's weakness to seize land and goods; see for example Ps. 137:7; Jer 49:7–22). The messy particularity of the genealogy, in Matthew as in Chronicles, serves as a reminder of God's consistent, persistent presence—even where that presence was not noted or sought, or even desired.

The genealogies in Chronicles have a definite structure, which demonstrates the Chronicler's purpose. 1 Chronicles 1:1—2:2 traces the line from Adam to Israel's twelve sons, the ancestors of the twelve tribes. Then, 5:1—9:44 lists the genealogies of the tribes, apart from

17

Judah. The royal tribe of Judah is placed at the center of the Chronicler's genealogies, in 2:3—4:23. The Davidic line comes in the middle of the Judah material (3:1–24), sandwiched between Judahite genealogical lists in 2:3–55 and 4:1–23. So, David and his line are the center and climax of the genealogies in 1 Chronicles 1—9. Although the Chronicler paints on a worldwide canvas, his focus never wavers from the line of David.

1:1—2:2
From Adam to the Sons of Israel

The Chronicler begins literally at the beginning, with Adam, the first human. The first major section of the genealogies traces the human lineage from Adam to the sons of Israel (1:1—2:2), with a short summary genealogy of Abraham inserted on the way (1:24–27). The information in these genealogical lists is taken from Genesis, and derives ultimately from a source sometimes called the Toledot Book, or the Book of Generations. The Chronicler follows Genesis faithfully. Minor differences between Chronicles and its source do not indicate disagreement, but rather show points at which the scribes have made common errors, such as the confusion of similar-appearing letters one for another.

From Adam to Abraham (1:1–27)
(//Gen. 5:1–32; 10:2–29; 11:10–26)

This section of the Chronicler's genealogies begins and ends with a list of ten names: first, the ten generations from Adam to Noah (1:1–4a), followed by the names of Noah's three sons; last, the ten generations from Noah's son Shem to Abraham (1:24–27). A kind of closure is brought by these two lists. After twenty generations, we have come to the end of the beginning of history. With Abram, the age of Israel has begun.

The line from Adam to Noah's sons (1:1–4) is taken from Genesis 5:1–32, though only the names of the males in direct line are given, without the narrative links Genesis provides. At this point, the genealogy branches out into a list of the descendants of Japheth (1:5–7), Ham (1:8–16), and Shem (1:17–23), from Genesis 10:2–29. Here, the Chronicler no longer is pursuing a single line, but rather shows how all the nations of the earth are descended from the sons of Noah.

18

Once again, narrative material from the source is mostly ignored, with two intriguing exceptions. First, the Chronicler pauses to take special note of Nimrod, son of Cush and grandson of Ham, who "was the first to be a mighty one on the earth" (1:10//Gen. 10:8). This interest in Nimrod, the world's first king (see Gen. 10:10–12), prefigures the Chronicler's interest in kingship, and specifically in David. Second, among the descendants of Shem, the Chronicler notes the significance of the name "Peleg" (meaning "division" in Hebrew): "for in his days the earth was divided" (1:19//Gen. 10:25). In Genesis, this name relates to the story of the tower of Babel (Gen. 11:1–9), where God confused the languages of the world's peoples, prompting them to divide across the earth into separate nations. But for the Chronicler, this name may also point grimly to other divisions: the breakup of David's united kingdom after Solomon's death, and the scattering of the exiles throughout the Babylonian empire following Jerusalem's destruction. The Chronicler's history of Israel follows a pattern of alternating light and darkness: a period of faith, followed by loss of faith and destruction, followed by reform and renewal. This pattern may be foreshadowed here, as Nimrod's greatness is followed by the fall Peleg witnessed. So, even as Chronicles lays out for us the origin of all the world's peoples, it retains as its aim the history and destiny of a particular people.

In 1 Chronicles 1:24–27, the focus tightens back down upon the ancestry of the people Israel. Returning to Shem, these verses move in a quick direct line from the ancestor of all the Semitic peoples to the specific ancestor of the people Israel, Abram—collapsing Genesis 11:10–26 into a terse list of ten names. The Chronicler reminds the reader that Abram is also called Abraham (1:27). The name "Abraham" first appears in Genesis 17:5, in the old Priestly account of God's covenant with the patriarch: "No longer shall your name be Abram, but your name shall be Abraham; for I have made you the ancestor of a multitude of nations." After this new name is given by God, the old name "Abram" no longer appears in Genesis. By telling the reader that Abram became Abraham, the Chronicler reminds us of God's covenant, and also neatly bridges the gap between his source in Genesis 11:26, where the patriarch is called Abram, and Genesis 25:12–18 (from which the list of Ishmael's descendants in 1:29–31 is taken), where he is called Abraham.

The Sons of Abraham (1:28–33)
(//Gen. 25:1–4, 12–18)

19

The Chronicler was fully aware that Abraham had more than one son. Before continuing the line as we would expect, through Isaac, the child of promise, Chronicles first turns to Abraham's other sons, beginning with the oldest, Ishmael (1:29–31//Gen. 25:13–16a). The explanatory material in Genesis 25:12, relating to the circumstances of Ishmael's birth to Hagar, Sarah's Egyptian handmaid, is not provided by the Chronicler. Here as elsewhere, Chronicles assumes that the reader knows the story. Next, Chronicles lists the descendants of Abraham through Keturah, the concubine that Abraham took after Sarah's death (1:32–33//Gen. 25:1–4)—including in particular Midian, whose descendants would provide a home for the fugitive Moses (Exod. 2:11–22). None of these, as the narrative in Genesis 25 reminds us, were regarded as heirs by Abraham. Though he acknowledged them, and helped provide for them while he was living, "Abraham gave all he had to Isaac" (Gen. 25:5). Yet all are listed here, before the Chronicler continues along the path of promise that leads through Isaac.

Today, when Christians think and talk about the continued tumult in the Middle East, we often focus on Israel, to the exclusion of Palestinian and broader Arab history and interests. It would be good for us to remember, as the Chronicler did, that Isaac was not an only child. Ishmael and Midian, too, are sons of Abraham, and deserve to be heard.

The Sons of Isaac (1:34–54)

Now, we come to Isaac, and so at last to his son, the eponymous ancestor of the people Israel (1:34). But again, our expectations are thwarted. Again, the Chronicler turns first to the less reputable line, tracing in 1:35–37 the descendants of Esau, Isaac's firstborn. Chronicles also provides at this point the genealogy of Seir (1:38–42) and lists the kings and clans of Edom (1:43–54). This is in keeping, not only with the faithfulness of the Chronicler to his source (Gen. 36), but also with the connection between Esau and the land of Edom (see Gen. 25:30; 27:39–40).

The Sons of Esau (1:34–37) (//Gen. 36:9–14). The Chronicler lists only the names of Esau's sons and grandsons, ignoring the other information from Genesis 36:9–14, such as the mothers' names. It would be a mistake, however, to read into this an anti-feminine bias on the Chronicler's part. As we have already seen in the case of Keturah, women do figure in many of the genealogies and lists that make up these first nine chapters. Rather, in the account of Esau's line, the Chronicler is once more stripping his source down to the bare frame, taking only what interests him: the names of the sons who carry the line.

The Sons of Seir (1:38–42) (//Gen. 36:20–28). In 1 Chronicles 1:38–42, as in the listing of the sons of Ham and Japheth, the Chroni-

20

cler steps outside the Israelite lineage to deal with the nations: here, with the descendants of Seir. Seir and Edom originally referred to distinct geographical regions: Edom to the agricultural plains to the southeast of Judah, Seir to the wooded highlands of the same area (Knauf 1992, 1072–73). When Edom became a nation state dominated by the wealthier people of the lowlands, this distinction was lost. The Genesis parallel to the Chronicler's list (Gen. 36:20–28) notes that Seir was a Horite, and that his sons were the ancestors of the Horite clans. Deuteronomy 2:12 claims that the Horites were defeated and expelled by the sons of Esau, so that what was formerly Seir became Edom. Elsewhere in the Hebrew Bible, the names Seir and Edom are used synonymously (Gen. 32:3; Num. 24:18; Ezek. 35:1–15). The Chronicler does not bother to identify Seir at all, but without explanation treats the list of Seir's sons, in union with the listing of Esau's sons, as a record of Edom's inhabitants.

The Kings and Clans of Edom (1:43–54) (//Gen. 36:31–43). Consistent both with the Chronicler's interest in kingship (already shown in 1:10) and with his faithfulness to his source, we now find a listing of Edom's kings and their capital cities, drawn from Genesis 36:31–39. The king list is followed by a list of the clans of Edom (1:51b–54//Gen. 36:40–43). Such clan lists also followed the record of the sons of Esau and Seir in Genesis 36, but those lists were ignored by the Chronicler. The inclusion of this one, then, is likely significant. Further, the Chronicler adds a statement not found in Genesis, which both brings the king list to an end and introduces the clan list: "And Hadad died" (1:51a).

The Hebrew word translated "clan" in the NRSV can also be rendered as "clan chief," which raises an intriguing interpretive possibility. Up through the time of Hadad, "before any king reigned over the Israelites" (1:43), Edom was governed by kings. However, after Hadad's death, Edom was governed by clan chiefs, not kings. A likely explanation relates to the rise of Davidic kingship in Israel. When David's line was established, Edom became a vassal state subject to the Davidic kings (2 Sam. 8:13–14). Thereafter, its rulers were not properly called kings, but rather merely chiefs (Japhet 1993, 64). Once again, it seems, the Chronicler's long view is directed toward David and his line.

The Sons of Israel (2:1–2)
(//Gen. 35:22b–26)

Now, at last, the reader is brought to the listing of Israel's sons, the twelve patriarchs of Israel. The names are not given by birth order (see

Gen. 29:31—30:24; 35:16–18)—indeed, the list jumps around in an odd fashion. The reason for this curious order becomes apparent when we examine the Chronicler's source: Genesis 35:22b–26. In the Genesis text, the sons of Leah are listed first, then the sons of Rachel, then the sons of Rachel's maid Bilhah, and finally the sons of Leah's maid Zilpah. The Chronicler follows this order (although Dan has been misplaced between Zebulun and Joseph), but leaves out the mothers' names, so that the pattern is obscured. Later, the Chronicler will trace the descendants of Israel's other sons. But first, in a complex series of genealogical lists drawn from a variety of sources, the Chronicler turns to the line of Judah (2:3—4:23).

2:3—4:23
The Line of Judah

That Judah should be treated first among the sons of Israel is a change in the pattern we have observed before in the genealogies. The Chronicler dealt with the descendants of all three sons of Noah before returning specifically to the line from Shem to Abraham. He treated Ishmael and the sons of Keturah before returning to Isaac, and Esau and Seir before returning to Israel. But now the line of Judah, ancestor of David, is given pride of place. This departure from the expected pattern serves to underline the significance of Judah, and of David, all the more. As we have already observed, the Judahite material forms the center section of the Chronicler's genealogies. Indeed, the record of David's line, at the heart of the Judah section (3:1–24), will be the climax of these genealogical lists.

The Descendants of Judah (2:3–55)

The list of the sons of Judah in 2:3–4 is taken from Genesis 46:12, and from the story of Judah and Tamar in Genesis 38. The story of Judah's seduction by his daughter-in-law is not retold by the Chronicler; however, it is deliberately evoked in several ways. First, the sons of Judah are grouped by their mothers: Bath-shua, called "the Canaanite woman" (2:3) and Tamar, identified as "his [that is, Judah's] daughter-in-law" (2:4). Second, in the only piece of the narrative taken from his source, the Chronicler records that "Er, Judah's firstborn, was wicked in the sight of the LORD, and he put him to death" (2:3//Gen. 38:7), letting Er's death stand for the fate of his brother Onan. The list of the

22

sons of Shelah, Judah's only surviving son by Bath-shua, is given as an appendix at the end of the Judahite genealogies, in 4:21–23. Third, the line from Judah through David and beyond is traced, in the lists that follow, through Tamar's son Perez. Thus, in a few swift, broad strokes, the Chronicler recalls to the reader's mind the whole story of Tamar's boldness, which preserved the line of Judah and ensured the birth of David.

Now, within the line of Judah, the Chronicler resumes the practice followed in the first chapter of the genealogies. Chronicles does not move directly to the object of its interest, David and his line, but rather approaches that goal in slow, wide spirals, which take the reader out to the furthest extent of the Judahite line that the Chronicler's sources touched. Therefore, before turning to the line of Perez, which leads ultimately to David, the Chronicler pursues the line of Zerah (2:6–8).

To his credit, the Chronicler does not appear to have invented genealogies outright: when his sources are silent (as, for instance, regarding the descendants, or lack thereof, of Perez's son Hamul [2:5]), he is silent. However, he is sometimes very creative in his use of sources. Consider the names of the five sons of Zerah (2:6). The name of the first son comes from Joshua 7:1, which tells of how "Achan son of Carmi son of Zabdi [Chronicles reads "Zimri"] son of Zerah, of the tribe of Judah" took some of the spoil from the city of Jericho, which had been devoted to the LORD. The names Chronicles gives for the other four sons of Zerah come from 1 Kings 4:31, where Solomon is said to have been "wiser than Ethan the Ezrahite, and Heman, Calcol, and Darda, children of Mahol." Evidently, the Chronicler understood "Ezrahite" to mean "descendant of Zerah," and disregarded the phrase "children of Mahol." With the four names in this verse (note that the Chronicler reads Dara for Darda) added to Zabdi/Zimri from Joshua 7:1, Zerah is given five sons, paralleling the five sons of his father Judah.

To us, this use of Scripture appears odd, even incomprehensible. Certainly, the Chronicler must have been aware that people listed as contemporaries of Solomon could not possibly be grandsons of Judah! However, this cheerful disregard for chronology is a common feature of the Chronicler's History. The Chronicler is not working with the "real" world of historical fact so much as with the world of text and tradition. That does not mean that Chronicles cannot be mined for useful historical information. It is a reminder, however, that the Chronicler's historical standards, and exegetical methods, are quite different from ours.

In 2:9, the Chronicler begins to treat the descendants of Hezron, son of Perez. The most important of these is the family of Ram, which the Chronicler traces swiftly down to David and his siblings (2:10–17). Here, the Chronicler follows the genealogy in Ruth 4:18–22 (see also

23

Num. 1:7) in form as well as substance, except for the identification of Nahshon as "prince of the sons of Judah" (2:11). This special identification may relate to Nahshon being brother-in-law to Aaron (Exod. 6:23), and hence a precursor of the connection between Judah and Levi, kingship and worship, which is a consistent motif of the Chronicler's History.

For the brothers and sisters of David, the Chronicler appears to make use of his own sources, which differ in some respects from the Deuteronomistic History. The first three sons of Jesse are as listed in 1 Samuel 16:1–9 and 17:13 (though Chronicles has Shimea rather than Shammah) and, in Chronicles as in 1 Samuel, David is the youngest brother. Chronicles lists David as the seventh son, while in 1 Samuel he is the eighth son. Both lists involve traditional patterns in folklore: the seventh son, and the youngest son with seven brothers.

David's sister Zeruiah with her three sons Abishai, Joab, and Asahel is mentioned in 2 Samuel 2:18, though the Deuteronomist does not mention her relationship to David. It is intriguing to note that, according to the Chronicler, Joab was David's nephew. This may go some way toward explaining their curious relationship: Joab's familiarity towards the king, and David's tolerance for Joab, make better sense if they were family.

Apart from this passage in Chronicles, there is no biblical mention of David's other brothers or sisters. Note, though, that David's sister Abigail is said to have married Jether the Ishmaelite, which takes us back again to Abraham's Arab descendants. Judah's "line" begins to appear more like a web of intricate interconnections.

The diversity of the Judahite lists preserved by the Chronicler is shown especially in 2:34–41, which deals with the lineage of the Jerahmeelite Sheshan. In 2:31, we are told that Sheshan had a son, Ahlai, through whom his line presumably continued. But in 2:34, Sheshan is said to have no sons, only daughters, and to have given one of his daughters to an Egyptian slave, named Jarha. Out of this marriage was born Attai, through whom the line then continues. Apparently the Chronicler identifies Attai with Ahlai, and so tries to reconcile two competing traditions. Significantly, the Chronicler does not discount one tradition in favor of the other, or emend them so as to present a single, self-consistent account. This harmonizing tendency, as we will see, is a common feature in the Chronicler's use of Scripture.

The Davidic Line (3:1–24)

Now, Chronicles spirals back at last to David's line, and we come to the midpoint and climax of the genealogies. Chapter 3:1–4 (//2 Sam. 3:1–5) records the first six sons born to David during his reign in Hebron. The only significant difference in the two lists is the name of the second son: Daniel in Chronicles, Chileab in Samuel. The LXX of 2 Samuel 3:3 reads Dalouia for the MT's Chileab, suggesting that all three are attempting to deal with a garbled, uncertain original. Following the list of David's first six sons, the Chronicler notes that David ruled in Hebron "for seven years and six months. And he reigned thirty-three years in Jerusalem" (3:4//2 Sam. 5:5). No explanation is given for the move from Hebron to Jerusalem; the Chronicler assumes that we know the story. Later, in 10—11, the text will step neatly over this messy period of civil war. The effect, there as here, is to heighten David's sovereignty by belittling or ignoring the opposition.

The following verses turn to the sons of David born in Jerusalem (a parallel to this list, with minor variations, appears in 14:3–7). Four sons are said to have been born to David and "Bath-shua, daughter of Ammiel" (3:5)—clearly Bathsheba, though nothing is said of their adultery, or of Uriah's murder. Second Samuel mentions only one son other than Solomon born out of this union: the child conceived in adultery, who bore David's punishment (2 Sam. 12:13–14). Nor is anything said outside of Chronicles of the other five sons, born to unnamed mothers, not to mention the unnamed sons born to concubines (3:9). However, the Chronicler's Davidic connections likely gave him access to sources unknown to the Deuteronomist. The tragically misused Tamar *is* mentioned, in 2 Samuel 13, as sister to Absalom and half-sister to her rapist, Amnon.

In 3:10–24, the Chronicler lists for us the direct line of David's descendants, from Solomon the temple builder to the Chronicler's contemporary, Anani. The list from Solomon to Josiah (3:10–14) is a linear representation of the Davidic kings taken straight from the Deuteronomistic History, each king being listed as the son of his predecessor. Then, with Josiah, the listings begin to branch out, perhaps because of questions concerning proper succession. Four sons are listed for Josiah: the otherwise unknown Johanan (who evidently did not survive), Jehoiakim, Zedekiah (whom we will discuss below), and Shallum. Upon Josiah's tragic death in battle against Pharaoh Necho at Megiddo, it was the youngest son Shallum who was popularly acclaimed as king, taking the throne name Jehoahaz (2 Kgs. 23:29–30). He ruled for only three months before being deposed by Necho, deported to Egypt, and replaced by his presumably more pliant older brother Jehoiakim (2 Kgs. 23:31–35; Jer. 22:10–12). Now, Chronicles lists the sons of Jehoiakim (3:16), who are also the last two kings in David's line: Jeconiah (also called Jehoiachin [2 Kgs. 24:6–17; 2 Chr. 36:8–9] and Coniah [Jer. 22:24]) and Zedekiah (see 2 Chr. 36:10, which also describes Zedekiah

25

as Jeconiah's brother). Note that this is in conflict with 2 Kings 24:17, which says that it was Jehoiachin's uncle Zedekiah (see 3:15; originally named Mattaniah, according to Kings), who was installed by Nebuchadnezzar of Babylon as king in place of his exiled nephew.

The confusion is easy to understand. Evidently, either the Deuteronomist or the Chronicler has confused Zedekiah son of Josiah with Zedekiah son of Jehoiakim. Second Kings is closer in time to the events surrounding Zedekiah's reign than the Chronicler; however, the Chronicler is closer to Davidic sources. Also, Chronicles has the support here of Zedekiah's contemporary, the prophet Jeremiah. Jeremiah consistently calls Jehoiakim the son of Josiah, but never applies that title to Zedekiah (Japhet 1993, 98). Since Jeremiah also confirms that Jehoahaz was called Shallum (a fact otherwise noted only by Chronicles), his support at this point as well may lead us to conclude that the Chronicler's account is accurate.

Now we come to the descendants of David from the beginning of the exile down to the period of the restoration. Jeconiah, who was taken away to Babylon in 597 B.C., had seven sons born in exile. One of them, Shenazzar, is apparently the figure called Sheshbazzar in Ezra 1:8–11 (each name being an alternate form of the same Babylonian name, Sin-ab-uṣur), who was the first Persian-period governor of Judah.

In the second generation of exiles, Zerubbabel son of Pedaiah is certainly the Zerubbabel under whose governorship the second temple was completed (Ezra 3:8; 5:2; Hag. 1:1; 2:1–4, 21–23; Zech. 4:6–10). Elsewhere, Zerubbabel is said to be the son of Shealtiel, not the son of Pedaiah. This may reflect the practice of levirate marriage. By this custom, if a man died without issue, his brother was obligated to marry the widow, and the first son born from their union was considered for purposes of inheritance the child of the deceased man (see Deut. 25:5–10). Hence, Zerubbabel could have been the biological son of Pedaiah, as Chronicles states, and still legally the son of his uncle Shealtiel.

Zerubbabel's second son Hananiah, in the third generation after the exile, is the one through whom the fourth generation, likely the first to be born after the return, is traced. At this point, the text becomes tricky. On the basis of the king list in 3:10–14, we could construe the list in 3:21 as a lineal descent, spanning five generations from Jeshaiah to Shecaniah—which is, in fact, what the LXX apparently does (see the Introduction). Or, guided by the similar structure in 3:16, we could see these men as brothers. In that case, Hananiah would have had six sons, all part of the fourth generation. The latter possibility is confirmed by 3:22, which is best read as listing the six sons of Shecaniah. Among them is Hattush, who returned from exile with Ezra (Ezra 8:2–3; ca. 458 B.C.).

Thus, 3:21 must refer to a single generation, since otherwise Hattush would date to quite some time *after* Ezra.

The Chronicler follows the list down to the birth of Anani, seventh son of Elioenai in the seventh generation since the exile—truly an auspicious birth! This may well be the same Anani who is mentioned in the papyrus documents left behind by the Jewish community at Elephantine (ca. 410 B.C.). Arguably, the Chronicler stops at this point because he has reached his own time. So the Davidic line, which will provide the plot line for the Chronicler's narrative in the chapters to come, also provides the connection between the Chronicler's "present day" and Israel's ancient heritage.

Miscellaneous Judahite Material (4:1–23)

Another set of Judahite genealogical lists both brackets the David material before it and introduces the tribal genealogies that follow. This chapter is a miscellany of lists, having little connection either with one another or with the previous Judahite material. Note, for instance, that the five sons of Judah listed in 4:1–2 bear little resemblance either to the five sons of Judah listed in 2:3–5, or to the first five generations of Judah's line.

The Chronicler is using old Judahite sources, not referred to elsewhere. Quite probably, these lists are very old indeed. The places mentioned were not part of postexilic Judah, suggesting that these lists were preserved from the time before Jerusalem's fall. Indeed, the list of the sons of Shelah, Judah's only surviving son by Bath-shua (4:21–23), states that the records are ancient (4:22). Contact between these sources and other material from our Scriptures may be found at 4:13//Judges 1:13, which speak of Othniel son of Kenaz (although the relationship between Kenaz and Caleb is unclear in the Chronicles lists; note that 4:15 mentions a Kenaz who is Caleb's grandson, rather than his brother, as Judges states), and at 4:15//Numbers 13:6, both of which describe Caleb as a son of Jephunneh (compare 2:9 and 18, where Caleb is a son of Hezron).

The lists collected here seem concerned with establishing the ownership of the land of Judah, by associating place names with the names of ancient worthies descended from Judah. The town of Bethlehem, birthplace of David, is incorporated into the genealogy in 4:4: "These were the sons of Hur, the firstborn of Ephrathah, the father of Bethlehem" (for the association of Bethlehem with Ephrathah, see also Ruth 4:11 and Mic. 5:2). In 2:19 as well, Hur is a son of Caleb by Caleb's second wife Ephrath, though Bethlehem is not mentioned (but, see 2:51).

27

Other southern place names incorporated into these lists include Tekoa (4:5; cf. 2:24), Ziph (4:16), and Eshtemoa (4:17).

The concern for land in this section is also reflected in the brief narrative concerning Jabez (4:9–10; note that Jabez as well is a Judean place name in 2:55). Although given a name of ill omen (the text punningly associates Jabez with Hebrew *ʿoṣeb*, meaning "pain"), Jabez is said to be "honored more than his brothers" (4:9)—perhaps because his birth had been so difficult. Jabez prayed, "Oh that you would bless me and enlarge my border, and that your hand might be with me, and that you would keep me from hurt and harm!" (4:10). The Chronicler assures us that God heard, and answered, this prayer. One is reminded of Jacob, also beloved by his mother, also given a dark name following a difficult birth (see Gen. 25:19–28; "Jacob" means "supplanter" or "heel-grabber"), but who also trusted God and received blessing. The brief vignette of Jabez establishes God's blessing upon the land and line of Judah generally. But Jabez also is an example of many to come in the Chronicler's narrative, who will trust the Lord, worshiping in sincere piety, and who will as a result be blessed.

Note, finally, the prominence of women in these lists. Here are Hazzelelponi, daughter of Etam; Ephrathah, mother of Hur and grandmother of Bethlehem; Helah and Naarah, the two wives of Asshur; the suffering, unnamed mother of Jabez; "Bithiah, daughter of Pharaoh, whom Mered married," as well as Bithia's daughter Miriam and Mered's unnamed Judahite wife; and "the wife of Hodiah, the sister of Naham": a remarkable and unprecedented list of the women of Judah's line. Women do appear in genealogies elsewhere, when a difficulty in the lineage necessitates distinguishing the sons of favored wives from the sons of less favored wives or concubines. But the women in 4:1–23, by and large, are listed in their own right.

Biblical genealogies generally follow the rule of patriliny: descent is traced through the father, not the mother. Later, probably in the Roman period, the rabbis would rule in favor of matriliny. Still today among Orthodox Jews, it is the children of a Jewish mother who are regarded as Jewish, and Jewish descent is traced through the mother's line. However, there are some indications of matriliny in the Hebrew Bible, from early on. Consider the story of Shiphrah and Puah, the Hebrew midwives (Exod. 1:15–21). The text says that because they resisted Pharaoh's cruelty, God made them clans (literally, "houses"; the translation "he gave them families" in the NRSV is far too weak). That is, at least two ancient Israelite clans traced themselves back, not to a man, but to a woman! Perhaps these old Judahite lists as well preserve some sense of a competing, matrilineal tradition. At the very least, however, they reflect an openness to women quite surprising and refreshing in this generally patriarchal material.

4:24—9:44
The Tribal Genealogies

Having followed the thread from Adam to Judah, and from Judah through David to his own time, the Chronicler returns to the list of Israel's sons in 2:1–2, and traces the lineage of the other tribes. Here, Chronicles draws by and large on biblical sources, particularly from the Genesis genealogies, the census material in Numbers, and the territorial allotments in Joshua.

Excursus: **Zebulun and Dan**

Curiously, only ten tribes are traced in these genealogies. Zebulun and Dan have dropped out of the sequence altogether. However, the tribe of Zebulun is at least mentioned in the genealogies (in the Levitical town lists; see 6:63, 77), and features in the narrative of Chronicles as well (1 Chr. 12:33, 40; 27:19; 2 Chr. 30:10, 11, 18). Some of the tribal lists are quite short: Naphtali, for instance, takes only a single verse (1 Chr. 7:13). If Zebulun's list was also brief, it could well have dropped out due to scribal error.

However, the tribe of Dan is not mentioned anywhere in the tribal genealogies. Note that in the list of Levitical towns in 6:54–81, the towns in the territory of Dan (Josh. 21:23–24) have not been enumerated by the Chronicler. Indeed, there are only three passing mentions of the tribe of Dan in the entire Chronicler's History: 12:35, which lists the troops from Dan who came to Hebron to acclaim David as king; 27:22, which identifies Azarel son of Jeroham as the leader of the tribal military division from Dan; and 2 Chronicles 2:13–14, where Huram's skilled artisan Huram-abi, commissioned to assist in the building of the temple, is said to be the son of a Tyrian man and a Danite woman (elsewhere, in 1 Chr. 21:2; 2 Chr. 16:4, and 30:5, Dan is a place name, not a tribe). Recall, too, that Dan was inserted out of order in the list of Israel's sons in 2:1–2—placed, intriguingly, after Zebulun, the other missing tribe in the genealogies. Taken together, this evidence suggests

29

that the genealogical lists in 1 Chronicles 1—9 originally made no mention of Dan at all, and that a later editor inserted Dan into the list of Israel's sons.

Chronicles' negative assessment of Dan is in keeping with other biblical texts, which also view Dan as suspect, particularly in the area of worship (see Johnstone 1998, 111). In Judges 17—18, Danite raiders kidnap a priest and steal a silver image to establish a temple in their own city of Dan. Judges 18:30 claims that the priests at this shrine were descendants of Moses, a claim sufficiently scandalous that later scribes altered the text to read Manasseh instead of Moses! When Jeroboam's followers broke away from Jerusalem's control to establish the separate northern kingdom of Israel, Jeroboam established two shrines for his people: the old shrine in Dan, and another in Bethel (1 Kgs. 12:29). This act is steadfastly condemned in the books of Kings as the sin of Jeroboam, which ultimately doomed the northern kingdom to destruction (for example, 1 Kgs. 13:34; 2 Kgs. 17:21–22). Little wonder that Chronicles, with its focus on right worship in the right temple, should also be suspicious of Dan.

Simeon (4:24–43)

The tribal genealogies begin with Simeon rather than the firstborn Reuben, who "is not enrolled in the genealogy according to the birthright" because he slept with his father's concubine (5:1; compare Gen. 35:22; 49:4). The list of the sons of Simeon in 4:24 comes (with slight variations) from Genesis 46:10, part of a list of the descendants of Israel who went down into Egypt (see also Exod. 6:15; Num. 26:12–13). This list is used throughout the tribal genealogies for the sons of the patriarchs. The account in 4:28–33, describing the regions in which the descendants of Simeon settled and the villages in that territory, is taken from the territorial allotments in Joshua 19:1–8.

The other material in the Simeon lists comes from sources unique to the Chronicler. One such source is mentioned in 4:33, which says that the Simeonites "kept a genealogical record." Another is implied in 4:34–43, which describes the movement of some groups associated with Simeon during the reign of Hezekiah. Elsewhere, the Chronicler demonstrates special, accurate knowledge of events during Hezekiah's reign (the digging of Hezekiah's famous tunnel, for instance; see 2 Chr. 32:30) in particular. This suggests that the Chronicler had access to Judean royalist sources.

Even while tracing the lineage of Simeon, Chronicles' pro-Judah bias remains evident. Note the observation that Simeon did not increase to the extent that Judah did (4:27), and the statement that the towns claimed by the Simeonites remained theirs "until David became king" (4:31)—the implication being that, once David's rule began, the land became his to apportion as he willed.

Reuben (5:1–10)

First Chronicles 5:1–2 recalls the story of Reuben's disgrace to explain why Simeon rather than Reuben comes first in the tribal genealogies. But of course, Judah's family had been listed even before Simeon. The Chronicler explains this priority: "Judah became prominent among his brothers and a ruler [David, of course] came from him" (5:2). Still, the Chronicler assumes that the reader knows the story of Joseph from Genesis 37—48, and so he notes that, despite the preeminence of Judah's line, the birthright among the sons of Israel belonged to Joseph. While this idea is not explicit in the Joseph story as told in our MT, it is certainly implied (particularly in Joseph's dreams; see Gen. 37:5–11) and appears in all of the Targums (translations of the Hebrew Bible for use in the synagogue by Aramaic speaking Jews; so Williamson 1977, 94). Instead of tracing Joseph's line, however, Chronicles traces the two tribes descended from Joseph (see Gen. 48:1–22): Manasseh (5:23–26; 7:14–19) and Ephraim (7:20–29). This pattern is found in many other tribal lists; compare, for example, the list of the tribes in Ezekiel 48:1–29, which includes Ephraim and Manasseh, with the tribal designations given to the twelve gates of idealized Jerusalem in Ezekiel 48:30–34, which refer instead to Joseph.

The names of the sons of Reuben come, as did the names of Simeon's sons, from the list of Israel's sons who went down into Egypt (5:3//Gen. 46:9; see also Exod. 6:14; Num. 26:5–6). The remainder of the Reubenite material (5:4–10) comes from sources peculiar to Chronicles. Two historical references punctuate the material. First, we are told that Beerah, the last chief of Reuben, was taken into exile by King Tiglath-pilneser of Assyria—evidently Tiglath-pilesar III, who conquered Gilead in 733 B.C. (5:6). Second, we learn of the battle between Reuben (under the leadership of Jeiel) and the Hagrites in the days of Saul (5:7–10). Here, we are able to check the Chronicles' sources against other evidence. According to a Moabite inscription called the Mesha stele, Aroer, Nebo, and Baal-meon (places 5:8 says were occupied by Reuben in the time of Saul) were held by Moab until the late ninth century B.C.—about two hundred years after Saul. Note, too, that in contrast to David and even the foreigner Tiglath-pilneser, Saul is neither called king nor said to reign in Israel. This is in keeping with the

31

attitude expressed in 10—12, where Saul's death and the beginning of David's reign are described. While Saul may have occupied a throne in Israel prior to David, Chronicles never regards Saul as king in any real sense. David is the first true king of Israel.

Gad (5:11–22) and the Half-Tribe of Manasseh (5:23–26)

Curiously, Gad and the half-tribe of Manasseh are placed before the Chronicler's lengthy and important treatment of the descendants of Levi, Israel's third son. In large part, this shift in the expected order is prompted by geography: like Reuben, Gad and a portion of the families of Manasseh were settled in the area east of the Jordan (note the close relationship among Reuben, Gad, and Manesseh in Num. 32:20–42; Josh. 13:8–33; 1 Chr. 5:18–22, 26). However, this unexpected movement also returns us to a pattern we have seen before in the genealogies: spiraling slowly toward topics of interest, rather than barrelling at them headlong.

Chapter 5:17 states that the descendants of Gad "were enrolled by genealogies in the days of King Jotham of Judah, and in the days of King Jeroboam of Israel." Apparently, it is these genealogies that the Chronicler is using. To be sure, Chronicles is not relying on our Bible here. The genealogy of Gad in 5:11–17 bears no resemblance to the Gadite lineages found elsewhere (compare Gen. 46:16; Num. 26:15). Further, the assumption that Jotham and Jeroboam II ruled at the same time is contrary to 2 Kings 15:32, which records that Jotham of Judah became king in the second year of Pekah of Israel—well after Jeroboam II had died. However, the chronology of the kings of Israel and Judah is a notoriously knotty problem; some scholars argue that the reigns of Jotham and Jeroboam II may well have overlapped. At any rate, it is clear that the Chronicler is following his own sources at this point.

The Chronicler presents two brief narratives regarding Gad and Manasseh. The first story, 5:18–22, is unique to Chronicles. The second, 5:25–26, is based on the accounts of Israel's decline and fall in the Deuteronomistic History (see 2 Kgs. 15:19–20; 17:6; 18:11). These stories illustrate the twofold theme of the Chronicler's History, which will be reiterated time and again: obedience to the Lord and sincere piety bring blessing, disobedience and false worship bring a curse. So, Reuben, Gad, and Manasseh were blessed in their wars with the Hagrites, "for they cried to God in the battle, and he granted their entreaty because they trusted in him" (5:20). However, when the three Transjordanian tribes "transgressed against the God of their ancestors,

32

and prostituted themselves to the gods of the peoples of the land, whom God had destroyed before them" (5:25), their end was destruction and exile. The fall of the northern kingdom, like the later fall of Judah, comes from false worship and disobedience to the word of the Lord. The grim fate of these tribes, which remained lost in exile "to this day" (5:26), stood as a warning to the Chronicler's own community not to take God's grace for granted. Jerusalem had received the marvelous and unexpected gift of a second chance. However, if the people returned to the ways of their forebears, they too would be lost.

Excursus: **The God of the Ancestors**

The expression "God of their ancestors" (5:25; literally, "God of their fathers") and related expressions such as "God of your ancestors" or "God of his ancestor David" are characteristic of the Chronicler's History. Of the sixty-six occurrences of this divine title in the Hebrew Bible, thirty-five are found in Chronicles and Ezra, compared to only four in the Deuteronomistic History (Josh. 18:3; Judg. 2:12; 2 Kgs. 20:5 [//Isa. 38:5]; 21:22).

After Chronicles and Ezra–Nehemiah, the God of the ancestors is mentioned most often in the Torah (25 times; the one remaining citation is Dan. 2:23). Evidently, this divine title is very old. It appears in what is probably the oldest text in Scripture, the Song of the Sea (Exod. 15:1–18):

> The LORD is my strength and my might,
>   and he has become my salvation;
> this is my God, and I will praise him,
>   my father's God, and I will exalt him. (Exod. 15:2)

The ancient idea of God as the divine kinsman formed the foundation of Israel's idea of covenant, by which "the rights and obligations, the duties, status, and privileges" belonging by right to family relations were extended to incorporate the entire people Israel as the family of God (Cross 1998, 3). This idea has implications as well for Israel's conception of God: "The Divine Kinsman, it is assumed, fulfills the mutual obligations and receives the privileges of kinship. He leads in battle, redeems from slavery, loves his family, shares the land of his heritage . . . , provides and protects" (Cross 1998, 7).

In the Torah, the God of the ancestors establishes the continuity of the covenant. Isaac worships the god of his father Abraham (Gen. 26:24). Jacob worships the God of his father Isaac (for example, Gen. 31:29; 46:1–3). The twelve patriarchs worship the God of their father,

33

Jacob (Gen. 43:23; 49:25; 50:17). This pattern of covenant continuity extends into Exodus, where the God of Abraham, Isaac, and Jacob proves faithful to the ancient promise of land, progeny, and blessing (3:6–16; 4:5). Similarly, in Deuteronomy the God of the ancestors guarantees the continuity of the ancient covenant into future generations (for example, 1:11; 6:3; 27:3), but also threatens the curse should the covenant be violated (29:25).

With its use of the title "God of the ancestors," Chronicles sounds this same note of continuity with tradition. Indeed, the major purpose of the genealogies, as we have seen, is to demonstrate the continuity of divine faithfulness from Adam to Anani, and extending outward through the entire people of Israel. However, the note of warning sounded in Deuteronomy and in the Deuteronomistic History (see especially Deut. 29:25; Judg. 2:12; 2 Kgs. 21:22) is also central to Chronicles. The God of the ancestors, who first established Israel in the land, also exiled the unfaithful. Now, even as the continuity of the line of promise lends comfort and assurance to the Chronicler's audience, they too are cautioned. The ancient story of Israel conveys curse as well as blessing. The God of the ancestors held the ancestors accountable for their actions; the Chronicler's community, too, must remain faithful if they wish to inherit the promise of blessing in the land.

Levi (6:1–81)

The section regarding the priestly tribe of Levi is longer than that devoted to any of the other tribes, apart from Judah. This is in keeping with the focus of the Chronicler on the temple and its cult, founded and preserved by David's line. The material in this section falls into two parts. The first part, 6:1–53, deals with the three major Levitical groups in the service of Jerusalem's cult: the priests (6:1–15), the Levites (6:16–30), and the temple singers (6:31–48). Each group is traced all the way back to Levi. Chapter 6:49–53 recalls the priesthood of Aaron, and reminds the reader of the distinction in sanctity between priests and ordinary Levites. The second part, 6:54–81, lists the Levitical cities and towns scattered throughout the territories possessed by the other tribes.

The Levitical Genealogies (6:1–53). The names of Levi's sons in 6:1 appear to have been taken from Genesis 46:11 (see also Exod. 6:16; Num. 26:57). Then, the Chronicler lists the sons of Kohath and of Kohath's son Amram, arriving at the famous siblings Moses, Aaron, and Miriam (6:2–3//Exod. 6:18, 20; see Num. 26:57–59).

The following verses (6:4–15) trace the lineage of the high priests,

34

from Eleazar the son of Aaron to Jehozadak, who "went into exile when the LORD sent Judah and Jerusalem into exile by the hand of Nebuchadnezzar" (6:15). Curiously, the Levitical genealogies do not trace the high-priestly lineage down to the Chronicler's own time. However, Nehemiah 12:10–11 picks up where this list leaves off, with Joshua son of Jehozadak (see Hag. 1:1; 2:2, 4), and follows the line down to Jaddua II (born ca. 420 B.C.), the Chronicler's contemporary.

The priestly families tended to use and reuse the same stock of names (note the recurrence of Amariah, Azariah, and Zadok). Unfortunately, this tendency of priestly names to repeat themselves has resulted in the corruption of the genealogy over time. The eye of a scribe could easily leap from one name to a similar name, skipping the names in between; or, a copyist could copy the same name twice without noticing the error. So, while three Azariahs are listed here, two others (one from the reign of Uzziah [2 Chr. 26:20] and one from the reign of Hezekiah [2 Chr. 31:10]) have been overlooked. Still, by reference to Josephus, who has a longer list (*Antiquities* 10.152–153), and to the narrative of the Deuteronomistic and Chronicler's Histories, the genealogy can be reconstructed in a fairly complete fashion.

Note that Zadok, who was named by David as one of the two high priests in the Jerusalem shrine (24:3), is listed in the high-priestly genealogy (6:8; see 6:50–53; 18:16). According to the Chronicler, Zadok's line goes back to Aaron's son Eleazar—a claim often rejected by scholars. Of particular influence has been the proposal that Zadok was a priest of Jebusite Jerusalem, and was retained as priest by David following his conquest of that city (Rowley 1939, 113–41). However, "Why would David who obviously attempted to draw all the old League traditions to his new religious establishment, turn and invite a pagan priest as one of the high priests of the national cultus?" (Cross 1973, 210). Most likely, David appointed Zadok to represent the dominant southern priestly house, and Abiathar to represent the dominant priestly house of the north. For the Chronicler, however, it is clearly the southern, Aaronid line that has preeminence.

Two other names of note are Azariah son of Johanan and Jehozadak son of Seraiah, who are connected with the only bits of narrative in this priestly genealogy. Of Azariah the Chronicler says, "it was he who served as priest in the house that Solomon built in Jerusalem" (6:10). So, Azariah marks the establishment of the first temple. Jehozadak, of course, witnessed the end of the temple, being priest at the time of its destruction (6:15). The two of them together, then, bracket the entire first temple period, which is the historical subject of Chronicles. Perhaps it is for this reason that the Chronicler does not at this point complete

35

the genealogy down to Jaddua. Once more, Chronicles' genealogies set before the reader a reminder of what has been, both of blessing and of curse. The Chronicler's community, living in the time of the second temple, would have gotten the point. Only through faithfulness to the tradition could the second temple be saved from the fate of the first.

Having traced the line of high priests, the Chronicler goes back to Levi to trace the other Levitical clans, divided into three great families: the descendants of Gershom (usually called "Gershon" outside of Chronicles), Kohath, and Merari. For Levi's sons and grandsons, Chronicles draws on Exodus 6:16–19 (///1 Chr. 6:16–19; see also Num. 3:17–20). Similarly, the line of Kohath's son Amminadab (evidently another name for Izhar; see Exod. 6:23) down to Ebiasaph is taken from Exodus 6:21, 24. The names of Gershom's and Merari's descendants, as well as the remainder of Kohath's line, are drawn primarily from the Chronicler's own sources. Of particular interest is the inclusion of Samuel in the line of Kohath (6:28). In 1 Samuel 1:1, as here, Samuel is said to be the son of Elkanah, son of Jeroham, but 1 Samuel places the prophet in the tribe of Ephraim, not the tribe of Levi. For the Chronicler, however, it doubtless seemed important for such a pivotal figure in David's story (see 11:3) to have unquestionable family credentials. Hence, the Chronicler baptizes Samuel into the sacral tribe of Levi.

Now, Chronicles leaps ahead to David's establishment of the temple musicians (6:31–48; see 16:4–7). The Chronicler insists upon an unbroken continuity of service from the tent shrine David established to the temple that Solomon built. So, although Solomon would build the temple, it was David who was the author of its liturgy.

Three leaders of the temple singers are mentioned, one from each of the three Levitical families: Heman of the Kohathites (6:33–38), Asaph of the Gershonites (6:39–43), and Ethan of the Merarites (6:44–48). These names may be familiar from the Psalms: Psalms 50 and 73—83 are attributed to Asaph, Psalm 88 to Heman, and Psalm 89 to Ethan. In addition, Psalms 42, 44—49, 84, 85, 87, and 88 are all associated with the Korahites, a subgroup of the Kohathites to which Heman belonged (see the title of Ps. 88; Exod. 6:24; 2 Chr. 20:19). Significantly, Chronicles lists Heman as the leader among the three, with his brothers Asaph and Ethan standing to his right and left (see Num. 4:1–4 for the preeminence of the Kohathites).

The Levitical genealogies conclude with a reference to the sanctity of Aaron and his descendants, who "made offerings on the altar of burnt offering and on the altar of incense, doing all the work of the most holy place, to make atonement for Israel, according to all that Moses the servant of God had commanded" (6:49). For the Chronicler, sacrificial priesthood is the exclusive province of the Aaronid priests. The empha-

36

sis upon obedience to the command of Moses—clearly a reference to the Torah—stands as a reminder of the importance of Scripture to the Chronicler. Following this reminder, Chronicles swiftly recaps the high-priestly genealogy, tracing the line down to David's time, and once more establishing Zadok's Aaronid credentials.

The Levitical Towns (6:54–81). The remainder of the Levite section is drawn (with some slight variations) from Joshua 21, the listing of Levitical cities and towns within the territory of the other tribes. Note that the Levitical towns in the territory of Dan (Josh. 21:23–24) have not been picked up by the Chronicler—suggesting, as we have already observed, that Dan is deliberately excluded from the genealogies. By assigning Levi scattered towns in the territory of other tribes rather than giving the tribe its own territory, Chronicles stands in continuity with ancient tradition (Num. 18:20–32; Deut. 18:1; Josh. 13:14). Since the Levites were given no inheritance in the land, their livelihood depended on the tithes and offerings of the other, secular tribes.

Issachar (7:1–5)

Once more, the account of the sons of the patriarch comes from Genesis 46 (7:1//Gen. 46:13; see Num. 26:23–24). The rest of Issachar's lineage appears to have been drawn from a military census, reworked as a genealogy. The listing of the number of Issachar's warriors "in the days of David" (7:2) foreshadows the assembly of the tribal armies in support of David's kingship (12:23–40).

The First Benjamin Genealogy (7:6–12)

The Benjaminite material is distributed among three sections in the tribal genealogies: at 7:6–12, 8:1–40, and 9:35–44 (actually, a copy of 8:29–38). We can identify a warrant for Benjamin's consideration in each separate place. However, the mere fact that so much space is devoted to Benjamin (more than to any tribe apart from Judah and Levi) is surely significant.

Throughout the Chronicler's History, faithful Israel is designated particularly as "Judah and Benjamin" (for example, 9:3; 2 Chr. 11:3; Ezra 1:5; Neh. 11:36). These were the tribes that remained faithful to David's line following Jeroboam's revolt. However, even before the kingdoms split in the Chronicles narrative, Benjamin serves as an example of loyalty to God's anointed. In 12:2, Benjaminite archers and slingers are among the first to follow David. Note, too, that in 21:6, Joab refuses to include Levi and Benjamin in David's census, having rightly perceived that the census is abominable to the Lord. Faithful Levi and Benjamin

37

are thus untainted by participation in David's rebellious act. The special attention to Benjamin in the genealogies, then, is consistent with the Chronicler's basic approach.

The placement of the first Benjaminite list (7:6–12) appears to follow from the Chronicler's sources. Like the Issachar material that immediately precedes it, this Benjaminite material derives the sons of Benjamin from Genesis 46 (Gen. 46:21//1 Chr. 7:6; see Num. 26: 38–40), and then reworks an old military census into a genealogy. Thus, Issachar and the first Benjamin list come from the same sources, and so have been kept together.

Naphtali (7:13)

This is the shortest of the genealogies, consisting simply of the sons of Naphtali as recorded in Genesis 46:24 (see Num. 26:48–49). Note, though, that the Chronicler nonetheless takes the time to mention Naphtali's mother Bilhah, the handmaid of Rachel (Gen. 46:25; see also Gen. 30:7–8; 35:25). In the Genesis 46 passage, "the sons of Bilhah" refers to Dan and Naphtali; in Chronicles, where Dan does not appear, these words refer to Naphtali's sons.

Manasseh (7:14–19)

Unlike the earlier Manassite account (5:23–24), which simply listed the settlements and chiefs of the Manassite clans east of the Jordan (see Num. 32:39–42; Josh. 1:12–17), this section deals with the descendants of Manasseh. Unfortunately, the genealogy is extremely tangled and corrupt, so that the relationships are often unclear. Many of the names found here (Machir, Gilead, Asriel, Shemida) are also found in Numbers 26:29–33, showing a general agreement as to the clans of Manasseh. However, in Chronicles these names are arranged into quite a different genealogy. So, for example, Asriel is the son of Gilead in Numbers, but the son of Manasseh himself in Chronicles. Another intriguing difference is the presence of women in the Manassite list. In contrast to the Numbers parallel, which mentions neither wives nor daughters, Chronicles lists Manasseh's nameless Aramean concubine, Maacah wife of Machir, Zelophehad's daughters, and Hammolecheth, who was apparently Machir's sister. As in the Judahite lists, this inclusion of women marks a welcome change from the unrelievedly patriarchal tone of most genealogies.

Ephraim (7:20–29)

38

As we would expect, the genealogy of Ephraim, the second son of Joseph, follows the listing of Joseph's first and eldest son, Manasseh (see Gen. 48:1–22). However, Ephraim's genealogy bears only a slight relationship to biblical sources (compare this text with Num. 26:35–36, where Shuthelah is listed as Ephraim's son, but no other names are held in common). Note that, further down in Ephraim's line, the Chronicler comes to Joshua (7:27). Although Joshua is everywhere called the son of Nun (for example, Exod. 33:11; Josh. 1:1; 1 Kgs. 16:34; Neh. 8:17), this is the only biblical genealogy supplied for him.

The most remarkable feature of the Ephraimite genealogical list is the narrative in 7:21b–23. Ephraim's entire family is wiped out in an abortive cattle raid on the people of Gath. After a long period of mourning, during which Ephraim is comforted by his brothers, Ephraim's wife again conceives, and the line is preserved. Still, Ephraim commemorates the terrible slaughter of his first family by naming his new son Beriah, meaning "disaster."

The story of Beriah is reminiscent of the story of Jabez in 4:9–10, and like it may well be very old. But the most intriguing feature of the Beriah story is the assumption that Ephraim lived in the land, when according to the story in Genesis, Ephraim was born, lived, and died in Egypt. The rabbis attempted to resolve this difficulty by proposing an early exodus for Ephraim (b. Sanhedrin 92.2). Certainly, it is clear that Chronicles here presents an alternative tradition to the Exodus story.

This narrative imagines the tribe of Ephraim as native to the land. Further, the Ephraimites in this story evidently live, at least in part, by raiding the wealthy inhabitants of the coastal plain. This fits the social picture of Palestine in the thirteenth century B.C., when Egypt's hold on the region was weakening, the Canaanite city-states were warring on one another, the marauding Sea Peoples were establishing settlements such as Gath along the coast, and lawless people were settling in the hill country. Archaeologists have recovered at Tell el-Amarna in Egypt numerous letters from the Canaanite city-states to Pharaoh Akhenaton, which help us to picture this time. The Amarna letters express concern about the outlaws living in the hills, who are called the *Habiru*. Many scholars believe this term to be related to the word "Hebrew." In short, the story of Ephraim's tragedy may well provide a window back onto the settlement of the Israelites in the land, from a quite different perspective than the mainstream view in the Pentateuch. The preservation of such an odd little nugget among the Chronicler's sources reminds us of the remarkable diversity of Israel's traditions. The use of this narrative here demonstrates the Chronicler's skill in weaving together a variety of sources and traditions.

Asher (7:30–40)

39

The names of the children of Asher and of his son Beriah are taken directly from Genesis 46:17 (see Num. 26:44–46). Note that Asher is said to be "enrolled by genealogies, for service in war" (7:40). Evidently, the Asher genealogy, like the genealogy of Issachar and the first Benjaminite list, has been taken from a military census.

The Second Benjamin Genealogy (8:1–40)

The second Benjaminite list draws upon different sources than the first. Note, for instance, that apart from Bela, there is no agreement between these two Benjaminite lists on the names or number of Benjamin's sons. Chapter 8:1–40 emphasizes the connection between Benjamin and the southern kingdom. So, in 8:13, the Benjaminites Beriah and Shemah are associated with Aijalon (a site that, according to 2 Chronicles 11:10, was fortified by the Judean king Rehoboam), while in 8:28 and 32, the chiefs of Benjamin's clans are said to live in Jerusalem. The placement of this list at the end of the tribal genealogies fits the broken birth-order arrangement of the first few tribes. So Benjamin, the youngest son of Israel, is treated last.

It is this second list that gives an account of Saul's place in the Benjaminite genealogy (8:33–34). Here as elsewhere (for example, 1 Sam. 9:1; 2 Sam. 21:14; 1 Chr. 12:1; 26:28), Saul is called the son of Kish. The name of Saul's grandfather is derived, either by the Chronicler or by his source, from 1 Samuel 14:49–51. Assuming that Abner was Saul's uncle rather than his cousin (a possible reading of 1 Sam. 14:50–51), Ner the father of Abner had to be Saul's grandfather (rather than Abiel, as stated in 1 Sam. 9:1; 14:51). The names of Saul's four sons in 8:33 come from 1 Samuel 14:49 (for Jonathan, Malchishua, and Ishvi/Ishbaal) and 31:2 (for Abinadab). Ishvi is apparently another name for Esh-baal (8:33; 9:39) or Ishbaal (for example, 2 Sam. 2:8; 3:7–8; 4:1). The MT of 2 Samuel refers to this son of Saul, who reigned in the north for seven and a half years after his father's death, as Ish-bosheth. Rather than referring to the son of an Israelite king as "man of Baal" (the literal meaning of Ishbaal), the scribes replaced the name of the Canaanite god with the word *bosheth*, which is Hebrew for "shame." Similarly, the son of Jonathan, called Mephibosheth in 2 Samuel (see 2 Sam. 4:4; 9:6; 10–13), is called Merib-baal in 1 Chronicles 8:34 and 9:40.

The Conclusion of the Tribal Genealogies (9:1–44)

40

Following the second Benjaminite list (8:1–40), the main body of the tribal genealogies concludes in 9:1, with the summary statement, "So all Israel was enrolled by genealogies; and these are written in the

Book of the Kings of Israel." Then, the reader is told of Judah's exile "because of their unfaithfulness." In the story of David, which begins in chapter 10 with the death of Saul, it is made clear that Saul as well "died for his unfaithfulness" (10:13). Thus, the end of the genealogies and the beginning of the narrative in Chronicles are connected by a firm reminder of the Chronicler's theme: faithfulness to the Lord and obedience to the Lord's word bring blessing and life, while unfaithfulness and disobedience bring destruction and death.

In an appendix to the tribal genealogies, 9:2–34 describes the returnees to Jerusalem, after the time of exile had ended. The list is not a general record of Jerusalem's resettlement, but rather focuses on the priests and the Levitical families. This list is found again later in the Chronicler's History, with some minor variations (Neh. 11:4–19). Its placement here, in the opening section of Chronicles, prefigures the eventual reestablishment of the temple and its worship following the disaster of exile. Like the Davidic genealogy in chapter 3, the list of returnees provides a connection with the "present day" of the Chronicler.

The genealogies conclude (9:35–44) with a section of the second genealogy of Benjamin (taken from 8:29–38) showing the ancestry and descendants of Saul. By repeating this portion of Benjamin's lineage at the end of the genealogies, the Chronicler provides a neat segue from the genealogies into the story of David, which opens with the death of Benjamin's most famous son, Saul (10:1–14).

By structuring the genealogical lists in such a way that David's line comes at the climax, the Chronicler demonstrated to his people the central place of David and his line in God's design. Further, as we have seen, the genealogies have already introduced us to the central theme of the the Chronicler's History: that faithful obedience and sincere piety lead to blessing, while disobedience and false worship lead to curse. Finally, the genealogies have shown us something of how the Chronicler reads Scripture. Rather than weighing texts critically, the Chronicler seems content to treat all of Scripture (and indeed, other sources not found in our Scriptures) as having equal weight and value. The Chronicler's approach is not analytical, but synthetic; both/and, rather than either/or. In the genealogies, the Chronicler assembled a bewildering variety of traditions into a new whole, in which each part complemented every other part. We will see these same ideas, attitudes, and approaches expressed in the Chronicler's treatment of David's story.

David

While the story of David in 1 Chronicles draws heavily upon the Deuteronomistic History, the Chronicler's narrative takes a quite different direction and shape. In Samuel–Kings, David appears in a number of roles: as the virtuous young hero, the valiant warlord, the good outlaw, the victorious king and, finally, the sad old man, a mere husk of his former glory. In Chronicles, however, David appears in one preeminent role. David is the founder of Jerusalem's temple liturgy. All else that he is or does is placed in service to this mission. The Chronicler is not particularly interested in David's politics, or even in David the man. However, the portrayal of David in Chronicles is not so much idealized as *focused*, narrowly and precisely, on one aspect: David as worship leader and founder. Although Solomon will actually build the temple, all that he and the later descendants of David will do to strengthen and preserve Jerusalem's shrine has already been prepared for by David himself.

Following a prologue that depicts the death of Saul (10:1–14), Chronicles presents David's story in three great movements (see Wright 1998, 49–59, though the outline followed in this study differs from his at several points). First, in 11:1—12:40, David is proclaimed king by all the tribes of Israel. Supported by "a great army, like an army of God" (12:22), he conquers Jerusalem and makes it his capital.

Next, in 13:1—21:30, the accomplishments and failures of David's reign are described. As is appropriate for the author of Jerusalem's liturgy, David's first and perhaps greatest act is to bring the sacred ark of the covenant into Jerusalem (13:1—16:43). David's victories in war and successes at home demonstrate that God's blessing rests on him. Indeed, God promises to preserve David's line forever (17:1–15). The promise is threatened by David's sin, when in his pride he undertakes a census of all Israel (21:1–30). But good comes from David's evil: the threshing floor of Ornan, where David sets up an altar and offers sacrifices to avert God's wrath, is revealed as the future site of God's temple (22:1).

43

The final act of David's story, in 22:1—29:30, is as much about Solomon as it is about David. But its primary focus is on the temple that Solomon will build. David assembles the materials needed for the temple's construction and the personnel needed for its maintenance and liturgy. Then, he gives to Solomon both the plans for the temple and the throne. Afterwards, David dies in peace and security.

10:1–14
(//1 Sam. 31:1–13)

Prologue: The Death of Saul

In Chronicles as in 1 Samuel, the story of kingship in Israel begins with Saul. However, the Chronicler does not regard Saul as king in any full sense. In Chronicles, the first person who is said to reign in Israel is David, not Saul (3:4). Even during Saul's putative reign, David was in fact in command (see 11:2//2 Sam. 5:2). Saul is mentioned because he must be, in order to establish the context for David's coming to power. From the genealogies, we have learned that while the Chronicler uses tradition creatively, he does not invent new traditions. Hence, Chronicles is faithful to what the tradition reveals about David's accession to the throne: that David was not the natural successor to kingship, but rather supplanted another line.

However, the Chronicler spends no more time on Saul than he has to, telling only the story of Saul's defeat and suicide at the battle of Gilboa. The Chronicler's account differs from his source text (1 Sam. 31:1–13) slightly, but significantly. In 1 Chronicles 10:6 (//1 Sam. 31:6), it is not all Saul's men who die, emphasizing the military scope of the loss, but "all his house." Similarly, in contrast to 1 Samuel, which records a mass exodus of Israelites "on the other side of the valley and those beyond the Jordan" (1 Sam. 31:7), Chronicles relates that only the Israelites in the valley (presumably, the valley below Gilboa) fled. These changes have a double effect. First, in the Chronicler's view, no one with a legitimate, dynastic claim to Saul's throne survived the battle of Gilboa. No impediment now remains to David's assumption of the throne. The seven years of civil war described in the first four chapters of 2 Samuel can thus be skipped over without a mention! Second, the depredations of the Philistines having been minimized, the extent of David's kingdom is from the first greater than that imagined in 1 Samuel.

44

In 10:10, Saul's head is placed in the temple of Dagon, which may involve some symbolic significance (Mosis 1973, 24–25). Note that in the ark narrative (1 Sam. 4:1—7:1), it is Dagon's head that is removed, a trophy of the warrior God of Israel whose glory accompanies the ark (1 Sam. 5:4). Perhaps, for the Chronicler, the defeat of Saul meant that Israel was humiliated before the Philistine god, just as Dagon had been humiliated before the ark. In any case, the heroism of the troops of Jabesh-gilead mitigates this disgrace; the remains of Saul and his sons are given a decent burial.

An interpretive conclusion in 10:13–14 affects the reading of the entire scene. Saul, we are told, "died for his unfaithfulness," specifically for his unfaithfulness to the word of the Lord (10:13, translated "command of the LORD" in the NRSV). Here again, the Chronicler's focus on Scripture is in view—though in a negative rather than a positive sense. Saul's rejection of the word of the Lord sets him against the mainstream of David's descendants, who will hear and respond to the divine word.

Rather than seeking the Lord through the legitimate means of prophetic word or Scripture, Saul tried to gain supernatural insight through forbidden means, by consulting a medium (1 Sam. 28:3–25). For this reason, "the LORD put him to death" (10:14)—a very harsh reading of the circumstances of Saul's suicide. Note that suicide is not condemned as such in the Hebrew Bible. The six suicides explicitly described—those of Abimelech, Samson, Saul and his armor-bearer, Ahithophel, and Zimri—have in common the purpose of avoiding or reversing shame, so that honor is preserved or restored. The death of Abimelech, like that of Saul, took place on the battlefield. Both were badly wounded. But Saul killed himself to escape torture, abuse, and humiliation. Abimelech's was an assisted suicide: he ordered his armor bearer to kill him, so that he would not be shamed by dying from a wound inflicted by a woman (Judg. 9:54)! Samson's suicide was more purposeful: in his death he killed more Philistines than he had in his entire lifetime as their enemy (Judg. 16:30), thus restoring the honor taken from him by his blinding and humiliation. The counselor Ahithophel, seeing that his wise advice was ignored by Absalom, foresaw David's return to power and avoided humiliation by (after carefully putting his affairs in order) hanging himself (2 Sam. 17:23). Finally, the northern king Zimri, seeing that his defeat by Omri was imminent, burned down his own palace with himself inside it (1 Kgs. 16:18). In none of these cases is the act in itself condemned, although only Samson's suicide is viewed heroically. The story of Saul's death, then, could be viewed as a tragedy, moving the reader to pity and regret.

But for the Chronicler, Saul's death should evoke from us not pity, but a grim satisfaction. The Chronicler's assessment of Saul's suicide is strongly reminiscent of what the Deuteronomist says of Zimri, who died "because of the sins that he committed, doing evil in the sight of the LORD, walking in the way of Jeroboam, and for the sin that he committed, causing Israel to sin" (1 Kgs. 16:19). However, the Chronicler goes still further, seeing the Lord as the agent responsible for Saul's death. Saul may have held the sword, but it is the Lord who, in the Chronicler's view, put him to death. Saul was unfaithful, and reaped the fruits of his unfaithfulness: just as unfaithful Judah would suffer eventual defeat and destruction (see 9:1). However, Saul's defeat is not God's last word—far from it! Out of the blood and death and destruction that bring Saul's story to an end comes the true beginning of Israel's greatness under David. Just so, in the flow of the Chronicler's History, the exile is not God's last word, but rather serves as the crucible of Israel's refinement and rebirth.

In the end, the Chronicler's assessment of Saul is in keeping with the assessment found in the Deuteronomistic History. Although that history made use of earlier sources sympathetic to Saul, the final form of the text views him as a madman, rebellious against the word of God, who fell in battle after having been rejected by God. With this view, the Chronicler is in full agreement. By eliminating the period of civil war following Saul's death from his purview, the Chronicler only continues the trend already evident in the final form of the Deuteronomistic History, to minimize the scale and significance of those seven years of conflict. Both the Deuteronomist and the Chronicler, it seems, were in a hurry to get to David; that the Chronicler's impatience is more pronounced is only a sign of the greater importance he gives to David and his line.

11:1—12:40

David Becomes King

With the death of Saul, David assumes the throne. Chapter 11:1–9 (//2 Sam. 5:1–10) describes the coronation of David and the conquest of Jerusalem. It is followed by a list of David's heroes: the Three, the Thirty, and a representative sample of his army (11:10–47), along with a report of some of their deeds. This list of the great warriors in David's service appears, with some variations, in 2 Samuel 23:8–39. The account of the exploits of David's heroes is followed by three stories about David's earliest supporters (12:1–22). Although these stories sometimes assume knowledge of Samuel–Kings, they are not taken from that source. Once more, the Chronicler is drawing upon sources and traditions unknown to us. Likewise unique to Chronicles is the enumeration by tribes of David's great army (12:23–40).

In Chronicles, David's reign is unopposed from the beginning. Jerusalem falls to him virtually without a struggle, and so is from the first David's city. In Israel, David is unanimously supported by all the tribes, and particularly by Israel's greatest heroes and warriors. In this way, the Chronicler establishes a firm foundation for the important acts that follow, particularly the transport of the ark to Jerusalem, the establishment of the liturgy and sacred personnel, and the assembly of plans and materials for the temple that David's son Solomon will build.

David Begins His Reign (11:1–9)
(//2 Sam. 5:1–10)

All the elders of Israel gather to David at Hebron, to declare him their king. In 2 Samuel, "Israel" refers to the northern tribes, which now after seven and a half years of civil war accept David's leadership. But in Chronicles, which does not mention the war, "Israel" is understood to refer collectively to north and south (see 12:23–40). The point is that David has the unqualified support of all the tribes. The Chronicler typically emphasizes that David was anointed in obedient response to the word of the Lord—related, in this instance, through the prophetic word of Samuel (11:3). From the first, David's kingdom is founded on the word of the Lord, just as Saul's had been doomed by his disregard of the divine word.

Of course, a king needs a palace, and a capital city. So David, accompanied by the united armies of all Israel (11:4), marches on the Jebusite stronghold of Jerusalem, then called Jebus. The Chronicler's account of the conquest is lean and direct. Although the Jebusites confidently declare, "You will not come in here," (11:5), the city is taken without incident. David had offered command over his armies to the first man to strike a blow against the Jebusites. By leading this first charge against the king's enemies, Joab earns his command. But Joab is more than a warrior in Chronicles. We are told that, while David personally oversaw construction of the central stronghold, including the terraces on the eastern slopes of Zion called the Millo (meaning "fill"), Joab "repaired the rest of the city" (10:8).

47

The acquisition of a fortified, defensible capital would of course be a necessity for any new king. But the Chronicler's long view is on the greater significance of Jerusalem, as the place of the Lord's temple. As we will see, the Chronicler moves very swiftly from David's enthronement and conquest of Jerusalem to the bringing of the ark into the city (chapter 13). It is for this reason, then, that the city must be conquered and repaired: not so much as a capital for David, but in preparation for the enthronement of the Lord in the shrine David would establish, and in the temple David's descendants would build and defend. So, the possession of Jerusalem is the beginning of David's greatness: after this, "David became greater and greater, for the LORD of hosts was with him" (11:9//2 Sam. 5:10).

David's Heroes (11:10–47)
(//2 Sam. 23:8–39)

In 2 Samuel, this list of the great warriors in David's service appears at the end of David's story. By placing the list at the beginning of David's reign, the Chronicler adds still more to the overwhelming sense of David's power, and of the support given to David by his followers, from the very first. Indeed, by noting that these great heroes are but the *chiefs* of David's warriors (11:10; compare 2 Sam. 23:8), the Chronicler implies power beyond even these great worthies. Like David's coronation itself, the support of these heroes for David is said by the Chronicler to be in keeping with the word of the Lord—regarding not David alone, but all Israel (11:10). The point is clear. Once more, from the beginning, David's unquestioned leadership over a unified Israel is stressed. David's authority is a crucial issue for Chronicles, because David was the founder of the Jerusalem temple liturgy. To ensure orthodoxy, it is vital that David be shown to have commanded respect and obedience from the first. Only then can the reader be sure that the liturgy David was inspired to authorize was indeed established and preserved, just as God had commanded.

The roll call of heroes begins with the exploits of the Three, David's closest companions and greatest warriors. The list in Chronicles is a bit confusing, as only two of the Three are mentioned: Jashobeam (11:11) and Eleazar (11:12–14). The third member of this elite group, Shammah (see 1 Sam. 23:11–12), is not mentioned in Chronicles. However, note that the exploits of Eleazar in Chronicles seem to be a combination of the deeds of Eleazar and Shammah recounted in 1 Samuel, suggesting that the two have been collapsed into one. Impressive as the Three may be (Jashobeam alone is said to have killed three hundred warriors at one time), the place of David as greatest of Israel's heroes

48

remains unquestioned. So, in Chronicles, Eleazar's victory is shared with David: the two took their stand together at Pas-dammim, "and the LORD saved them by a great victory" (11:14).

The story of the Bethlehem well (11:15–19//2 Sam. 23:13–17) illustrates perfectly both the love of these heroes for their leader, and the qualities in David that earned such fierce loyalty. The setting is the cave of Adullam, which was David's military headquarters during his years as a bandit in flight from Saul (see 1 Sam. 22:1; titles of Pss. 57 and 142). The Chronicler has not described this period, but assumes that the reader is familiar with David's entire story. Adullam is only about fifteen miles from Bethlehem, David's birthplace and hometown. Being so close to home, but unable to go there because of the Philistine garrison quartered in Bethlehem, David began to reminisce about the taste of the water from the communal well his family had used when he was a boy. The Three overhear David's wistful request ("O that someone would give me water to drink from the well of Bethlehem that is by the gate!" 11:17) and decide to grant it. They launch a lightning-swift raid, breaking into the enemy camp just long enough to draw water from the well, and then fight their way back home with the water. David's reaction is priceless. Instead of drinking the water, David pours it out as a drink offering before the Lord—showing, in so doing, that this is a gift too precious for any human to accept. Then, David declares, "My God forbid that I should do this. Can I drink the blood of these men? For at the risk of their lives they brought it" (11:19). This flashback to David's hard years reminds the reader that, even before he became king, David had earned the love and loyalty of the people.

Having demonstrated the heroism of the Three, the Chronicler now turns to the deeds of the Thirty, David's elite corps of warriors. First among these heroes is Abishai, brother of Joab and commander of the Thirty (11:20–21). Also among the Thirty is Benaiah, whose exploits include the single-handed slaying of a lion in the wintertime, when the beast would have been lean, hungry, and particularly fierce (11:22); and the besting of an Egyptian champion nearly eight feet tall, armed with "a spear like a weaver's beam" (11:23; compare 1 Sam. 17:4–7; 1 Chr. 20:5). Benaiah's victory against this foreign giant, using no weapon but a staff, is strongly reminiscent of the story of David's victory over the Philistine giant Goliath, also won using the weapon of a shepherd (a sling, in David's case; see 1 Sam. 17: 1–58).

After the mention of these representatives of the Thirty comes a sampling of the rank and file. The list of David's warriors is a bit longer in Chronicles than in the parallel text in Samuel, which ends with Uriah

49

the Hittite, husband to Bathsheba. Just as the Chronicler lists only two of the Three, and only two representatives of the Thirty, so this list, long as it is, is intended to be a representative sample. It was warriors of this caliber, in such great numbers, who flocked to David to acclaim him as king. The glory of these great heroes, drawn as they are into David's orbit, demonstrates the power and glory of the king they served.

David's First Followers (12:1–22)

As in the story of the Bethlehem well, the Chronicler flashes back to the days when David was an outlaw, on the run from Saul. Even then, when David was at his weakest, he was able to attract great warriors to his cause—even from among Saul's own people. So, first among those listed as David's first followers are archers and slingers from Benjamin, "Saul's kindred" (12:2). Also from among those who would have been expected to follow Saul were veteran infantry officers from Gad, "whose faces were like the faces of lions, and who were swift as gazelles on the mountains" (12:8). The hard-bitten Gadites were not fair-weather converts to David's cause. They came to join him in the spring, when the Jordan was in flood and the crossing was difficult and dangerous (12:15). These eleven Gadite heroes supported David, quite literally, through hell and high water!

Chapter 12:16–18 relates the arrival of troops from Benjamin and Judah at David's stronghold. David says to them, "If you have come to me in friendship, to help me, then my heart will be knit to you; but if you have come to betray me to my adversaries, though my hands have done no wrong, then may the God of our ancestors see and give judgment" (12:17). The word rendered "friendship" in the NRSV is the Hebrew *shalom*, which means well-being, health, and peace. To those who offer him peace and friendship, David promises his own personal dedication and commitment: "my heart will be knit to you." In the ancient Israelite view of humanity, the heart was the seat of the will and the center of the self. To bind one's heart to another, as David here pledges to do, was not a sentimental or romantic act. It was, rather, an assurance of loyalty and commitment.

David makes no threat to counterbalance this promise. Should these troops come to betray rather than to befriend, David trusts "the God of our ancestors" to "see and give judgment" (12:17; see the excursus on the God of the ancestors, above). David's confidence in God stands in strong contrast to the faithlessness of Saul, who sought guidance in the cult of the dead rather than trusting in the ancient tradition of Israel's faith.

David's trust proves well-founded, for the Lord takes action and answers David's question in dramatic fashion. Suddenly the leader of these soldiers, Amasai (here called "chief of the Thirty," but see 11:20–21//2 Sam. 23:18), is overcome by the spirit and prophesies. The Hebrew means, literally, "the spirit clothed itself with Amasai." This metaphorical use of the verb "clothe" appears only three other times in the Hebrew Bible. The first, from Judges 6:34, involves Gideon's empowerment as a war leader; there, the NRSV reads "the spirit of the LORD took possession of Gideon." The second, in Job 29:14, involves Job's assertion of innocence and righteousness: "I put on righteousness, and it clothed me." The third is also from Chronicles (2 Chr. 24:20), and like 1 Chronicles 12:18 involves a spontaneous prophetic pronouncement—this time from Zechariah the priest. One might also remember the language of the apostle Paul, who says that believers have "put on the Lord Jesus" (Rom. 13:14), and insists, "As many of you as were baptized into Christ have clothed yourselves with Christ" (Gal. 3:27). These New Testament texts and the LXX of the Hebrew Bible texts listed above all use forms of the same Greek word, suggesting that Paul is using here an idea drawn, in particular, from Chronicles. At any rate, in all of these passages the point is the same. Job insists that his righteousness defines him—Job has virtually *become* righteousness. Similarly, Paul urges believers to be immersed in Christ, so that Jesus stamps their very being with his character. The language of possession used by the NRSV in the Judges parallel may seem odd or extreme. Still, it expresses the central idea in all of these texts: that one has in some sense given over one's identity to another controlling power.

In short, Chronicles affirms that the spirit of God took Amasai over, and spoke through him. There is no indication that Amasai either expected or intended this. He was a warrior, not a prophet! But still, the spirit spoke through him in words that echo David's longing for *shalom*:

> We are yours, O David;
>   and with you, O son of Jesse!
> Peace, peace [*shalom*] to you,
>   and peace to the one who helps you!
> For your God is the one who helps you.

With this fervent declaration of *shalom*, Amasai and his people are accepted into David's service and become officers in his army. Once more, David's mission has been affirmed by the word of the Lord.

In 12:19–22, the Chronicler moves us up in time to the battle at Mount Gilboa in which Saul and his house came to an end. The Chronicler assumes that the reader knows the story of David's career as a

51

mercenary with the Philistine army (see 1 Sam. 27:1—28:2). He does not trouble to tell it again, apart from reminding us that David took no part in the battle, having been warned off by the Philistines themselves (12:19; compare 1 Sam. 29:1–11). Although the Philistines had worried about David deserting to Saul, what happened instead was that a contingent of troops from Manasseh deserted Saul to follow David! These soldiers went with David to his former base at Ziklag, and then helped David track down and defeat the Amalekite marauders who had looted and burned the town in his absence. The full story (though without mention of assistance from Manassite deserters) is found in 1 Samuel 30:1–31; the Chronicler again assumes we know who the "band of raiders" (12:21) were, and why David was pursuing them.

This extended flashback concludes with an affirmation of popular support for David: "Indeed from day to day people kept coming to David to help him, until there was a great army, like an army of God" (12:22). The point here is twofold. First, David's authority once more is bolstered by the affirmation of support from all Israel, north and south, even before he officially became king. Second, the statement that David's army was "like the army of God" (a better reading than the indefinite form used in the NRSV) conveys the sense present throughout these chapters, that God is with David in all he does. In 11:9, we were told that "David became greater and greater, for the LORD of hosts was with him." Now, the hosts of heaven are paralleled by the hosts of David. That David's army is like God's emphasizes not only the irresistible power of David's forces, but also the rightness of David's cause.

David's Army (12:23–40)

Having told us that David amassed "a great army, like an army of God" (12:22), the Chronicler now describes the extent of this "great army," in some detail. This material is unique to Chronicles, evidently based upon traditions otherwise unknown to us. The numbers are unrealistically large (see the discussion of large numbers in Chronicles in the Introduction). However, the significance of this text is not to be found in its historical accuracy, or lack of accuracy. The Chronicler effectively demonstrates support for David from all the tribes—twelve (counting Ephraim and Manasseh instead of Joseph) plus Levi. In terms of the story line of Chronicles, this section returns us in time and space to David's coronation at Hebron, where soldiers have come from all Israel "to turn the kingdom of Saul over to him, according to the word of the LORD" (12:23).

Several features of this list are worthy of note. First, while the nearby tribes of Judah and Benjamin contribute relatively modest support, the most distant northern and Transjordanian tribes send huge contingents: compare 6,800 troops from Judah and 3,000 from Benjamin with 120,000 from Reuben, Gad, and the half-tribe of Manasseh, or 28,600 from distant Dan. In this way, Chronicles emphasizes the support of all Israel for David. Far from holding back their loyalty, the northern tribes demonstrate even more enthusiasm for David than his own tribe!

Chronicles does not entirely ignore the sectional strife that would continue to plague Israel. In 12:29, another reason for the small contingent from Benjamin is given: these, after all, were "the kindred of Saul . . . of whom the majority had continued to keep their allegiance to the house of Saul." This is as close as the Chronicler comes to acknowledging the divisive period of civil war that came between Saul's death and David's enthronement.

However, Benjamin is the exception. The eighteen thousand troops from the half-tribe of Manasseh living west of the Jordan "were expressly named to come and make David king" (12:31). Similarly, Issachar "had understanding of the times, to know what Israel ought to do" (12:32). This statement may remind Christian readers of Jesus' words on the importance of reading the signs of the times (Matt. 16:2–3; Luke 12:54–56). Wise Issachar had the discernment to perceive God's hand upon David, the wisdom to sense the direction of the Spirit's leading, and the courage to act. Finally, note that Zebulun came "to help David with singleness of purpose" (12:33). The expression translated "with singleness of purpose" in the NRSV means literally "without a double heart," or, given the Hebrew connotations of the heart, "without double-mindedness." This expression is also found in Psalm 12:2, which prays God's deliverance from those who speak "with flattering lips and a double heart." Similarly, the Letter of James declares that "the doubter, being double-minded and unstable in every way, must not expect to receive anything from the Lord" (Jas. 1:7). In Zebulun, however, such double-mindedness was lacking. As we would say, the fifty thousand soldiers from Zebulun gave David their wholehearted support.

Indeed, 12:38 affirms that the entire company, 339,600 troops from all the tribes of Israel, "came to Hebron with full intent to make David king over all Israel; likewise all the rest of Israel were of a single mind [literally "of one heart!"] to make David king." It is a joyous, festive occasion, with all David's multitude joining together to eat and drink. The troops not only came to David in full battle gear, ready to fight for him; they also came with abundant food and wine to share with one another, "for there was joy in Israel" (12:40).

13:1—21:30
David's Reign

Now that David is secure on his throne in Jerusalem, the Chronicler turns to the great events of his reign. David's first and greatest act as king is the transport of the ark to Jerusalem, and the inauguration of services of worship before the ark (13:1—16:43). Following this, Chronicles relates God's promise of an eternal dynasty for David (17:1–15), and David's prayer of thanksgiving in response (17:16–27). David's successes, both in the field of war and in the peaceful administration of his kingdom (18:1—20:8), demonstrate God's blessing. Unfortunately, the Chronicler also must relate David's one great failure: his disobedience to God's will regarding the census (21:1–30). This failure, however, will prove to be the springboard for David's greatest legacy: the plans and preparations for the great temple in Jerusalem, which David's son Solomon will build.

The Ark Comes to Jerusalem (13:1—16:43)

With his kingship established, David turns his attention to the ark of God, the most sacred object in Israel's ancient traditions. The ark was an ornately decorated box, containing (among other sacred items) the tablets of the Ten Commandments—hence the frequent designation "ark of the covenant" (twelve times in Chronicles alone; for example, 1 Chr. 15:25–29; 2 Chr. 5:2, 7). However, the ark was revered not so much for what it contained as for what it represented. Atop the ark was placed the *kapporeth*, usually translated "mercy seat": a slab of gold surmounted by the images of terrible semidivine beings called cherubim (Exod. 25:17–22). The outstretched wings of the cherubim formed a throne, above which the Lord was believed to be invisibly present—as the divine title "the LORD, who is enthroned on the cherubim" indicates (13:6//2 Sam. 6:2; see also 1 Sam. 4:4; Ps. 80:1; Ezek. 10:1). The ark served as the Lord's footstool, the place where the divine feet touch the earth. Hence, the ark was the intersection of divine and human worlds, and so was identified as the place of the Lord's special presence. Indeed, in the days of Israel's wilderness wandering, the ark had been the place where Moses and Aaron encountered the Lord (Exod. 25:22). By bringing the ark into Jerusalem, David was establishing this city as the place of God's enthronement. Jerusalem was to be not merely the capital of a kingdom, but the center of the world.

54

While the material in 13:1—16:43 is drawn from 2 Samuel 5:11—6:20, the Chronicler has rearranged the stories somewhat. In 2 Samuel, the accounts of David's friendship with Hiram of Tyre, the building of David's palace, and the defeat of the Philistines come before the story of the two attempts to bring the ark to Jerusalem. But in Chronicles, these accounts are sandwiched between the two ark stories, so that the first, failed attempt at transporting the ark comes first.

This change has two major effects. First, David's coronation, the conquest of Jerusalem, and the bringing of the ark follow one after another in swift sequence in Chronicles. Following his conquest of Jerusalem, David's first act as king is to bring the ark into his new capital. In this way, it is made clear that David's first priority was the establishment of Jerusalem's worship. Second, the Chronicler deals with a question posed by David himself: "How can I bring the ark of God into my care?" (13:12//2 Sam. 6:9). The reader could well conclude that Uzzah's death was a sign of God's disfavor toward David. But by moving the stories of David's successes in war and diplomacy to a position following the failed first attempt to bring the ark to Jerusalem, the Chronicler makes it clear that this was not the case. God's hand continued to rest upon David in blessing, as David continued to be faithful and obedient to the divine word. In fact, as we will see, it is David himself who learns the cause of the first failure, and remedies it by reinstituting the proper religious authorities.

The First Attempt (13:1–14) (//2 Sam. 6:2–11). In 1 Chronicles 13:1, David consults with "the commanders of the thousands and of the hundreds." Earlier (11:1–9), the armies of Israel had come to David at Hebron to declare him king, and had followed him to the conquest of Jerusalem. Now, after an extended flashback demonstrating David's glory through the fame and power of his army, the Chronicler returns us to the time after Jerusalem's conquest and repair.

David tells the leaders of the assembled armies what he intends to do. The priests and Levites, now scattered through the country in the "cities that have pasture lands" (13:2; see 6:54–81), are to be summoned to Jerusalem—indeed, all the inhabitants of Israel are to be urged to come. "Then," David says, "let us bring again the ark of our God to us; for we did not turn to it in the days of Saul" (13:3). Once more, the faithlessness of Saul's reign is placed in contrast to the pious devotion of David. Not only does David intend to bring the long-abandoned ark to the city, but the summoning of the priests and Levites shows David's resolve to establish Jerusalem as the religious center of his kingdom.

David asks his commanders for their support in this enterprise. He is resolved to bring the ark to Jerusalem, but he will do this only "If it seems good to you, and if it is the will of the LORD our God" (13:2).

55

Ominously, Chronicles assures the reader only of the first condition: "The whole assembly agreed to do so, for the thing pleased all the people" (13:4). The failure to ensure God's will in this matter will have tragic consequences.

The people come to Jerusalem from across the length and breadth of David's kingdom, "from the Shihor of Egypt to Lebo-hamath" (13:5). In Numbers 34:5 and 8, the farthest extent of the territory promised to Israel by the Lord is marked by Lebo-hamath to the north, and the Wadi of Egypt to the south (see also Ezek. 47:19–20; Amos 6:14). The Chronicler claims that these borders applied from the very beginning of David's reign. Further, he understands "the Wadi of Egypt" to refer, not to the Wadi el-Arish, which ran through the desert between the Negeb and the Sinai wastes, but to Shihor—that is, the Nile (Josh. 13:3; Jer. 2:18; Isa. 23:3)! Not only are all Israel's tribes loyal to David from the first, but all Israel's rightful territory and more is already in his possession.

The account of the ark's journey to Jerusalem comes from 2 Samuel 6:2–11. Most of the variations between Chronicles and Samuel are due to the different text Chronicles is using as a source, not to changes made by the Chronicler. So, in the MT of 2 Samuel 6:2, we are told that David and the people went to Baale-Judah for the ark. This is awkward, as 1 Samuel 6:21—7:1 states that the ark had been left at Kiriath-jearim. Chronicles follows the reading of the old Palestinian text (now available to us in a fragmentary text of Samuel from Qumran, called 4QSam[a]), which identifies Baalah with Kiriath-jearim.

The ark, riding on a new ox-drawn cart, is accompanied by a singing, dancing throng, led by David himself. But the rejoicing is stilled by tragedy when Uzzah, riding on the cart with the ark, puts out a hand to steady the sacred chest. In that moment, "The anger of the LORD was kindled against Uzzah; he struck him down because he put out his hand to the ark; and he died there before God" (13:10//2 Sam. 6:7). To a Christian reader, this seems savagely unfair. Recall, however, the significance of the ark in ancient Israel. The ark, as the footstool of God, is charged with the very power and presence of the Divine. Note that David and his company, dancing and singing around the ark, are said to be "dancing before God" (13:8)—the ark is identified unambiguously with the presence of the Lord! Just so, Uzzah "died there before God" (13:10), a victim of the dangerous holiness, beyond human comprehension or endurance, manifested in the ark.

That God should be dangerous, terrible and terrifying, may disturb many readers. However, the Bible often describes an encounter with God as terrifying. For example, following his dream at Bethel, Jacob "was afraid, and said, 'How awesome [the KJV reads, 'How *dreadful*'] is this place'" (Gen. 28:17). At the burning bush, Moses "hid his face, for he was afraid to look at God" (Exod. 3:6). In the New Testament, the disciples fall to the ground in terror when God speaks from heaven, affirming that Jesus is his son (Matt. 17:6). They are also terrified when Jesus reveals his power by stilling the storm (Mark 4:40–41).

The point, in all of these texts, is that standing in the presence of God is at once wonderful and terrifying. Religion scholar Rudolf Otto (1958, 12–19) has defined the Holy as the *Mysterium Tremendum*, Latin for "the terrible mystery." The holiness of God is awful in the ancient sense: full of awe; wonderful and terrible at the same time. We are at once drawn to God by strong cords of love and adoration, and frightened of God, filled with the overwhelming awareness that God is *GOD*, after all, and entirely unlike anything in our world.

The death of Uzzah brings a halt to David's grand procession. David is understandably angry, fearful, and dismayed. Rather than taking the ark on into Jerusalem, he entrusts it into the keeping of Obed-edom, the Gittite (13:13//2 Sam. 6:11). This appears to be an act of terror and desperation, as though David were abandoning the ark of God to a stranger rather than continuing with it for a step further. But Chronicles mitigates the disgrace considerably by providing for Obed-edom a Levitical pedigree, among the singers and gatekeepers of the Korahite clan (for example, see 15:18; 16:38; 26:4–5). In any case, it becomes swiftly evident that the fault had not lain with the ark itself. Far from suffering under the burden of the ark's safekeeping, Obed-edom and his house are blessed (13:14//2 Sam. 6:11).

God Blesses David (14:1–17) (//2 Sam. 5:11–25). Indeed, David as well experiences blessings from God, proving that, despite the failed attempt to bring the ark into Jerusalem, he is not under God's wrath. This is shown first of all by the friendship of King Hiram of Tyre, who sends materials and skilled laborers to build David a palace (14:1). The effect this generosity had on David is striking: "David then perceived that the LORD had established him as king over Israel, and that his kingdom was highly exalted for the sake of his people Israel" (14:2). In its context in Chronicles, hard on the heels of Uzzah's death and David's failure, this expression of confidence is particularly striking. Not only is David's kingdom blessed, but David is also blessed personally, by many wives and children (14:3–7//2 Sam. 5:13–16; see 1 Chr. 3:5–8).

David's successes earn the enmity of his former masters, the Philistines. Now that David has been "anointed king over all Israel" (14:8), he is a rival who must be put down. The Philistines attack at Rephaim. But, before David goes out against them, he seeks the will and guidance of the Lord (14:10)—something that he had failed to do regarding the first abortive attempt at transporting the ark. Only when David has learned that the Lord favors the assault and assures Israel of

57

victory does David attack, winning a great victory at Baal-perizim. In their panic, the routed Philistines leave behind their gods, which David and his men then burn (14:12). Note that the Chronicler has David and his men deal with the alien gods as commanded by the Torah: "break down their altars, smash their pillars, hew down their sacred poles, and burn their idols with fire" (Deut. 7:5; see also Deut. 12:3).

The name Baal-perizim, we are told, comes from David's exclamation, "God has burst out against my enemies by my hand, like a bursting flood" (Baal-perizim meaning "the lord of bursting out"; 14:11). Again, the contrast with the Uzzah story is significant. The place where Uzzah died was called Perez-uzzah (understood in 13:11 to mean "the bursting out against Uzzah"; see Mosis 1973, 60–61). As there, the anger of the Lord had burst forth against David's servant Uzzah, so here, the Lord's anger bursts out against David's enemies.

Once more, the Philistines rally for the attack; once more, David inquires of the Lord what he should do. This time, instead of a frontal assault, David and his army are commanded to attack by surprise, bursting out of the cover of a balsam grove. God gives the signal for the attack: "When you hear the sound of marching in the tops of the balsam trees, then go out to battle; for God has gone out before you to strike down the army of the Philistines" (14:15). This time, the Philistines are routed out of Israelite lands "from Gibeon to Gezer," and forced to retreat to their own territory. As a result of David's victory over the Philistines, "[t]he fame of David went out into all lands, and the LORD brought the fear of him on all nations" (14:17). Only now, with David's place in God's plan firmly established and all doubts about David's worthiness removed, does the Chronicler turn to David's second attempt to bring the ark to Jerusalem.

The Ark Comes to Jerusalem (15:1—16:43). Once again, the ark is brought to Jerusalem, though this time successfully (15:1–29). The account of the second attempt at transporting the ark is far longer than the first. The preparations that ensured success are carefully described, as are the celebrations which inaugurated Jerusalem's shrine (16:1–43). While the outline of the narrative and much of the content comes from 2 Samuel, the final form of the narrative is uniquely the Chronicler's.

David's Preparations (15:1–24). First Chronicles 15:1 records that David built palaces for himself, and also erected the sacred tent for the Lord. With these actions, Jerusalem was prepared to become the political and spiritual center of the people Israel. All that remains is the Lord's entry into the city in full splendor. Once more, David prepares to bring the ark into his city. This time, however, he is ready. There will be no further tragedies to mar this joyous occasion.

58

This time, David is determined to handle the ark in accordance with the Torah. Chapter 15:2 states, "Then David commanded that no one but the Levites were to carry the ark of God, for the LORD had chosen them to carry the ark of the LORD and to minister to him forever." This is in keeping with Deuteronomy 10:8, which assigns to the Levites responsibility for bearing of the ark, as well as ministry to the Lord and the giving of the blessing (see also Deut. 31:25). For the Deuteronomist, carrying the ark is understood as a form of priestly service (Deut. 31:9; see also 1 Sam. 6:15; 2 Sam. 15:24–25; 1 Kgs. 8:4). In priestly texts as well, the bearing of the ark is a task given to the Levites, although as a group they are subservient to the Aaronid priests (Num 3:31; 4:4–20). In 15:4, David "gathered together the descendants of Aaron and the Levites," to ensure that all was done properly.

It is an unusual group that David assembles. Ordinarily, as we have seen, the Levites are divided into three clans, descended from Gershom, Kohath, and Merari, the three sons of Levi. However, in 15:5–10, six Levitical clans are described: in addition to the familiar three, we find the clans of Elizaphan, Hebron, and Uzziel. Hebron and Uzziel are two of the four sons of Kohath, the other two being Amram, ancestor of Aaron, and Izhar/Amminadab (Exod. 6:18//1 Chr. 6:18; see also Num. 3:19). Elizaphan is evidently the son of Uzziel (Exod. 6:22). Apparently these three Kohathite clans had attained sufficient prominence as to be listed in their own right, apart from the other Kohathite families. Among them, these six Levitical clans total 862 people, all of whom have come to Jerusalem at David's command.

Addressing himself to the leaders of the six clans, as well as to the priests Zadok and Abiathar, David says, "sanctify yourselves, you and your kindred, so that you may bring up the ark of the LORD, the God of Israel, to the place that I have prepared for it" (15:12). David has learned that the reason for the previous disaster was that the ark was not given "proper care" (15:13): literally, "we did not seek it according to the ordinance." This represents another point of contrast between David's reign and Saul's. In 13:3, we learn that Israel did not "turn to" (literally, "seek") the ark "in the days of Saul." Then, in the first attempt, David and his people seek after the ark, but wrongly, without observing the stipulations concerning the ark's transport in the Torah. Now at last, thanks to David, the ordinances are properly observed (Japhet 1993, 301).

According to Exodus 25:12–15, the ark was fitted with rings and poles, so that it could be carried by hand. In priestly tradition, the Levitical clan of Kohath was responsible for carrying the ark, as well as the most holy of the other items within the tabernacle (Num. 4:2–16). Further, the ark was to be carried on the shoulders of the Levites (Num. 7:9). In all of this, David did "as Moses had commanded according to the word of the LORD" (15:15).

Once more, the ark is accompanied by a triumphal procession. But this time, the musicians are Levites, specially called to this task (15:16–24). Note that, along with the Levitical musicians, three other groups are mentioned in this list: the gatekeepers (15:18, 23–24), the Levites "of the second order" (15:18), and the priests who "were to blow the trumpets before the ark of God" (15:24).

In Chronicles, the gatekeepers are simply designated as Levites. However, in the Deuteronomistic History the keepers of the threshold are called priests (contrast 2 Kgs. 12:9 with its parallel in 2 Chr. 24:8, and 2 Kgs. 22:4 with 2 Chr. 34:9; the two other references to the keepers of the threshold, 2 Kgs. 23:4 and 25:18, have no parallel in Chronicles). Chronicles is here in continuity with Numbers 3:14–39 and Ezekiel 44:11, 14, which also assign the task of guarding the temple gates to Levites, not priests. Two tasks are explicitly given to the guardians of the threshold in 2 Kings: they are to guard the gate into the inner court, where the altar is, and they are to collect the contributions of the people for the upkeep of the temple.

Perhaps the preexilic guardians of the threshold should be distinguished from the postexilic gatekeepers. After all, according to 9:22, 212 gatekeepers returned from exile (compare Ezra 2:42, which lists 139; Neh. 7:45, with 138; and Neh. 11:19, which has 172); yet, 2 Kings 25:18 speaks of only three guardians going into exile. However, in 2 Chronicles 15:18 as in 2 Kings 23:4, the "second order" and the temple guardians appear together, suggesting a connection between these groups in Chronicles as well.

In 2 Kings 23:4, the second order are called priests. The expression "second order" also appears in 2 Kings 25:18, where we are told that Seraiah the chief priest and the three guardians of the threshold were taken captive together with Zephaniah, "a priest of the second order" (a better translation of the Hebrew than the NRSV's "the second priest"). The duties of the second order are nowhere stated explicitly. The context of 2 Kings 23:4, however, is suggestive. The high priest Hilkiah, the second order, and the guardians have been summoned by Josiah to cleanse the temple: to remove from it all the images and worship objects used in the worship of Baal, Asherah, and the host of heaven. This suggests that the duties of the second order were related to the maintenance of the temple itself—as does the association of this group with the guardians, who were responsible for collecting funds for temple maintenance. Note, too, that Ezekiel 40:45–46 describes two distinct

60

priestly groups: "the priests who have charge of the temple," and "the priests who have charge of the altar." The latter group is further specified as "the descendants of Zadok, who alone among the descendants of Levi may come near to the LORD to minister to him" (Ezek. 40:46). Ezekiel's first group, the temple clergy as opposed to the altar clergy, could well be the priests of the second order.

In Chronicles, however, only the clergy serving at the altar are called priests. Curiously, blowing the trumpets before the ark of God is also a task given to priests (15:24; 16:6). However, this is in keeping with the responsibilities of the priests elsewhere in Scripture. So, in Numbers 31:6, Aaron's grandson Phineas was given responsibility for the war trumpet (see 2 Chr. 13:12, where the battle trumpets are blown by priests), while in Joshua 6:9, 13, it is the priests who blow the trumpets at Jericho. Once more, the Chronicler draws upon the whole of Scripture to relate his story.

Excursus: **Priests and Levites**

Evidently, the second order and the gatekeepers maintained the temple's life and conducted its liturgy. But in Chronicles they, like the temple musicians, are called simply "Levites," never priests. The tension between the Chronicler's History and the Deuteronomistic History on this point is rather like that encountered in the Torah between Deuteronomy, which understands priesthood to belong to the whole tribe of Levi (Deut. 18:1), and the priestly traditions, in which priesthood is restricted to the sons of Aaron (for example, Exod. 28:40–41; 40:12–15; Num. 17:1–11). To understand this shift, we need to look swiftly back over the history of Israel's priesthood.

Using the evidence contained in competing traditions in the Hebrew Bible, we can reconstruct a long-standing, often bitter rivalry between two priestly houses in Israel (Cross 1973, 195–215). One traced its descent from Moses and held sway at Shiloh and Dan, as well as in local shrines in Arad and Kadesh. The other held Aaron to be its founder, and was in power at Bethel and Hebron. When David first united the tribes of the north and south into a single kingdom in around 1000 B.C., he established two high priests in the Jerusalem shrine (2 Sam. 20:25; see also 1 Chr. 15:11; 18:16; 24:6): Abiathar, who belonged to a northern Levitical family descended from Moses, and Zadok, who (as we have seen) represented southern priestly claims associated with Aaron. In this way, both the southern and northern tribes, and both the Mushite and Aaronid priestly houses, had a representative in Jerusalem.

Unfortunately, this dual priesthood was brought to an end by

61

David's son Solomon. When David was on his deathbed, his oldest son Adonijah claimed the throne, supported by Abiathar (1 Kgs. 1:7). David, however, declared his younger son Solomon (supported by Zadok; see 1 Kgs. 1:8) to be the rightful heir. When Solomon came to the throne, therefore, he exiled Abiathar to Anathoth (1 Kgs. 2:26–27; significantly, there is no parallel to any of this in Chronicles), and Zadok became the sole high priest.

For over three hundred years, the descendants of Zadok, called the Zadokites, would remain in control of the Jerusalem temple. In contrast to the exclusivity of these Aaronid priests, the Mushite priestly families held a more inclusive notion of priesthood, embracing all Levites. Though largely denied the rights of sacrifice and leadership in worship, the Levitical families continued to teach and to preserve their traditions; the book of Deuteronomy and the northern traditions preserved in the Torah are likely the work of these northern Levites. When Jerusalem fell to Babylon in 587 B.C., the Zadokites, as the priestly house loyal to David's line, were taken away into exile. The old northern Levitical families, apparently, were left in place.

At the end of the exile, the returning Zadokite priests, acting with the authority and support of the new Persian government, took control and rejected the claims of the Levitical priests in the land, denying them any role in the restored temple. The tensions brought by this return are powerfully depicted in two texts from this period, the final form of Ezekiel 40–48, or the Law of the Temple (Ezek. 43:12; see Tuell 1992, 44–46), and the book of Malachi. Representing the ideas and attitudes of the returning Zadokite priests, the Law of the Temple absolutely bars the Levites from priesthood: "They shall not come near to me, to serve me as priest, nor come near any of my sacred offerings, the things that are most sacred" (Ezek. 44:13). However, "the descendants of Zadok, who kept the charge of my sanctuary when the people of Israel went astray from me, shall come near to me to minister to me; and they shall attend me to offer me the fat and the blood, says the Lord GOD" (Ezek. 44:15). For his part, the Levite Malachi accuses the postexilic priesthood of ritual uncleanness and political corruption (Mal. 1:6–13). In place of the exclusivistic claims of the Zadokites, Malachi calls for a return to the covenant of Levi, wherein all Levites, rather than just a single Levitical family, are given the opportunity to serve as priests (Mal. 2:4, 8; see also Deut. 18:1; Jer. 33:19–22).

In its final form, the Torah is a compromise between these competing ideas. Deuteronomy, with its inclusive notions of priesthood, is left standing side by side with the priestly traditions that restrict priesthood to the line of Aaron. However, Aaron's line extends through *two*

62

sons: not only Eleazar, who is ultimately the ancestor of the Zadokites, but also Ithamar.

In the Torah, Eleazar is responsible for supervision of the Kohathite Levitical clan, which carries the most holy objects and accoutrements from within the tabernacle (including the golden altar and the ark) when the tribes are on the move (Num. 4:2–16); he is personally held responsible for the oil, the incense, and the regular meal offering. Ithamar, on the other hand, is given responsibility for the Gershonites and the Merarites, who do the heavy work of hauling the tent, its frame, and other bulky (and less sacred) items (Exod. 38:21; Num. 4:28, 33; 7:6–8). In brief, Eleazar is associated with the most sacred items, particularly those pertaining to sacrificial service; Ithamar is associated with nonsacrificial items. The distinction between the priestly lines of Eleazar and Ithamar is reminiscent of the twofold division of temple clergy and altar clergy described in Ezekiel 40:45–46, and of the priests of the second order, mentioned in the Deuteronomistic History. Possibly, Ithamar represents old Mushite priestly claims recognized by the Aaronids (so McBride 1973).

Chronicles, too, strives to smooth over old conflicts (see Hanson 1975, 270). Although the title priest is restricted to the descendants of Aaron, the Chronicler is deeply interested in the ministry of the Levites, and ascribes great dignity and importance to their work. Note, too, that in 24:3, Ahimelech son of Abiathar is placed in the line of Ithamar! To be sure, the Chronicler has little choice in the matter. If, as his sources claim, Abiathar was a priest, and if, as the Chronicler always affirms, only Aaronids are priests, then Abiathar must connect up to Aaron somehow. Like the priestly traditions in the final form of the Pentateuch, the Chronicler is prepared to recognize the members of some non-Zadokite Levitical clans as priests. However, the distinction between priest and Levite remains.

The Ark Enters the City (15:25—16:6//2 Sam. 6:12–16). David's hosts join in the joyous procession from the house of Obed-edom. Seven bulls and rams are offered to the Lord. Chronicles provides a particular motive for this sacrifice: "because God helped the Levites who were carrying the ark of the covenant of the LORD" (15:26). The relief of the Levites at not having met Uzzah's fate is palpable! One is reminded of Christian essayist Annie Dillard's observation, "I often think of the set pieces of liturgy as certain words which people have successfully addressed to God without their getting killed" (1984, 59).

David is dressed, the Chronicler tells us, in both "a robe of fine linen" and "a linen ephod" (15:27; note that in 2 Sam. 6:14, David is wearing only the ephod). Also robed in linen are the Levites carrying the ark, and the Levitical musicians accompanying the procession. David is thus numbered among the ark's sacral attendants. He is also, however, set apart by the linen ephod, a priestly garment (see 1 Sam. 22:18; Exod. 28:31; 39:22). David, it appears, is regarded by the Chronicler as an honorary priest.

Overall, the Chronicler's account of the ark entering Jerusalem is more orderly and staid than the description in 2 Samuel. Note that while both texts say that the ark was brought into the city with shouting and blasts on the shofar, or ram's horn, Chronicles adds "trumpets, and cymbals, and . . . loud music on harps and lyres" (15:28). However, these represent not a spontaneous outpouring, as in 2 Samuel, but the performances of authorized Levitical musicians. As Paul would admonish centuries later, the worship of the ark procession was "done decently and in order" (1 Cor. 14:40).

The contrast is important for understanding the reaction of Michal, daughter of Saul and wife of David, to the king's dance (15:29//2 Sam. 6:16). In 2 Samuel, Michal's contempt is prompted by the wild, bawdy spectacle of the king of Israel dancing in an ephod that scarcely covers his nakedness (2 Sam. 6:20). But in Chronicles, there is no such reason for Michal's scorn. David's dancing, while joyous and exuberant, is not indecent. Michal's contempt becomes, like her father Saul's unfaithfulness, a demonstration of the contrast between pious David and the impious lineage he had replaced.

Finally, the ark is carried into the tent-shrine David had prepared for it. Sacrifices are offered, and gifts of food are presented to all the people (16:1–3//2 Sam. 6:17–19). But in Chronicles, the celebration is just getting under way. Following an account of the Levites and priest-musicians appointed by David to serve in the Jerusalem shrine (16:4–6), the Chronicler turns to the psalms sung to dedicate the shrine.

Worship before the Ark (16:7–43//Pss. 105:1–15; 96; 106:1, 48). Three psalms are quoted in 16:8–36: 105:1–15 (//1 Chr. 16:8–36); 96 (//1 Chr. 16:23–33); and the first and last verses of 106 (//1 Chr. 16:34–36). All three songs are attributed by the Chronicler to "Asaph and his kindred" (16:7), with whom many of the psalms are associated (see Pss. 50; 73—83). But Asaph and his kindred sing their songs at David's command. It is David who is the founder of Jerusalem's liturgy (16:7).

In form, Psalm 105 is a hymn: a song of praise to God. The motivation for praise in this psalm is the memory of God's mighty acts of deliverance for the people Israel. Psalm 96 is likewise a hymn, but in this psalm, praise is motivated by the Lord's power as judge and ruler of the world. Psalm 106, a communal psalm of thanksgiving, forms an interpretive pair with Psalm 105. These two psalms appear together in both the book of Psalms and in 1 Chronicles 16, and both contain the expression "Hallelujah" (rendered in the NRSV as "Praise the Lord"; see Pss. 105:45; 106:1, 48). But most importantly, both psalms recall the events of Israel's past—though from strikingly different perspectives. Psalm 105 emphasizes Israel's past as the history of God's salvation and deliverance. In Psalm 106, however, that same past is seen as the history of Israel's rebellion (see also Ps. 78; Ezek. 20:1–26)! Viewing these psalms together, the reader finds the righteousness of God contrasted with the sinfulness of God's people. In this pair of psalms, then, Israel's remembered past is used by the psalmists to call forth a response of faith and commitment. As James Mays observes of Psalms 105 and 106, "The first calls for trust, the second for repentance" (Mays 1994, 337).

Together, the three psalms quoted in chapter 16 express the central theme of Chronicles. Because God is the righteous judge and ruler of the world, the reader is assured that God will respond with blessing to those who are faithful. However, also because of God's justice, unfaithfulness and disobedience will result in destruction. Like Psalms 105 and 106, Chronicles finds the theme of divine justice and righteousness demonstrated in the history of God's people. Indeed, it is for this purpose that the Chronicler retells Israel's story.

In 16:8–13(//Ps. 105:1–6), the service to consecrate David's shrine opens with an extended invitation to praise the Lord. In the first two verses, the community is called to "make known his deeds among the peoples" and "tell of all his wonderful works": specifically, of God's saving deeds in Israel's history. The community called to sing and to remember are the "offspring of his servant Israel, / children of Jacob, his chosen ones" (16:13). In Psalm 105:6, Abraham is used in place of Israel, which fits the psalmist's point: that God's faithfulness to the promise made with Abraham becomes the key to Israel's entire history. However, the pairing of Jacob and Israel found in Chronicles is by far more typical of biblical usage (for example, Num. 24:5; Deut. 33:10; Isa. 41:8). Note that, in Chronicles, the father of the twelve patriarchs is always called Israel; the name "Jacob" appears only here, in this extended quote from Psalm 105 (16:13, 17). For the Chronicler, the designation Israel would be important, as one of Chronicles' major concerns is the unquestioned unity of all Israel under David.

In 16:13, Israel is called the servant of God. This apparently humble designation, however, is paired with a title that is anything but humble. The children of Jacob are called God's "chosen ones" (16:13). Indeed, God refers to the people Israel as "my prophets," and even as "my anointed ones": that is, my *messiahs* (16:22)! A similar statement is found in Isaiah 55:3, where the Lord promises, "I will make with you an everlasting covenant, / my steadfast, sure love for David." Here, as in the psalm the Chronicler has adapted, the old idea of the eternal

65

covenant with David has been transformed. For Second Isaiah, it is with the *people* that God swears an everlasting covenant; they are the rightful heirs of the "steadfast, sure love" God had at first shown to David.

The Chronicler, for whom the line of David remains a crucial link to Israel's traditions, would not go as far as this. Nonetheless, it is clear that not only are David and his heirs God's anointed ones, but that the entire community has been anointed, each of them specially chosen for a task no one else could perform. The apostle Paul spoke of the church as the body of Christ (1 Cor. 12:12–31), and of being crucified with Christ (Gal. 2:19–20). Paul's point was that the life and ministry of Christ continue in the believer. Similarly, David is for the Chronicler a model of faithful response to God that the community is called upon to emulate.

Chapter 16:14–18 brings us to to the body of the hymn, in which God is praised for God's mighty acts of deliverance in Israel's history:

> He is mindful of his covenant forever,
>> of the word that he commanded, for a thousand generations,
> the covenant that he made with Abraham,
>> his sworn promise to Isaac. (vv. 15–16)

That God is faithful to God's promise is apparent right away. The covenant with Abraham was also sworn to Abraham's son Isaac, and confirmed to Isaac's son Jacob (16:17). Should there be any question as to the content of that promise, the psalm makes its meaning clear: "To you I will give the land of Canaan, / as your portion for an inheritance" (16:18). This promise would have had particular relevance to the Chronicler's community, reclaiming the land after the Babylonian exile.

The story of God's covenant with Abraham begins in Genesis 12:1–3. Note that this promise is a covenant of grant: an outright gift, a promise made to Abraham on God's initiative, with no strings attached. The covenant of grant involved the free gift of land from an overlord to a vassal and his descendants, as a sign of the lord's favor. Just so, God gives to Abraham the unconditional promise that his descendants will be a great nation, and that they will have a land of their own. David's reign, and specifically David's establishment of the Jerusalem liturgy, marks for the Chronicler the complete fulfillment of this promise (recall the borders of the land attributed to David's kingdom in 1 Chr. 13:5). For the Chronicler, the ancient story of God's faithfulness recalled in this psalm is the key to understanding Israel's past, and a source of hope for Israel's future. God made a promise, and God keeps God's promises.

66

In Psalm 105:12–45, the history of Israel is selectively retold. Although the introduction of the psalm stresses the promise to Abraham, little attention is paid to him in the psalm, or for that matter to any of the Patriarchs. Only four verses speak, very generally, of Israel in the time prior to the Egyptian captivity (Ps. 105:12–15). However, it is precisely these verses that the Chronicler chooses to quote. The remainder of the psalm, which deals principally with the events of the Exodus, is ignored. It would be a mistake, however, to conclude from this that the Chronicler is inimical to the Exodus traditions. As we have already seen time and again, the Chronicler assumes that his readers are familiar with the sources he cites. Later in the Chronicler's History, in the books of Ezra and Nehemiah, exodus themes will assume greater importance. For now, the Chronicler's interests are focused on David, and the traditions that can support and interpret David's reign. The unconditional promise of God to Abraham will be mirrored in 17:1–15 by God's unconditional promise to David. Further, the picture of nomadic Israel in the days of the Patriarchs doubtless struck a chord with the Chronicler's community. They, too, had known what it was to be

> few in number,
>> of little account, and strangers in the land,
> wandering from nation to nation,
>> from one kingdom to another people.
>> (16:19–20)

Yet, just as God had protected Abraham, Isaac, and Jacob, God had protected the exilic community, and had established them again in the land. By citing these verses of Psalm 105, the Chronicler reminds his community of God's promise.

Next, the Chronicler turns to Psalm 96, a hymn that offers praise for God's justice and authority. The structure of this hymn is somewhat unusual, as it has not one invitation to praise, but two (16:23–24 and 16:28–30a). Appropriately, the psalm also offers two motivations for praise: the Lord's supremacy over all idols (16:25–27), and the Lord's just rule over both the natural world and all the nations (16:30b–33).

Together with Psalms 24, 29, 47, 93, 95, and 97—99, Psalm 96 is an *enthronement song*. In the enthronement songs, God is acclaimed as ruler over all heaven and earth, often with the shout, "The LORD is king!" (see Pss. 93:1; 96:10; 97:1; and 99:1). That the Chronicler should include an enthronement song among the songs sung at the inauguration of the ark's tent-shrine is scarcely surprising. The ark was understood to be the footstool of the Lord, above which God was invisibly enthroned (for example, Exod. 25:22; 2 Sam. 6:2; Ps. 80:1; Isa. 37:16). Psalm 96 itself quotes from an earlier enthronement song, Psalm 29 (compare Ps. 96:7–9 to Ps. 29:1–2)—although, as we will see below, with some intriguing changes.

67

Chapter 16:23 presents an invitation to the worshiping community: "Sing to the Lord, all the earth. / Tell of his salvation from day to day." In the United Methodist Church, 16:23–24 is used in the prayer over the water in the service of baptism and reaffirmation of baptism (see *The United Methodist Hymnal* 1989, 36, 41–42, 51–52). The idea of the covenant community constituted by baptism is certainly appropriate to the mood and context of Chronicles, which likewise involves a worshiping community constituted by the Lord's saving acts.

In 16:25–27, God's supremacy over idols (the first of the two motives for praise in this psalm) is affirmed. The word translated "idols" in the NRSV means, literally, "worthlessness." All claims on human worship are worthless compared to the one true God, who "made the heavens" (for a similar perspective, see Isa. 40:18–26). According to the Chronicler, the worship of idols led to the destruction of the northern kingdom (5:25). Similarly, unfaithfulness resulted in Judah's destruction (9:1), and reliance on the cult of the dead rather than seeking guidance from the Lord led to Saul's demise (10:13–14). David's destruction of the Philistine images, by contrast, demonstrates the proper attitude toward worthless idols (14:12).

Note that, while Psalm 96:6 reads "strength and beauty are in his sanctuary," the parallel in 1 Chronicles 16:27 says "strength and joy are in his place." Quite probably, this marks a deliberate reworking of the psalm for its context. Remember that, in the Chronicler's narrative, the psalm was being sung in the tent-shrine of the ark. The temple sanctuary had not yet been built.

The second invitation to praise (16:28–30a) is adapted from Psalm 29, a very old psalm that applies imagery associated with the Canaanite storm god Baal to the Lord. The opening verses of this psalm call upon all the gods to honor the Lord:

Ascribe to the LORD, O heavenly beings,
  ascribe to the LORD glory and strength.
Ascribe to the LORD the glory of his name;
  worship the LORD in holy splendor. (29:1–2)

In 16:28–30a//Psalm 96:7–9, nearly identical words appear. However, it is not the heavenly beings but the "families of the peoples" who are called upon to give honor to the Lord. The change makes perfect sense, in light of the statement earlier in the psalm that the "gods" are empty, worthless idols (16:26). So, in the following verses, it is not the heavenly beings who are called to assemble in the divine court, but the worshiping community which assembles before the Lord (that is, in the context in Chronicles, before the ark).

In 16:30b–31, the lines from Psalm 96:10–11 are somewhat rearranged, and the statement "He will judge the peoples with equity" (Ps. 96:10) is missing. Similarly, the lines "He will judge the world with righteousness, / and the peoples with his truth" (Ps. 96:13) are missing in Chronicles, suggesting that these excisions are not accidents of transmission, but deliberate editorial revisions by the Chronicler. After all, the Chronicler's focus is not on the Lord's judgment of all peoples, but on the Lord's judgment of Israel in particular. Still, the pronouncement of the Lord's reign is to be made, not in the heavens or in the tent shrine, but "among the nations" (16:31//Ps. 96:13), just as David's victory over the Philistines "brought the fear of him on all nations" (14:17). What God does among the people Israel, for good or ill, is done on a world stage, in the sight of all peoples.

In the following verses, the reign of God is demonstrated in both the natural and the human worlds. The order and stability that are evident in the natural world demonstrate the reliability of God's reign. The Chronicler is confident that God's control of the human world will ultimately be shown to be just as reliable.

In 16:32–33, all nature is invited to join in praising God (compare Isa. 55:12–13). However, nature praises God in particular for God's justice in the human realm: "for he comes to judge the earth" (16:33). Similarly, in Romans 8:18–25, Paul says that "the creation waits with eager longing for the revealing of the children of God" (Rom. 8:19). Human justice and injustice have consequences for the natural world. Through waste and pollution of our natural resources, human decisions can threaten the future of life on this planet. Little wonder that the establishment of God's just order should be applauded by ocean, field, and forest!

In Chronicles, the citation of Psalm 96 stands as a check on the promises in the Psalm 105 citation. Throughout Israel's history, God has always been faithful. However, as the judge of the earth, God will also hold Israel accountable. It is this message that is expressed by the final psalm citation, from Psalms 106:1 and 48 (1 Chr. 16:34–36; note that the first "Hallelujah" is missing, suggesting that it may have been added to the psalm after the Chronicler's time).

On their own, these verses express the proper attitude for the Chronicler's community: thankfulness for what God has done, together with a humble prayer for God's continued help and deliverance. However, they also bracket a psalm that sees Israel's history as a history of rebellion: "Both we and our ancestors have sinned; / we have committed iniquity, have done wickedly" (Ps. 106:6). Uncompromisingly, the psalm recalls all the murmuring and rebellion in Israel's story, from

69

their bondage in Egypt down to their bondage in Babylon. It is a history calculated to drive Israel to its knees in repentance. Psalm 106 completes the picture the Chronicler wants his community to see. Israel's past demonstrates both God's love and God's justice. God's love has brought the Chronicler's community back to the land of promise, and given them another chance. However, God's justice should stand as a spur, to urge the community onward in faithful obedience to the Lord.

The last line of Psalm 106 has been cleverly reworked by the Chronicler to fit the context. Rather than an invitation to praise and submission ("Let the people say, 'Amen!' Praise the LORD!"), it has become a statement of the community's response to the tent's dedication: "Then all the people said 'Amen!' and praised the LORD" (16:36).

The worship before the ark is not intended to stand alone. Rather, this day of celebration marks the beginning of a continuing tradition: "David left Asaph and his kinsfolk there before the ark of the covenant of the LORD to minister regularly before the ark as each day required" (16:37). Curiously, however, the sacrificial service to the Lord performed by Zadok and the other priests is conducted, not before the ark in Jerusalem, but "before the tabernacle of the LORD in the high place that was at Gibeon" (16:39). Although the ark had been brought to Jerusalem, no mention is made in the Chronicler's sources of any of the other sacred furnishings being carried there. So, the Chronicler assumes that the tabernacle and the altar of burnt offering were left where they were, at Gibeon (see 21:29; 2 Chr. 1:3–6, 13). Only in Chronicles is Gibeon said to be the location of the tabernacle and its altar. Perhaps the Chronicler assumes this, in order to explain why Solomon offered a thousand burnt offerings at Gibeon (1:6//1 Kgs. 3:4).

Only now, with the tent-shrine duly consecrated and provision made for continual service to the Lord, do the people and their king return to their households (16:43//2 Sam. 6:19b–20a). It is important for the Chronicler that the entire community was present to witness David's liturgy. The tradition is thus confirmed as reliable by eyewitnesses. Further, it is clear that for the Chronicler, worship is truly "the work of the people"—the literal meaning of the Greek *leitourgia*, from which our word "liturgy" is derived. It is the community's responsibility to remember, and to keep the traditions faithfully. Note, as we observed above, that Chronicles does not record the byplay between Michal and David (2 Sam. 6:20–23). In this way, Michal's scorn is directed, not at any purported indecency on David's part, but at David's fervent piety. She stands as a negative example of the way of unfaithfulness that led her father to his death, and would lead Judah to destruction and exile.

David's Successes (17:1—20:8)

The pattern established in the Chronicler's ark narrative is followed in these chapters, which describe God's promise of eternal kingship to David, and the successes of David's reign. Just as the first, failed attempt at transporting the ark was followed by a confirmation of David's worthiness, so the second, successful attempt is followed by God's confirmation of David's line, through prophetic word and military and political accomplishments. In 14:1–7, David was affirmed, first by Hiram's contributions toward a house for Israel's king, and then by the birth of children. So, in the following chapter, God will promise to build David a house (17:10): that is, an eternal dynasty. David's sons will reign after him as a demonstration of God's faithfulness to David their ancestor. Further, in 14:8–17, David's victory over the Philistines confirmed David's power and authority. Likewise, in the chapters ahead, David will prove triumphant over all his enemies (18:1–13; 19:1—20:8), as well as just and fair in his administration (18:14–17).

Nathan's Oracle: David Is Promised an Eternal Dynasty (17:1–15) (//2 Sam. 7:1–17). In its original context, Nathan's oracle served to affirm God's unconditional promise that David's line would reign forever. This idea is also reflected in such texts as Psalm 89:36–37:

> His line shall continue forever,
>   and his throne endure before me like the sun.
> It shall be established forever like the moon,
>   an enduring witness in the skies.

Of course, this affirmation became a serious problem when, in 587 B.C., the Babylonians conquered Jerusalem, destroyed the palace, murdered the reigning king's sons, and took the king away in chains to Babylon. In fact, never again after that did a descendant of David sit on the throne in Jerusalem. The shock and bewilderment of the people of Israel is painfully apparent in the latter part of Psalm 89:

> But now you have spurned and rejected him;
>   you are full of wrath against your anointed.
> You have renounced the covenant with your servant;
>   you have defiled his crown in the dust. (vv. 38–39)

What could God's everlasting covenant with David possibly mean now?

Clearly, the promise did not mean what they had thought it meant: the political survival of Israel in perpetuity. Later Christian interpreters

71

would see the promise of David's eternal reign as fulfilled in Jesus Christ, who through the power of his resurrection lives and reigns forever (for example, Mark 12:35–37; Acts 2:25–36; Rev. 5:5). However, within the Hebrew Bible as well, God's covenant with David came to be understood in new ways. In the final form of the Deuteronomistic History, the wickedness of the people and their kings, particularly Manasseh (2 Kgs. 21:10–15), brings on the covenant curses of Deuteronomy, including exile (Deut. 28:63–68); implicitly, the hope is that a return to faithfulness will bring a restoration of God's blessing. In the Psalms, a shift takes place from the exaltation of the earthly king on Zion (for example, Ps. 2) to praise of the heavenly king, the Lord (for example, Pss. 95—99). In the prophets, the unconditional, eternal promise of blessing comes to be seen, not as between David and the Lord, but as between the Lord and the entire people Israel (for example, Jer. 32:40; Ezek. 37:25–26; Isa. 55:3).

We should expect, then, to find in Chronicles as well a rethinking of God's unconditional promise to David. Surprisingly, we do not—at least, not in any radical sense. To be sure, there are differences between 17:1–15 and its source text in 2 Samuel 7. However, many of these differences are minor, explainable either as scribal errors or as instances of the Chronicler's source text differing from the MT of 2 Samuel. At bottom, both texts make the same fundamental affirmation. In 1 Chronicles as in 2 Samuel, David's line is eternal.

The unit begins with David "settled in his house" (17:1//2 Sam. 7:1), at home in his newly built palace. Unlike his source (2 Sam. 7:1), the Chronicler makes no mention of David being given rest from his enemies at this point (see also 17:10//2 Sam. 7:11). This may be because such rest is already assumed from David's victory over his enemies the Philistines (14:16–17). More likely, however, the Chronicler does not speak of rest from David's enemies because more battles are yet to follow (18—20). Israel's rest will not come until the reign of David's son, Solomon (22:9; 23:25).

David's ease in his own house prompts him to reflect on the comparative humility of the Lord's dwelling, the tent-shrine of the ark. He summons his prophet Nathan and declares his thoughts; Nathan replies, "Do all that you have in mind, for God is with you" (17:2//2 Sam. 7:3). Although it is never stated, David's intention is clear: the king will build for the Lord a temple, a house of cedar like his own great palace.

But that night, Nathan receives a message for David from the Lord: "You shall not build the house for me to live in" (17:4). Though the NRSV chooses to render the text as referring to "a house" (following the LXX as well as the 2 Sam. parallel), the MT of 17:4 reads "*the* house": an explicit reference to the one, specific temple in Jerusalem. Expanding

72

on this prohibition, the Lord states, "I have not lived in a house since the day I brought out Israel to this very day, but I have lived in a tent and a tabernacle" (17:5).

In contrast to 2 Samuel 7:6, Chronicles does not mention Egypt, prompting some scholars to view 17:5 as one of many "instances in which the Chronicler omits, or at least narrows, the role of the Exodus" (Japhet 1993, 330). However, one must see that the meaning of the text is unchanged. The reader would of course know that the place from which Israel was "brought out" was Egypt, and that the exodus was intended. Further, the importance of the law of Moses for the Chronicler makes it unlikely that Chronicles rejects the exodus (indeed, see the reference to the Exodus in 17:21). Perhaps what we find here instead is a *broadening* of the exodus idea. By not mentioning Egypt by name, the text leaves open to the reader the possibility of finding God's deliverance as a sign of divine presence in many circumstances. For the Chronicler's community, the deliverance from Babylon in particular showed God's gracious deliverance, as Ezra–Nehemiah demonstrates.

First Chronicles faithfully records from the source text the statement that the Lord does not require a temple, and so has never commanded anyone to build one (17:5–6). However, for the Chronicler, it is not the institution of temples in general that is in question here. Rather, it is the right of David in particular to build the temple in Jerusalem. The question is not whether or not the temple should be built, but rather who should build it. God has denied David's request. Later, we will be told the reason for this prohibition (22:8).

That God forbids David to build the temple does not mean that David is in any way unfaithful or unworthy, any more than David's initial failure to bring the ark into Jerusalem meant this. First Chronicles 17:6–10 affirms David's election by God. It was God who had taken him from his former humble position as a shepherd and elevated him to kingship; it is God, further, who declares, "I will make for you a name, like the name of the great ones of the earth" (17:8). David's exaltation is linked to the exaltation of his people, who are promised stability, security, and victory over all David's enemies (17:9–10).

Now we come to the second main point of the oracle. While David is forbidden to build a house for the Lord, he is assured that "the LORD will build you a house" (17:10). David is promised a son, who will continue his line. It will be this son (clearly Solomon) who, the Lord declares, "shall build a house for me, and I will establish his throne forever" (17:12). Note that the parallel in 2 Samuel 7:13 reads "a house for my name." Given the importance of the name of God in Deuteronomistic theology, it might be thought that here again the Chronicler's source is a different, perhaps more original, text than the MT of

73

2 Samuel. However, 22:10, which also refers to 2 Samuel 7:13–14, reads "He shall build a house for my name," showing that the Chronicler's source did have this reading. Apparently, the Chronicler regards the presence of the name of the Lord and the presence of God as identical, so that "me" and "my name" are interchangeable. The Deuteronomists, however, used the name to avoid identifying God too unambiguously with any earthly institution. So God does not literally dwell in the temple; rather God's name is established there (see Deut. 12:5; 1 Kgs. 8:18–19, 27–30). However, as we have already seen regarding the ark, the Chronicler *does* identify the presence of God, in a fairly straightforward fashion, with the liturgy conducted in Jerusalem's shrine. For the Chronicler, the temple *is* the house of the Lord (see 22:6).

The most significant departure from the 2 Samuel text, however, comes in the following verses. In contrast to 2 Samuel 7:14–15, Chronicles makes no mention of God chastening David's descendants. To some scholars this has seemed to correct the unconditional promise in 2 Samuel 7, that though God might punish particular descendants of David's line, the line itself would be eternal (for example, Japhet 1993, 334). To be sure, we might expect to find such a correction. The Chronicler was certainly aware that David's line had not ruled forever—that, indeed, there was no Davidic king on Israel's throne in his own time. Note, however, that in Chronicles, God still affirms of David's descendant that "his throne shall be established forever" (17:14). Curiously, the unconditional promise of an eternal Davidic line is retained.

How, then, does the Chronicler account for the end of Davidic kingship in 587 B.C.? Why doesn't chapter 17 mention God's chastening? A likely explanation is provided by two other shifts in Chronicles. In 17:14 (compare with 2 Sam. 7:16), it is not David's house and kingdom that is established forever, but God's. Further, God declares concerning David's son, "I will confirm him in my house and in my kingdom forever, and his throne shall be established forever" (17:14). It is Solomon's throne that is "established forever" here, not David's.

These demonstrations of the Chronicler's perspective alter Nathan's oracle in two major ways. First, the emphasis on *God's* house and kingdom leads to a more spiritualized, less historically specific view on kingship in chapter 17. While the political kingdom of David would certainly have its failures (indeed, those failures have in large measure provided the occasion for the Chronicler's History), God's kingdom would endure. Further, as an affirmation of God's faithfulness, David's line would endure. In its earliest incarnation, the Chronicler's History apparently sought to legitimate the temple-building carried out by the Davidide Zerubbabel, making support for David's line crucial. Later, as the genealogies in chapters 1—9 demonstrate, David's line continued

74

to serve for the Chronicler's community as a sign of God's ongoing grace, and a connection to Israel's past, even though David's descendants no longer ruled. Here as elsewhere, the Chronicler is far less concerned with politics than with faith.

Second, with the focus narrowly on Solomon rather than broadly on the entire Davidic line, the punishments described in 2 Samuel 7 become, for the Chronicler, irrelevant. In sharp contrast to the Deuteronomist, who views Solomon with a somewhat jaundiced eye, the Chronicler (as we will see) regards Solomon as the obedient son of David, who fulfills his calling by building the temple (see 2 Chr. 8:16). In Chronicles, Nathan's oracle involves not a critique of temple ideology, but rather a statement of who may, and who may not, build the temple in Jerusalem. That task is given to David's son Solomon. For the Chronicler, the way now is prepared for David's successor.

David's Prayer of Thanksgiving (17:16–27) (//2 Sam. 7:18–29). David's response to Nathan's oracle is a remarkable prayer of praise and thanksgiving to God, for God's grace to David and to Israel, and for God's promise of a dynasty. Apparently, the setting for this prayer is the tent-shrine of the ark, which in Chronicles has just been erected and consecrated (16:1–43). David enters the shrine and sits before the Lord to offer his prayer. The tone of the prayer is set from the beginning: David is fully aware that neither he, nor his family, nor Israel itself deserves God's favor. David's blessing, and Israel's very existence, are a testament to the love of God for God's people, offered freely and graciously. The words of David's prayer bring to mind one of the best-loved hymns of the church, John Newton's "Amazing Grace." Newton, a reformed drunkard, brawler, and slave trader, reflected with awe on God's unexpected and unmerited love for him:

> Amazing grace! How sweet the sound
> That saved a wretch like me!
> I once was lost, but now am found,
> Was blind, but now I see.

So, too, David expresses wonder at God's gracious election: "Who am I, O LORD God, and what is my house, that you have brought me thus far?" (17:16).

Despite David's humble origins (recalled in Nathan's oracle; see 17:7), God regards him "as someone of high rank" (17:17//2 Sam. 7:19; the text is difficult in both passages, but the NRSV rendering of Chronicles seems best). Therefore, David has become a person of high rank: indeed, he has been made king over all Israel! But David has no illusions about his own innate greatness or worthiness; "You know your servant," he says to God (17:18). Still, God has done great things for God's

75

servant, and promised greater still to come. The language is strongly reminiscent of the Psalms, particularly Psalm 139. David's confidence before God rests, not in any self-righteousness, but in God's love and grace.

The most dramatic demonstration of that love and grace is the existence of Israel itself: "Who is like your people Israel, one nation on the earth whom God went to redeem to be his people" (17:21). Alone among all the world's peoples, Israel is a nation created by God. God's mighty acts, manifest in victory over Israel's enemies, but particularly in the deliverance from Egypt (17:21//2 Sam. 7:23; note that, while the NRSV does not reflect this, Egypt is mentioned in the MT of 2 Sam. 7:23), show Israel to be a people much loved by God. But Israel's past is also a reminder of Israel's dependence upon God's grace, and so a reminder of the need for faithfulness.

Reflection upon God's faithfulness to Israel, manifested particularly in the exodus, gives David confidence that God's promises regarding his own line are also reliable. To God's promise, David adds his own Amen: "And now, O LORD, as for the word that you have spoken concerning your servant and concerning his house, let it be established forever, and do as you have promised" (17:23). David's line, and Israel's continuing faithful witness, will prove in ages to come a continuing testimony to God: "Thus your name will be established and magnified forever" (17:24).

God's grace is not only the subject of David's prayer, it is the foundation that makes prayer possible: "For you, my God, have revealed to your servant that you will build a house for him; therefore your servant has found it possible to pray before you" (17:25). It is because David knows of God's grace and love for him that it is possible for him to pray at all. Otherwise, how could he dare even to address the Lord of the universe? Similarly, the author of Hebrews states that it is God's grace manifest in Christ that enables the believer to "approach the throne of grace with boldness, so that we may receive mercy and find grace to help in time of need" (Heb. 4:16). In the parable of the Pharisee and the tax collector (Luke 18:9–14), Jesus taught that prayer based on our own self-righteousness is no prayer at all; it is when we recognize our unworthiness, and our absolute dependence on God's grace, that our prayers have meaning and power. David's prayer, then, is both a model for prayer, and a theological statement of the meaning of prayer.

The conclusion of David's prayer in Chronicles represents a subtle but significant departure from the source text. In 2 Samuel, God's blessing is regarded as future: "with your blessing shall the house of your servant be blessed forever" (2 Sam. 7:29). However, in Chronicles, David praises God for the blessing already received, a blessing which redounds to God's own glory: "For you, O LORD, have blessed and are blessed forever" (17:27). So, in Chronicles, the security and serenity of David in God's grace are emphasized. Although David's desire to build a temple has been rebuffed, David has confidence in God's plan for his life, and for the lives of his descendants.

David's Accomplishments, at Home and in the Field (18:1— 20:8). This account of David's successes consists of military exploits (18:1–13; 19:1—20:8), sandwiched around a brief account of David's just administration (18:14–17). A glance at the list of parallels in the following headings reveals that the Chronicler is being more selective in his use of source material here than in any other part of David's story. A glance at the Chronicler's source shows why this is the case. Second Samuel 9, which is not used in Chronicles, describes David's generosity to Jonathan's crippled son Mephibosheth. Although Mephibosheth is listed in the Chronicler's genealogies (where he is called Merib-baal; see 8:34; 9:40), neither he nor any other descendant of Saul plays any role in the Chronicler's narrative. Chronicles downplays the period of civil war following Saul's death, and indeed claims that all of Saul's house perished on Mount Gilboa (10:7). Further, David and Jonathan's friendship is not mentioned in the Chronicler's History. Little wonder, then, that the Chronicler chooses not to describe David's dealings with Mephibosheth. Likewise skipped by the Chronicler is material critical of David: the entire Bathsheba episode (2 Sam. 11:1—12:25) and the whole complex of material concerning the rebellions of Absalom and Sheba (2 Sam. 13:1—20:22).

However, as we have observed before, it does not do to suggest that the Chronicler is trying to present us with a whitewashed, expurgated portrait of David. The Chronicler, after all, assumes that the reader is familiar with all these stories. Instead, the Chronicler provides a focused, pointed account, preserving those aspects of David's story that matter for his purpose. Rabbi Herbert Tarr imagines the Chronicler's defense against the charge that he has passed over great chunks of Israel's story: "I've chronicled not all that actually happened, but what truly mattered. The world is drowning in facts, suffocating in statistics. What's needed is *meaning*" (Tarr 1987, 499).

The meaning of David's story, as we have seen, is for the Chronicler found in the establishment of the Jerusalem temple liturgy. So, Chronicles follows the story of the ark and its shrine with the promise of blessing to David, and with signs of that blessing. In our own time, we have seen any number of tell-all biographies and exposés, in which heroes and heroines of the past have been shown to be flawed, pitiful

77

women and men. While we of course should not idolize anyone, there is something coarse, voyeuristic, and shabby about this obsession with exposing weakness wherever it can be found. David's failings were well known, and were already recorded in sad detail in Samuel–Kings. The Chronicler was determined, however, that these faults and crimes should not detract from David's real accomplishments.

David's Victories (18:1–13//2 Sam. 8:1–14). David conducts victorious campaigns against the Philistines (18:1), the Moabites (18:2), King Hadadezer of Zobah (18:3–4), the Arameans (18:5–8), and the Edomites (18:12–13). His victory over Hadadezer earns the gratitude and generosity of Hadadezer's enemy Tou of Hamath, who adds his own contribution to the wealth that David has gained through his conquests (18:9–11). This hoard, "together with the silver and gold that he had carried off from all the nations, from Edom, Moab, the Ammonites, the Philistines, and Amalek," is dedicated to the Lord (8:11).

Differences between Samuel and Chronicles through this section can largely be attributed to scribal errors, to the Chronicler simplifying his source (the obscure Philistine town of Metheg-ammah in 2 Sam. 8:1 becomes the better-known and more significant Gath in 18:1), or to the source text of Chronicles differing from the MT of Samuel (the reference to chariots in 18:4, though not found in the MT of 2 Sam. 8:4, is found in the LXX and in 4QSam[a]).

Three points, however, deserve special mention. First, in 18:2, Moab is defeated by David, subjugated, and forced to give tribute. But in 2 Samuel 8:2, the Moabite troops are forced to lie in lines on the ground and be measured with a length of cord. For every three cord lengths of troops measured, only one cord length is left alive. In other words, two-thirds of Moab's defeated military force is executed! The Chronicler does not mention this gruesome scene. Perhaps the slaughter of the Moabites was not present in the Chronicler's source. However, since this scene is found in the LXX of 2 Samuel, it is more likely that the Chronicler has skipped it. This may be because, like the stories of adultery, murder, and rebellion in 2 Samuel which Chronicles also avoids, this account puts David in a bad light. It is also possible, however, that the Chronicler knows, from his special Judean sources, that this grim report is legendary.

Second, 18:8 says of the bronze taken as spoil from Hadadezer that "with it Solomon made the bronze sea and the pillars and the vessels of bronze." This sounds very like an expansion from the Chronicler, since it certainly suits the Chronicler's purpose. The spoil taken in David's wars is set aside explicitly for use in Solomon's temple-building. Note, however, that the LXX of 2 Samuel 8:11 also has this observation. Probably, the Chronicler's source already said that Hadadezer's bronze hoard was used by Solomon for temple furnishings and accoutrements. Once more, Chronicles proves faithful to its source.

Third, it is intriguing that, while 2 Samuel 8:13 attributes the victory over Edom to David himself, 18:12 gives the credit to Abishai son of Zeruiah, the commander of the Thirty (see 11:20–21). While it is possible that this switch comes from a scribal error, it is perhaps more likely that we find here the Chronicler's use of his own, more accurate Judean sources. At any rate, the victory is followed up by David's establishment of troop garrisons in the region, with the result that Edom, like Moab, becomes subject to David's authority.

The point of this opening section is clear. As 18:13 states, "the LORD gave victory to David wherever he went." David's victories demonstrate God's blessing, already promised in the preceding chapter. Meanwhile David, out of faithfulness to the Lord, sets aside the spoil taken in battle for use in the temple that his son will build, also in accordance with God's promise.

David's Just Administration (18:14–17//2 Sam. 8:15–18). In faithfulness to his source, the Chronicler now turns from the account of David's military victories to a description of the court bureaucracy. The point of this brief reference is stated at the outset: "So David reigned over all Israel; and he administered justice and equity to all his people" (18:14). Not only is David a successful commander in the field, he is also an exemplary ruler at home.

David's bureaucracy appears to have been based on an Egyptian model (Myers 1965, 138). By this model, Jehoshaphat (called the "recorder" in the NRSV) would have been David's "chief of protocol," responsible for all matters involving access to the king; perhaps a good contemporary parallel would be the White House Chief of Staff. Shavsha, the only official for whom no father is listed, may have actually been an Egyptian (Myers 1965, 135). As the king's secretary, he would have handled all royal correspondence, as well as proclamations, laws, and decrees.

Many of the key figures in David's administration are familiar. Joab we already know as David's commanding general (see 11:6). Benaiah son of Jehoiada, one of the Three (see 11:22–24), is also a familiar name. The Cherethites and the Pelethites (18:17), under the leadership of Benaiah, were evidently a foreign mercenary bodyguard, perhaps made up of Sea Peoples like the Philistines (the Cherethites, for example, may have originally come from Crete). Once David had served as just such a mercenary, in service of the Philistines. Now, he has his own troop of swords for hire.

Zadok and Abiathar, too, we know; however, it is clear that the text of 18:16 (// 2 Sam. 8:17) is confused. Zadok's contemporary under David

79

was Abiathar, not Ahimelek (15:11). Further, the order of the names (Zadok-Ahitub-Ahimelek-Abiathar) has suggested to some an original connection with 1 Samuel 22:9, 20, where Abiathar is said to be the son of Ahimelek the son of Ahitub. Many scholars think that the original text read "Abiathar son of Ahimelek son of Ahitub, and Zadok"; a Zadokite partisan has reversed the order, to give preeminence to Zadok and to provide him with a legitimate priestly ancestor (Ahitub; see Cody 1969, 89). Wellhausen concludes that the Zadokites "were originally illegitimate (if one may venture to apply a conception which at that time was quite unknown), and did not inherit their right from the fathers, but had it from David and Solomon" (1957, 139).

However we do have, in the corrupted text of 2 Samuel 8:17, a legitimate line for Zadok. We can reconstruct, on ordinary text-critical principles, an original text identifying "Zadok son of Ahitub and Abiathar son of Ahimelek" (Cross 1973, 213–14; see 6:8, 52–53). The Ahitub identified as Zadok's father would not, of course, be the Ahitub who was Abiathar's grandfather; rather, we find here yet another instance of the tendency in priestly circles to use and reuse the same stock of names. The Chronicler, however, not only faithfully follows the mistaken text of 2 Samuel 8:17, but applies it consistently in the narrative that follows. While Zadok and Abiathar are David's priests in 15:11, in 24:3 and 6 it is Zadok and Ahimelek who fill this role.

Note finally that, while the MT of 2 Samuel 8:18 refers to the sons of David as priests, 18:17 states that they were "the chief officials in the service of the king." While one might suspect this to be another instance of the Chronicler's fiddling with the text, the LXX of 2 Samuel also describes David's sons merely as royal officials, suggesting that the Chronicler is faithful to his source.

David's Victories Continued (19:1—20:8//2 Sam. 10:1–19; 11:1; 12:26, 30, 31; 21:18–22). Primarily, these chapters deal with David's Ammonite campaign. First, we are told the circumstances which brought about war with Ammon. David had sent official mourners to the court of the new King Hanun following the death of his father Nahash, saying "his father dealt loyally with me" (19:2). The Chronicler assumes that the reader knows Nahash had been an enemy of David's enemy, Saul (see 1 Sam. 11). Hanun's royal officials convinced the young king that the mourners were in fact spies, so Hanun publicly humiliated them (shaving their hair and cutting their robes short so that their private parts were exposed) and sent them back home.

80 Realizing that "they had made themselves odious to David" (19:6), the Ammonites decided to launch a preemptive strike. Hiring a large band of thirty-two thousand mercenary charioteers from Aram, the Ammonites set out to do battle with the armies of Israel. According to

Chronicles, the battle took place at Medeba, a Moabite city (19:7; see Num. 21:30; Josh. 13:9), although it is difficult to understand why a battle involving Israel, Aram, and Ammon would have been fought so far south (so Japhet 1993, 359).

Faced with both the Ammonite army and the Aramean mercenaries, Joab divided his own forces to meet the threat. Evidently judging the Arameans to be the greater threat, he took personal command of a contingent of picked troops and aligned them against the chariotry. The other wing Joab entrusted to his brother Abishai (who had earlier defeated the Edomites; see 18:12), and directed him to attack the Ammonites. Pinched between the two armies, Joab and Abishai are able to reinforce one another's lines as needed, so turning their disadvantage into an advantage (19:12). Joab, who trusts the result of the battle to God (19:13), wins an overwhelming victory. Abishai occupies the city, while Joab returns to Jerusalem.

The defeat of the Aramean mercenaries prompts Hadadezer (see 18:3–4) to organize an Aramean alliance under his general Shophach and launch a face-saving assault. This time, David takes personal command of Israel's armies (19:17), and sets up his battle lines to the east of the Jordan. The Aramean assault fails, and Hadadezer's army flees with heavy casualties. Hadadezer is forced to acknowledge David's supremacy, and "the Arameans were not willing to help the Ammonites any more" (19:19).

With the loss of their Aramean allies, the Ammonites are vulnerable to an invasion, which begins as soon as the winter rains have ended and the roads are dry: "In the spring of the year, the time when kings go out to battle" (20:1). The notice that David sent Joab into battle while he remained behind in Jerusalem carries an implicit rebuke in 2 Samuel 11:1. There, this passage opens the Court History (2 Sam. 11—1 Kgs. 2), a section of the Deuteronomistic History that is highly critical of David. Indeed, it is because David remained in Jerusalem that he became embroiled in his affair with Bathsheba. However, in Chronicles no special meaning is attached to this statement at all. David's confidence in his generals has already been demonstrated (see 18:13; 19:8), as has David's continued prowess in battle (19:17). So it is not at all unusual that David should entrust the siege of Rabbah to Joab.

From his source, the Chronicler selects the news of the siege's success (20:1b//2 Sam. 12:26), and of David's actions following Rabbah's defeat (20:2–3//2 Sam. 12:30–31). He passes over Joab's threat to claim the city for himself if David does *not* come and occupy it (2 Sam. 12:27–29)— since, for the Chronicler, there was no shame in David's entrusting the conquest to Joab. Still, as in Abishai's conquest of Edom (18:12–13), David is assumed to be there at the end, to take responsibility for the actual

81

occupation. The MT of 20:2//2 Samuel 12:30 says that, after occupying Rabbah, David took the crown of their king and placed it on his own head—a reasonable enough action on the part of a conqueror, save that the crown is said to have "weighed a talent of gold" (20:2): over seventy-five pounds! A more likely reading, suggested by the Latin, Arabic, and some Greek versions and followed by the NRSV, is that David took the crown from the image of Milcom, the national god of Ammon (1 Kgs. 11:5, 33; 2 Kgs. 23:13). Like the Phoenician gods Melchart and Molech, Milcom was evidently a form of the old Canaanite storm god Baal. All three names are derived from the same Semitic root as *melek,* the Hebrew word for "king": in fact, the phrase "their king" and the name Milcom are nearly identical in Hebrew. These are evidently confused elsewhere (see Jer. 49:1, 3; Zeph. 1:5; in each case, though the Hebrew literally means "their king," the NRSV rightly reads "Milcom"), making it more likely that here as well, Milcom should be read. By defacing the image of Ammon's god, and claiming for himself Milcom's crown, David completes the subjugation and humiliation of Ammon.

The population of Rabbah, and indeed of "all the cities of the Ammonites" (20:3), is turned into a labor force by David, "to work with saws and iron picks and axes." Harsh as this seems, the MT of 20:3 suggests even more horrific treatment: the Hebrew evidently means, "he *sawed* them with saws"! (Emphasis added.) However, the word occurs only here, suggesting the possibility that it may be a scribal error. The parallel in 2 Samuel 12:31 definitely has "set them to work with saws and iron picks and iron axes," suggesting this should be the reading in 1 Chronicles as well. Finally, putting an entire population to torture seems impossibly extreme, even for the cruelest of ancient despots. It is entirely out of character for David.

With Ammon pacified, the text turns to David's continuing conflict with the Philistines. This conflict, however, has mythic overtones, for the stories center, not around conflict between armies over territory, but around single combat with giants. While the MT of 2 Samuel 21:18–22 describes the Philistine champions simply as "descended from the Rapha," or perhaps "from Harapha" (translated "giants" in the NRSV), the Chronicler refers to them explicitly as the Rephaim (1 Chr. 20:4; NRSV reads "the descendants of the giants"). This term is used in the Hebrew Bible both for the ancient, pre-Israelite inhabitants of Canaan (Gen. 14:5; 15:20; Deut. 2:10–11) and for the dead in the underworld (for example, Ps. 88:10; Isa. 14:9). The connection between these two concepts is found in old Canaanite mythology, where the Rephaim are the line of fallen heroes and kings from ancient days, now consigned to the place of the dead (Smith 1992, 675–76). Deuteronomy

3:11 states that the iron bedstead of Og of Bashan, last of the Rephaim, was on display in Rabbah. The bed is said to measure nine cubits by four cubits: about fourteen feet by six feet! Clearly, the Rephaim could be regarded as giants.

The mythic stature of the Rephaim is also stressed in Deuteronomy 2:11, which identifies the Rephaim with the Anakim. The Anakim were in turn described in Numbers as the Nephilim, before whom "we seemed like grasshoppers, and so we seemed to them" (Num. 13:33). Finally, the Nephilim were the monstrous progeny produced "when the sons of God went in to the daughters of humans" at the dawn of time (Gen. 6:4). All of these connections, it appears, are in back of the Chronicler's description of the Philistine champions as the Rephaim.

In 2 Samuel, it is possible to think of the children of Rapha as huge human warriors. But by identifying these Philistine heroes as the Rephaim, the Chronicler adds a rich, mythological undertone to the story—the Philistines are championed by the remnants of a lost race of ancient monsters! Still, David's heroes Sibbecai, Elhanan, and Jonathan prove more than equal to the task. The giants are slain, and the Philistines are subjugated.

One intriguing difference between 1 Chronicles and 2 Samuel deserves consideration here. In 2 Samuel 21:19, the giant slain by Elhanan is "Goliath the Gittite, the shaft of whose spear was like a weaver's beam" (compare 11:23; 1 Sam. 17:4–7). In 20:5, Elhanan slays Lahmi, Goliath's brother. Often, this has been viewed as a deliberate change by the Chronicler in the service of David's honor, as it was David, of course, who had killed Goliath (1 Sam. 17). However, the Chronicler does not tell or refer to the story of David and Goliath. Further, as we have seen, the Chronicler usually is not troubled by discrepancies among his sources. It is more likely that the change had already been made in the Chronicler's source, either by accident (the consonants of the two texts in Hebrew are very similar) or, more likely, by design.

David's Failure: the Census and Its Aftermath (21:1–30)

As we have observed, Chronicles follows a pattern of alternating periods of good and evil, blessing and curse. David's reign, to this point, has been uniformly blessed. Even the death of Uzzah was not a sign of divine disfavor toward David; indeed, it was David who figured out what had gone wrong, and who set it right by arranging for the ark's proper transport by the proper religious personnel. But now comes David's great sin, in the Chronicler's view: the census.

83

Once more, the Chronicler proves selective in use of his source. David's song (2 Sam. 22//Ps. 18) and last words (2 Sam. 23:1–7) are passed over by the Chronicler, in preference for his own account of David's final actions and words (see 22:1—29:30). The list of warriors in David's service from 2 Samuel 23:8–39, remember, is placed by the Chronicler toward the beginning of David's story (11:10–47). The Chronicler's account of the census, the plague, and David's sacrifice at the threshing floor of Ornan are drawn from 2 Samuel 24:1–25. Though Chronicles and the MT of 2 Samuel differ substantially here, comparison with 4QSam[a] and LXX confirms that the Chronicler is generally faithful to his source.

David Orders a Census (21:1–6) (//2 Sam. 24:1–9). Having decided to undertake a census of all Israel, David commands Joab and his commanders, "Go, number Israel, from Beer-sheba to Dan, and bring me a report, so that I may know their number" (21:2//2 Sam. 24:2). No political or economic motivation is given for this decision, either in Chronicles or in its source. Both agree, however, that the census is evil. A modern reader may find this odd. However, the perception that censuses are wicked is not restricted to these parallel passages. According to Exodus 30:11–16, when a census must be taken, a half-shekel ransom is to be paid to the sanctuary by each person, "so that no plague may come upon them for being registered"! In Acts 5:37, Gamaliel recalls to the council the bloody revolt of Judas the Galilean, launched in response to the census conducted by Quirinius around 6 A.D.

It is not difficult to understand why censuses should have such a vile and dangerous reputation. A king would need to count his people for three major reasons, none of them good news for the ordinary subject. First, the census count enabled the ruler to set tribute: a census usually meant that taxes were about to increase. Second, a census could determine the size of a population available as a forced labor pool (2 Chr. 2:17; remember, too, the use to which David put the citizens of Rabbah). Third, the census gave the government a sense of how large a force could be conscripted into military service (Num. 1:3; 26:2; 2 Chr. 25:5–6). David's census was evidently of this third sort: note that it was carried out by the military, and that the people numbered were "men who drew the sword" (21:5; compare 2 Sam. 24:9). The point, for the Chronicler as for his source, is that the census is an evil act, which will bring down divine retribution on Israel.

After an initial protest (21:3), Joab obeys his lord, and carries out the census. However, he is selective in his obedience. In Chronicles, Joab deliberately excludes Levi and Benjamin from the census (21:6). By not counting Levi, Joab is following the Torah, which exempts Levi from any military census (Num. 1:49). The reasons for excluding Benjamin are more complex. As we have already seen, Benjamin plays a special role in the Chronicler's History (see the commentary on 7:6–12). In the genealogies, three separate lists are devoted to Benjamin; only Judah and Levi are treated in greater detail. Further, throughout the History, "Judah and Benjamin" is the Chronicler's designation for faithful Israel. Another reason for excluding Benjamin may be that the high place at Gibeon was located in Benjaminite territory (Josh. 18:25). According to the Chronicler, the tabernacle and its altar were located at Gibeon (16:39; 21:29; 2 Chr. 1:3–6, 13), which therefore remained the site of sacrificial worship in Israel until the building of Solomon's temple. Respect for the Lord's altar could have prevented Joab from carrying out on Benjaminite land a command he knew to be wrong (Myers 1965, 147).

Perhaps because of the exclusion of Levi and Benjamin, the numbers in 21:5 differ significantly from those in 2 Sam. 24:9. Second Samuel records 800,000 troops from Israel in the north and 500,000 from Judah in the south, for a total of 1,300,000. In Chronicles, "*all* Israel" (not, as in 2 Sam. the northern tribes alone) could field 1,100,000 troops, of whom 470,000 came from Judah. Note the emphasis on the unity of all Israel in Chronicles, as well as the 200,000-troop deficit. Perhaps the Chronicler assumes that these 200,000 belong to the two missing tribes; the deficit in Judah could be due to some of Benjamin's troops being associated with Judah (see 8:1–40).

Excursus: **Satan**

In 2 Samuel 24:1, it is the Lord who in fury against Israel prompts David to take the wicked step of ordering a census of all Israel. However, in Chronicles, "Satan stood up against Israel, and incited David to count the people of Israel" (21:1). This raises two questions for the reader: who is this "Satan," and why is it that in Chronicles he, not the Lord, prompts David's census?

Christians will be quick—indeed perhaps *too* quick—to identify David's tempter with the personal devil and spiritual adversary of the New Testament, where the personal name Satan is used thirty-five times. In the Hebrew Bible, however, this term often appears with reference to a human enemy (the Hebrew term *śaṭan* is translated "adversary" in the NRSV of 1 Sam. 29:4; 2 Sam. 19:22; 1 Kgs. 5:4; 11:14, 23, 25; and as "accuser" in Ps. 109:6). *Śaṭan* is definitely used to designate a heavenly being in three cases. The first involves the angel of the Lord, who becomes for a time a *Śaṭan* (the NRSV reads "adversary") to the prophet Balaam (Num. 22:22, 32). In the other two cases, Job 1—2 and Zechariah 3:1–2, *śaṭan* appears with the article, as a title: "the *śaṭan*." In both places, the NRSV uses the proper name Satan; however, a better rendering of the Hebrew would be "the Adversary" or "the Accuser." In each case, the *śaṭan* is a member of the Lord's heavenly court, and functions as a kind of celestial prosecuting attorney. So, in the book of Job, the *śaṭan* accuses the righteous Job of serving the Lord out of self-interest, because God has always blessed him. "But stretch out your hand now, and touch all that he has," the *śaṭan* claims, "and he will curse you to your face" (Job 1:11). Similarly, until rebuked by the Lord, the *śaṭan* stands ready in Zechariah 3 to accuse the high priest Joshua.

This brings us to 21:1. Here, instead of *the śaṭan*, the text reads simply *śaṭan*. Most interpreters take this to mean that Satan here is a proper name—the first such occurrence in Scripture, and the only one in the Hebrew Bible. However, it is also possible to translate the term as "an adversary" (Japhet 1993, 374–75). In that case, some nameless, human advisor would be responsible for influencing David's decision. Favoring this mundane reading is the absence of any other trace of a personal Satan in Chronicles. On the other hand, the LXX of 1 Chronicles 21:1 reads *diabolos* here, a Greek word generally translated as "devil" in the New Testament. This is not definitive, as the LXX uses *diabolos* three times with reference to a human enemy (the nameless accuser in Ps. 109:6; Haman in Esth. 7:1; 8:1; and Antiochus in 1 Macc. 1:36). But elsewhere, *diabolos* is the LXX rendering in all the Hebrew references to a heavenly, supernatural *śaṭan*, suggesting that the figure in 1 Chronicles was also understood by the LXX translators to be a supernatural adversary (note, too, Wis. 2:24: "but through the devil's [Greek *diabolos*] envy death entered the world, / and those who belong to his company experience it"). Other elements of the supernatural in chapter 21 (David's conversation with God via Gad in 21:8–13; the angel with a drawn sword and the fire from heaven in 21:18–27) further support the likelihood that Satan, too, is a supernatural being.

But whether David's *śaṭan* was a supernatural being or not, the question of why Chronicles attributes David's temptation to this figure rather than to God remains. One answer may be that the Chronicler is uneasy with attributing evil to God. Note, though, that Chronicles leaves intact other stories of God acting deliberately to deceive or to bring about evil ends: consider, for example, the story of the lying spirit from the Lord who speaks through Ahab's prophets (2 Chr. 18:18–22// 1 Kgs. 22:19–23). While such stories may be disturbing to the modern reader, they are an inescapable part of Israel's radical confession that God alone is sovereign. So, Second Isaiah writes:

86

> I am the LORD, and there is no other.
> I form light and create darkness,
> I make weal and create woe;
> I the LORD do all these things.
> (Isa. 45:6c–7)

The Chronicler is not so much troubled by ascribing evil to God as he is determined that David be held accountable for his actions. In Chronicles, David is no passive puppet, manipulated by God. When enticed by Satan, he yielded to the temptation, and carried out an act he knew to be wrong—an act, furthermore, that his general Joab warned him against (21:3). The Chronicler's position on temptation here is reminiscent of that held by James in the New Testament: "No one, when tempted, should say, 'I am tempted of God'; for God cannot be tempted by evil and he himself tempts no one" (Jas. 1:13). For James, God's only involvement in temptation is empowering us to triumph over it, so that, having "stood the test," we might "receive the crown of life that the Lord has promised to those who love him" (1:12).

Like the Chronicler, James insists that blaming temptation upon God denies our responsibility for our own spiritual welfare. Testing can lead to endurance, and endurance to maturity and wholeness (Jas. 1:3–4). However, yielding to desire leads to sin, and sin, to use James's striking image, "gives birth to death" (1:15). The fault lies not in the temptation itself, nor in the desires that give temptation its power, but in surrendering to temptation. The temptation of Jesus in the Gospel narratives (Matt. 4:1–11; Luke 4:1–13) demonstrates this principle. Satan was able to tempt Jesus to turn the stones into bread because Jesus was hungry. He could tempt Jesus to throw himself from the pinnacle of the temple because Jesus knew the angels would indeed save him. Satan could even tempt Jesus to turn aside from God and worship him, because God's road led to Golgotha, and Jesus did not want to suffer and die! None of these desires was sinful in itself. Only if his desires had led Jesus to yield to temptation would Jesus have sinned. But Jesus triumphed over temptation. Therefore, as the author of Hebrews says, Jesus understands our struggles, having been "in every respect tested as we are, yet without sin" (Heb. 4:15–16).

Satan's temptation strikes at David's desires and weaknesses: particularly, it seems, at his pride. Joab's response to David's command is a rebuke to such overweening pride: "May the LORD increase the number of his people a hundredfold! Are they not, my lord the king, all of them my lord's servants? Why then should my lord require this? Why should he bring guilt on Israel?" (21:3). David's need to count his people, like the compulsion of a miser to count his gold, speaks at once of

87

possessive pride, and of neurotic insecurity. God has promised to preserve David's kingdom. Why then should David worry about how many swords he can place in the field? In Chronicles, David in his righteousness was a model for the Chronicler's community. So also, in his pride and rebellion, David stands as a warning. If even David could fall, and had to face the consequences of his failure, the Chronicler's community needed to be all the more attentive and obedient to the will of the Lord.

God's Judgment (21:7–30) (//2 Sam. 24:10–25). In Chronicles, God's displeasure comes not before the census, as its cause, but afterwards as its consequence (21:7). When God begins to strike out at Israel, David realizes his sin, and prays for forgiveness. God's answer comes by David's seer, Gad. David is given a choice of three punishments: either there will be three years of famine, three months of devastation while David flees before his enemies, or "three days of the sword of the LORD, pestilence on the land, and the angel of the LORD destroying throughout all the territory of Israel" (21:12). David makes his choice: he will accept the punishment that comes directly from the Lord—that is, the pestilence. This may seem to the reader an act of cowardice, particularly as David asks "let me not fall into human hands" (21:13). Why should the people suffer for David's sin? However, note that David also says, "let me fall into the hand of the LORD." David does not seek to save his own life. After all, David's death would not threaten the promise: his son Solomon, though young, was ready to take over. But if Israel were overrun by an enemy, or decimated and bankrupted by lengthy famine, Solomon would have no kingdom to inherit. Further, David trusts in the Lord, "for his mercy is very great." Even in his punishment, David submits to the will of God.

The pestilence sweeps through the land, taking seventy thousand lives. But then, after sending the destroyer against Jerusalem itself, the Lord commands a halt. David sees, towering above the threshing floor of Ornan, "the angel of the LORD standing between earth and heaven, and in his hand a drawn sword stretched out over Jerusalem" (21:16). In response to this awful vision, David cries out for God to hold him and his house alone accountable: "It is I who have sinned and done very wickedly. But these sheep, what have they done?" (21:17). To spare Jerusalem, David is willing to give up all that God had promised him.

God's response comes through the angel, by way of David's prophet Gad (21:18; compare 2 Sam. 24:18). The notion of a heavenly being conveying the divine word is very old—indeed, in Hebrew the word translated "angel" also means "messenger." However, the idea of an angel delivering God's message to a prophet reflects the influence of late prophecy: particularly Zechariah, where an angel whom the prophet calls "the angel who talked with me" serves as Zechariah's guide and interpreter in his visions (for example, Zech. 1:9; 2:3–5; 4:11–14; in contrast, see such earlier texts as Isa. 6:1–13; Jer. 1:4–10; and Ezek. 2:1—3:3, where the prophet is addressed by God directly). Angelic intermediation will later be a key feature in apocalypses such as Daniel (for example, Dan. 8:15–17) and Revelation (for example, Rev. 1:1).

Just as, following Korah's rebellion, Aaron had stood between Israel and the Lord with an offering to avert the plague (Num. 16:46–50), so Gad instructs David to purchase the threshing floor of Ornan, set up an altar to the Lord there, and offer sacrifices to turn aside God's judgment. In Chronicles, Ornan and his sons also see the angel; however, while his sons run from the vision of the angel, Ornan goes on threshing grain (21:20)! When David declares why he needs the threshing floor, Ornan spontaneously offers to give his king not only the ground, but his oxen and grain for the sacrifice, and his yokes and threshing-sledges for wood. The grain is not mentioned in 2 Samuel; however, its mention in Chronicles is in keeping with the directives in Torah to include a meal offering with every burnt offering (so Myers 1965, 149; see Exod. 29:38–41; Num. 15:1–10).

Despite Ornan's generosity, David recognizes that a sacrifice is no sacrifice at all if it costs nothing, and so he purchases the ground. Unlike 2 Samuel 24:24, where David buys oxen and land together for fifty shekels of silver, in 1 Chronicles 21:25 David pays six hundred shekels of gold for the site alone. The great rabbinic Bible scholar Rashi, noting that the price in gold paid in Chronicles was twelve times the price in silver paid in 2 Samuel, suggested that David paid fifty shekels for each tribe. To be sure, the increase is a reflection of the Chronicler's view: first, of David's fairness and generosity (Ornan has certainly received "the full price" [21:24] for his field); and second, of the preciousness of this sacred site.

When David had built the altar and placed his offerings upon it, "He called upon the LORD, and he answered him with fire from heaven on the altar of burnt offering" (21:26). Plainly, this dramatic demonstration of God's acceptance is influenced by the story of Elijah's prophetic duel in 1 Kings 18, where the Lord answered the prophet with fire from heaven that consumed his offering. It is joined to a vision that simply and powerfully expresses God's grace: "Then the LORD commanded the angel, and he put his sword back into its sheath" (21:27). But, even though the sword has been sheathed, David remains terribly aware of its presence (21:30). The wrath and the grace of God have both been shown here at the threshing floor of Ornan. Surely, this

89

means that God has chosen this site in Jerusalem, rather than the tabernacle's location in Gibeon, as the place of God's particular presence.

22:1—29:30
The End of David's Reign

First Chronicles 22:1 marks the transition to the end of David's reign. From now on, all that the king does will be focused toward his successor, and specifically toward the building of the Jerusalem temple. The material throughout this section is unique to Chronicles, though allusions to other texts can be found at numerous points.

This final unit in David's story is structured around three farewell speeches of David: to Solomon (22:6–19), to the court officials (28:1–21), and to all Israel (29:1–9). Also to be found here is a long list of temple and court officials (23:1—27:34). Many scholars regard much of this material as secondary expansion to Chronicles (for example, Mosis 1973, 44). Certainly, the Chronicler draws on a variety of material throughout this section, and the various sources used do not always agree with one another, or with other materials elsewhere in Chronicles. By now, however, this should be no surprise. The techniques in evidence throughout this section, and its overall themes, are consistent with the Chronicler's method and theology elsewhere.

Preparations for the Temple (22:1–19)

In keeping with the Chronicler's pattern, good comes from David's evil. The threshing floor of Ornan, where David offered his sacrifice to avert the plague from Jerusalem, is revealed as the site where Solomon's temple is to be built (22:1). The next several chapters all deal, in one way or another, with the temple establishment set up by David for his successor Solomon. However, this opening section deals specifically with preparations for the temple's construction.

Materials for the Building of the Temple (22:2–5). Having learned the location of the temple, David begins preparations for its building, stockpiling iron and bronze, collecting cedar logs from the Phoenicians, and arranging for the quarrying and dressing of great blocks of stone. As part of the preparations, David mobilizes a body of forced laborers, specifically for the difficult, dangerous quarry work (22:2). Note that, according to the Chronicler, neither David nor

Solomon used native Israelites as forced labor. Instead, foreigners were used for this purpose (for example, 20:3; 2 Chr. 2:17).

These preparations are necessary, David declares, because while the temple must be magnificent, Solomon is "young and inexperienced" (22:5). David, though old, is still at the peak of his powers in Chronicles. He is able to command the respect necessary for successful trade and negotiations, and so to procure the needed materials. It will take time for Solomon to gain such confidence. So, as his last kingly act "before his death" (22:5), David makes the necessary arrangements.

David's First Farewell Speech (22:6–19). David's first farewell speech is principally addressed to his son, Solomon. The burden of the speech is given in its introduction: "Then he called for his son Solomon and charged him to build a house for the LORD, the God of Israel" (22:6). David's farewell to his son is focused, as was David's own reign, on provision for right worship. This is quite a contrast to David's final farewell to Solomon in 1 Kings 2:1–9, where the main body of the speech deals with eliminating enemies and potential rivals! But David's speech is appropriate to its context and setting in Chronicles. While the Deuteronomistic History describes the political chaos and uncertainty of the transition from David to Solomon, the Chronicler stays with the certitude of the divine promise. Solomon of course must become king, for God had said it. Just so, as Nathan's oracle had decreed, Solomon will build the temple.

David begins his speech by recalling the circumstances of Nathan's oracle in chapter 17, where David was told that he could not build the temple. Now, we learn why permission was denied. The Lord, David says, had told him, "You have shed much blood and have waged great wars; you shall not build a house to my name, because you have shed so much blood in my sight on the earth" (22:8). This explanation is unique to Chronicles. In 1 Kings 5:3, Solomon tells Hiram of Tyre that David's wars had prevented him from building the temple. But the statement in Chronicles goes far beyond stating that war kept David too busy to engage in temple building. Rather, because of his wars, God *forbade* David to build.

In Chronicles, war can be a sign of God's wrath and a consequence of sin (so 2 Chr. 16:9). Curiously, though, David's wars were never a cause for disapprobation in the Chronicler's account of David's reign. Indeed, as we have seen, victory in battle was one of the signs of God's blessing and favor upon David. Some interpreters have proposed that David's problem was related to ritual uncleanness. According to Israel's ancient law, the life of a creature is in the blood, and so the blood belongs to God, and cannot legitimately be used or handled by any human (Lev. 17:10–16;

91

see also Gen. 9:4–6; Deut. 12:15–16). As a bloody man, then, David was ritually defiled and so unable to build God's pure and holy dwelling.

It is more probable, however, that David was forbidden to build the temple in Chronicles because his vocation was to be a warrior, not a man of peace. The temple declares God's victory over chaos and evil (see Pss. 29; 46), and so is a place of peace, not conflict. Therefore, the temple must be built by a man of peace. In chapter 17, David is not said to have been given rest from his enemies (in contrast to the Chronicler's source in 2 Sam. 7:1, 11). That rest is reserved for Solomon (22:9; see also 23:25). Indeed, Solomon's very name, which in Hebrew sounds much like *shalom*, shows him to be the man of peace during whose reign the Lord "will give peace and quiet to Israel" (22:9). A Christian reader may be reminded of Paul's statement in 1 Corinthians 12:27–31 that, while there are a variety of gifts and callings in the body of Christ, all are apportioned by God through the one Spirit. So, it was David's gift to be a warrior—a calling which, unfortunately for David, made it inappropriate for him to build the temple. Solomon, however, whose calling was to be a man of peace, could carry out God's command to build "a house for my name" (22:10; see the commentary on 17:12–14, above).

However, just as David's glory had not been due to any inherent greatness of his own, but rather to God's grace (17:17–18), so Solomon would succeed in building the temple only if the Lord was with him (22:11). To this end, David prays, "may the LORD grant you discretion and understanding, so that when he gives you charge over Israel you may keep the law of the LORD your God" (22:12). David's prayer that Solomon be given "discretion and understanding" foreshadows Solomon's own prayer for wisdom (2 Chr. 1:10; compare 1 Kgs. 3:9). Most significant, however, is David's prayer that Solomon observe the law. Saul's reign had crashed to ruin because of his failure to heed the word of God (10:13). In contrast, David's reign had begun in obedience to divine word (11:3), and continued in success so long as David sought after God's will. So now, David prays that Solomon will remain faithful to God's word revealed in the Torah.

David's speech in 22:13 partially reflects the king's last words to Solomon in the Deuteronomistic History (1 Kgs. 2:2–3). There as well, David urges his son to be strong, and to observe the statutes and ordinances of Moses. However, the closest parallel to this text, as many scholars have observed, is to be found in God's words to Joshua in Joshua 1:6–9. Arguably, this implies that the Chronicler had in mind a typological parallel. Just as the authority of Moses had passed to Joshua, so now David's authority passes to Solomon. The comparison of David and Moses is particularly striking, however. Both are, for the Chronicler, founders of Israel's liturgy: Moses in the ultimate sense, as the one through whom the Torah was revealed; David as the one at last empowered to put Moses' principles in action. As we will see in David's second farewell speech (28:1–21), this parallel is particularly applicable to temple-building. For the Chronicler, David and Moses stand together as the ultimate authorities for what constitutes right worship.

Next, David describes to Solomon the preparations he has made for the temple, both in materials (22:11–14) and in skilled and unskilled labor (22:15–16). All that remains is for Solomon to "begin the work" (22:16). The amounts of material David has collected are staggering: one hundred thousand talents (about 3,775 tons) of gold, and one million talents (37,750 tons) of silver, as well as bronze and iron "beyond weighing." The figures are obviously exaggerated: today the gold alone would be worth over thirty-four billion dollars! Yet David instructs his son, "To these you must add more" (22:14)! The point is clear. God's temple demands and deserves the best and the most that human beings can supply: to recall Oswald Chambers, our utmost for God's highest. Contemporary readers may well be offended by this extravagance. Shouldn't our resources rather be used to combat injustice, to feed the hungry and clothe the naked? Perhaps we should recall Jesus' words when his followers were offended by an alabaster jar broken, its precious contents wasted (Matt. 26:6–13; Mark 14:3–9). While we are always and everywhere called to use our resources to aid the needy, our highest calling, in the words of the Westminster Catechism, is "to glorify God and to enjoy him forever." Extravagance in the service of God's glory is no waste!

In an aside to the leaders of Israel (perhaps the same group who will be addressed by David in 28:1–21), David calls upon them to support Solomon in his calling from God. David's words here reflect the theology of the conquest of the land in Numbers 32:22 (Japhet 1993, 403). Only now, under David, has the land at last been "subdued before the LORD and his people" (22:18). Now, in the peace that David has won, space and time is provided for Solomon, the man of peace, to fulfill his vocation and build the temple. Just as David had once led Israel in seeking after the ark (13:3; 15:13), so he directs the leaders of Israel: "Now set your mind and heart to seek the LORD your God. Go and build the sanctuary of the LORD God so that the ark of the covenant of the LORD and the holy vessels of God may be brought into a house built for the name of the LORD" (22:19).

Preparations for the New King (23:1—28:21)

In Chronicles as in the Deuteronomistic History, Solomon begins his reign as David's coregent (23:1). But in Chronicles, David remains confident and strong to the end: "old and full of days" (23:1), he declares

93

Solomon king. The transition of power, therefore, is seamlessly smooth and peaceful. David first assembles his sacral and political administration (23:2—27:34); then he addresses to them his second farewell speech, urging them to support their new king as he builds the temple (28:1–21).

Sacral and Political Administration (23:2—27:34). Just as David made preparations for Solomon's temple-building by stockpiling materials and gathering laborers, so he prepared for Solomon's assumption of power by assembling a reliable bureaucracy. Having made Solomon his coregent, David summons "all the leaders of Israel and the priests and the Levites" (23:2). The purpose of this summoning is made clear in the following chapters, as (in an order roughly opposite to the listing in 23:2), the sacral and political administration of David and Solomon's kingdom is set forth. The material which follows can be divided into two major sections. The first, largest, and most important concerns the organization of the Levites and priests for worship and administration (23:2—26:32). The second deals with the military and political structure of David's government (27:1–34).

Sacral Administration (23:3—26:32). The importance given to the Levites throughout this section has often led scholars to propose that the Chronicler was a Levite (or a Levitical school). Recall, however, that in Chronicles the distinction between priest and Levite is steadfastly maintained (see the excursus on priests and Levites above). Nowhere in the Chronicler's History is it suggested (as it is, for example, in Deuteronomy and in Malachi) that priesthood should be the province of the entire tribe of Levi. Chronicles is closer in spirit to the priestly sources of the Pentateuch, the Law of the Temple in Ezekiel 40—48, and the postexilic prophets Haggai and Zechariah. To be sure, however, Chronicles is far more conciliatory in its approach, and so far more positive about the Levites, than any of these other texts.

Levitical Clans and Duties (23:3–32). A census taken of the Levites totals thirty-eight thousand men "thirty years and upward" (23:3). The Levites were exempt from any military census, as their service to Israel was regarded as fulfilled by their work in the temple (Num. 1:49). Therefore, as we have seen, Joab rightly did not count the Levites when David ordered his census (21:6). Now, however, they are counted for a legitimate reason: to assign them their places in temple service.

The age of eligibility given here for Levitical service is intriguing. Like 23:3, Numbers 4:3, 23, and 30 also place the lower limit on Levitical service at thirty (though Numbers also stipulates a retirement age of fifty). Note, however, that Numbers 8:24 lowers the age of eligibility to twenty-five, while 1 Chronicles 23:24 and 27 drop it to twenty! Apparently, there were a variety of alternate traditions pertaining to the

94

age at which a Levite could begin service. This age of eligibility could fluctuate up or down, depending on the number of Levites available. It is possible that the Chronicler is using multiple sources here, and (as is frequently the case in chapters 1—9) placing them side by side with no attempt to harmonize them. But the "thirty" in 1 Chronicles 23:3 could also be a scribal error, prompted by the number thirty-eight thousand preceding it, so that the text should read "twenty" there as well (Japhet 1993, 412). This reading is supported by 27:23, which states that in his tragic census, "David did not count those below twenty years of age," and by 2 Chronicles 31:17, where the Levites of Hezekiah's time begin service at twenty.

Perhaps the change in the age of service in chapter 23 reflects the changed circumstances described in verse 26. Tremendous maturity, patience, and wisdom, as well as physical strength, were required for the proper transport of the tabernacle and its contents (as the Chronicler's ark narrative demonstrates). But with the building of the temple, portage of the tabernacle and its contents would no longer be necessary. As a result, it might be thought that younger, less mature Levites would now be able to serve successfully. The lack of an upper age limit to Levitical service in chapter 23 may also be due to these changed circumstances. As the heavy labor of transporting the tabernacle will no longer be a Levitical responsibility, it will no longer be necessary for Levites to retire at fifty.

David divides the Levites into four groups. The largest, twenty-four thousand strong, is assigned to "have charge of the work in the house of the LORD" (23:4). These may be the "second order" of 15:18. Next come the administrators: six thousand Levites are appointed to serve as "officers and judges" (23:4; see 26:20–32). Finally, four thousand Levites each are assigned to duty as gatekeepers (23:5; see 26:1–19), and as temple musicians (23:5; see 25:1–31). Note that these last three groups are dealt with in the following chapters, in reverse order.

In 23:6–23, the divisions of the Levites are set forth, based on the Levitical clans. The clan list here bears a general similarity to other such lists in Chronicles and elsewhere, being divided overall into three groups, derived from the three sons of Levi: Gershon, Kohath, and Merari (23:6; see 6:16; 15:5–7). However, this list does not quite coincide either with the Levitical clan list given in 15:5–10 or with the Levitical genealogy in 6:16–30 (note, for instance, the differences in the descendants of Gershon). Also, as is common with genealogical lists, there are scribal errors and other difficulties (such as the confusion regarding the descendants of Ladan and Shimei in 23:9–10). Still, none of this requires one to think that this list is a later addition to the text.

95

More likely, 23:6–23 is yet another demonstration of the Chronicler's reliance upon multiple sources.

Two features in this list are of particular interest. Among the sons of Amram, "Aaron was set apart to consecrate the most holy things, so that he and his sons forever should make offerings before the Lord, and minister to him and pronounce blessings in his name forever" (23:13). Therefore, Aaron's lineage is not given here among the Levitical clans, but is treated separately, in the account of the twenty-four courses of the priesthood that follows this Levitical list (24:1–19). A similar organizational principle may be at work here to that observed in the Judah section of the Chronicler's genealogies (2:3—4:23). Just as there, the line of David (3:1–24) was bracketed by two Judahite genealogical lists (2:3–55 and 4:1–23), so here the line of Aaron (24:1–19) is bracketed by two Levitical lists (23:3–22 and 24:20–31).

While Aaron's line is treated separately, the descendants of Aaron's brother Moses are "reckoned among the tribe of Levi" (23:14)—yet another indication of the Chronicler's place in Israel's ancient debate concerning the priesthood. David's selection of Zadok and Abiathar as priests at the central Jerusalem shrine was a diplomatic attempt to mediate between two great priestly houses: the Moses priesthood at Shiloh, represented by Abiathar, and the Aaron priesthood at Hebron, represented by Zadok. Although historically the house of Zadok prevailed, the debate continued in Israel's sacred literature. The Chronicler's position is clear. As much as he respects "Moses the man of God" (23:14), he rejects the priestly claims of Moses' descendants. In distinction from the descendants of Aaron, who alone are priests, the descendants of Moses are simply Levites. However, as we have observed before, it is interesting that in 1 Chronicles 24:3, Abiathar's family is incorporated into Aaron's lineage.

Of particular interest is the statement of Levitical duties, responsibilities, and privileges laid out in 23:24–32. The Levites have been enrolled and placed in divisions for an important purpose: "to do the work for the service of the house of the Lord" (23:24). The word translated "work" in the NRSV (*'abodah* in Hebrew) is typically used in the priestly traditions of the Pentateuch to describe the hard physical labor of disassembling, transporting, and reassembling the tabernacle and its contents (Milgrom 1970, 61–76; see especially Num. 4). However, now that Jerusalem has been established as the place of the Lord's shrine, the Levites no longer need to be responsible for this portage: "The Lord, the God of Israel, has given rest to his people; and he resides in Jerusalem forever" (23:25).

With the establishment of a permanent shrine to the Lord in Jerusalem, the Levitical "work" has taken on a new meaning. Now, the

96

Levites will labor in service to the Lord, not physically, but spiritually: in the liturgy, maintenance, and administration of the Jerusalem temple. The double meaning of the English word "service" expresses something very like this transformation. We can use "service" to describe labor or duty (as in a "self-service" gas station, or a person in the military being "in the service"), or to describe a gathering for worship (Sunday "services"). Just so, David declares, Levitical service will henceforth be performed in the worship services of the Jerusalem temple. 23:28–32, which both begins and ends with the expression "for the service (Hebrew *'abodah*) of the house of the LORD," describes the character and content of Levitical labor in this new circumstance.

The NRSV of 23:28 reads that the Levites are "to assist the descendants of Aaron for the service of the house of the LORD," suggesting that the Levites are subservient to the priests. However, the Hebrew is better translated by the JPSV, which reads that the Levites are to serve "alongside the Aaronites." The Levites in Chronicles are not priests. However, neither are they temple servants or "janitors" (as Myers 1965, 161, puts it). Rather, the Chronicler "portrays levitical and Aaronide responsibilities as generally complementary" (Knoppers 1999, 59). The situation described in chapter 23 sounds a great deal like that described in Ezekiel 40:45–46, where temple clergy and altar clergy serve side by side—save that the Chronicler, unlike Ezekiel, does not refer to his temple clergy as priests.

The specific Levitical responsibilities laid out in 23:28–32 are in some cases drawn from the traditions in Torah, and in others are quite unique and unexpected. So, that the Levites are responsible for "the care of the courts and the chambers, the cleansing of all that is holy, and any work for the service of the house of God" (23:28) sounds reminiscent of the "second order" in the Deuteronomistic History, and more than a little like janitorial service! However, the temple chambers are elsewhere reserved for priests, suggesting an expansion of Levitical responsibility and access here (Knoppers 1999, 65). Similarly, 23:29 says that the Levites are "to assist also with the rows of bread, the choice flour for the grain offering, the wafers of unleavened bread, the baked offering, the offering mixed with oil" (see also 9:29–32). The terminology used here is drawn from priestly traditions. Outside of Chronicles, however, the Levites are never mentioned in connection with any of these special offerings. Indeed, the "rows of bread," elsewhere called "the bread of the presence," are strictly reserved in the Torah as the sole responsibility of the priests (Lev. 24:8–9; see Knoppers 1999, 65).

Particularly striking is the statement that the Levites are responsible for maintaining just and proper measures (23:29). Just weights and measures are repeatedly urged in the Hebrew Bible, and the use of false

97

weights is called an abomination, abhorred by God (for example, Lev. 19:35–36; Prov. 11:1; Amos 8:5). In the ancient Near East the maintenance of standard weights and measures was typically a royal responsibility. So, in the prologue to the ancient Sumerian law code of Ur-Nammu, we read that among his other accomplishments, Ur-Nammu "fashioned the bronze *silá*-measure, he standardized the one mina weight, (and) standardized the stone-weight of a shekel of silver *in relation to* one mina" (translated by Finkelstein 1969, 523–24). Likewise, the Law of the Temple holds the leader of the community, the prince, accountable for "justice and right practices"; specifically, by ensuring a just system of measurement (Ezek. 45:9–12). Only here in Chronicles is the maintenance of just measures a Levitical responsibility.

Chapter 23:30–31 gives the Levites responsibility for conducting the liturgy: "And they shall stand every morning, thanking and praising the LORD, and likewise at evening, and whenever burnt offerings are offered to the LORD on sabbaths, new moons, and appointed festivals, according to the number required of them, regularly before the LORD." Doubtless this involves particularly the Levitical singers and musicians. The ascription of Psalms to Asaph (Pss. 50 and 73—83), Heman (Ps. 88), Ethan (Ps. 89), Jeduthun (Pss. 39, 62, and 77), the Korahites (Pss. 42, 44—49, 84, 85, 87 and 88), or simply "To the leader" (an ascription found fifty-five times—nearly as often as David, to whom seventy-three Psalms are attributed) supports a strong leadership role in worship for the Levites.

Finally, the Levites are to "keep charge of the tent of meeting and the sanctuary" (23:32). The terminology is priestly (Num. 3:28; 18:4–5), but the context in Chronicles requires a new interpretation (Knoppers 1999, 63–64). In Numbers, keeping charge of the sanctuary is a Kohathite responsibility, relating to the transport of the most sacred items from the tabernacle. When the tabernacle was at rest, only the priests could enter the holy sanctuary. But in Chronicles a permanent shrine is in view, and the responsibility to keep charge of the sanctuary is given not to the Kohathites, but to the Levites generally. The implication is that the Levites are to have access to the sanctuary itself. Note, by the way, that the Hebrew expression translated "keep charge" is very like that found in Ezekiel 40:45–46, where it designates "the priests who have charge of the temple" and "the priests who have charge of the altar."

The mention of the ancient tent of meeting in union with Solomon's temple might be thought to indicate that the Chronicler is, after all, only playing with texts here—combining information from his sources in a creative, and ahistorical, fashion. However, the tent of meeting, or the tabernacle, was brought into the temple by Solomon, along with the ark and "all the holy vessels that were in the tent" (2 Chr. 5:5//1 Kgs. 8:4). Indeed, the dimensions of the space under the outspread wings of the giant cherubim in the most holy place of Solomon's temple, where the ark was kept, correspond to the dimensions of the tabernacle (see Friedman 1987, 174–87, who proposes that the tent was actually incorporated into the temple structure, pitched beneath the cherubim in the most holy place). In his statements of Levitical responsibilities as well, the Chronicler is not engaging in ahistorical fancy. He is recalling a complementarity between priest and Levite that once existed, and which he hopes might exist once again.

The Twenty-four Courses of the Priesthood (24:1–19). Having completed his treatment of the Levitical clans and their duties, the Chronicler returns to the priestly line of Aaron. Unlike the high-priestly genealogy in 6:4–15, which deals only with the line of Eleazar, 24:1 lists all four sons of Aaron: Nadab, Abihu, Eleazar, and Ithamar (Exod. 6:23; Num. 3:2). The bizarre circumstances of the deaths of Nadab and Abihu (Num. 3:4) are not mentioned by the Chronicler; only that they died childless, so that Aaron's line continued through Eleazar and Ithamar.

Next, Chronicles jumps ahead to David's time, and to the two heads of the priestly houses descended from Eleazar and Ithamar, Zadok and Ahimelech (see 18:16). Although the house of Eleazar is more numerous than that of Ithamar (sixteen Eleazarite families, as opposed to only eight Ithamarite families), the two are treated equally, their order of leadership in sacrificial service being determined by lot (24:5). This means of organizing sacrificial service is reflected in Luke 1:9, where Zechariah, father of John the Baptist, is chosen by lot to offer incense in the sanctuary. The Chronicler's approach here is distinct from the priestly traditions of the Torah, where Eleazar and Ithamar are possessed of different levels of sanctity (for example, Exod. 38:21; Num. 4:2–16). But in 24:5, each house is said to contain both sacrificial ("officers of God") and nonsacrificial ("officers of the sanctuary") clergy, so that there is no basis for a preference of Eleazar over Ithamar.

Still, there is a clear basis for the distinction between priest and Levite. As Ralph Klein observes, "The duties of the priests were given by God, as revealed to Aaron. The duties of the Levites in ch. 23 are assigned by David" (Klein 1993, 638). Similarly, while David himself organizes (Hebrew verb *(halaq)* the Levites in their divisions, the divisions of the priests, being organized (again, *(halaq* in Hebrew) by lot, are left in the hand of God (24:5). Often in Scripture, drawing lots is used as a means of determining God's will (for example, Num. 26:55; 1 Sam. 10:17–26; Acts 1:26). Indeed, an important priestly task was the keeping and use of the sacred lot, the Urim and Thummim (see Exod. 28:30; Num. 27:21; 1 Sam. 14:41). For the Chronicler, then, priestly service is possessed of greater sanctity, and of more ancient attestation, than Levitical service. While Levite and priest fill complementary roles in Chronicles, their roles are never interchangeable.

Another Levitical List (24:20–31). This second Levitical clan list, as we have seen, brackets the line of Aaron between two Levitical lists. Its relationship to the first Levitical list in 23:3–32 is uncertain. As the second list extends some of the families in the earlier list, while leaving Hebron (24:23//23:19) and Mushi (24:30a//23:23) unchanged, 24:20–31 may be a supplement to the earlier list (Myers 1965, 166). Note, however, that an entirely new line has appeared under Merari (24:27), while Gershon is not mentioned at all. This suggests that 24:20–31 is not a supplement, but an alternate list.

Like the priestly list in 24:1–19, the second Levitical list involves organization by lot (24:31) rather than, as in 23:6, by royal decree. The order of service for both the temple musicians (25:8) and the gatekeepers (26:13) is also determined by a lottery, described in language similar to that found in 24:31 (compare "the chief as well as the youngest brother" in 24:31 with "small and great, teacher and pupil alike" in 25:8; and "small and great alike" in 26:13). However, different terminology is used in these three passages (in each, the Levites "cast lots") than was used in either 23:1 or 24:5 (where priest and Levite are "organized," whether by David or by lot), suggesting that no conflict is intended between David's organization of the Levites, and the determination of their order of service by lot.

Still, while the lotteries in 24:5; 25:8; and 26:13 all have the purpose of determining the order in which Levitical or priestly families will serve, no such justification is given for the lottery in 24:31, leaving it unclear for what purpose the lots are drawn here. Probably, 24:31 is an editorial expansion, added by the Chronicler to his source text in 24:20b–30 to bring the two Levitical clan lists into greater harmony with the priestly list (Japhet 1993, 423). Indeed, the text states that the Levites "cast lots corresponding to their kindred, the descendants of Aaron" (24:31). Intriguingly, Josephus speaks of twenty-four courses of Levites, corresponding to the twenty-four priestly courses (*Antiquities* 7.17). Perhaps the parallel between 24:1–19 and 20–31, established by the expansion at verse 31, suggested that the numbers should also be parallel, though it is unclear how the names in 24:20–31 could be juggled to yield twenty-four.

100

The Temple Musicians (25:1–31). This is the fifth list of the Levitical musicians in Chronicles, which shows something of their importance to the Chronicler's view of right worship. The association of David with music and poetry is certainly not unique to Chronicles: David appears as a musician and poet in 1 Samuel 16:14–23 and 2 Samuel 1:17–27, and seventy-three psalms are ascribed to him. Still, as Chronicles attributes Jerusalem's liturgy to David, his role as a patron of music and poetry is particularly important here.

The first list of temple musicians, in 6:31–48, is a reverse genealogy, tracing David's singers Heman, Asaph, and Ethan back to Levi through, respectively, Kohath, Gershom, and Merari. The second list, in 15:16–22, treats the appointment of Heman, Asaph, and Ethan by the Levitical leaders, at David's command. In 16:4–6, David places Asaph in charge of the liturgy before the ark; 16:37–42 describes the continuation of praise before the ark, led by Asaph, as well as continuing services before the tabernacle at Hebron, conducted by Heman and Jeduthun—evidently, another name for Ethan (recall that Pss. 39, 62, and 77 are attributed to Jeduthun).

The fifth list, 25:1–31, purports to give a breakdown of the temple musicians under the leadership of these same three. Note that here again, the third singer is called Jeduthun; indeed, the name "Ethan" does not appear again in the Chronicler's History. However, the fictional character of the list is plain. The singers are presented in a schema of twenty-four courses, like the Aaronid priests. To fill out the list, the Chronicler has manufactured names, many of them blatantly artificial. In particular, the purported "sons" of Heman (25:4) are actually, from Hanani onwards, either a series of song titles or a strange little poem. After some slight rearrangements, the "names" of Heman's sons translate as follows:

> Be gracious to me, Yahweh, be gracious to me;
> My God art thou.
> I have magnified and I will exalt [my] helper;
> Sitting in adversity I said,
> Clear signs give plentifully.
>   (Myers 1965, 173)

The Chronicler apparently doesn't mind the reader seeing through his artifice. His point remains: as in 23:28, so here, the liturgical ministry of the Levites is complementary to the sacrificial ministry of the priests.

Two other odd features of 25:1–31 deserve mention. First, it is certainly strange that "the officers of the army" (25:1) should be involved with David in setting the musicians apart for their service. However, the word translated "army" here by the NRSV is used elsewhere of the Levites gathered for sacred service (Japhet 1993, 439; for example, Num. 4:3; 8:24–25). Quite probably, then, 25:1 simply restates 15:16,

101

where it is "the chiefs of the Levites" who are responsible for appointing Asaph, Heman, and Ethan/Jeduthun.

The other curious feature relates to the description of the temple musicians' ministry as "prophecy" (25:1 and 3). Asaph, it is said, "prophesied under the direction of the king" (25:2), while Heman is called "the king's seer" (25:5). Actually, in early Israelite prophecy, the link between prophet and musician was not unusual at all. Moses' sister Miriam, who is called a prophet (Exod. 15:20; see also Num. 12:1–16; 1 Chr. 6:2–3; Micah 6:4, which emphasize Miriam alongside Moses and Aaron), plays a tambourine and leads the women of Israel in singing and dancing (Exod. 15:20–21). In 1 Samuel 10:5, Samuel tells Saul that he will encounter "a band of prophets coming down from the shrine with harp, tambourine, flute, and lyre playing in front of them; they will be in a prophetic frenzy." Saul is caught up in the spirit of the Lord with the prophets, and he as well prophesies. Similarly, in 2 Kings 3:15, Elisha calls for a musician, and prophesies while the musician is playing. In short, the association of music with prophecy is not as odd as it may at first appear. Indeed, surely our own experience of worship has taught us of the capacity of music to strike deep chords within us, and bring us to a heightened awareness of the presence, power, love, and majesty of God. As hymnist Fred Pratt Green has written,

> How often, making music, we have found
> a new dimension in the world of sound,
> as worship moved us to a more profound
> Alleluia!
> (*The United Methodist Hymnal* 1989, no. 68)

Evidently the Levitical musicians, playing under the inspiration of the Lord's spirit, were believed also to be channels of the divine word.

The Gatekeepers (26:1–19). This is the fourth list of gatekeepers in Chronicles. The first, in 9:17–32, deals with the gatekeepers who returned to Jerusalem from exile; four families are listed, totaling 212 people. However, this list also expounds to some degree on the responsibilities of the gatekeepers, which evidently went beyond mere guard duty to assisting in a variety of ways with the appurtenances of temple worship (see 9:28–32). The second list, at 15:18b, 23, mentions four names in association with David's ark procession: Obed-edom, Jeiel, Berechiah, and Elkanah. The third list, at 16:38, lists two families of gatekeepers in David's time, Obed-edom and Hosah, and mentions sixty-eight members of Obed-edom's family who worked as gatekeepers (see the discussion of Obed-edom in 13:13–14). The fourth list, at 26:1–19, is in form like the list of temple musicians: first presenting a clan list, then describing the drawing of lots to determine the order of service, and the gates that each family will guard. Here, three families are in view, totaling ninety-three people: sixty-two in the family of Obed-edom, eighteen in the family of Meshelemiah, and thirteen in the family of Hosah (26:8–11).

There is some controversy as to whether or not the gatekeepers were originally regarded as Levites: Obed-edom, for instance, is in 2 Samuel 6:10–11 called a Gittite. However, as we have seen (see the commentary on 15:18, 23–24), the gatekeepers may be related to the Levitical keepers of the threshold in the Deuteronomistic History (2 Kgs. 12:9; 22:4; 23:4; 25:18). At any rate, guard duty over the sanctuary is a Levitical task in Torah as well (see Num. 1:50–53; 3—4). There is, then, clear precedent for the assignment of Levites as guards of the temple gates in the Chronicler's History.

The Temple Administrators (26:20–32). Finally, Chronicles relates the assignment of Levites to the tasks of administration and finance crucial to the maintenance of the temple. As every pastor knows, administration is neither easy nor glamorous; however, it *is* a ministry, and an essential one to the life of the community of faith. The text first lays out the assignments for the Levitical treasurers (26:20–28). In particular, they are responsible for booty taken in battle and dedicated to the Lord (see 18:8), going back to the reign of Saul (26:28). It is intriguing to find here also donations from Abner, Ishbaal's general during the seven and a half years of conflict following Saul's death. Although the Chronicler makes no mention of the civil war, he assumes that his readers are aware of it, and know who Abner was.

Next, 26:29–32 speaks of Levites in political and judicial roles: the Izharites, "appointed to outside duties for Israel, as officers and judges" (26:29), and the Hebronites, who were given "oversight . . . for all the work of the LORD and for the service of the king" both west and east of the Jordan (26:30, 32; for the Levitical pedigree of Izhar and Hebron, see 6:2, 18; 23:12, 18–19). In the Pentateuch's priestly traditions, the Levites do not serve as judges. However, service in the law courts is an important part of the Levitical priesthood in both Deuteronomy (17:8–13; 21:5) and the Law of the Temple in Ezekiel 40—48 (Ezek. 44:24). Unlike either the Deuteronomist or Ezekiel's Zadokite editors, the Chronicler does not regard judgeship as a priestly responsibility. Still, the appointment of Levites as judges and officials is taken with great seriousness. The Chronicler stresses that every attempt was made to find the best people to serve (see 26:31).

Together, the lists of the Levites and priests serve as the necessary counterpart to the material preparations for the temple described in chapter 22. David bequeaths to Solomon an intact and functioning temple establishment, from priests and liturgists to administrators and temple guards. All that is lacking is the temple itself.

103

Political Administration (27:1–34). Having finished his treatment of the Levitical appointments, the Chronicler turns now to David's secular officials. The political administration of Israel is treated in four parts: the military (27:1–15), the tribal leaders (27:16–24), David's stewards (27:25–31), and David's personal advisors (27:32–34). Many scholars regard this material as a secondary addition to Chronicles, since it does not deal with the temple or its personnel. However, there is ample precedent in Israel's sacred literature for mixing religion and politics. In Deuteronomy, the responsibilities of the king (Deut. 17:14–20) are given in close association with those of the priest (Deut. 18:1–8) and the prophet (Deut. 18:9–22). Similarly, in the Law of the Temple, the responsibilities of priests and Levites (Ezek. 44:1–31) and those of the prince (Ezek. 45:7—46:18) are closely related.

In fact, the structure of 23:1—28:21 requires the inclusion of the secular as well as the sacred leadership of Israel. In 23:2, David summons "all the leaders of Israel and the priests and the Levites." The following chapters, as we have seen, deal in reverse sequence with the Levites (23:3–32; expanded in 24:20—26:32) and the priests (24:1–19); it is to be expected that next, the leaders of Israel will be discussed. Further, in 28:1, we read, "David assembled at Jerusalem all the officials of Israel, the officials of the tribes, the officers of the divisions that served the king, the commanders of the thousands, the commanders of the hundreds, the stewards of all the property and cattle of the king and his sons, together with the palace officials, the mighty warriors, and all the warriors." These are the very groups discussed in chapter 27. We have, then, no reason to regard 27:1–34 as a later addition.

The Military (27:1–15). The Chronicler begins by laying out the divisions of David's army, and their commanders. The text sets forth twelve divisions, each numbering twenty-four thousand, which serve in monthly rotation (27:1). The names of the twelve division commanders all appear among the first sixteen names in the list of David's heroes (11:10–30). The Chronicler refers to these men as "the chiefs of David's warriors" (11:10); now, those chiefs are matched up with their commands. Scholars differ as to whether the Chronicler is drawing on an actual source here, describing an actual practice at some point in Israel's history, or (as in the list of the temple musicians) creating an idealized presentation for ideological effect. Either way, the function of the text in Chronicles remains the same. David bequeaths to Solomon an intact, functioning, fully viable military. While David was forced to carve out his kingdom with the edge of a sword, Solomon will begin his reign in strength and security, enabling him to be the man of peace who will build the temple.

104

The Tribal Leaders (27:16–24). The second group of Israel's leaders listed by the Chronicler is the tribal officials. The same principle observed in 2:1–2 (///Gen. 35:22b–26; see Num. 1:5–15) is used for the ordering of the tribes here, though the Joseph tribes, Ephraim and Manasseh, are listed separately, and Dan is in its proper place. In keeping with the distinction between priest and Levite consistently maintained by the Chronicler, the tribe of Levi is divided into Levi and Aaron (27:17). Manassah also is divided into two half-tribes (27:20b–21a), reflecting geographical reality. The one change in the expected order, the shift of Naphtali from the end of the list to a position after Zebulun (27:19), may also reflect geographical concerns (Japhet 1993, 471). Gad and Asher are missing; probably, they were dropped from the end of the list by a scribal error.

The list of tribal leaders ends with an odd note concerning David's census. First, we are told that "David did not count those below twenty years of age, for the LORD had promised to make Israel as numerous as the stars of heaven" (27:23; see also 23:24, 27). Apparently, David's census did not count those under twenty, since even without them God's blessing would ensure a huge number—a presumptuous and prideful assumption. Despite the census, then, the population of the tribes is not listed here: both because, since Joab refused to count Levi and Benjamin, the census was never finished (21:6), and because "wrath came upon Israel for this" (27:24)—that is, for the census, not for Joab's failure to finish it (21:7–17; for a different view, however, see Wright 1998, 54–55).

By the Chronicler's time, the tribal system no longer existed. But this listing of the tribal officials is, nonetheless, important. That all the leaders of all the tribes served willingly under David's authority makes again the Chronicler's point that all Israel supported David's rule. In Chronicles, David bequeaths to Solomon an intact and unified kingdom.

David's Stewards (27:25–31). The last two groups of leaders listed are the ones closest to the throne: those who handle the king's property, and those who have the king's ear. First, David's stewards are listed, together with their areas of responsibility. Apart from serving as an impressive demonstration of David's wealth, this passage has an important function in the Chronicler's narrative. The security of David's personal fortune is assured. Therefore, he can bequeath to Solomon economic as well as military and political stability. Solomon can *afford* to build the temple!

David's Personal Advisors (27:32–34). Apart from Joab and Abiathar (and, possibly, Benaiah son of Jehoiada; see below), this list of David's advisors does not correspond to the king's administration as set forth in 18:14–17. While that list details the public administration, these may be David's "private advisors" (Myers 1965, 185). They are a curious group. David's uncle Jonathan appears only here in Scripture. Jehiel, who "attended the king's sons" (27:32) and so was apparently Solomon's tutor, is not mentioned in any narrative about either David or Solomon. Jehoiada son of Benaiah is also an enigma, unless his name is a scribal error for Benaiah son of Jehoiada, a renowned warrior among the Thirty and chief of David's bodyguard (11:22–25; 18:17).

Yet, mysterious as these otherwise unknown advisors are, the familiar names are perhaps still more mysterious. Ahitophel is praised as the wisest of counselors in 2 Samuel 16:23; however, he lends his counsel to David's treacherous son Absalom, and defects to Absalom when the prince revolts against his father (2 Sam. 15:12, 31; 16:15—17:4). The revolt fails in large measure because Hushai (who is called "the king's friend" in 27:33; see 2 Sam. 15:37), pretending also to go over to Absalom's side, counters Ahitophel's wise counsel with bad advice (2 Sam. 15:32–37; 17:5–14). Ahitophel, seeing his counsel rejected and knowing Absalom's cause is doomed, commits suicide (2 Sam. 17:23). Abiathar, though an old friend from David's mercenary days (1 Sam. 22:20–23) and one of David's high priests in Jerusalem, sides with Solomon's rival Adonijah in his bid for David's throne (1 Kgs. 1:7). Joab, to be sure, is a far more attractive figure in Chronicles than in the Deuteronomistic History; however, on the one occasion in Chronicles that Joab gives his king advice (in 21:3, concerning the census), David refuses it! According to 1 Kings 2:13–35, Solomon would order Benaiah son of Jehoiada to assassinate Joab, and would exile Abiathar to Anathoth. The advisors, then, are a most ironic bequest.

Perhaps, in the end, David's advisors are actually a message to the Chronicler's community. Even the wisest and best make mistakes. Even the most faithful and trusted can prove false. As always, Chronicles offers a warning together with the promise. Like Solomon, the Chronicler's community had inherited a great tradition, and built a temple. But the threat of faithlessness and sin was also a part of their heritage. They could not afford to relax their vigilance, for if they did, the grim past would repeat itself.

David's Second Farewell Speech (28:1–21). David's second farewell speech is principally addressed to the leaders of Israel listed in chapter 27. In many ways, this passage recalls David's first speech, addressed principally to Solomon, and Nathan's oracle in chapter 17. Again, David recalls his desire to build the temple, and God's refusal on the grounds that David has shed blood (28:2–3). However, David and his line have nonetheless been chosen for kingship. Out of all the tribes of Israel, God had chosen Judah, and out of all the families of Judah,

God had chosen David's house. Now, out of all David's sons ("for the LORD has given me many"; 28:5), the Lord has chosen Solomon.

However, while in 17:14 the promise of eternal kingship for Solomon and his descendants was unconditional, here the Lord states, "I will establish his kingdom forever if he continues resolute in keeping my commandments and my ordinances, as he is today" (28:7). The survival of Solomon's kingdom depends upon faithfulness in following God's word. Intriguingly, however, the verbs in 28:8 are *plural:* it is not Solomon but the leaders addressed in this speech who are commanded, with God and the entire assembly of Israel as witnesses, to "observe and search out all the commandments of the LORD your God; that you may possess this good land, and leave it for an inheritance to your children after you forever." Quite probably, the Chronicler is addressing his own community here, and calling them to faithfulness. They knew all too well what faithlessness had ultimately cost Solomon's descendants.

David's first farewell speech recalled the first conquest of the land (22:18; compare Num. 32:22). This second speech also recalls those early days, especially as described in the book of Deuteronomy (for example, 15:4–5); in particular, note that the expression "the good land" occurs, apart from 28:8, only in Deuteronomy (1:35; 3:25; 4:21–22; 9:6) and in Joshua (23:16). Perhaps the closest parallel to the language used here, however, is Deuteronomy 4:21–22. After urging Israel to obey the law revealed on Horeb, Moses speaks of his impending death: "For I am going to die in this land without crossing over the Jordan, but you are going to cross over to take possession of that good land" (Deut. 4:22). In 1 Chronicles 28, it is David who is about to die, leaving the completion of his greatest work to others. However, just as Joshua led the people on into the land of promise, Solomon would build the temple. Once more, as in the first speech, the parallel between David and Moses is clear.

In 28:9–10, Solomon is addressed in an aside—just as, in the first speech directed to Solomon, the leaders were addressed as well (22:18–19). Solomon is urged to be devoted to the Lord, who "searches every mind, and understands every plan and thought" (28:9; see 17:18). In a statement that could be regarded as the "golden text" of Chronicles, David assures his son, "If you seek him, he will be found by you; but if you forsake him, he will abandon you forever" (28:9). The double edge of promise and threat in this text is, as we have often seen and will see again, the Chronicler's theme. A Christian reader will doubtless be reminded of Jesus' words in the Sermon on the Mount: "Ask, and it will be given you; search, and you will find; knock, and the door will be opened for you" (Matt. 7:7). However, the assurance of God's presence

107

to the sincere and earnest seeker is in Chronicles joined to a grim warning that faith, once laid aside, may not lightly be taken up again. In the New Testament, this warning is sounded in the terrifyingly harsh words of Hebrews 6:4–6: "For it is impossible to restore again to repentance those who have once been enlightened . . . and then have fallen away, since on their own they are crucifying again the Son of God and are holding him up to contempt" (see also Heb. 10:26–31). Of course, these hard words are mollified by other texts, in both testaments, which give assurance of God's forgiveness. But it would be a mistake to gloss over the harsh tones of wrath and finality, either in Chronicles or in Hebrews. For the Chronicler, as for the preacher of Hebrews, faith is no casual matter! The believer is called to commitment, in absolute terms. What this commitment means for Solomon is plain. Once more, as in his first speech, David urges his son to "be strong and act" (28:10; compare 22:13)—that is, to build the temple in accordance with his calling.

The parallel between David and Moses emerges once more in 28:11–19. Just as the pattern (Hebrew *tabnith*) of the tabernacle had been revealed to Moses and preserved in the written Torah (Exod. 25:9, 40), so also the plan (also Hebrew *tabnith*) of the temple was revealed to David, and passed on by him in written form to Solomon (28:11, 12, 18, 19; see de Vries 1988, 626). As in Exodus, the plan revealed to David lays out the pattern for the shrine (28:11–12) and all its furnishings (28:13b–18). However, the divinely revealed plan also involves "the divisions of the priests and of the Levites, and all the work of the service in the house of the LORD" (28:13a). David is not only the architect of the temple building and the designer of its appurtenances. He is the author of the temple liturgy, and the one responsible for establishing the structures of authority and personnel that ensure that liturgy's performance and preservation.

This statement, however, may be misleading. David's plan is not credited to his own ingenuity. Rather, like Moses, David is said to pass on the pattern that was revealed to him. Intriguingly, the pattern is revealed to David as a written text: "All this, in writing at the LORD's direction, he made clear to me—the plan of all the works" (28:19). Precedence for this idea comes from the prophet Ezekiel (Ezek. 2:8—3:3). In his call vision, Ezekiel sees a scroll covered front and back with "words of lamentation and mourning and woe" (Ezek. 2:10). He is commanded to eat this scroll, and its words become a part of him. Ezekiel's prophecy, thus, is self-consciously literary. While earlier prophetic texts are clearly collections of oral performances, Ezekiel has written a book.

108

The Chronicler stands in this same tradition. The emphasis on God's revelation as a written text in 28:19 is consistent with our observations throughout Chronicles. The Chronicler is a student of Scripture and understands the will of God to be expressed through the written word. Little wonder, then, that the plan for Israel's shrine and its personnel should come to David as a text. In the Chronicler's History, the portions that deal with the postexilic restoration of Judah (that is, Ezra–Nehemiah) continue this same theme. With the exception of Haggai and Zechariah, prophets and prophecy no longer function as the means of God's revelation. So, Ezra is not a prophet, but rather "an inspired text interpreter" (Schniedewind 1995, 250). The text of Scripture has become the means of divine revelation. The great Temple Scroll from Qumran marks a far point on this continuing trajectory. This text, a plan for a massive temple complex, presents itself as the *tabnith* originally revealed to Moses, then handed on to Solomon by David (Yadin 1983, 177 and 182). For the Qumran community, not only were the revelations to Moses and David seen as one and the same, but this unified revelation was contained not in a vision, but in a book!

The address to Solomon resumes at 28:20–21. Yet again, Solomon is urged, "Be strong and of good courage, and act" (28:20). However, the new king is assured that he is not alone. Solomon can count on divine help; furthermore, he can rely on the support of the priests and Levites, the skilled assistance of volunteers, and the aid of officials and people alike. In short, the groups described in the preceding chapters, and addressed earlier in this second farewell speech, are at Solomon's service, to ensure that the work is carried out.

The Kingdom Passes to Solomon (29:1–30)

We come now to the end of David's story, as he passes his crown on to his son Solomon. Just as David's reign had begun with the affirmation of the people (11:1–2), so it ends with David calling upon the people to affirm his successor. Still, although this chapter fits well into the final form of Chronicles, it seems likely that much of it it was added at a later stage in the composition of this work. The word translated "temple" in 1 Chronicles 29:1 and 19 (Hebrew *biyrah*) is a late Hebrew loanword from the Persian language. Elsewhere, *biyrah* usually refers to the fortified citadel in the Babylonian city of Susa, and appears in some of the youngest books of the Hebrew Bible: Nehemiah (1:1), Esther (ten times; for example, 1:2; 2:8; 9:12), and Daniel (8:2). It is used for the temple fortress in Jerusalem only here (29:1, 19) and in Nehemiah (2:8; 7:2). Further, the references throughout this chapter to rich contributions from wealthy donors reflect, not the difficult, impoverished early days of the Judean Restoration (see Hag. 1:1–11), but the greater

109

wealth of the period after 450 B.C. (Meyers and Meyers 1993, 22–26). Probably, then, much of this final chapter in David's story comes from the last stages in the composition of the Chronicler's History.

David's Third Farewell Speech (29:1–9). In this final speech, the whole assembly of Israel is addressed. Like the second speech, this third speech recalls the language and themes of the earlier speeches, as well as the description of David's preparations for the temple (22:2–5, 11–16). Once more, David states that Solomon is "young and inexperienced" (29:1; compare 22:5), and so is in need of the help and support of the entire community. David issues a challenge to the assembly: "Who then will offer willingly, consecrating themselves today to the LORD?" (29:5). First, however, he serves as an example for giving, by dedicating his own personal fortune to the temple (29:3–4). The people respond enthusiastically, led by the tribal, military, and political officials (the people addressed, in short, in the second speech). Two features of this list of contributions are particularly interesting. First, the donations are given in darics, a coin introduced by Darius around 515 B.C. (Klein 1993, 645). This anachronism clearly points to a time of composition in the Persian period, no sooner than the late sixth century. Second, the Levitical supervision of donations, led by Jehiel the Gershonite (29:8), reflects the role of Levites as treasurers spelled out in 26:20–28, especially verses 21–22.

David's Last Words (29:10–22a). It is certainly appropriate that, in Chronicles, David's last words are words of praise to God, and an invitation to the people to join in worship and praise. Chapter 29:11 will sound particularly familiar: "Yours, O LORD, are the greatness, the power, the glory, the victory, and the majesty; for all that is in the heavens and on the earth is yours; yours is the kingdom, O LORD, and you are exalted as head above all." The concluding doxology of the Lord's Prayer—"For thine is the kingdom, and the power, and the glory, forever"—plainly comes from this passage. In David's last words, however, these words do not conclude his prayer, but rather begin it. God's kingship is the beginning point of David's prayer. God is the source of all power and rulership, as well as the source of all wealth (29:12–13).

David asks, "But who am I, and what is my people, that we should be able to make this freewill offering?" (29:14; compare 17:16–18). In contrast to God's great glory, "we are aliens and transients before you, as were all our ancestors; our days on the earth are like a shadow, and there is no hope" (29:15). As in his prayer of thanksgiving in 17:16–27, David here states that Israel is entirely dependent upon God. Even Israel's offerings to God had come first from God, "[f]or all things come from you, and of your own have we given you" (29:14b). David's words, set to music by an anonymous Christian composer, form one of the most familiar offertory sentences in Christendom, "All Things Come of Thee" (*United Methodist Hymnal* 1989, 588).

This theology of giving derives ultimately from Leviticus 25. There the land, though promised from of old to Abraham, Isaac, and Jacob, is revealed not to be the property of Israel after all. Rather, the Lord declares, "the land is mine; with me you are but aliens and tenants" (Lev. 25:23; compare 29:15). The terms "aliens and tenants" usually refer to non-Israelites who lived in the land. Having no land of their own, they were dependent upon the Israelites for their livelihood, often working as bondservants or slaves. As these people were dependent upon Israel, so Israel was dependent upon the Lord. The Israelites did not own the land, any more than the tenant farmers who tilled the soil for their Israelite masters owned the land.

Similarly, David declares that he and his people are "aliens and transients," without home or hope apart from God's grace. To the Chronicler's community, for whom the exile was still a recent memory, these words would have had particular resonance. By rebuilding the temple, they were not doing God any favors—as though God needed their worship. Indeed, "all this abundance that we have provided for building you a house for your holy name comes from your hand and is all your own" (29:16). But although God needs nothing that Israel can offer, God is pleased by Israel's righteousness and devotion. Therefore David prays, not just for himself and his generation, but for all future generations: "O LORD, the God of Abraham, Isaac, and Israel, our ancestors, keep forever such purposes and thoughts in the hearts of your people, and direct their hearts toward you" (29:18). The Chronicler's community, clearly, is included in and challenged by this prayer.

One last time, David prays for his son Solomon (29:19). He prays, first, that Solomon will be single-mindedly devoted to following "your commandments, your decrees, and your statutes": clearly a reference to the Torah. David had begun his own reign in obedience to the divine word, and he prays that his son will be likewise faithful. Second, David prays that Solomon will indeed complete the project that David has begun—that the temple will be built.

In 1 Chronicles 29:20, David calls upon the entire assembly to bless the Lord. They respond with a tremendous offering of one thousand bulls, lambs, and rams—an extravagant demonstration of devotion and dedication. However, this is no grim day of deprivation. The Chronicler says that all Israel "ate and drank before the LORD on that day with great joy" (29:22a). One is reminded of what Paul says about giving: "Each of you must give as you have made up your mind, not reluctantly or under

111

compulsion, for God loves a cheerful giver" (2 Cor. 9:7). A life of service to the Lord should be a life of joy and celebration.

Reaffirmation of Solomon's Kingship (29:22b–25). The Chronicler has already had David declare Solomon king once, in 23:1. Now, Solomon is anointed king for a second time. Note, though, that while the phrase "a second time" appears in the MT, the LXX lacks this statement. It does appear most probable that the final section of the Chronicler's history of David's reign is meant to be read as a single occasion. The statement in the MT of 29:22b that Solomon is being anointed a second time could, then, reflect a simple misunderstanding by a scribe. However, as we have seen, it also appears probable that the account of David's third speech and his last words were added at a later point in the composition of the Chronicler's History, probably at the same time that Nehemiah's memoirs were added. It is possible, then, that the "second time" refers to this second, later ending to David's story and second account of Solomon's accession to the throne.

In any case, the transition of power is smooth and seamless. Not only the leaders of Israel, but specifically the other sons of David all pay homage to Solomon. Further, we are given a foreshadowing of the successes of Solomon's reign: "he prospered, and all Israel obeyed him" (29:23); indeed, "The LORD highly exalted Solomon in the sight of all Israel, and bestowed upon him such royal majesty as had not been on any king before him in Israel" (29:25).

The Death of David (29:26–30). At last, "in a good old age, full of days, riches, and honor," David dies (29:28). The Chronicler declares that David had ruled over all Israel for forty years: seven in Hebron, forty-three in Jerusalem. Once more, Chronicles ignores the period of civil war, when David actually ruled only the territory of Judah.

Now, for the first time, we encounter a pattern that will be followed throughout Chronicles. At the end of each king's reign, the Chronicler usually records the sources allegedly used for that king's history. The seven exceptions to this rule are notable. No sources are listed for the evil monarchs Jehoram, Ahaziah, and Athaliah (2 Chr. 21—23), the assassinated king Amon (2 Chr. 33:21–25), the deposed king Jehoahaz (2 Chr. 36:1–4), the exiled king Jehoiachin (2 Chr. 36:9–10), or for the reign of Judah's final king, Zedekiah (2 Chr. 36:11–21). The significance of these absences will be discussed in context.

For David's reign, the Chronicler claims to have consulted the records of the seer Samuel, the prophet Nathan, and the seer Gad (29:29). It is not altogether clear that these are actual sources, separate from the biblical texts which we know that the Chronicler has used. For example, as we will see, Solomon's story is drawn entirely from our book of Kings, and yet the Chronicler cites three distinct prophetic sources for Solomon's deeds (2 Chr. 9:29; see Klein 1992, 996). The Chronicler does, at times, make use of sources otherwise unknown to us. However, it is most likely that 29:29 and similar texts elsewhere are making a statement, not about the Chronicler's extrabiblical sources, but about the nature of Scripture as divine revelation. The pattern for Israel's temple and its liturgy came to David, remember, as a text. The Chronicler understands prophets as authors of texts, and text as the means by which God's word is made known. Hence, he assumes that his biblical sources for David's reign, in the Deuteronomistic History, are composed by the prophets who figure prominently in David's story: Samuel (11:3), Nathan (17:1–15), and Gad (21:9–13, 18–19).

God's prophetic word concerning David has significance far beyond David and his line. The Chronicler states that these records concern "accounts of all his rule and his might and of the events that befell him and Israel and all the kingdoms of the earth" (29:30). God's plan for David ultimately will involve great nations far beyond Israel's borders: Assyria, Egypt, Babylon, and distant Persia. Like Second Isaiah, who refers to Cyrus of Persia as the Lord's anointed (Isa. 45:1), the Chronicler understands God to be active on a global scale to accomplish God's purposes.

The significance of David for the Chronicler cannot be overstated. David is the first and greatest king of united Israel. His family forms an unbroken line of connection from the Chronicler's own time back to the glory days of Israel's greatness, and indeed, as the genealogies in 1 Chronicles 1—9 demonstrate, further back to the very dawn of history.

But most importantly, David stands, together with Moses, as the founder of Israel's worship; he is the author of Israel's liturgy, and the architect of Israel's temple. The remainder of the Chronicler's story is but the unwinding of themes already revealed here, in the history of David. Solomon will actually build the temple. Other kings will be praised for their faithfulness in supporting and renewing the temple and its liturgy, or damned for acting faithlessly, and so bringing corruption and ruin to the temple. But David remains always in the background, in warning and in promise, the image of what once was, and the ideal expression of what might be again. In Chronicles, the long shadow of David is cast over all the kings and all the years that follow.

113

2 Chronicles

Solomon

Regarding Solomon, as regarding his father David, the Chronicler's attention is sharply focused. Just as David is in Chronicles the author of Jerusalem's liturgy, Solomon is the builder of Jerusalem's temple. Already in David's story, Solomon has been presented to us as the one commissioned by God to build the temple (1 Chr. 17:12). Repeatedly, the dying David urged his son to carry out this commission (1 Chr. 22:16; 28:10, 20; 29:19). It should be no surprise, then, to discover that the Chronicler's account of Solomon's reign is focused on this task. Of the nine chapters in 2 Chronicles that concern Solomon, six deal with the preparations for the temple, its construction, and its dedication. The bulk of Solomon's story, then, is concerned with temple-building.

To this end, the Chronicler has been selective in the use of his source, our book of 1 Kings. Unlike the situation with 2 Samuel, where the Chronicler appeared to have access to a different (and better) Hebrew text than the MT, it seems probable that for Kings, the Chronicler's source was more or less the same as the Hebrew text we have before us. In the Solomon account, that source has been slightly rearranged and in places expanded, though overall the Chronicler's editing has produced a shorter, more pointed narrative. As was the case with David, Chronicles shows little interest in Solomon the man. Few stories illustrating Solomon's legendary wisdom are selected by the Chronicler for retelling (1 Kgs. 3:16–28 and 4:29–34 are missing, though 2 Chr. 9:1–12 recounts Solomon's relationship with the queen of Sheba from 1 Kgs. 10:1–13). Nor does Chronicles record the abuses and peccadilloes that marred Solomon's reign, such as his use of Israelite forced labor (1 Kgs. 5:13–14) or his many wives and the temples he built for them (1 Kgs. 11:1–13). The result is a text that focuses more deliberately on the temple-building, which is for the Chronicler the point of Solomon's story.

Second Chronicles begins with an account of Solomon's accession to the throne (1:1–17). Appropriately, Solomon's first act as king is an

117

act of piety: he offers a thousand sacrifices to the Lord on the ancient bronze altar of Bezalel at Gibeon. There, in response to Solomon's prayer, God grants the king wisdom and knowledge, as well as promising material blessings. A brief description of Solomon's wealth and power demonstrates that God's promise is kept, and confirms that Solomon has the means and the authority to build a temple for the Lord.

The second, and major, section of Solomon's story concerns the temple. Solomon's preparations for the building, including negotiations with Huram of Tyre, are found in 2:1–18. Then, the actual building of the temple and its description follows in 3:1—5:1. Finally, in 5:2—7:22, the ark of the covenant is carried into the completed structure, and the temple is dedicated.

Once the temple is built, the Chronicler considers a few broader issues relating to Solomon's reign (8:1—9:31). Solomon's construction projects, his military accomplishments, his marriage to Pharaoh's daughter, his piety, and his successes in commerce and diplomacy are all briefly described. Greater attention is paid to the visit of the queen of Sheba (9:1–12), perhaps because this visit demonstrates the extent of Solomon's fame, as well as witnessing to his legendary wisdom. Finally, the Chronicler returns to the matter of Solomon's great wealth, which was raised at the beginning of his account (9:13–28), and winds up his story with the king's death (9:29–31).

1:1–17

Solomon Becomes King

The closing chapters of David's story emphasize the smooth, seamless transition from David to Solomon. In particular, we are told that David's other sons accepted Solomon's kingship (1 Chr. 29:24). The story of Solomon in Chronicles begins, then, not with squabbles about succession, but with Solomon in firm control. The opening words of 2 Chronicles 1:1 in Hebrew are nearly identical to the opening words of 1 Kings 3:1. In Chronicles, however, instead of Solomon's marriage to an Egyptian princess, the story begins with a clear statement of Solomon's authority: "Solomon son of David established himself in his kingdom; the LORD his God was with him and made him exceedingly great" (2 Chr. 1:1).

The account of Solomon's sacrifices at Gibeon and his prayer for wisdom are drawn from 1 Kings 3:1–15, with some editing so as to pre-

118

sent Solomon as already a mature and capable ruler (1 Kgs. 3:7, where Solomon says, "I am only a little child; I do not know how to go out or come in," is not used by the Chronicler). The description of Solomon's wealth in 2 Chronicles 1:14–17 comes from the end of Solomon's story in the Deuteronomistic History (1 Kgs. 10:26–29)—just as the account of David's heroes and warriors was moved by the Chronicler from the end of David's story to the beginning. David's rule was defined by his military might, which confirmed God's blessing upon him. David the warrior was able to carve out a kingdom, and particularly, as his first kingly act, to conquer Jerusalem as the place of God's shrine. Solomon, however, is a man of peace. His rule will be defined by his great wealth, which likewise confirms God's blessing upon Solomon. This wealth, as the second part of Solomon's story will reveal, is placed in service to God through the building of the temple: Solomon's first kingly act. The wealth of Solomon ensures the magnificence of God's temple.

God Grants Solomon Wisdom (1:1–13) (//1 Kgs. 3:1–15)

At Solomon's decree, "all Israel" assembles at Gibeon to offer sacrifices (1:2–3). Similarly, at the beginning of David's reign, all Israel had come to Hebron to acknowledge David's rulership (1 Chr. 11:1), and had followed him to Jerusalem, to conquer that city (1 Chr. 11:4). Perhaps the closest parallel to this scene, however, is the gathering of the whole assembly to carry the ark into Jerusalem (1 Chr. 13:1–5, recalled in 2 Chr. 1:4). Solomon, too, begins his reign with a pilgrimage and an act of worship. In Chronicles, no apology need be given for sacrifices made at Gibeon (compare 2 Chr. 1:3–6 with 1 Kgs. 3:2–4). Until the completion of the temple in Jerusalem, Gibeon was the proper place for sacrificial service, as the altar and the tent of meeting were there (2 Chr. 1:5; see also 1 Chr. 16:39; 21:29). Indeed, the bronze altar before the tent is here said to be the very altar that Moses' master craftsman, "Bezalel son of Uri, son of Hur," had fashioned, following the pattern revealed to Moses (2 Chr. 1:5; see Exod. 35:30–33; 38:1–2). This is a fitting place, then, to seek the will of the Lord—which is the reason Solomon and the assembly have come to Gibeon (2 Chr. 1:5).

The Lord responds dramatically to Solomon's magnificent sacrifice (one thousand burnt offerings; see 2 Chr. 1:6//2 Kgs. 3:4). That night, God appears to the king in a vision, with a remarkable offer: "Ask what I should give you" (1:7). This astonishingly open-ended offer calls to mind similar passages from the Gospels: "Whatever you ask for in prayer with faith, you will receive" (Matt. 21:22); "So I tell you, whatever you ask for in prayer, believe that you have received it, and it will

119

be yours" (Mark 11:24); "If in my name you ask me for anything, I will do it" (John 14:14). What is a believer to make of such texts—particularly since our personal experience reveals that prayers often are not answered in the way that we wish?

In Chronicles, the point comes not in God's offer, but in Solomon's response: "Give me now wisdom and knowledge to go out and come in before this people, for who can rule this great people of yours?" (2 Chr. 1:10; compare 1 Kgs. 3:9). What Solomon wants is to be what God has called him to be. Solomon's calling is clear, having been revealed long before to his father David (1 Chr. 17:16); indeed, Solomon attributes his own reign to God's "great and steadfast love to my father David" (2 Chr. 1:8//1 Kgs. 3:6). Solomon's desire is to rule wisely and well. God is very pleased with Solomon's request—so much so that God promises to give him not only the abilities he has requested, but also "riches, possessions, and honor, such as none of the kings had who were before you, and none after you shall have the like" (2 Chr. 1:12//1 Kgs. 3:13).

God's reply to Solomon's request calls to mind the teaching of Jesus in the Sermon on the Mount: "But strive first for the kingdom of God and his righteousness, and all these things will be given to you as well" (Matt. 6:33). This, indeed, seems to be the point of those remarkable, open-ended promises in the New Testament. The object for the believer is not how to get more out of God. Rather, we are challenged to ask ourselves: what do we really want? Are our desires in keeping with God's desires for us? Do we trust God's direction for our lives? If so, then like Solomon, we can surely count on finding fulfillment in God's will for us.

Now, with God's assurance of wisdom, knowledge, power, and abundance, Solomon goes to Jerusalem to begin his reign (1:13). The following verses will demonstrate God's faithfulness. Solomon is given wealth and power to supplement his wisdom. The demonstration of Solomon's wisdom, for the Chronicler, will be the building of God's temple.

Solomon's Wealth (1:14–17)
(//1 Kgs. 10:26–29)

The horse-drawn, armored chariot was the pinnacle of military technology in the Iron Age. Wherever there was room for the chariots to roll, chariotry would prevail over infantry every time. Solomon's ability to field fourteen hundred chariots (2 Chr. 1:14//1 Kgs. 10:26) demonstrates his military strength and security.

However, security can be won at the expense of the general welfare. Doubtless for this reason, Deuteronomy 17:16 forbids the king to make slaves of his own people "in order to acquire more horses." Chronicles, however, insists that such was not the case with Solomon. Rather, the king's security and wealth led to the enrichment of his entire kingdom: "The king made silver and gold as common in Jerusalem as stone, and he made cedar as plentiful as the sycamore of the Shephelah" (1 Chr. 1:15). The sources of this wealth are described in 2 Chronicles 1:16–17. Solomon acquired horses from Que, a region famed for its horseflesh, and chariots from the expert artisans of Egypt. Then, he sold them to other kingdoms, notably the Hittites and the Arameans. In short, Solomon was an arms dealer—a curious trade for a man of peace! The Chronicler draws no moral lessons from this exchange; certainly, there is no trace of any criticism of Solomon on this account. The purpose of this text in Chronicles is to demonstrate the Lord's faithfulness. Just as God had promised, Solomon has become rich.

2:1—7:22
Solomon Builds the Temple

This largest segment of Solomon's story concerns the preparations for the temple, its construction, and its dedication. The unit begins in 2:1, with the statement that "Solomon decided to build a temple for the name of the LORD, and a royal palace for himself." In 7:11, the completion of these projects is announced: "Thus Solomon finished the house of the LORD and the king's house; all that Solomon had planned to do in the house of the LORD and in his own house he successfully accomplished." The unit then concludes with an epilogue, in which God answers Solomon's temple dedicatory prayer with words of promise and warning (7:12–22). Although this unit begins with Solomon's decision to build both the temple and a royal palace, and closes with the statement that he has succeeded in both projects, the only other mention of Solomon's palace is in Huram's letter (2:12). It is the temple that occupies Solomon's attention throughout these chapters.

Here again, the Chronicler has abridged his source. By moving directly from Solomon's vision at Gibeon to his temple preparations (skipping 1 Kgs. 4), Chronicles emphasizes Solomon's role as temple-builder. The building of the temple becomes Solomon's first kingly act, and the premier demonstration of his wisdom (Japhet 1993, 523 and 536). Curiously, the Chronicler's editing is particularly marked with regard to the description and measurement of the temple complex: the

121

text of Chronicles through this section is only about half as long as the source text in 1 Kings. This may appear odd, even startling. Hasn't the building of the temple been the aim of Chronicles to this point? Why, then, should the Chronicler shortchange the description of this structure?

In fact, it is not the temple as a building that is of interest to the Chronicler. Rather, it is the temple as the center of Israel's worship (Myers 1965, 16). The emphasis on the temple's liturgy is found already in Solomon's correspondence with Huram: "Who am I to build a house for him, except as a place to make offerings before him?" (2:6). While David's liturgy is conducted in Solomon's temple, it is the liturgy, not the temple, that the Chronicler deems of greatest importance.

The temple section of Solomon's story is divided into three parts, with an epilogue. The first part describes Solomon's temple preparations, specifically the conscription of foreigners as forced laborers and the acquisition from Huram of Tyre both of rare woods for the temple and of the fabulously skilled craftsman Huram-abi (2:1–18). Next, the actual temple structure and its appurtenances are described (3:1—5:1). Finally, the temple is completed by bringing the ark into the most holy place, and prayers of dedication are offered (5:2—7:11). In the epilogue, the Lord appears to Solomon in response to his temple dedicatory prayer (7:12–22). The Lord reiterates the promise to hear prayers directed toward the temple, and issues a stern warning that faithlessness and idolatry will lead to exile and destruction.

Solomon's Preparations for the Temple (2:1–18) (///1 Kgs. 5:1–12)

Solomon had been instructed by his father to prepare for the building of the temple, adding to the already-extensive preparations David had made (1 Chr. 22:14). Just as David had gathered precious woods and metals and conscripted foreigners to quarry stone for the building (1 Chr. 22:2–5), so Solomon arranges for materials and skilled labor from Tyre (2 Chr. 2:3–10), and assembles a crew of forced laborers from among Israel's foreign population, particularly to work as stonecutters (2 Chr. 2:2, 17–18).

The two accounts of Solomon's conscript labor force frame the Chronicler's description of Solomon's temple preparations, coming before and after the king's correspondence with Huram, king of Tyre (2:3–16; elsewhere, the king of Tyre is called Hiram). Chronicles does not deny that Solomon and his father David made use of forced labor. However, Chronicles insists that the conscripts were foreigners, not Israelites (2 Chr. 2:17–18; compare 1 Chr. 20:3; 22:2). The Chronicler's

122

view thus stands in contrast to his source, in which Solomon does use Israelites as slave laborers (1 Kgs. 5:13–18).

Solomon initiates contact with Huram of Tyre by recalling that Huram had provided the cedar for David's palace (2 Chr. 2:3; see 1 Chr. 14:1). He does not need to explain why David himself did not go on to build a temple for the Lord (compare 1 Kgs. 5:3–4), since in Chronicles David was not called to that task; the building of the temple is reserved for Solomon. The king stresses to Huram the temple's importance, both for the conduct of Israel's liturgy (2 Chr. 2:4), and as a demonstration of the Lord's majesty, "for our God is greater than other gods" (2:5). In this connection, Chronicles prefigures Solomon's prayer at the temple's dedication by including language from that prayer in the letter to Huram: "But who is able to build him a house, since heaven, even highest heaven, cannot contain him? Who am I to build a house for him, except as a place to make offerings before him?" (2 Chr. 2:6; compare 6:18//1 Kgs. 8:27).

In Chronicles, Solomon makes two requests of Huram. First, he asks for "an artisan skilled to work in gold, silver, bronze, and iron, and in purple, crimson, and blue fabrics, trained also in engraving, to join the skilled workers who are with me in Judah and Jerusalem, whom my father David provided" (2 Chr. 2:7; for David's provision of skilled laborers, see 1 Chr. 22:15–16). Second, he asks for rare and precious woods for the temple, "cedar, cypress, and algum timber from Lebanon" (2 Chr. 2:8; compare 1 Kgs. 5:6), as well as skilled timberers to fell the trees and prepare them for shipping. In exchange, Solomon offers to provide for the workers "twenty thousand cors of crushed wheat, twenty thousand cors of barley, twenty thousand baths of wine, and twenty thousand baths of oil" (2 Chr. 2:10; cf. 1 Kgs. 5:11–12, where only the wheat and oil are mentioned). In Kings this provision is given annually to Hiram, and appears to be part of a treaty between Jerusalem and Tyre. But the Chronicler, typically, is not interested in the politics of the arrangement. In Chronicles, the sole point of this correspondence is to make provision for the temple. Still, the dependence of Tyre upon Palestinian produce appears historically accurate (see also Ezek. 27:17).

Huram's response praises Solomon extravagantly: "Because the LORD loves his people he has made you king over them" (2:11). In particular, Huram praises Solomon's wisdom (2:12), which is presumably evident in his plans for the temple. Intriguingly, the foreign king also praises the Lord: "Blessed be the LORD God of Israel, who made heaven and earth" (2:12; compare 1 Kgs. 5:7). The language used here is reminiscent of Darius's monumental inscriptions, which typically begin, "A great god is Ahuramazda, who created this earth, who created

123

yonder heaven" (Boyce 1984, 290). In turn, this language seems to be reflected in the Persian-period Aramaic documents preserved in the book of Ezra, in which the Persian monarchs Darius (Ezra 6:9–10) and Artaxerxes (Ezra 7:12, 21, 23) refer to the Lord as "the God of heaven" (see also the Hebrew version of Cyrus's decree in 2 Chr. 36:23//Ezra 1:2). Huram, then, is speaking of the Lord in language similar to that used by the Persian rulers of the Chronicler's time.

Huram agrees to all Solomon's proposals. The lumber will be built into rafts and floated down the coast to Joppa (2:16). In response to Solomon's request for a skilled master artisan, Huram will send the remarkably able Huram-abi, who is "trained to work in gold, silver, bronze, iron, stone, and wood, and in purple, blue, and crimson fabrics and fine linen, and to do all sorts of engraving and execute any design that may be assigned him" (2:14).

In Chronicles, Huram-abi is said to be the son of a Tyrian man and a Danite woman, while in 1 Kings 7:13–14 (where he is called Hiram), he is said to be from the tribe of Naphtali. Confusion of one tribe for the other would have been easy: both Dan and Naphtali were descended from Rachel's handmaid Bilhah, and both were settled in the far north, near Tyre. However, it is more likely that the Chronicler has made Huram-abi a Danite to parallel Oholiab, Bezalel's coworker in the construction of the tabernacle and its appurtenances (for example, Exod. 31:6; note too the mention of Bezalel in 2 Chr. 1:5). Jewish rabbinical exegetes such as Pseudo-Rashi viewed Huram-abi as a descendant of Oholiab, reflecting this same idea (Japhet 1993, 541). Another reason for connecting Huram-abi with Dan may have been uncovered by the discovery of ancient metal works at Dan. According to archaeologist Avraham Biran, "the king of Tyre was trying to show Solomon that the man really is an expert, he comes from a tradition of metalworkers. He comes from the tribe of Dan, which had already excelled in metalworks" (Shanks 1999, 74).

The Temple Is Built (3:1—5:1)
(///1 Kgs. 6:1–30; 7:15–51)

His preparations completed, Solomon began to build the temple "on the second day of the second month of the fourth year of his reign" (3:1). The building site is identified as the spot revealed to David, that is, the threshing floor of Ornan (see 1 Chr. 21:28—22:1). It is also identified as Mount Moriah: presumably, the mountain in the land of Moriah where Abraham was commanded to sacrifice Isaac (see Gen. 22). The association of the temple mount with the mountain of Isaac's sacrifice assumed in traditional Jewish interpretation (for example, Tar-

124

gum Jonathan and the commentary of Rashi) evidently derives from this text (Japhet 1993, 551). For the Chronicler, the location of the temple was not chosen lightly. The holiness of this spot and its association with sacrifice go back beyond David to the very beginnings of Israel's traditions.

The dimensions of the temple are given "in cubits of the old standard" (3:3). Evidently, the length of the cubit in the Chronicler's time was not the same as it had been in Solomon's. A likely explanation is that the Persians had imposed a new standard, different from Israel's traditional units of measurement (for another indication of a longer, Persian-period cubit, see Ezek. 40:5 and 43:13; so Tuell 1992, 27–29). For his readers to visualize Solomon's temple properly, the Chronicler needs to remind them that it was the *old* cubit, not the new Persian standard, that was used by Solomon.

The temple description in Chronicles is a quick, sketchy outline drawn from 1 Kings 6:1—7:51 (though skipping the construction of Solomon's palace, 1 Kgs. 7:1–12; the craftsman Huram, identified in 1 Kgs. 7:13–14, has already been introduced in 2 Chr. 2:13–14). The overall dimensions of the temple are given, followed by the description of the vestibule (3:3–4a). The statement that the vestibule was 120 cubits high is certainly a textual corruption; even given the tendency of the Chronicler to exaggerate numbers, this figure is simply ridiculous.

Chronicles next moves on to the paneling and gilding of the temple interior (3:4b–7//1 Kgs. 6:14–18, 21–22, 29–30). Some details are unique to Chronicles: particularly, the precious stones (3:6; taken over from the description of Solomon's palace in 1 Kgs. 7:9–11). The sheer quantity of the gold used in Chronicles is astonishing: "six hundred talents of fine gold" are used to overlay the temple's interior (3:8). Given the reference to the "upper chambers" in 3:9, it appears most likely that this figure applies to the whole interior, and not merely to the most holy place; even so, it is an extravagant amount (Japhet 1993, 555). According to 3:9, "The weight of the nails was fifty shekels of gold." Like the height of the vestibule, it appears doubtful that this is mere exaggeration: a fifty-shekel nail would weigh twenty ounces—a spike, rather than a nail! Nor, on the other hand, would fifty shekels' weight suffice for all the nails needed to place gold panels over the temple interior. Probably, as gold is too soft a metal to use for nails in any case, what is intended here is that even the nails were gilded; fifty shekels of gold should suffice for that purpose (Japhet 1993, 555). Clearly, Chronicles aims to awe the reader with the temple's opulence—the entire interior was covered in gold panels, fastened with golden nails!

Of particular importance is the most holy place with its enormous cherubim, whose wings would overshadow the ark (3:8–13//1 Kgs.

125

6:19–28). The cherubim stand side by side facing the main chamber of the temple, with their inner wings touching and their outer wings stretching out to the chamber walls. In this way, the cherubim formed an enormous throne, like the cherub thrones portrayed in ancient Near Eastern art (for example, on an ivory plaque from Megiddo from the thirteenth to twelfth century B.C.; see the illustration in *Harper's Bible Commentary* 1988, A4). However, the throne was empty: no image of the Lord occupied the most holy place. Rather, the Lord was believed to be enthroned invisibly above the cherubim, with the divine feet resting on the ark.

In Chronicles, the doorway into the most holy place is covered by a "curtain of blue and purple and crimson fabrics and fine linen," embroidered with cherubim (3:14). However, according to 1 Kings 6:31–32, Solomon's temple had olivewood doors. Probably, the Chronicler is here describing a feature of the second temple (see the reference to the temple curtain in Matt. 27:51//Mark 15:38//Luke 23:45).

Having completed the description of the temple interior, the text moves to the temple forecourt to describe the monumental bronze structures placed here by Solomon: the pillars, the altar of burnt offering, and the molten sea (3:15—4:6). First, the two bronze pillars, Jachin and Boaz, are described (3:15–17; compare the more detailed account in 1 Kgs. 7:15–22). The summary character of the entire temple description in Chronicles is vividly demonstrated in the dimensions of the bronze pillars. The height of the pillars in 3:15 appears to be derived from the dimensions in 1 Kings by adding them all together: eighteen cubits high plus five cubits for the capital plus twelve cubits around equals thirty-five cubits (Japhet 1993, 557). The purpose of these free-standing pillars is unknown. Probably, Jachin and Boaz were gateposts, marking the entry into sacred space unapproachable by any but the priests (Meyers 1992, 598). That the bronze pillars were given names suggests that they may have been personified as guardians of the temple threshold (see Ps. 24:7–10).

Next the Chronicler turns to the bronze altar of burnt offering (4:1). The bronze altar is mentioned only twice in the Deuteronomistic History (1 Kgs. 8:64 and 2 Kgs. 16:14–15). It does not appear in the description of Solomon's temple; nor, curiously, is the altar listed among the bronze items broken up and carried off by the Babylonians (2 Kgs. 25:13–17). Perhaps the altar is downplayed in Kings because the Deuteronomistic History was written from the perspective of Levites, or "temple clergy," rather than that of "altar clergy." In Chronicles, however, the altar *must* be described, given the significance of sacrifice in the temple liturgy (see 1 Chr. 21:18–27; 2 Chr. 2:4–6; also, note the significance of the bronze altar of Bezalel in 2 Chr. 1:5). Another descrip-

126

tion of the altar of burnt offering is found in Ezekiel 43:13–17 (though it is not said to be made of bronze; see, however, Ezek. 9:2, where the altar before the temple is called the "bronze altar"). If the base of Ezekiel's altar (Ezek. 43:13) was a sunken foundation, the height given there for the altar would match the description in 2 Chronicles 4:1 (Albright 1920, 139). But while the altar in Ezekiel is twelve cubits square, the altar in Chronicles is twenty cubits square. The dimensions in Chronicles may have originally referred to the larger altar, modeled on the altar at Damascus, built by King Ahaz (2 Kgs. 16:10–16; not paralleled in Chronicles)—or, they may simply reflect the Chronicler's tendency to exaggeration.

The molten sea (4:2–5//1 Kgs. 7:23–26) was a huge bronze basin of fresh water, placed in the temple forecourt to the south of the altar (4:10). It was supported on the backs of twelve bronze oxen, arranged so that three faced in each direction—symbolizing, perhaps, the twelve tribes of Israel. The designation "molten" means that the sea was cast out of molten bronze, as opposed to being beaten with hammers out of a thin bronze sheet (the usual way of making bronze bowls and vessels). The sheer size of the sea makes it unlikely that it was cast in one piece, however.

The NRSV translates the terms used for the decorations under the lip of the sea as "panels" (4:3//1 Kgs. 7:24). Actually, in Chronicles, the decorations are figures of bulls or oxen, while in Kings, they are round, gourdlike knobs (see the NIV or the JPSV on these passages). It is possible that the difference may involve a scribal error; two of the terms used are somewhat similar in Hebrew. However, given the horror of Jeroboam's bull images in the Deuteronomistic History (see 1 Kgs. 12:25–33), it is more likely that the Chronicler accurately describes the sea, and the final form of 1 Kings has altered the description.

Chronicles and Kings give the same figures for the height, diameter, and circumference of the bronze sea (given the dimensions of the circular vessel, the Israelites put the value of *pi* at 3; the true value, carried out to four decimal places, is 3.1416). However, the volume of the sea in Chronicles is three thousand baths: a thousand baths greater than that given in 1 Kings. While some scholars have proposed that the difference can be accounted for by different shapes imagined for the sea (a hemisphere in Kings, a cylinder in Chronicles), it is more likely either that the Chronicler is again exaggerating, or that (as with the cubit) the Chronicler's standard measure of volume is different from that presumed by his source.

127

Chronicles goes on to describe briefly the ten smaller basins that accompanied the monumental sea (4:6//1 Kgs. 7:38–39; the detailed description of the wheeled stands for the basins in 1 Kgs. 7:27–37 does not appear in Chronicles). The purpose of both the basins and the sea, we are told, is for ritual cleansing: the smaller basins are for washing the sacrifices, while the sea is for the ablutions of the priests. The purpose given for the sea seems unlikely, however, as the lip of the basin would have been some ten feet off the ground (the Mishnah gets around this problem by providing the sea with spigots, fashioned by the priestly craftsman Ben Kattin; see for example *b. Yoma* 25b; 37a). The molten sea was far too big for any practical use.

Much more likely is a symbolic function, indicated already by the name given to this huge bronze cauldron: the sea. In the ancient Near East, the sea was regarded as a symbol of the primordial chaos that ruled before the gods imposed order on the world. The authority of the creator god over the waters of chaos was emphasized in myth and poetry, and symbolized concretely by placing a large vessel of fresh water in the temple precincts. In Babylon, this vessel was called the *apsû*, or the waters of the abyss. As the waters of chaos beneath the earth were also considered the source of the earth's fruitfulness, these temple vessels further symbolized the god's control over fertility (Stinespring 1962, 541). The Lord's victory and supremacy over the waters of the sea is acclaimed throughout the Hebrew Bible, especially in the Psalms (see, for example, Pss. 24; 46). Further, the bull imagery associated with the sea in Chronicles is a common fertility motif throughout the ancient Near East. Most likely, then, the sea represented the Lord's victory over the waters of chaos, and—because of that victory— the Lord's control over the life-giving waters of fertility.

Finally, Chronicles describes the golden lampstands, tables, and vessels used within the temple (4:7–8), and, in summary fashion, the construction of the various courts with their bronze doors (4:9; in contrast to the golden doors in the temple itself, 4:22//1 Kgs. 7:50). Chronicles presumes that the temple is surrounded by two walls, forming an inner courtyard, "the court of the priests," and an outer courtyard, "the great court," accessible to the laity. Intriguingly, the great temple built by Herod the Great featured *three* courtyards: the inner Priest's Court, the Court of Israel, and the outermost Women's Court.

Having completed the description of the temple and its contents, the Chronicler in rapid summary fashion ascribes all the bronze work of the temple precincts to Huram (earlier called Huram-abi; 4:11–18//1 Kgs. 7:40–47). The precious gold work of the furnishings within the temple, however, is ascribed directly to Solomon (4:19–22//1 Kgs. 7:48–50). The completion of the work is affirmed in 5:1 (//1 Kgs. 7:51): "Thus all the work that Solomon did for the house of the LORD was finished." The precious stuff accumulated by David is stored in the tem-

128

ple treasuries. Now, all that remains is for the Lord to enter and claim the Lord's house.

The Temple Is Dedicated (5:2—7:11)

With the physical work of the temple's construction finished, the time has come for the building to be completed by the Lord's presence. Here Chronicles, following its source in 1 Kings 8:1–66, fits the model of other temple texts in Israel and the Near East. In Exodus 40:34–38, when the tabernacle was finished, the tent was filled with the cloud of the Lord's glory. In Ezekiel's vision of the glorified temple, after the temple structure had been revealed to the prophet, the glory of the Lord filled the sanctuary (Ezek. 43:5). Just so, when the ark was carried in procession into the most holy place, Solomon's temple was filled with the cloud of the glory, and so inhabited by the divine presence (5:13–14//1 Kgs. 8:10–11). In each setting, the nearly tangible manifestation of the Lord's presence, called the "glory" (the Hebrew term *kabod* carries a connotation of weight and forceful presence), is said to "fill" the sanctuary. Only then is the sanctuary truly complete.

A similar pattern appears elsewhere in the ancient world. In the old Canaanite myth of the building of Baal's temple, the storm god, rejoicing, moves in as soon as the structure is completed, summoning all the gods and goddesses for a magnificent feast (Herdner 1963, 4.6.44–59). The Gudea cylinders from the twenty-second century B.C. illustrate the antiquity of this conception. After the detailed description in Cylinder A of the building of the temple and the opulence of its materials and furnishings, Cylinder B details the coming of the god to inhabit the newly built structure. Gudea prays, "Ningirsu, I have built here your house for you, / May you enter it in joy!" (translated by Jacobsen 1987, 427). The following lines detail the preparations that follow: sacrifices, special offerings, and libations are made, the path of the processional is prepared and purified, the people bow down. Then, the coming of the god is described:

> The warrior Ningirsu entered the house,
> the owner of the house had come,
> a very eagle catching sight of a wild bull!
> The warrior's entering his house
> was a storm roaring into battle.
> Ningirsu roamed through his house,
> it was [the sound of] the Apsu temple precincts
> when festivals are celebrated.
> The owner was ready to come out from his house—
> it was like the sun rising over Lagash land!
> (translated by Jacobsen 1987, 429)

Only when the image of the god in procession had entered the temple and the deity had taken possession of it could the temple truly be said to be finished.

The pattern of the Gudea cylinders is reflected in the Chronicler's account of Solomon's temple. We have already had the description of the temple, emphasizing its magnificence and opulence (3:1—5:1). But, without the Lord's glory, the temple remains empty and without enduring significance. It is merely a building—a very pretty and expensive building, granted, but only a building nonetheless. Now, we come to the rites whereby the temple will be occupied by the Lord. Of course, in Israel, there is no image of the Lord to carry in procession. Instead the ark, the footstool of the Lord, is carried into the most holy place, to symbolize the Lord's taking ownership of the sanctuary (5:2—6:2). The cloud of the glory, the manifestation of God's presence, shows that this is no empty rite: the Lord is here, and this temple has now become God's house. Solomon's response to the overwhelming manifestation of the Lord's glory sounds remarkably like the words of Gudea: "I have built you an exalted house, a place for you to reside in forever" (6:2//1 Kgs. 8:13).

The procession of the ark is followed by Solomon's prayer of dedication and consecration (6:3–42). After addressing the assembly (6:3–11), Solomon offers a lengthy and ponderously theological prayer to the Lord (6:12–42). Then come the sacrifices, offered not only by the king, but by the people as well (7:1–10). Only when all of the rites of dedication are finished is the temple truly completed; only then can it be said "Thus Solomon finished the house of the Lord" (7:11).

The Procession of the Ark (5:2—6:2) (//1 Kgs. 8:1–13). Once more, all Israel is assembled at Solomon's command, to take part in a solemn pilgrimage (5:2–3; compare 1:2–3). This time, they assemble not in Gibeon, but in Jerusalem, to carry the ark from David's tent shrine into the temple Solomon has built. Parallels to David's ark procession are apparent. Just as all Israel had assembled then to bring the ark into Jerusalem (see 1 Chr. 13:1–4; 15:3), all Israel assembles now to bring the ark into its permanent home. Note, too, that in 2 Chronicles 5:4, as in 1 Chronicles 15:2, the ark is carried in procession by the Levites (in contrast to 1 Kgs. 8:3, where priests perform this duty; for more on bearing the ark as a Levitical rather than priestly responsibility in Chronicles, see the discussion above on 1 Chr. 15:2). By bringing the ark into the temple he has built, Solomon finishes what David had begun.

The occasion for the ark's processional is "the festival that is in the seventh month" (2 Chr. 5:3): that is, Sukkoth, or the Festival of Booths (see Lev. 23:33–35). Later in the Chronicler's History, the first sacrifices offered after the return from exile, on the newly rebuilt altar of burnt offering, will also be in celebration of Sukkoth (Ezra 3:1–6). Further, this festival will follow the first public reading of Ezra's Torah (Neh. 8:1–18)—appropriately enough, as according to Deuteronomy 31:10–13, every seven years the law is to be read to the assembly of all Israel during the Festival of Booths. That Solomon's temple should be dedicated during this festival of the law may seem strange at first. We tend to separate right worship and right action, as though the pursuit of social justice and the celebration of God's grace were two different, distinct spheres of action. In Scripture, however, these realities are always held together. So, in Psalm 24:4, the ones who may ascend to the Lord's temple to worship and receive blessing are "Those who have clean hands and pure hearts, who do not lift up their souls to what is false, and do not swear deceitfully." Similarly, James baldly states, "For just as the body without the spirit is dead, so faith without works is also dead" (Jas. 2:26). In Chronicles, this principle finds reflection in the linkage of Moses the lawgiver and David, recipient of God's gracious promise of kingship (see 1 Chr. 22:13; 28:11–19). For Solomon's temple to be dedicated during Booths recalls again this connection.

Solomon's ark procession, like David's, involves sacrifices. But while Solomon sacrificed "so many sheep and oxen that they could not be numbered or counted" (2 Chr. 5:6//1 Kgs. 8:5), David had offered a single sacrifice of seven bulls and rams (1 Chr. 15:26//2 Sam. 6:13 in 4QSam[a]; the MT of 2 Sam. 6:13 has evidently been altered to more closely resemble 1 Kgs. 8:5). Solomon's tremendous wealth, and the wealth of his kingdom, are once again used in service to the Lord.

The ark was carried to its resting place beneath the overshadowing wings of the cherubim. The long, gilded poles used to carry the ark were left in place. When one looked into the most holy place from the main room of the temple, the near ends of the poles could just be glimpsed, looming out of the blackness of the inner room. There they remain, we are told, "to this day" (5:9//1 Kgs. 8:8). It is strange that Chronicles should preserve this statement from Kings. In the Chronicler's day, of course, there were no poles; indeed, the ark itself was only a distant, painful memory. When Jerusalem fell to Babylon in 587 B.C., the ark vanished from history. Probably, it was stolen and broken apart for the gold. Still, the memory of the ark and what it had symbolized remained powerful for the people of Israel. Despite the loss of the premier symbol of God's kingship, they had experienced God's forgiveness, grace, and deliverance, and knew that God still reigned. But though they had now returned to the land, and rebuilt their temple and their lives, the experience of defeat and exile had changed them irrevocably. Nothing would ever be as it once had been. 2 Chronicles 5:9 serves as a reminder to the community of what was lost and could never be regained.

131

Curiously, 5:10 states that there was nothing in the ark but the tablets of the law. Chronicles here renders faithfully the source text in 1 Kings 8:9, which was evidently written before the addition of the priestly traditions involving a jar of manna (Exod. 16:32–34) and Aaron's miraculous budding rod (Num. 17:10–11) being placed within the ark (see also Heb. 9:4). Indeed, as the Chronicler does not supplement his source at this point, it may be that the Torah had not yet reached its final form when Chronicles began to be written, supporting an earlier date for the first stages of the Chronicler's History. However, as the Chronicler is elsewhere faithful to his sources, even when they run counter to his own ideas, not too much can be made of this.

Much of the material in 5:11–13 is unique to Chronicles. Here, as was the case in David's ark procession (1 Chr. 15:16–24), an important role is played by the Levitical singers and musicians. Once more, they are led by Asaph, Heman, and Jeduthun (see 1 Chr. 16:4–6, 37–42; 25:1–31). That the climax of the ark's procession, the placement of the ark in the most holy place, should be accompanied by music shows the vital role that music played in worship for the Chronicler. Remember that David's musicians were called prophets (1 Chr. 25:1–5)! In Chronicles, God communicates through music, which tells us something important, not only about music, but about *God*. The deepest truths about God and life are not rational—as important as reason is to faith. As Isaiah 55:8–9 affirms:

> For my thoughts are not your thoughts,
> nor are your ways my ways, says the LORD.
> For as the heavens are higher than the earth,
> so are my ways higher than your ways
> and my thoughts than your thoughts.

If it is to be in any way adequate to our experience of the incomprehensible God, worship must speak on a level deeper than reason. Art, poetry, and music are not added frills. They are indispensable means of expressing and evoking the full range of our encounter with the divine.

The Levitical choir sings "in praise to the LORD, 'For he is good, for his steadfast love endures forever'" (5:13). Apart from Jeremiah 33:11 (in a section of that book generally deemed a late addition by scholars), this familiar refrain occurs only in the Chronicler's History and the Psalms (Pss. 106:1; 107:1; 118:1–4, 29; and as a repeated refrain throughout Ps. 136). The word rendered "steadfast love" in the NRSV (Hebrew *ḥesed*) is impossible to render simply in English. While *ḥesed* does mean "love," it should not be understood in our sentimental Western fashion. Usually, *ḥesed* expresses the commitment that the participants in a treaty owe to one another; "covenant loyalty" may be as good a translation as "steadfast love." That God is committed to God's people, and promises to love them loyally and steadfastly, is indeed good news!

In the Chronicler's History, praise for the Lord's goodness and constancy belongs particularly in the context of worship in Jerusalem's temple. God's committed love is experienced in, and proven by, the ancient liturgy established by David, and preserved by his descendants. In Chronicles, the refrain "O give thanks to the Lord, for he is good; for his steadfast love endures forever" is first sounded in the worship following David's installation of the ark in his Jerusalem shrine (1 Chr. 16:34, citing Ps. 106:1). It is sung by the musicians under Heman and Jeduthun, as part of the sacrificial liturgy established by David and conducted, until the completion of Solomon's temple, at the altar in Gibeon (1 Chr. 16:41). In 2 Chronicles 5:13, the couplet "For he is good, for his steadfast love endures forever" is sung once more in connection with the ark, this time as it is brought to its final resting place in the most holy place of Solomon's temple. Later in the temple dedication service, these words are sung by the congregation of Israel when fire from heaven consumes Solomon's sacrifice (2 Chr 7:3). As David's Levitical singers begin service in Solomon's newly completed temple (2 Chr. 7:6), this refrain expresses the nature of their ministry. Similarly, in Ezra 3:11, when the foundations of the rebuilt temple are laid, the congregation sings "For he is good, / for his steadfast love endures forever toward Israel." Indeed, the only reference to this phrase not associated directly with the temple liturgy is its use by the singers accompanying Jehoshaphat's army as it marches to war against the Edomites (2 Chr. 20:21). Even there, however, the singers are part of a holy war, commanded by the Lord through a revelation to Zechariah the Levite—a revelation given in response to Jehoshaphat's prayer before the temple (2 Chr. 20:5–17). It is in the ancient liturgy of Jerusalem's temple that God's steadfast love is demonstrated and properly celebrated.

As the ark is carried into the most holy place, to the accompaniment of music and song, the presence of the Lord becomes overwhelmingly apparent: "the house, the house of the Lord, was filled with a cloud, so that the priests could not stand to minister because of the cloud; for the glory of the Lord filled the house of God" (2 Chr. 5:13–14). The Lord has come home, and the temple has become God's house.

In response to this manifestation of the Lord's glory, Solomon exclaims, "The Lord has said that he would reside in thick darkness. I have built you an exalted house, a place for you to reside in forever" (6:1–2//1 Kgs. 8:12–13). The word rendered "thick darkness" in the

133

NRSV refers elsewhere to the incomprehensible, inaccessible cloud of God's heavenly dwelling (for example, Exod. 20:21; Ps. 97:2; Job 22:12–14). Perhaps this reference to the "thick darkness" of the Lord's dwelling has been prompted by the cloud that filled the sanctuary. On the other hand, the "thick darkness" could be a reference to the most holy place, the windowless inner chamber of the temple. Most likely, a bit of both is intended. After all, for the Chronicler, the one is made symbolically present by the other. In the blackness of the most holy place, above the cherubim whose wings overshadow the holy ark, the "thick darkness," the cloud of the Lord's glory, has come to dwell.

The doubtless ancient couplet included in Solomon's temple prayers explicitly describes the Jerusalem temple as an earthly dwelling place for the Lord: an "exalted house" in which the Lord will live forever. As we will see, this concept conflicts with the Deuteronomistic theology of Solomon's prayer that follows, in which care is taken to distinguish the symbol from the reality (6:12–42; especially v. 18). While the Chronicler will render the subsequent prayer faithfully, it is clear that his heart remains with this old poetic fragment. For the Chronicler, God is present in the worship of God's people, in a very real sense.

Solomon's Prayer of Dedication (6:3–42) (//1 Kgs. 8:14–53). Now that the ark has been carried into the most holy place, and the Lord has taken possession of the temple, the house is dedicated by prayer. Solomon begins by blessing the assembly (6:3–11). In his blessing, the king recalls Nathan's oracle (1 Chr. 17:1–15), as well as David's three farewell speeches (1 Chr. 22:6–19; 28:1–21; 29:1–9). These promises have now all come true: "Blessed be the LORD, the God of Israel, who with his hand has fulfilled what he promised with his mouth to my father David" (2 Chr. 6:4). After generations during which the Lord had chosen no single place of worship and no kingly line for Israel, God's promise to David had ushered in a new day. To him the Lord had declared, "I have chosen Jerusalem in order that my name may be there, and I have chosen David to be over my people Israel" (2 Chr. 6:6). The fullness of God's promise to David, however, has only now become plain. Solomon is the first Israelite born to be king; in him, God's promise to build a house for David has been fulfilled. Further, Solomon has fulfilled his own calling by doing what David could not do: he has built a house for God, and brought the ark into a permanent dwelling (2 Chr. 6:10–11).

134   After blessing the assembly, Solomon turns to address God (6:12–42). Mounting a bronze dais (6:13; not mentioned in Kings), Solomon kneels before the altar and, lifting his hands to the heavens, begins to pray. This prayer, which expresses the central tenets of

Deuteronomistic theology, is one of the most important texts in the Deuteronomistic History. Although the Chronicler does not agree with the assessment of the temple in Solomon's prayer, the twin themes of promise and threat running through this text are very appropriate to Chronicles' overall theology. Therefore, Chronicles follows this source faithfully until the final verses, where the Chronicler provides his own conclusion (compare 1 Kgs. 8:50b–53 with 2 Chr. 6:40–42).

Solomon begins by praising God's faithfulness and constancy, particularly evident in the fulfillment of God's promises to David (6:14–17). Solomon prays that God's steadfast love would continue to rest upon David's house. But then, Solomon's prayer turns to the other promise God had made to David: the construction of the temple. Earlier, Solomon had described God's temple as "an exalted house, a place for you to reside in forever" (6:1–2). Now, however, he asks, "But will God indeed reside with mortals on earth? Even heaven and the highest heaven cannot contain you, how much less this house that I have built!" (6:18; see also 2:6).

In the Deuteronomistic theology of Solomon's prayer, God is not, indeed cannot be, literally present in the temple. However, God has established the divine name in this place. Therefore, God is particularly attentive to the temple in Jerusalem, so that prayers directed toward the temple are heard (6:19–21—what J. J. M. Roberts has whimsically called "the microphone theory" of divine presence). Chronicles differs from this position substantially, holding for a real presence of the Lord in the temple. However, as we have seen, that presence is in Chronicles linked not so much to the temple itself as to the worship conducted there; it is in the liturgy of Israel that God's presence is experienced. For the Chronicler as for the psalmist, the Lord is "enthroned on the praises of Israel" (Ps. 22:3).

God's attentiveness to the Jerusalem shrine and its altar means that oaths sworn before the altar are binding. Such oaths are sworn in God's hearing, with God as witness. Therefore, whoever swears falsely before the altar will be punished, and the party in the right will be vindicated (2 Chr. 6:22–23). This principle serves as a legal precedent for the remainder of the prayer. Just as God hears oaths sworn before the altar, God will be attentive to other matters brought there.

So, when Israel has sinned and as a result experienced defeat in battle, if they "turn again to you, confess your name, pray and plead with you in this house," God will hear, forgive, "and bring them again to the land that you gave to them and to their ancestors" (2 Chr. 6:24–25). Defeat is here assumed to result from sin—the flip side of the affirmation in Chronicles that victory in battle demonstrated God's blessing (see 1 Chr. 18:13; for defeat as punishment, see 1 Chr. 5:25–26;

135

10:1–14; 21:12). Further, the promise that God will bring a penitent people back to the land clearly presupposes the exile, and would have been particularly meaningful to the Chronicler's community.

Other crises in Israel's collective life are likewise understood to be punishments from God brought on by sin; however, Solomon's prayer gives assurance that prayers of repentance directed toward the temple will lead to forgiveness and restoration. So, drought may be averted by prayer and repentance (6:26–27). Likewise famine, whether caused by "plague, blight, mildew, locust, or caterpillar," or by besieging armies, may be turned aside by prayer (6:28–31). Indeed, not only the needs of the community, but the personal needs of individuals may be brought before the Lord at the altar, in confidence that God will "hear from heaven, your dwelling place, forgive, and render to all whose heart you know, according to all their ways, for only you know the human heart" (6:30). Solomon's prayer assumes that God cares, not just for Israel collectively, but for each person individually. This affirmation is central to the teaching of Jesus, who taught his followers to address God personally, as "Father" (Matt. 6:7–15//Luke 11:1–4), and to lift their needs and wants before God in confidence that they would be heard (Luke 18:1–8).

Perhaps the most astonishing statement in Solomon's prayer is found in 6:32–33: "Likewise when foreigners, who are not of your people Israel . . . come and pray toward this house, may you hear from heaven your dwelling place, and do whatever the foreigners ask of you." Nothing is said here of these foreigners being proselytes. Rather, the text affirms that God's attentiveness to the Jerusalem shrine is inclusive and unconditional: *all* prayers directed toward Jerusalem, even those of foreigners, are heard. On the other hand, the text does not support mere relativism, with all creeds and cultures regarded as equivalent. The foreigners who pray toward the temple are those who have "come from a distant land because of your great name, and your mighty hand, and your outstretched arm" (6:32)—terms that in Deuteronomy refer to God's special deliverance of Israel from bondage (see, for example, Deut. 4:34; 26:8). Israel retains its particular role as the one nation specially established by God, and hence as the witness to the world of God's grace and power. Further, Jerusalem's temple remains the essential connecting point between our world and God. Still, Solomon's prayer affirms that God does hear the prayers of foreigners. Indeed, Solomon urges God to be as responsive to those prayers as to the prayers of Israel, in order that "they may know that your name has been invoked on this house that I have built" (6:33).

136

Similar notions are reflected elsewhere in Scripture, particularly in the book of Isaiah. In Isaiah 2:1–4, "the mountain of the LORD's house" is affirmed as the center of the world; there, one day, the nations will find wisdom and unity, and lose their warlike ways. Isaiah 56:7, a text roughly contemporaneous with Chronicles, affirms that "my house shall be a house of prayer for all peoples." Jesus quoted this passage as expressing God's intention for the temple in his own day (Mark 11:17). In our contemporary situation of pluralism, when many cultures and many faiths impinge upon the church from all sides, this is an important consideration. While we should never compromise or apologize for the gospel we proclaim, we must also remain aware that God is larger than our conceptions, and God's spirit is at work in places and in ways we do not know. God hears and answers prayer—not just our prayers, but *all* prayers.

Reflection upon the foreigner prompts consideration of another crisis calling for prayer: when Israel is at war with a foreign enemy. Solomon urges God to support the people in their battles. However, there is a condition: "If your people go out to battle against their enemies, *by whatever way you shall send them*" (2 Chr. 6:34—emphasis added). Solomon's prayer assumes that Israel will fight as directed by God, in obedience to the divine will—just as David had (see 1 Chr. 14:8–17). Should that not be the case, Israel can of course expect nothing but defeat (as Solomon's prayer has already confirmed; see 2 Chr. 6:24–25).

Finally, Solomon asks God's mercy upon his people "[i]f they sin against you—for there is no one who does not sin—and you are angry with them and give them to an enemy, so that they are carried away captive to a land far or near" (2 Chr. 6:36). The threat of exile is a standard covenant curse (see Deut. 28:32–33), so in Kings this passage need not have come from the time of the exile. For the Chronicler's community, however, the reference to the exile in Babylon was clear and unmistakable. What is here expressed as a hope had been their actual experience; their prayers from captivity had been heard and answered, and they had been able to return to Jerusalem.

In Kings, the plea that God will hear Israel's prayers even from exile in a foreign land leads to the conclusion and climax of the prayer. God will surely be gracious to Israel, and cause Israel's enemies to act graciously, because of God's ancient promise: "For you have separated them from among all the peoples of the earth, to be your heritage, just as you promised through Moses, your servant, when you brought our ancestors out of Egypt, O Lord GOD" (1 Kgs. 8:53). It is because of God's covenant with Israel through Moses that God will hear and deliver. The references to the exodus in the conclusion of Solomon's prayer mirror similar references at the prayer's beginning, in 1 Kings 8:21 (note that the statement "when he brought them out of the land of Egypt" does not appear

137

in 2 Chr. 6:11, which parallels this text). Reference to Moses' Sinai covenant is consistent with the legal basis of this prayer. As we have seen, the foundation of Solomon's prayer is the legal precedent that, because God hears prayers directed toward the altar, oaths sworn before the altar are binding. Similarly, in 1 Kings 8:54–61, observance of God's Law—the "commandments, statutes, and ordinances"—is enjoined upon the community. It is the Torah given to Moses that is the background and basis for God's attentiveness to the temple, and to the prayers directed thereto.

Rather than grounding hope in Torah observance by memorializing the exodus (1 Kgs. 8:50b–53), Chronicles finds a ground for hope in God's presence in the temple liturgy. This emphasis is focused, as is the Chronicler's wont, through a quote from Scripture: in this case, from Psalm 132:8–10, 16. The psalm is appropriate to the Chronicler's purpose in several ways. First, Psalm 132 is one of the Songs of Ascents (see Pss. 120–134), a collection of songs in the Psalter that appears to have been intended for use by pilgrims going up to Jerusalem. The importance of Jerusalem in this psalm, and in all the Songs of Ascents, certainly fits with the centrality of Jerusalem in this prayer. Second, this is a psalm in praise of David, and of God's faithfulness to David—a central theme in Chronicles thus far, and one reemphasized already in Solomon's blessing on the assembly, as well as in the opening words of his prayer.

Most particularly, however, Psalm 132 deals with David bringing the ark into Jerusalem. The specific verses quoted by the Chronicler begin by memorializing this event: "Now rise up, O LORD God, and go to your resting place, / you and the ark of your might" (2 Chr. 6:41a//Ps. 132:8). In the context in Chronicles, of course, this poem refers to Solomon bringing the ark into the temple. Indeed, the language is particularly appropriate to Solomon's temple. As a permanent dwelling rather than a tent, Solomon's temple is far more appropriately called a "resting place" than David's tent shrine. Further, recall that in Chronicles "rest" is not given to David, or to Israel during his reign (see the discussion of 1 Chr. 17:1). It is Solomon, the man of peace, who brings rest to Israel, and under whom, then, the ark may properly be said to have found its own resting place (see 1 Chr. 22:9; 23:25).

The significance of the temple as the resting place both for God and for the ark finds expression later in the psalm:

> For the LORD has chosen Zion;
>   he has desired it for his habitation:
> "This is my resting place forever;
>   here I will reside, for I have desired it."
>   (Ps. 132:13–14)

Although these verses are not quoted in Chronicles, the Chronicler likely assumes, here as elsewhere, that the reader is familiar with the entire poem. Psalm 132 is an apt expression of the theology of presence we have already found expressed in Chronicles. God is really present in this place, as the ark symbolizes, and as the cloud of the glory demonstrates. However, the divine presence is not necessarily connected to the structure of cedar, stone, and gold Solomon has built. God's presence here is a gracious gift, manifest in and through the worship of God's people.

The next lines in Chronicles address the worshiping congregation and its leaders: "Let your priests, O LORD God, be clothed with salvation, / and let your faithful rejoice in your goodness" (2 Chr. 6:41b). Here, the Chronicler appears to be adapting his source. The description of the priests combines verses 9 ("Let your priests be clothed with righteousness") and 16 ("Its priests I will clothe with salvation") of Psalm 132. God's salvation and deliverance, the subject of much of Solomon's prayer, is here connected with the priesthood of Solomon's temple. As for the Lord's faithful, they do not merely shout for joy (as in Ps. 132:9, 16), they "rejoice in your goodness." As 2 Chronicles 5:13 and its parallels throughout the Chronicler's History affirm, it is in worship before the temple that God's goodness is experienced and celebrated.

The expressions rendered by the NRSV as "do not turn away the face of your anointed one" (Ps. 132:10) and "do not reject your anointed one" (2 Chr. 6:42) are in Hebrew nearly identical. However, in the MT of 2 Chronicles 6:42, the word translated "anointed one" is actually plural, so that the Hebrew reads "do not reject your anointed ones." Most scholars (including the translators of the NRSV) regard this as a scribal error, and read the word as singular, following Psalm 134:10, the LXX, and numerous Hebrew manuscripts. However, we may be able to identify a motivation for the change in Chronicles.

In 1 Chronicles 16, David's successful transport of the ark into Jerusalem was celebrated and his tent shrine for the ark was dedicated by a service of worship, which also featured the singing of psalms. There, in a quote from Psalm 105:15, God rebukes the nations and their kings, saying "Do not touch my anointed ones; / do my prophets no harm" (1 Chr. 16:22). Perhaps the modified psalm in 2 Chronicles 6:41–42 is meant to parallel that earlier reference, linking Solomon's temple dedication to the dedication of David's shrine. In both contexts, the "anointed ones" are plainly the people of the worshiping congregation. In 2 Chronicles 6:42, this reading is further supported by moving the reference to "your servant David" (the "anointed one" in Ps. 132:10) from the first line of the verse to a new line of the Chronicler's own composition.

139

In Chronicles, a new second line added to this verse concludes Solomon's prayer: "Remember your steadfast love for your servant David" (1 Chr. 6:42). In Kings, Solomon's prayer is bracketed by references to the exodus and to Moses; in Chronicles, the prayer begins and ends with David. For the Chronicler, it is not so much the Torah of Moses as the liturgy of David that ensures God's presence in the Jerusalem temple. Like the reference to God's goodness added to the preceding verse, the mention of God's steadfast love in 2 Chronicles 6:42 recalls the refrain "O give thanks to the LORD, for he is good; for his steadfast love endures forever"—a refrain that in Chronicles consistently refers to worship in the Jerusalem temple. The temple and its liturgy are the final demonstration of God's steadfast love to David. By building the temple, and bringing the ark into it, Solomon has accomplished his calling, and fulfilled God's promises to his father.

Sacrifices of Dedication (7:1–11) (//1 Kgs. 8:54—9:1). The final stage of the temple dedication is the offering of sacrifices by Solomon and his people. The Chronicler provides his own introduction to this section. In 2 Chronicles 7:1–3, two miraculous signs, to which the people respond with awe, reveal God's presence. As in the Chronicler's version of Solomon's prayer, the focus remains on worship (in contrast to 1 Kgs. 8:54–61, where Solomon exhorts the people to observe the Law).

First, fire falls from heaven and consumes Solomon's offerings (2 Chr. 7:1a; note that the content of Solomon's offering is not presented until 2 Chr. 7:5). Earlier, David's offering at this same site was also consumed by fire from heaven (1 Chr. 21:26; see also 1 Kgs. 18). This dramatic demonstration of divine approval, both for Solomon's temple and for his prayer, once more places Solomon and his father in parallel. Next, the glory of the Lord again fills the temple, so that the priests are unable to enter (2 Chr. 7:1b–2; see 5:13–14). This second reference to the Lord's occupation of the temple undergirds the affirmation in Chronicles of the Lord's real presence in the Jerusalem shrine.

In response to the fire from heaven and to this second manifestation of the divine glory, the people "bowed down on the pavement with their faces to the ground, and worshiped and gave thanks to the LORD, saying, 'For he is good, / for his steadfast love endures forever'" (7:3; see Ezek. 40:17–18; 42:3, where the pavement is located in the outer court). The words of the congregation, here as elsewhere in the Chronicler's History, affirm God's faithful presence in Israel's worship. Yet that presence is not taken for granted, but calls forth awe, wonder, and terror—the people fall on their faces, like Moses before the burning bush (Exod. 3:6).

Now, Chronicles resumes its use of the narrative in Kings (2 Chr. 7:4–10//1 Kgs. 8:62–66). Solomon's offering is stupendous: "twenty-two

140

thousand oxen and one hundred twenty thousand sheep" (7:5). Indeed, so great is the sacrifice that the bronze altar is not large enough to offer it all. Solomon consecrates a large area of the temple forecourt to serve as a temporary altar, and burns the sacrifices there on the ground (7:7). Participating in this sacrifice are not only the priests, but the Levitical singers and musicians (7:6—a verse unique to Chronicles). Intriguingly, as in David's time, the task of blowing the trumpets falls not to Levites, but to priests (see 1 Chr. 15:24; 16:6). Chronicles reminds us that it was David who had commissioned these musicians, provided their instruments, and charged them already during his own reign to give "thanks to the LORD—for his steadfast love endures forever." The continuity of Levitical service is further confirmation of God's faithfulness. The singing of the now-familiar temple refrain, the participation of the Levitical musicians, and the mention of the priestly trumpeters connects this passage to 2 Chronicles 5:12, where the ark was carried into the most holy place of Solomon's temple. Here, as there, David's liturgy and the divine presence are linked.

In 7:9–10, the Chronicler addresses questions relating to the timing of the temple dedication and of the Feast of Booths (Japhet 1993, 611–13). Although the temple dedication is set at the time of the feast (5:3), nothing in the dedication itself corresponds to the accepted patterns of that celebration. The Chronicler therefore proposes that the seven days of the dedication actually preceded the seven days of the feast (7:9; note that Chronicles refers to "the dedication of the altar" here, emphasizing once more the importance of the sacrificial liturgy). On the eighth day after the beginning of Booths, Solomon conducts a "solemn assembly," as priestly tradition required (see Lev. 23:36; contrast 1 Kgs. 8:66, where the people are sent away on the eighth day). Then, "[o]n the twenty-third day of the seventh month," the people are sent to their homes rejoicing. Since Booths would have been celebrated beginning on the fifteenth day of the seventh month, this date confirms the pattern: the temple dedication must have begun on the eighth, and the assembly must have been held on the twenty-second. Of course, this conflicts with the date of the dedication given earlier, which had been taken from Kings (2 Chr. 5:3//1 Kgs. 8:2), but the Chronicler, as we have seen, is not unduly concerned with consistency among his sources.

In 2 Chronicles 2:1, the account of Solomon's temple-building began with the statement that "Solomon decided to build a temple for the name of the LORD, and a royal palace for himself." Now, that work has been completed: "Thus Solomon finished the house of the LORD and the king's house; all that Solomon had planned to do in the house

141

of the LORD and in his own house he successfully accomplished" (7:11). Solomon has fulfilled his calling.

Epilogue: the Lord Answers Solomon's Prayer (7:12–22) (//1 Kgs. 9:2–9)

With the temple dedication completed, Solomon's temple is truly finished at last. Now, in an epilogue to the account of Solomon's temple-building, the Lord responds to the king's prayer of dedication. Once more, the Chronicler is, overall, faithful to his source; however, an expanded introduction gives a different spin to the Lord's response in Chronicles (compare 7:12–15 with 1 Kgs. 9:2–3).

The Lord assures Solomon, "I have heard your prayer, and have chosen this place for myself as a house of sacrifice" (7:12). The emphasis on the sacrificial liturgy conducted at Solomon's temple has been consistent in Chronicles. From the first, in his letter to Huram, Solomon had said that the house he would build for God would serve "as a place to make offerings before him" (2:6). In the temple description, Chronicles provides a description of the bronze altar that is lacking in Kings (2 Chr. 4:1). Similarly, in the temple dedication, the seven days of the dedication ritual are said to be for "the dedication of the altar" (7:9). This idea continues to find expression later in the Chronicler's History; note that in Ezra 6:3, the temple is described as "the place where sacrifices are offered and burnt offerings are brought." For the Chronicler, Solomon's temple is a "house of sacrifice;" by means of the sacrificial liturgy established by David, the worshiping community experiences God's presence in the temple.

In Kings, God's words to Solomon refer back to the beginning of the young king's reign, when the Lord appeard to him at Gibeon (1 Kgs. 9:2). Chronicles, however, establishes a direct connection between the Lord's words and Solomon's prayer, by making explicit references back to that prayer. Three potential disasters are described, each of which (as in Solomon's prayer) is understood as a punishment sent from God. The first, drought, is described in nearly identical terms in 7:13 and in Solomon's prayer (6:26). The second, the locust plague, is mentioned in both 7:13 and 6:28, though different terms for "locust" are used in each context. The third, pestilence, is also found in both 7:13 and 6:28; further, both texts use the same term for "pestilence." In Chronicles, God speaks in answer to Solomon's prayer.

In his prayer, Solomon had asked God to respond to the prayers the people directed toward the temple and its altar. In answer, the Lord declares, "if my people who are called by my name humble themselves, pray, seek my face, and turn from their wicked ways, then I will hear from heaven, and will forgive their sin and heal their land" (7:14). The concept introduced here, that true repentance begins with humility, is characteristic of Chronicles (Japhet 1993, 615). The importance of humbling oneself before God will be emphasized throughout the final section of this book, where the kings of Judah who humble themselves receive grace and forgiveness for themselves and for their land (for example, see 2 Chr. 12:12; 32:26).

To "seek [God's] face" is a "religious idiom for worship in the temple" (Allen 1999, 500; see Pss. 24:6, 27:8). In particular, this idiom appears in Psalm 105, one of the psalms sung at the dedication of David's shrine for the ark: "Seek the LORD and his strength, seek his presence [literally, "face"] continually" (Ps. 105:4//1 Chr. 16:11). For the Chronicler, prayer and repentance are not a private affair. If one truly wishes to seek God's face, the proper context for that search is worship before the temple among the people "who are called by [God's] name," participating in David's ancient liturgy.

The promise of God's response is likewise communal. As the people pray in humility, seek God's face in worship, and "turn from their wicked ways," God in turn promises to heed their prayers, "forgive their sin, and heal their land." Sincere repentance and faithful worship will bring health and wholeness upon the entire nation.

That the Lord's words are an explicit response to Solomon's prayer is, finally, confirmed in 7:15. Note that this verse repeats the wording of 6:40, save that what was there phrased as a request of Solomon ("Now, O my God, let your eyes be open . . .") is here stated by the Lord as a first-person affirmation: "Now my eyes will be open and my ears attentive to the prayer that is made in this place" (Japhet 1993, 600 and 615). Solomon's prayer has been answered; God will respond to the prayers of God's people offered at the temple.

Now, Chronicles resumes its use of the source in Kings. The Lord confirms the significance of the temple: "For now I have chosen and consecrated this house so that my name may be there forever; my eyes and my heart will be there for all time" (7:16; 1 Kgs. 9:3 lacks the word rendered "I have chosen"). Chronicles emphasizes that the temple in particular, as well as Jerusalem in general, is the place of God's choice. Solomon is urged to remain faithful, following the example of his father David, so that God's covenant with David might be kept—that is, that David's line might continue to rule in Jerusalem (7:17–18).

Up to this point, God's message for Solomon has been positive. But now, the Lord describes the consequences of faithlessness and disobedience. Should Israel "turn aside and forsake my statutes and my

143

commandments that I have set before you, and go and serve other gods and worship them" (7:19), the people will be exiled from the land, and the temple will be forsaken. The abandoned temple will become "a proverb and a byword among all peoples" (7:20); it will serve as a lesson to all who see it, that the Lord holds the people accountable for their actions. Of course, for the Chronicler's community, the grim truth of this warning was only too well known. Now that they had returned to the land and rebuilt their temple, it was vital that they remember the fate of the first temple. As glorious as Solomon's temple had been, God had abandoned it to destruction because of Israel's faithlessness. The same fate would befall the second temple, if God's people proved faithless once more.

8:1—9:31

Solomon's Reign

Having focused thus far on the temple alone, the Chronicler turns at the end of the story to other matters relating to Solomon's reign. Attention is paid first to a variety of royal projects, including the conquest of Hamath-zobah, the only military endeavor attributed to Solomon in Chronicles (8:1–18). Then, the Chronicler devotes considerable space to the relations between Solomon and the queen of Sheba (9:1–12). Finally, the account of Solomon's reign ends as it had begun, with a record of Solomon's fabulous wealth (9:13–28; see also 1:14–17). Nothing is said of Solomon's wives (1 Kgs. 11:1–8), or of God's displeasure with Solomon, which would ultimately result in the loss of the northern tribes (1 Kgs. 11:9–13, 26–40). In place of the account of Solomon's wars with Edom and Damascus (1 Kgs. 11:14–25), the Chronicler provides a summary affirmation of Solomon's secure rule over "all the kings from the Euphrates to the land of the Philistines, and to the border of Egypt" (9:26). The Chronicler is not attempting a whitewash; as we will see, he assumes that his readers know all this. But retelling it would serve no purpose, and indeed would cloud the Chronicler's central point: that Solomon fulfilled his calling by building the temple and putting David's liturgy into action. So, in Chronicles, the account of Solomon's reign ends as it had begun, with the wealth and wisdom that confirmed God's faithfulness to David's son.

144

Solomon dies having accomplished all that he was meant to accomplish (9:29–31). No explicit blame is laid at Solomon's door for the breakup of David's united kingdom, which would take place during the reign of Solomon's son Rehoboam (but, see the discussion of 9:29, below). By realizing David's plans and dreams for the temple, Solomon had preserved his father's legacy.

Solomon's Royal Projects (8:1–18) (///1 Kgs. 9:10–28)

The account of Solomon's activities and accomplishments begins with a rehearsal of his greatest project: the construction of "the house of the LORD and his own house" (8:1). This is the Chronicler's fourth mention of Solomon's palace (see also 2:1, 12; 7:11), though once again, no description is given. In Chronicles, the focus remains on the temple alone. The scale of Solomon's greatest achievement is indicated by the time required for this project: it took him twenty years to build the palace and the temple.

Next, Chronicles turns to another massive project. Solomon, we are told, rebuilt and resettled several cities given to him by Huram of Tyre (8:2). The Chronicler's account here is in direct conflict with his source. In 1 Kings 9:11–14, Solomon gives twenty cities to *Hiram*, for 120 talents of gold; moreover, the cities are despised by the Phoenician king! It may be that Chronicles describes a situation later than the one described in Kings; since Hiram was so displeased with his purchase, he may have returned the cities to Solomon, who then rebuilt and repopulated them (Myers 1965, 47). This, however, is unlikely. It is more probable that the Chronicler, given his attitudes toward Solomon and Huram, deemed it improbable that Solomon had sold land to Huram, and so corrected his source (Bickerman 1962, 23). Earlier, in his account of the correspondence between Huram and Solomon, the Chronicler showed no interest in the politics of their relationship. Here as well, whatever may have prompted this land deal historically, its only purpose in Chronicles is as an example of Solomon's public works. At any rate, this sort of resettlement and rebuilding in peacetime is unique in the Hebrew Bible (Japhet 1993, 621–22). Perhaps it reflects the experience of the Chronicler's own community, who knew all about rebuilding and repopulating ruined towns.

The conquest of Hamath-zobah (2 Chr. 8:3) presents three major problems. First, the name itself is curious, appearing only here in the Hebrew Bible. In 1 Chronicles 18:3, David campaigns against "Zobah toward Hamath" (the LXX reads "Zobah-hamath"); however, "Hamath" is absent in the parallel text (2 Sam. 8:3), as well as in some versions of the Chronicles passage. Second, in David's campaign against Zobah, Hamath was David's ally. How then does it happen that in 2 Chronicles these two enemies are linked as one, in opposition to David's heir? Perhaps the odd

145

combination of Zobah and Hamath in 2 Chronicles 8:3 reflects the situation in the Chronicler's time, when Zobah was part of the Persian province of Hamath (Myers 1965, 47). Third, Chronicles has to this point emphasized a contrast between David and Solomon. David was a warrior, a man of blood, and so was barred from building the temple; Solomon was the man of peace, commissioned by God to carry out this project. If Solomon too was a warrior, how was he able to do what David could not? Remember, though, that David was not punished for being a warrior; in fact, his victories in battle proved that God's favor rested on him. It was David's calling to be a warrior. Solomon, on the other hand, was called to build the temple.

Chronicles sets up a literary parallel between Solomon and David here. David's victories in the regions of Zobah and Hamath are described among his successes after the ark was brought to Jerusalem. Similarly, in 2 Chronicles 8:3, Solomon's victory over Hamath-zobah follows his establishment of the ark in the completed temple.

Still, Solomon's conquest of Hamath-zobah may have a historical basis as well. Solomon's northern border is set at Lebo-hamath (or perhaps, "the entrance to Hamath;" 2 Chr. 7:8//1 Kgs. 8:65), which "presupposes conquests at this far end of the kingdom" (Japhet 1993, 622). In 2 Kings 14:25, Jeroboam "restored the border of Israel" to Lebo-hamath, suggesting not only that the northern border had been located there previously, but also that the northern border was uncertain, and subject to contest. Even the role of Solomon in Chronicles as the man of peace may support the historicity of 2 Chronicles 8:3: if the conquest had not happened, why would the Chronicler cite it (so Japhet 1993, 622)? Perhaps, in the Chronicler's view, Solomon was not acting as a conqueror at Hamath-zobah, expanding the borders of his kingdom; rather, he was preserving control over a rebellious territory, earlier conquered by his father David (see 1 Chr. 13:5, where David's territory extends "from the Shihor of Egypt to Lebo-hamath"). In that case, Solomon's role as the man of peace would be preserved.

In its account of Solomon's building programs, Chronicles once more condenses and emends its source. Tadmor (later called Palmyra) was a significant trade center, an oasis located on the caravan route between Damascus and the Euphrates. Appropriately, in Chronicles this northern location is placed in conjunction with "all the storage towns that he built in Hamath" (2 Chr. 8:4). The MT of 1 Kings 9:18 reads "Tamar": a minor town in Judah to the south. However, later tradition held that when the text was read aloud, "Tadmor" was to be substituted for the word "Tamar" in the written text. This substitution has the effect of exalting Solomon as builder of an important trade center, and of supporting Solomon's northern border claims.

Second Chronicles 8:6 summarizes Solomon's success at building fortifications, store cities, bases for his cavalry and chariotry, "and whatever Solomon desired to build, in Jerusalem, in Lebanon, and in all the land of his dominion." So many building projects required a large labor pool. The labor was provided, however, not by Israelites, but by "the Hittites, the Amorites, the Perizzites, the Hivites, and the Jebusites, who were not of Israel, from their descendants who were still left in the land, whom the people of Israel had not destroyed" (8:7–8). In short, the remnants of the land's original occupants (see, for example, Exod 3:8, 17) served as slave laborers, to carry out Solomon's building projects. Once more, the people of Israel are expressly said not to be used as slave laborers; instead, "they were soldiers, and his officers, the commanders of his chariotry and cavalry" (8:9). Israelites also served as "the chief officers of King Solomon" (8:10)—that is, as the royal officials in charge of the slave laborers. The number of these officials is uncertain; 2 Chronicles 8:10 reads 250, while 1 Kings 9:23 has 550. The texts are sufficiently similar in Hebrew for one or the other to be a textual error. It is intriguing to note, however, that in 2 Chronicles 2:18 the number of non-Israelite overseers is 3,600, while the parallel text in 1 Kings 5:16 has 3,300, so that the total number of officials and overseers in both is 3,850 (Elmslie 1916, 200). Apparently, the scribes have kept the numbers in balance.

Next comes the first mention in Chronicles of Solomon's marriage to an Egyptian princess (2 Chr. 8:11//1 Kgs. 9:24; see also 1 Kgs. 3:1; 9:16–17). Solomon has built a house for his wife, outside of "the city of David." The reason for these separate quarters, according to Chronicles, is that "the places to which the ark of the LORD has come are holy" (8:11). Evidently, the presence of Pharaoh's daughter in the same precincts as the ark of the Lord is deemed inappropriate, even defiling. But, why should this be?

Later in the Chronicler's History, intermarriage with foreigners will become an important issue. Ezra will order a wholesale divorce of all foreign wives (Ezra 10:3–14), while Nehemiah will deal with intermarriage more leniently, taking no action against existing marriages but forbidding the practice in the future (Neh. 13:23–27). This attitude finds its roots in texts such as Deuteronomy 7:3–4, where the Lord says of the original inhabitants of Canaan, "Do not intermarry with them, giving your daughters to their sons or taking their daughters for your sons, for that would turn away your children from following me, to serve other gods." Similarly, Deuteronomy 23:3–6 details who may and who may not participate in the assembly of the Lord. Ammonites and Moabites "[e]ven to the tenth generation" are barred from the congregation (Deut. 23:3). Edomites and Egyptians are permitted to be counted in the assembly after living for three generations among the people Israel (Deut. 23:8). The intent behind these regulations, as Deuteronomy 7:4 makes clear, was not to preserve racial purity, but to maintain right worship. Intermarriage with the foreign nations, and swift acceptance of foreigners into the worshiping congregation, could lead to the corruption of Israel's worship by alien practices and ideas. (On this concern, see also Num. 25:1–15; 1 Kgs. 11:1–13.) Under no circumstances can these biblical prohibitions be understood as a warrant for racism!

Intermarriage is not universally deplored in the Hebrew Bible. Deuteronomy 21:10–14 describes the practice of marrying foreign women taken as prisoners in wartime, insisting that such war brides be treated with respect. Indeed, many heroes of Israel took foreign wives, without being criticized. In Numbers 12:1–16, Aaron and Miriam object to Moses' foreign-born wife; God, however, supports Moses, and Miriam is stricken with leprosy for speaking against her brother. Remember, too, the story of Ruth, the Moabite widow, who faithfully followed her mother-in-law Naomi back to Naomi's home in Bethlehem. Ruth married the Judean landowner Boaz, and became the great-grandmother of King David.

In 2 Chronicles 8:11, Solomon belongs in this same company. After all, if the Chronicler had been disturbed by the ethnicity of Solomon's Egyptian wife, he could simply have ignored this reference to Pharaoh's daughter—as he has ignored other references to her and to Solomon's other wives. That he does not do so suggests that it is not her Egyptian heritage that the Chronicler finds objectionable.

Another possibility is that Pharaoh's daughter is assigned separate quarters, not because she is an Egyptian, but because she is a woman. By Israel's law, a woman became ritually unclean every month during menstruation, and for seven days after. In case of vaginal bleeding due to illness, her defilement persisted until her bleeding had stopped (Lev. 15:19–33; see also Mark 5:25–34). Women were also rendered ritually unclean by childbirth, and remained unclean for seven days if the child was a boy, two weeks if she was a girl (Lev. 12:2–8). During these times of defilement, a woman was of course barred from any role in worship. However, even when women were not ritually unclean, contact with them was deemed risky, since a man was ritually defiled by sexual intercourse (Deut. 23:10–11). So, when Moses consecrates the congregation at Sinai, he strictly charges the males, "do not go near a woman" (Exod. 19:15). Similarly, in 1 Samuel 21:4–5, David's hungry troops are permitted to eat the sacred bread of the presence, if they have kept themselves from women.

148

Even so, the building of separate quarters may seem extreme.

Note, however, that in Chronicles the objection is not to Pharaoh's daughter living in the city of David—women, after all, did live in Jerusalem—but to her living in "the house of King David of Israel" (8:11). Apparently, in the days of the monarchy, the palace and the temple were part of a single complex (note that the building of temple and palace are consistently linked in Chronicles as a single project). The Chronicler understands the separate quarters built for Pharaoh's daughter as a way of maintaining the ritual purity of this complex.

Solomon not only builds the temple and brings the ark into it, he also sees to it that the liturgy of David is established and preserved (8:12–15). Once more, Moses and David are linked. Israel's sacred calendar, and the sacrifices required "for the sabbaths, the new moons, and the three annual festivals," come from the Torah of Moses (8:13). However, "the divisions of the priests for their service, and the Levites for their offices of praise and ministry alongside the priests as the duty of each day required, and the gatekeepers in their divisions for the several gates" are all as David had decreed (2 Chr. 8:14; see 1 Chr. 23:3–26:32). The expression "man of God," used here of David, typically refers to a prophet (for example, see 2 Chr. 11:2; 25:7, 9). In particular, Moses is called the man of God (Deut. 33:1; Josh. 14:6; the title of Ps. 90; in the Chronicler's History, see 1 Chr. 23:14; 2 Chr. 30:16; Ezra 3:2). David is only called a "man of God" three times in Scripture: all in the Chronicler's History, and all in relationship to the service of priests or Levites in David's liturgy (2 Chr. 8:14; Neh. 12:24, 36). Like Moses, David is a prophet, to whom God has given a revelation of how God is to be worshiped (see 1 Chr. 28:11–19). Solomon faithfully puts his father's vision into practice: "They did not turn away from what the king had commanded the priests and Levites regarding anything at all" (2 Chr. 8:15). With the proper liturgy established in the proper temple, Solomon has truly fulfilled his calling; now, from the Chronicler's perspective, "all the work of Solomon was accomplished" (2 Chr. 8:16).

Faithful to its source, Chronicles turns next to Solomon's profitable trade agreements with Africa (2 Chr. 8:17–18//1 Kgs. 9:26–28). In cooperation with Huram of Tyre, Solomon has commenced trade with the kingdom of Ophir. The port of Ezion-geber was located at the northernmost tip of the Gulf of Elath, a long finger of the Red Sea. Through this port, Solomon had access to the ports of the African kingdoms on the Red Sea. While the amounts involved (in 2 Chr. 8:18, 450 talents, or nearly 169 tons, of gold) are exaggerated, the African trade certainly would have been highly profitable. Further, it is perhaps through this trade that Solomon attracts the attention of the queen of Sheba (9:1–12).

149

The Visit of the Queen of Sheba (9:1–12)
(//1 Kgs. 10:1–13)

Sheba, or Saba, was a Semitic kingdom on the southwest coast of the Arabian peninsula, in what is today known as Yemen. The Sabeans were famous for their trade with Africa and India in gold and precious gems, and were perfectly situated on the caravan route for trade in myrrh and frankincense (Boraas 1985, 920). All of this made Sheba a place of legendary wealth (see Isa. 60:6; Ezek. 27:22–23).

The queen of Sheba comes to Jerusalem with a rich train, a caravan "bearing spices and very much gold and precious stones" (9:1). However, she has not been drawn to Solomon as a potential trading partner. Rather, she has come to see for herself if what she has heard about Solomon's great wisdom is true. What the queen learns surpasses her expectations; Solomon's accomplishments take her breath away (with the JPSV; the NRSV of 9:4 reads more woodenly, "there was no more spirit left in her"). She exclaims, "Happy are your people! Happy are these your servants, who continually attend you and hear your wisdom! Blessed be the LORD your God, who has delighted in you and set you on his throne as king for the LORD your God" (9:7–8a).

The queen of Sheba's words in praise of Solomon call to mind the words of Huram, from early in Solomon's story (2 Chr. 2:11). Just as Huram had said, "Because the LORD loves his people he has made you king over them," the queen of Sheba declares more fulsomely, "Because your God loved Israel and would establish them forever, he has made you king over them, that you may execute justice and righteousness" (2 Chr. 9:8b). This praise of Solomon, from kingdoms on opposite ends of the ancient world, demonstrates that God's promise to Solomon has been kept; God has given him "honor, such as none of the kings had who were before you, and none after you shall have the like" (2 Chr. 1:12).

The queen of Sheba gives to Solomon a wealth of the gold, precious stones, and particularly the spices in her caravan: "there were no spices such as those that the queen of Sheba gave to King Solomon" (2 Chr. 9:9). The unparalleled wealth of spice brought into Solomon's kingdom by the queen of Sheba prompts reflection on the wealth pouring into Solomon's kingdom through his cooperative trading endeavours with Tyre: not only the gold and jewels from Ophir, but the rare algum wood from Lebanon (see 2 Chr. 2:8; 1 Kgs. 10:11–12 has "almug wood," attributed to the trade with Ophir). This rare wood, prized for harps and lyres, was made into steps for the temple—yet another indication of the opulence of Solomon's shrine. The abundance of algum wood from Tyre, like the abundance of spices from Saba, is without parallel: "there never was seen the like of them before in the land of Judah" (2 Chr. 9:11). Not only praise, but wealth comes to Solomon from the furthest reaches of the ancient world.

However, Solomon is not regarded in any sense as a debtor, to Tyre or to Saba. Out of his own wealth, "King Solomon granted the queen of Sheba every desire that she expressed, well beyond what she had brought to the king" (2 Chr. 9:12). While this may reflect an historical trade relationship between Saba and Israel, there is no question in Chronicles of an equivalent exchange. As with Solomon's relationship to Huram, the politics of the relationship with Saba do not interest the Chronicler. The wealth of Saba is *given* to Solomon, unconditionally, as a token of the queen's great respect. Solomon, for his part, will not be outdone, in wisdom, wealth, or generosity.

Solomon's Wealth Revisited (9:13–28)
(//1 Kgs. 10:14–29)

Apart from a few scribal errors, Chronicles is generally faithful to its source through this section. The magnificence of Solomon's court is expressed in a series of vivid images. First, Solomon's annual income, from tribute and trade, is placed at 666 talents of gold: worth about 235 million dollars today. Some of this fabulous wealth was used to decorate Solomon's palace, "the House of the Forest of Lebanon" (9:16). The walls of the palace were hung with golden shields (9:15–16). Solomon's throne was made of ivory overlaid with gold. A lion figure stood to either side of the throne's armrests; twelve other lions, two flanking each of the six steps leading up to the throne, evidently represented the twelve tribes of Israel. In the Hebrew Bible, the lion is associated with royalty, and especially with the royal tribe of Judah. For example, in Jacob's deathbed blessing, he says of his son Judah:

> Judah is a lion's whelp;
>   from the prey, my son, you have gone up.
> He crouches down, he stretches out like a lion,
>   like a lioness—who dares rouse him up?
> The scepter shall not depart from Judah;
>   nor the ruler's staff from between his feet.
>   (Gen. 49:9–10)

It is appropriate, then, that the royal throne of David's line was built using a lion motif.

Even Solomon's tableware was all made of gold; "silver," we are told, "was not considered as anything in the days of Solomon" (9:20). To add

151

to the opulence of Solomon's court, the trade ships from Solomon's cooperative endeavour with Huram returned every three years with "gold, silver, ivory, apes, and peacocks" (9:21). Further, following the example of the queen of Sheba, rulers came to Solomon from all the kingdoms of the world, to learn from Solomon's wisdom and to give him gifts (9:22–24).

2 Chronicles 9:22–28 returns us to the discussion of Solomon's great wealth in 1:14–17. Again, we are told of Solomon's chariots and horses, and of his trade in horseflesh—although here, nothing is said of anything going out of Solomon's kingdom; the accent falls altogether on Solomon's accumulation of wealth. Once more, we are told that Solomon "made silver as common in Jerusalem as stone, and cedar as plentiful as the sycamore of the Shephelah" (2 Chr. 9:27; see 1:15). In Chronicles, Solomon's personal fortune was not earned at the expense of his citizenry; all Israel shared in the prosperity of the king.

Solomon's Death (9:29–31) (//1 Kgs. 11:41–43)

In contrast to his father, who was said to have "died in good old age, full of days, riches, and honor" (1 Chr. 29:28), Solomon's death is described quite matter-of-factly. After a reign of forty years, "Solomon slept with his ancestors and was buried in the city of his father David; and his son Rehoboam succeeded him" (2 Chr. 9:31//1 Kgs. 11:43; "the city of David" was the term used for the burial place of Israel's kings). In contrast to the evident affection that he has for David, the Chronicler seems fairly cool toward Solomon, despite his wealth and wisdom.

However, the only trace of the Deuteronomistic History's polemic against Solomon to be found in Chronicles comes in the statement of the prophetic sources for Solomon's story (2 Chr. 9:29). As was the case with David (see 1 Chr. 29:29), it is doubtful that these are actual, separate sources—particularly as, in the Chronicler's account of Solomon's reign, it is apparent that the only substantive source is the book of 1 Kings. Rather, the Chronicler assumes that the story of Solomon was produced by writing prophets.

The first prophetic source listed by the Chronicler is "the history of the prophet Nathan." Nathan, of course, delivered the oracle promising David a successor, who would build the temple (1 Chr. 17:11–12). The purpose of Solomon's whole life, for the Chronicler, is the fulfillment of this promise.

The second prophetic source is "the prophecy of Ahijah the Shilonite." Ahijah the Shilonite has not yet been mentioned in Chronicles. However, he plays an important role in 1 Kings 11—15, especially in 11:26–40. It is Ahijah who prophesies to Jeroboam, "thus says the

LORD, the God of Israel, 'See, I am about to tear the kingdom from the hand of Solomon, and will give you ten tribes'" (1 Kgs. 11:31). The reason for this, Jeroboam is told, is that Solomon has worshiped false gods, and "has not walked in my ways, doing what is right in my sight and keeping my statutes and my ordinances, as his father David did" (1 Kgs. 11:33). None of this is retold in Chronicles. But the reference to Ahijah the Shilonite in 2 Chronicles 9:29 shows that the Chronicler presupposes it, and assumes that his readers are aware of it.

The referrent for the third prophetic source, "the visions of the seer Iddo concerning Jeroboam son of Nebat," is far less clear. No visions of Iddo are described in either Chronicles or Kings, although he is cited as a source for the reigns of Rehoboam (2 Chr. 12:15) and Abijah (2 Chr. 13:22) as well as Solomon. An Aramaic inscription from around 800 B.C. has a term similar to "Iddo" in combination with the word "seer" (the title given to Iddo in 2 Chr. 9:29 and 12:15); evidently the term describes some kind of prophetic activity (see the translations of Rosenthal 1969, 655, and Lipinski 1978, 230). The name "Iddo" has a good prophetic pedigree in the Hebrew Bible as well; the prophet Zechariah was the "son of Berechiah son of Iddo" (for example, Zech. 1:1).

Josephus refers to the anonymous "man of God" in 1 Kings 13 as "Iddo" (Greek *Iadon;* see *Antiquities* 8.4.5), as do some rabbinic sources (Japhet 1993, 645). While this identification may itself be dependent upon 2 Chronicles 9:29, it is certainly suggestive, as this man of God predicts the eventual desecration and destruction of Jeroboam's altar at Bethel (1 Kgs. 13:2–3; for the prophecy's fulfillment, see 2 Kgs. 23:16–17). Between them, then, Ahijah the Shilonite and Iddo the seer would sum up the course of the northern kingdom, from its beginning to its dissolution.

Ultimately, the three sources listed for Solomon's story sum up the significance of Solomon, for good and ill. Of all the kings treated in the Chronicler's History, only David and Solomon ruled over "all Israel" (1 Chr. 29:26; 2 Chr. 9:30). Solomon's reign marks the end of David's united kingdom; after this, the descendants of David would rule only over the southern kingdom of Judah. Still, despite this great failure, Solomon had fulfilled his calling, as laid forth in Nathan's oracle. The temple had been built; the priests and Levites were in place; David's dream was now a reality. How the descendants of David dealt with this precious legacy will be the subject of the remainder of Chronicles.

The Kings of Judah

The final section of Chronicles deals with the period of the divided kingdom, from the accession of Solomon's son Rehoboam to the destruction of Jerusalem and its temple by the Babylonians in the days of King Zedekiah. Once more, the primary source for this history is 1 and 2 Kings. However, this section also marks the clearest example of the Chronicler's selective use of that source. In Chronicles, virtually nothing is said of the northern kingdom; indeed, the north and its kings are only mentioned when they directly impact the fortunes of the southern kingdom, Judah.

The reasons for this selectivity are plain. As we have already seen, the Chronicler's primary concern is for right worship in the right temple. He is interested in David as the founder of Jerusalem's liturgy, and in Solomon as the builder of the temple. David's descendants are the guarantors of that temple and liturgy; therefore, the Chronicler stays with the story of the house of David, and largely ignores the northern kingdom.

Still, many scholars have insisted that Chronicles, in sharp distinction to Ezra–Nehemiah, is positively inclined toward the north (so especially Williamson 1977, 139–140). In particular, it is claimed that in Chronicles, "Israel" always includes the northern tribes, while in Ezra–Nehemiah, "Israel" refers only to Judah and Benjamin (Williamson 1977, 69). Further, the story of the divided kingdom is bracketed by speeches calling the northern kingdom to repentance (2 Chr. 13:4–12: Abijah; 30:6–9: Hezekiah), which could "indicate the Chronicler's openness to Northern participation in the Jerusalem cult" (Klein 1992, 998).

Still, Chronicles rejects the northern cult and priesthood as illegitimate (2 Chr. 11:13–15; 13:8–12). Indeed, Amaziah is commanded by a prophet to reject military assistance from the north, "for the LORD is not with Israel—all these Ephraimites" (2 Chr. 25:7). The attempt by Hezekiah, following the Assyrian conquest, to win back the remnants

155

of the northern kingdom is met with derision by the northerners (2 Chr. 30:10–12). Those refugees who do take part are able to do so only because Hezekiah prays for them to be accepted (2 Chr. 30:18–20); just as in Ezra, separation from defilement is the prerequisite for full participation (Ezra 6:21). Further, as we have seen, the emphasis on Judah and Benjamin is found in Chronicles as well as in Ezra–Nehemiah (see the discussion above on 1 Chr. 7:6–12 and 21:6; and below, for example, on 2 Chr. 11:3 and 15:2), while Ezra as well as Chronicles can speak of the twelve tribes (Ezra 6:17; see Blenkinsopp 1988, 52). Ideally, "all Israel" meant the descendants of all twelve of Israel's sons. However, rebellion and apostasy had placed the ten northern tribes beyond the pale; only through repentance and ritual purification could they be included once more among the faithful congregation of the true Israel. In Chronicles as in Ezra–Nehemiah, the north lies outside the borders, both geographically and ideologically, "to which any loyal believer must adhere" (Ackroyd 1985, 164).

Throughout this section, one finds material regarding the kings of Judah that is unique to Chronicles, which again raises the question of the Chronicler's sources. On the one hand, much of this material is historically accurate: for example, Hezekiah's tunnel (2 Chr. 32:30), or the goal of Pharaoh Necco's campaign against Josiah (2 Chr. 35:20; see Klein 1994, 996). On the other hand, the Chronicler's reports concerning Judah's kings are not evenhanded. Successful building programs in 2 Chronicles appear to be restricted either to kings evaluated positively by the Chronicler (Rehoboam [?], 2 Chr. 11:5–12; Asa, 14:5–6; Jehoshaphat, 17:12–13; Hezekiah, 32:5), or, if a king is evaluated both positively and negatively, during the positive period of the king in question (Uzziah, 2 Chr. 26:9–10; Manasseh, 33:14; so Welten 1973, 42–52). Similarly, the five war reports in 2 Chronicles without a parallel in Kings come either during the reigns of "good" kings, or, if the report is mixed, during the positive part of the king's reign (Abijah, 2 Chr. 13:3–20; Asa, 14:9–15; Jehoshaphat, 20:1–30; Uzziah, 26:6–8; Jotham, 27:5–6; so Welten 1973, 166–175). One could argue, then, that the Chronicler freely composes stories, or uses his extrabiblical sources selectively, to prove his assertion that faithfulness leads to blessing. However, this argument proves circular. Does the Chronicler describe the kings he favors as engaging in building projects and being successful in war, or does he favor them, and assess them positively, *because of* their building activities and successes in war? One could well ask why, for example, such a minor figure as Abijah would have been evaluated positively by the Chronicler, "had he not had some previous account of his victory over the North" (Klein 1992, 998).

In the commentary that follows, the historicity of the Chronicler's claims for each of Judah's kings is evaluated. However, primary attention is given to the theology evident throughout the Chronicler's History. Here as elsewhere, Chronicles emphasizes the vital importance of Jerusalem's temple and its worship, and the necessity of heeding the divine word. The word of the Lord, in this section of Chronicles as in the book to this point, is expressed in Scripture and in the words of prophets (see the discussion of 1 Chr. 10:13, above). Those who heed the divine word demonstrate their faithfulness by support for David's liturgy and Solomon's temple and are blessed. Faithlessness, shown by rejection of the divine word, corruption of the liturgy, and defilement of the temple, leads to curse—and ultimately, to the ultimate curse of exile and destruction.

10:1—12:16
Rehoboam (///1 Kgs. 12:1–33; 14:21–22, 25–28)

Rehoboam's reign is ill-starred from the first. While David was declared king in his own capital at Hebron (1 Chr. 11:1), and Solomon at Jerusalem (2 Chr. 1:13), Rehoboam journeys to Shechem, an old northern sacred site some forty-one miles north of Jerusalem (see Josh. 24:1, 25; 1 Kgs. 12:25). Rather than the northern tribes coming to Rehoboam, Rehoboam goes to them. This suggests that his hold on the north was already tenuous, even before his reign had officially begun.

Among those who come to Shechem from "all Israel" is Jeroboam, son of Nebat. Jeroboam comes from Egypt, "where he had fled from King Solomon" (2 Chr. 10:2; see also 1 Kgs. 11:40). While the Chronicler has not retold the story of Jeroboam's revolt against Solomon, prompted by the word of the Lord from Ahijah the Shilonite (see 1 Kgs. 11:26–40), he clearly assumes that his readers are aware of it.

Jeroboam, joined by all Israel, places a condition upon fealty to Rehoboam: "Your father made our yoke heavy. Now therefore lighten the hard service of your father and his heavy yoke that he placed on us, and we will serve you" (10:4). But on the recommendation of the young hotheads on his staff, Rehoboam takes a hard line: "My father made your yoke heavy, but I will add to it; my father disciplined you with whips, but I will discipline you with scorpions" (10:14). In response to this brutal rejection of their concerns, "all Israel departed to their tents," rejecting David's line (10:16). "All Israel" clearly refers here to

157

all of the northern tribes, in contrast to "the people of Israel who were living in the cities of Judah," who remained loyal to Rehoboam (10:17). Both were "Israel" (Williamson 1977, 108–10)—at least, ideally. However, with the execution of Hadoram, Rehoboam's official in charge of forced labor in the north (10:18), northern Israel was "in rebellion against the house of David"—as it remains, says the Chronicler, "to this day" (10:19). The true, faithful Israel now became the southern kingdom of Judah, where Solomon's temple stood and David's descendants reigned (see 11:3).

In Kings, the grounds for Jeroboam's complaint ("Your father made our yoke heavy"; 1 Kgs. 12:4//2 Chr. 10:4) are clear. Solomon had used his own citizens as forced labor, to carry out his building projects (1 Kgs. 5:13–18)—as Jeroboam, whom Solomon had given "charge over all the forced labor of the house of Joseph" (1 Kgs. 11:28), was well aware. The Chronicler, however, denies that Solomon ever used Israelites as slave laborers (see 2 Chr. 2:2, 17–18; 8:7–10), which robs Jeroboam's revolt of its legitimacy. Rather than the justly motivated act of the oppressed northern tribes, the rebellion is an act of God, "so that the LORD might fulfill his word, which he had spoken by Ahijah the Shilonite to Jeroboam son of Nebat" (2 Chr. 10:15; see 9:29; 1 Kgs. 11:29–39). The reference to Ahijah's prophecy makes clear that God has broken up David's kingdom because of Solomon's faithlessness—even though the Chronicler does not describe the particular acts of faithlessness that resulted in this judgment. But while the rebellion of the northern tribes has been used by God, the rebellion itself remains illegitimate (see 2 Chr. 13:4–7). Perhaps for this reason, the Chronicler does not refer to Jeroboam's acclamation as king in the north (compare 1 Kgs. 12:20; see, though, 2 Chr. 13:1, where he is called "King Jeroboam"). Although God uses Jeroboam to punish David's descendants, his rebellion remains a sinful and tragic waste. The words of Matthew 26:24 regarding Judas express a similar ambiguity: "The Son of Man goes as it is written of him, but woe to that one by whom the Son of Man is betrayed! It would have been better for that one not to have been born." Just so, Jeroboam's revolt was the inevitable result of Solomon's sin and Rehoboam's arrogance. However, the Chronicler does not excuse Jeroboam from guilt or responsibility.

In response to Jeroboam's revolt, Rehoboam assembles an army of 180,000 troops from faithful Judah and Benjamin. However, before they can march, a word of the Lord comes to Shemaiah "the man of God" (11:2). Shemaiah's message is directed to Rehoboam and to "all Israel in Judah and Benjamin" (11:3; compare 1 Kgs. 12:23): now, "all Israel" refers to the southern tribes! Shemaiah's prophecy forbids Rehoboam's campaign to put down the rebellion: "Thus says the LORD:

158

You shall not go up or fight against your kindred. Let everyone return home, for this thing is from me" (11:4). Two features of Shemaiah's prophecy are particularly significant in Chronicles. First, the rebellion is again confirmed as ordained by God: "this thing is from me." In Chronicles, David's united kingdom did not collapse because of a rebellion for just cause. The kingdom collapsed because God made it collapse, just as Ahijah the Shilonite had said. Second, note that while 1 Kings 12:24 forbids battle against "your kindred the people of Israel," 2 Chronicles 11:4 reads simply "your kindred." As 11:3 suggests, while the Chronicler may follow convention and refer to the northern kingdom as "Israel," the *true* Israel is now Judah and Benjamin.

To this point, the Chronicler's account of Rehoboam's reign has faithfully followed 1 Kings 12:1–24. Now, the Chronicler turns to another source, unknown to us, for a list of fifteen fortified cities, built up for Judah's defense (2 Chr. 11:5–12). Although these fortifications are attributed by the Chronicler to Rehoboam's early reign, none defends against Israel to the north. All are within Judean territory, "strategically located to protect the kingdom of Judah from an attack on its western front" (Na'aman 1986, 5). It is more likely, then, that they belong to the time of Hezekiah's defense against the Assyrian invasion in 701 B.C. This probability may be strengthened by the fact that jars stamped with Hezekiah's royal seal are found in these same locations.

We will return to the subject of Hezekiah's wars and fortifications when we discuss Hezekiah's reign. For now, it is enough to note that the Chronicler evidently used as his source a list of fortified cities from Hezekiah's time, which he ascribed to Rehoboam. In its context in Chronicles, this list confirms the stability and security of the southern kingdom, from the very first. While Rehoboam did not retake the rebellious northern territories, this was because of the Lord's command through Shemaiah, and not because of military weakness or lack of preparation. Under Rehoboam, Judah remained strong and well defended (11:12).

Jeroboam's most infamous act was the establishment of shrines at Bethel and Dan, and the installation at these shrines of golden bull images (1 Kgs. 12:26–33). Second Chronicles 11:13–17 views Jeroboam's policies on religion from the Judean perspective. First Kings 12:31 states that Jeroboam "appointed priests from among all the people, who were not Levites" (see also 2 Chr. 11:14–15). Where, then, did the faithful priests and Levites go? According to the Chronicler, they came to Judah and Jerusalem (11:14). As for Jeroboam's shrines, Chronicles is even more vehement than Kings on their illegitimacy. What were worshiped there, according to the Chronicler, were "goat demons" (see Lev. 17:7; Isa. 13:21; 34:14): sinister denizens of ruins and waste places. The faithful

159

priests and Levites bring south with them "[t]hose who had set their hearts to seek the LORD God of Israel" (11:16). Their coming further legitimates the temple in Jerusalem as the one place of legitimate sacrifice "to the LORD, the God of their ancestors" (11:16); here, and here alone, are the ancient traditions of Israel's God truly preserved. That the faithful have all come south underlines, once more, the apostasy of the north, and lends even greater strength to Judah.

God's answer to Solomon's temple dedicatory prayer had affirmed that the security and wholeness of the land depend upon the faithfulness of its inhabitants (see 2 Chr. 7:14). Just so, for three years the faithful of Judah and Benjamin "made Rehoboam son of Solomon secure, for they walked for three years in the way of David and Solomon" (2 Chr. 11:17). Note that it was the people, not Rehoboam, who "walked . . . in the way of David" (compare 2 Chr. 29:2 and 34:2–3). Further, that there were *only* three years of security ominously portends an end to that security. In Rehoboam's fifth year, Shishak of Egypt invaded Judah; so, presumably, it was in Rehoboam's fourth year that his fall from faithfulness took place (see 2 Chr. 12:1–12; Braun 1988, 360).

But first, from yet another source, the Chronicler provides a list of Rehoboam's many wives, concubines, and children (2 Chr. 11:18–23). This list demonstrates God's blessing upon Rehoboam through those first three years. Similarly, in 1 Chronicles 14:3–7, God's blessing upon David was demonstrated by his large family. Also like David, Rehoboam wisely guards against squabbles over succession by naming his own successor, Abijah son of Maacah (2 Chr. 11:22; note that Abijah, like Solomon, was not the eldest son). However, the king does not sour the other princes toward his designated heir by showing Abijah undue favoritism. Important responsibilities are entrusted to all of Rehoboam's sons; also, "he gave them abundant provisions, and found many wives for them" (2 Chr. 11:23). Little wonder that, like his father Solomon, Rehoboam is commended for his wisdom (1 Chr. 11:23; but, see Sir. 47:23, where Rehoboam is condemned as "broad in folly and lacking in sense").

In Rehoboam's fifth year, his kingdom was invaded by Shishak of Egypt (2 Chr. 12:2//1 Kgs. 14:25)—evidently, Pharaoh Sheshonk I, founder of Egypt's Twenty-second Dynasty, who ruled from 945 to 924 B.C. We know of Shishak's invasion, not only from the biblical account, but also from the Bubastite Portal: a relief celebrating Shishak's victories located in the great temple to Amon at Karnak. The Chronicler says that Shishak's army included Ethiopians, Libyans, and the Sukkiim, who were Libyans from the western desert regions (12:3; Klein 1993, 661). The participation of Libyans in Shishak's army is historically probable, as Shishak was himself a Libyan nobleman (Horn and McCarter

1999, 130). Also accurate is the Chronicler's statement that Shishak "took the fortified cities of Judah and came as far as Jerusalem" (12:4). Although the Bubastite Portal inscription does not mention Jerusalem, Shishak apparently did head for that city initially. Among the cities conquered and laid waste by Shishak were Gezer, Aijalon, Beth-horon, and Gibeon, all located along "the usual northern approach" to Jerusalem (Horn and McCarter 1999, 132). Shishak's invasion was not directed at the southern kingdom, however; his armies ranged throughout Canaan, north and south, as well as eastward across the Jordan. According to the Bubastite Portal, Shishak's invasion was prompted by attacks from the east, threatening Egypt's frontier; perhaps this is a reference to Solomon's fortifications (Horn and McCarter 1999, 131). In any case, Shishak's invasion aimed to reestablish Egyptian hegemony over Canaan.

But the Chronicler, once more, is disinterested in politics. In Chronicles, Shishak's invasion, like Jeroboam's revolt, is God's doing: "When the rule of Rehoboam was established and he grew strong, he abandoned the law of the LORD, he and all Israel with him. . . . [B]ecause they had been unfaithful to the LORD, King Shishak of Egypt came up against Jerusalem" (12:1–2). Comfort, security and prosperity pose unanticipated threats to faithful living. When all is well, it is all too easy to trust in ourselves, to take credit for our blessings, and to forget that all we have is a gift from God (see 1 Chr. 29:14). This is a common theme in Scripture. For example, when the people of Israel were about to leave the dangers of the wilderness for the security of the land, Moses had warned them, "When you have eaten your fill, take care that you do not forget the LORD, who brought you out of the land of Egypt, out of the house of slavery" (Deut. 6:10–12).

Unfortunately, Rehoboam falls prey to the temptations of easy living, and forgets his God. As is usual in Chronicles, God's displeasure is communicated to the king by a prophet. Shemaiah comes to Rehoboam and his officials in Jerusalem, where they are gathered awaiting Shishak's assault, to announce, "Thus says the LORD: You abandoned me, so I have abandoned you to the hand of Shishak" (12:5).

That Jerusalem escaped conquest is doubtless due to Rehoboam's decision to pay tribute. Shishak "took away the treasures of the house of the LORD and the treasures of the king's house; he took everything. He also took away the shields of gold that Solomon had made" (12:9//1 Kgs. 14:26). However, the Chronicler attributes Jerusalem's deliverance to God. When Rehoboam and his officials respond to Shemaiah's message by humbling themselves and acknowledging the rightness of the Lord's actions, the Lord declares through Shemaiah, "They have humbled themselves; I will not destroy them, but I will grant them

161

some deliverance, and my wrath shall not be poured out on Jerusalem by the hand of Shishak" (12:7). Still, the Lord permits Shishak to reestablish Egyptian hegemony in the region, "so that they may know the difference between serving me and serving the kingdoms of other lands" (12:8). Sadly, Judah does not learn from this mistake, and so will be forced into submission to other foreign powers: Assyria, Babylonia, and ultimately Persia. But at least for the remainder of Rehoboam's reign, all is well. Despite diminished circumstances (bronze shields now replace the gold ones that had once decorated the king's palace; 12:10–11//1 Kgs. 14:27–28; see also 2 Chr. 9:15–16), "conditions were good in Judah" (12:12).

Chapter 12:13–16 briefly summarizes the reign of Rehoboam. He reigned seventeen years "in Jerusalem, the city that the LORD had chosen out of all the tribes of Israel to put his name there" (2 Chr. 12:13//1 Kgs. 14:21; see also Deut. 12:5–7). Only in Jerusalem can the Lord be rightfully worshiped; once more, the northern shrines of Jeroboam are implicitly rejected as illegitimate. Rehoboam's mother, we learn, was Naamah the Ammonite (2 Chr. 12:13//1 Kgs. 14:21; see also 1 Kgs. 14:31)—another foreign-born bride of Solomon's, not mentioned elsewhere by the Chronicler. The Chronicler's summary judgment on Rehoboam's reign is, not surprisingly, poor: "He did evil, for he did not set his heart to seek the LORD" (12:14). In Chronicles, Rehoboam's problem is inconstancy. He was easily swayed by his young advisors into a rash act that lost him the northern tribes, and was easily lulled by his first three years of blessing and prosperity into forgetting the Lord. Still, he did humble himself, so saving himself and his city, so that God's blessing did not entirely depart from his reign. Therefore he is buried in a place of honor, with his father Solomon and grandfather David, in the royal cemetery called "the city of David" (12:16; see 9:31).

The sources for Rehoboam's reign, according to 12:15, were "the records of the prophet Shemaiah and of the seer Iddo, recorded by genealogy." Shemaiah played a critical role in both of the major crises of Rehoboam's reign. It was he who spoke in the name of the Lord in opposition to Rehoboam's campaign to put down Jeroboam, and who spoke for the Lord during Shishak's invasion. Shemaiah, then, is appropriately named here. Indeed, "the records of the prophet Shemaiah" may refer to an actual document, perhaps the source of the Chronicler's information about Shishak's invasion. The second prophetic source, Iddo, was also mentioned as a source for Solomon's story (2 Chr. 9:29). If Iddo was indeed the nameless prophet who predicted the fall of the northern kingdom in 1 Kings 13, his mention in conjunction with Rehoboam's story is certainly appropriate. Evidently, it is to Iddo that the Chronicler ascribes the genealogical information in 11:18–23 (so Japhet 1993, 682–83).

13:1–22
Abijah (///1 Kgs. 15:1–2, 6–8)

The transition from Rehoboam to Abijah is smooth and uneventful: Rehoboam dies, and his designated heir Abijah becomes king (2 Chr. 12:16; see also 11:22). From the first, however, the great crisis of Abijah's short rule is foreshadowed. Abijah's reign is dated by the regnal years of Jeroboam, his enemy to the north (13:1). Throughout the reign of Rehoboam, he and Jeroboam had remained in a state of war (12:15). So, too, according to Kings, warfare between Judah and Israel was constant in Abijah's time (1 Kgs. 15:6–7; note that in 1 Kings, Rehoboam's heir is called Abijam).

However, in Chronicles, matters between Abijah and Jeroboam come to a head in one, great battle. The battleground is the slopes of Mt. Zemaraim: in Benjaminite territory, along the disputed border between Israel and Judah (see Josh. 18:22). Before the fighting begins, Abijah speaks: "Listen to me, Jeroboam and all Israel! Do you not know that the LORD God of Israel gave the kingship over Israel forever to David and his sons by a covenant of salt?" (13:4–5). Abijah addresses "all Israel." This could be a reference to the northern kingdom, Israel as opposed to Judah. However, it appears likely that both sides of the conflict are called upon here to remember and affirm God's covenant with David's line. The only other mention of a "covenant of salt" is in Numbers 18:19, where the priestly portion of the sacrifices is described as "a perpetual due; it is a covenant of salt forever before the LORD for you and your descendants as well." The parallel between David's line and Aaron's line is certainly appropriate in the thought world of Chronicles. The Chronicler defends the Davidic kings as the guarantors of right worship in Jerusalem, and as the guardians of Solomon's "house of sacrifice" (see 2 Chr. 7:12). God's covenant with David, then, is linked to God's covenant with Aaron.

In Abijah's speech, Jeroboam's revolt is explicitly condemned. Jeroboam is called a faithless servant, who had rebelled against his master; his fellow revolutionaries are dismissed as "certain worthless scoundrels" (13:6–7). These persons, Abijah declares, took advantage of his father's inexperience, "when Rehoboam was young and irresolute

163

and could not withstand them" (13:7). The Hebrew phrase rendered "irresolute" in the NRSV means literally "weak of heart." Rehoboam, remember, was condemned for his inability to "set his heart to seek the LORD" (12:14). This irresolution, Abijah claims, was taken advantage of by Jeroboam and his followers.

However, it is Jeroboam's apostasy that earns him Abijah's harshest condemnation. Jeroboam, he says, is counting on his numbers (800,000 to Abijah's 400,000) and on the power of his golden bulls to bring him victory. However, Abijah declares, the shrines of the golden bulls are served by false priests. All the true Aaronid priests, together with the Levites, have been driven out of the north. Jeroboam has replaced them with his own "priesthood," consisting of anyone who is able to come up with the price of the consecration offering (13:9; see also 11:14–15)! These not-priests, moreover, preside over the shrines "of what are no gods" (13:9). Spiritually, then, the northern kingdom is entirely bereft and powerless.

In contrast, Abijah states, Judah has abandoned neither the Lord nor the Lord's priesthood. In Jerusalem, true priests descended from Aaron and true Levites serve in the true temple, insuring that the Lord is truly worshiped, in the way that the Lord had revealed to Moses and David (13:10–11). The daily temple ritual is summarized in 13:11. Sacrifice and tending the temple lamps are priestly tasks (for priestly responsibility for the lamps, see Num. 8:2–3); however, preparing the rows of bread is in Chronicles a Levitical responsibility (see 1 Chr. 9:32; 23:29). As we have seen, priest and Levite serve side by side in Chronicles. Right worship is a combination of priestly and Levitical roles and responsibilities. In Jerusalem, the right liturgy is performed by the right personnel in the right temple; therefore, Abijah can declare, "we keep the charge of the LORD our God, but you have abandoned him" (2 Chr. 13:11).

Now, Abijah comes to his point: "See, God is with us at our head" (13:12). The true priests of Aaron's line are about to blow their war trumpets; once that has been done, and battle has been joined, there can be but one outcome. Abijah implores the northern army, "O Israelites, do not fight against the LORD, the God of your ancestors; for you cannot succeed" (13:12).

The claim that "God is on our side" has been used to justify far too many atrocities for us to be altogether comfortable with Abijah's rhetoric. Still, the God of the Scriptures doesn't sit back at a distance, watching human history unfold as an impartial referee. The creation, the Exodus story, and ultimately the Christian confession of the incarnation all proclaim that God is passionately involved in our world. Further, God takes sides—with the poor and needy against the rich and callous; with the oppressed against their oppressors. This is good news!

However, we must be very careful that this good news does not lead to spiritual arrogance. To say that God takes sides in the world is not, necessarily, to say that God is on *our* side—no matter who the "our" might be. The question rather must be, are we on God's side?

Abijah's speech winds up affirming Israel's ancient unity. After all, he reminds the northerners, the Lord is "the God of *your* ancestors" (emphasis added), not of ours alone. However, the rebellion of Jeroboam, and particularly the erection of the golden bulls, has effectively broken that unity. Now, if the people of "Israel"—that is, the northern kingdom—take up the sword against Judah, they will be rejecting their own heritage as Israel, and more importantly, they will find themselves opposing Israel's God.

While Abijah has been speaking, Jeroboam has begun deploying troops to launch a surprise attack from behind Judah's lines (13:13). Still, when the battle is joined, the northern kingdom's forces are soundly defeated. There is, of course, no question about the source of this victory: "God defeated Jeroboam and all Israel before Abijah and Judah. The Israelites fled before Judah, and God gave them into their hands" (13:15–16). Following up on his victory, Abijah lays claim to disputed Benjaminite territory along his northern border, including "Bethel with its villages and Jeshanah with its villages and Ephron with its villages" (13:19; see also Josh. 18:22). Jeroboam never recovers, and for the remainder of his brief, three-year reign, Abijah is secure.

Theologically, the Chronicler's point is clear. Abijah, who trusted in the Lord and preserved right worship in the right temple, was blessed with victory in battle, as well as with wives, sons, and daughters (13:21), and in death was honored by burial in the city of David (14:1). Jeroboam, who rejected the Lord, suffered defeat in battle and personal disaster: "the LORD struck him down, and he died" (13:20; cf. 1 Chr. 10:14, where Saul as well is said to have been killed by the Lord). It is possible that the Chronicler only means to say that Jeroboam's death was a judgment from God, not that he predeceased Abijah. However, Jeroboam does not appear again in Chronicles, suggesting that the Chronicler is emending his source at this point (in Kings, Jeroboam outlives Abijah; compare 1 Kgs. 15:8–9 with 2 Chr. 14:1). Abijah is the third and last Judean monarch for whom the Chronicler cites Iddo as a source (13:22; intriguingly, Iddo is called a prophet here, rather than a seer), doubtless because Iddo's message about the northern kingdom's defeat seemed appropriate in connection with Abijah's victory over Jeroboam.

But, was there an actual victory of Abijah over Jeroboam, or is this entire incident a literary creation by the Chronicler for theological effect? The account in Chronicles is certainly exaggerated. Israel's 500,000 casualties are a hundred thousand more than were suffered by

165

U.S. forces in the whole of World War II (Klein 1993, 664)! On the other hand, it is difficult to see why the Chronicler would have manufactured this story. In 1 Kings, Abijam is a minor figure, described in sharply negative terms as a virtual clone of his father (1 Kgs. 15:1–8). For the Chronicler to regard Abijah so positively, in sharp contrast to his source, surely would have required knowledge of traditions not found in Kings. Further, for the Chronicler to regard Abijah so positively, in the face of his early death, would have required a compelling motivation; we would expect the Chronicler to see Abijah's brief reign as a sign of divine disfavor. Probably, then, the Chronicler had access to a source that related a victory of Abijah over Jeroboam. The Chronicler has told that story, however, in his own way, and for his own purposes.

14:1—16:14
Asa (//1 Kgs. 15:11–24)

Asa is the first of four reforming kings in Chronicles, who set out to restore and purify Judah's worship (the others are Jehoshaphat, Hezekiah, and Josiah). The groundwork for this view of Asa was already present in the Chronicler's source, where the king "put away the male temple prostitutes out of the land, and removed all the idols that his ancestors had made" (1 Kgs. 15:12). Indeed, so great was Asa's zeal that he "removed his mother Maacah from being queen mother, because she had made an abominable image for Asherah" (1 Kgs. 15:13//2 Chr. 15:16). However, in Chronicles the account of Asa's reforms has been considerably reworked and expanded, so that it foreshadows the later reforms of Jehoshaphat, Hezekiah, and Josiah.

In the Chronicler's account, Asa's reign begins in peace and security: "In his days the land had rest for ten years" (14:1). Not since Solomon had rest been given to any of Judah's kings (see 1 Chr. 22:9). This renewed peace was the result of a restored faith. The specific actions Asa undertook—removing foreign altars and high places, breaking down pillars, hewing down sacred poles—are mostly in keeping with the stipulations of Deuteronomy (see, for example, Deut. 7:5; 12:3). The word translated "incense altar" in the NRSV of 14:5 does not appear in Deuteronomy or the Deuteronomistic History; however, in Leviticus 26:30 it appears, together with the high places, as falling under the Lord's condemnation: just as it does here in Chronicles. Asa's reforms, then, are in keeping with both priestly and Deuteronomic stipulations regulating worship.

In addition to doing away with the trappings of false worship, Asa's reforms also had a positive bent: Asa "commanded Judah to seek the LORD, the God of their ancestors, and to keep the law and the commandment" (2 Chr. 14:4). This directive is first given in Chronicles by David (1 Chr. 22:19; 28:8). Asa's fellow reformers Jehoshaphat (2 Chr. 17:7–9), Hezekiah (2 Chr. 30:6–9), and Josiah (2 Chr. 34:29–32; see Japhet 1993, 706–7), as true inheritors of David's greatness, also act as David did, to ensure right worship, faithful to Scripture and to ancient tradition.

In Chronicles, Asa is not only a religious reformer, but also an able military leader. Taking advantage of his years of peace and security, Asa acts to strengthen his kingdom, through the building of fortified cities (14:6) and the establishment of a large standing army (300,000 heavy infantry from Judah, and 280,000 archers from Benjamin: 14:8). However, he does not regard these as the ultimate source of Judah's security. Rather, Asa says, "the land is still ours because we have sought the LORD our God; we have sought him, and he has given us peace on every side" (14:7).

Both Asa's faith and his defenses are put to the test by an invasion from the south. Zerah the Ethiopian attacks Judah with overwhelming force: "an army of a million men and three hundred chariots" (14:9). In the face of this threat, Asa rightly turns to the Lord. This does not mean that Asa's military preparations have been needless, or worse, a sign of faithlessness. Repeatedly, the Scriptures urge us to trust in God. However, trusting in God does not mean that we abandon all caution, or that we cease to plan ahead. Later in the Chronicler's History, Nehemiah will go about his plans to rebuild Jerusalem carefully and cannily (see especially Neh. 2:9–20). In Matthew 10:16, Jesus warns his followers, "See, I am sending you out like sheep into the midst of wolves; so be wise as serpents and innocent as doves." Similarly, in Luke 14:25–33, Jesus urges those who would follow him first of all to plan ahead and count the cost, like a builder beginning work on a tower or a king preparing for war. Careful, constructive planning is an important first step if we really want to make a difference in our world.

But while Asa has prudently built up Judah's defenses, he does not rely on them alone. Rehoboam's wealth and security had led him to trust in his own power, and to abandon God's commandments (2 Chr. 12:1–2). However, like his father Abijah, Asa knows that strength, and victory in battle, come from the Lord. So, he prays, "O LORD, there is no difference for you between helping the mighty and the weak. Help us, O LORD our God, for we rely on you, and in your name we have come against this multitude" (2 Chr. 14:11). Asa's prayer recalls David's last words, where the ancestor of Judah's kings praised God as the

167

source of all "power and might" (1 Chr. 29:12). Like his ancestor David, Asa realizes that whatever strength he has to defend his kingdom comes from God, and so he trusts God for deliverance.

Asa's trust is vindicated. As in the days of his father Abijah, the Lord defeats Judah's enemy. Asa and his army pursue the fleeing host as far as Gerar to the south, sacking its villages and taking rich booty (2 Chr. 14:12–15). The entire host of Zerah the Ethiopian is slain.

As with Abijah's victory over Jeroboam, many features of this story are obviously exaggerated: in particular, the numbers are, once more, completely unrealistic. Further, the story has clearly been shaped to parallel Abijah's battle against the north. There, Jeroboam's forces outnumbered Abijah's two to one; here, Asa's 580,000 are met by Zerah's one million. After the Lord won the victory against Jeroboam, Abijah pursued his fleeing troops and gained territory to the north. After the Lord's victory against Zerah, Asa pursues and gains territory to the south. A parallel may also be intended between the invasion of Zerah the Ethiopian in Asa's reign and the invasion of Shishak the Egyptian in the days of Rehoboam. Faithless, vacillating Rehoboam was just barely saved, when he humbled himself in repentance before the Lord; even then, he was forced to give up all his treasure as tribute. Faithful Asa, however, prevailed over his southern enemy—indeed, the Lord eliminated all of Zerah's vast host.

On the face of it, then, there appears to be little if any historical basis for the Chronicler's account of Asa's victory over Zerah the Ethiopian. Indeed, history knows of no Ethiopian leader called "Zerah." However, while the Chronicler has definitely used this incident for his own theological purposes, it is difficult to see why he would have invented it—particularly given the importance he ascribes to the rest the land enjoyed in Asa's reign. Some scholars, noting that Ethiopians made up a part of Shishak's invasion force (see 2 Chr. 12:3), have proposed that Zerah was a mercenary in Shishak's employ, left behind with a contingent of Ethiopian troops to defend Egypt's northern frontier (Bright 1981, 235). Another possibility is that Zerah and his army were not Ethiopian at all. The word rendered "Ethiopian" in the NRSV is actually "Cushite." Cush can refer in the Hebrew Bible to Ethiopia; but it also may be used for a region in northern Arabia, sometimes called Cushan (see Hab. 3:7). "Zerah" cannot be an Egyptian name (that language has no equivalent for the letter "z"), but it is a good Semitic name: for example, one of Judah's sons (1 Chr. 2:4, 6) and two Levites (1 Chr. 6:21 and 41) were called "Zerah." Zerah could have been an Arab raider out of the southern deserts: a possibility supported by the mention of tents and camels in the description of Asa's victory

168

(2 Chr. 14:15). Perhaps, then, there is a historical core to the account of Zerah's invasion.

Following his victory over Zerah, a word of the Lord comes to Asa through the prophet Azariah son of Oded (2 Chr. 15:2–7). Azariah's prophecy begins by reaffirming the theme of Chronicles: "Hear me, Asa, and all Judah and Benjamin: The LORD is with you, while you are with him. If you seek him, he will be found by you, but if you abandon him, he will abandon you" (2 Chr. 15:2). These words are strikingly similar to what we have called the "golden text" of Chronicles, in David's second farewell speech: "If you seek him, he will be found by you; but if you forsake him, he will abandon you forever" (1 Chr. 28:9). Their positive truth has already been borne out in the early years of Asa's reign: God has responded to Asa's faithfulness and reforming zeal by giving rest to his land, and by giving Asa victory over his enemies. The negative truth of these words, as we will see, is borne out in the latter part of Asa's reign.

Azariah goes on to recall Israel's past before kingship: "For a long time Israel was without the true God, and without a teaching priest, and without law" (2 Chr. 15:3). These three essential elements were linked in the reign of David, Israel's first true king, who sought the Lord in truth, in obedience to Torah, and established the priests Zadok and Abiathar in Jerusalem. The responsibility of the priests to teach Torah is found throughout Scripture (for example, Lev. 10:10–11; Deut. 33:8–10; 2 Kgs. 17:27–28; Ezek. 44:23–24). However, before David established the teaching priesthood, the people could not learn Torah, and so could not seek the true God. "In those times," Azariah declares, "it was not safe for anyone to go or come, for great disturbances afflicted all the inhabitants of the lands. They were broken in pieces, nation against nation and city against city, for God troubled them with every sort of distress" (2 Chr. 15:5–6). This lawless period, vividly depicted in the book of Judges (especially Judg. 17—21), is succinctly summarized in Judges 21:25: "In those days there was no king in Israel; all the people did what was right in their own eyes." The Hebrew phrase rendered "it was not safe" in the NRSV of 2 Chronicles 15:5 could be literally rendered "there was no peace" (Hebrew *shalom*). In the spontaneous prophetic pronouncement of Amasai, David was promised *shalom* by the spirit of the Lord (1 Chr. 12:18). Azariah's prophecy regards the time before David as a time when there was no *shalom* in the land.

The turning point came "when in their distress they turned to the LORD, the God of Israel, and sought him"; then, "he was found by them" (2 Chr. 15:4). As we have seen, seeking the Lord is a persistent theme in Chronicles, and refers specifically to worship before the temple.

169

David led Israel in seeking after the ark of the Lord, to bring it to Jerusalem (1 Chr. 13:3; 15:13), and directed Israel's leaders to "seek the LORD your God" by building the temple (1 Chr. 22:19). So now, Azariah builds to the climax of his oracle: "But you, take courage! Do not let your hands be weak, for your work shall be rewarded" (2 Chr. 15:7). These words call to mind 1 Chronicles 22:13 and 28:10, where David exhorts Solomon to take courage, be strong, and act by building the temple.

But Azariah's words also represent a clear allusion to Zechariah 8:9–13, an oracle that begins, "Thus says the LORD of hosts: Let your hands be strong," and ends "Do not be afraid, but let your hands be strong" (Japhet 1993, 721). Zechariah's oracle describes the time before the rebuilding of the temple as being much like the lawless period before kingship (Zech. 8:10; compare 2 Chr. 15:5–6). However, the Lord assures Zechariah, now that the temple has been built, "there shall be a sowing of peace; the vine shall yield its fruit, the ground shall give its produce, and the skies shall give their dew; and I will cause the remnant of this people to possess all these things" (Zech. 8:12). The point is plain. In the Chronicler's story, Asa is being encouraged to engage in temple-building and reform, an exhortation that he understands and follows. At the same time, the Chronicler's community is being presented with the parallel between ancient times and their own. Like David, they had been called to bring the land out of lawlessness and Godlessness by heeding the Torah of the true "teaching priests." Like Solomon, they had built the Lord's temple. Now, like Asa, they are called to preservation and reformation.

While the Chronicler may have known of a prophet named Azariah son of Oded (note that the name "Oded" appears again in connection with a prophetic figure, in 2 Chr. 28:9–15), the oracle of Azariah is certainly the Chronicler's own composition. Similarly, in ancient Greek histories, or for that matter in the Deuteronomistic History, we often find speeches placed in the mouths of ancient worthies, expressing essential themes and ideas. Azariah's oracle is a marvelous example of the Chronicler's use of Scripture. The oracle is a *pastiche* of references and allusions to biblical prophecy. In addition to the allusion to Zechariah 8:9–13, cited above, 2 Chronicles 15:3 is structured following Hosea 3:4 (both involve a long period of lawlessness, due to the lack of three "elementary institutions"); 15:4 reflects Hosea 5:15; and 15:7b alludes to Jeremiah 31:16 (for these and other prophetic allusions in Azariah's oracle, see Japhet 1993, 719–21). It is doubtful that the Chronicler was actually flipping through these texts to assemble Azariah's oracle, in cut-and-paste fashion. Rather, he was so steeped in prophetic literature and idioms that the language of the Scriptures flowed easily from his pen.

John Wesley called himself *homo unius libri:* "a man of one book," the Bible. Although he rarely cited explicit text references, Wesley's sermons are an intricate web of biblical quotes and allusions. Similarly the Chronicler, immersed in Israel's ancient Scriptures, thought biblically, and his compositions resonate with biblical images and ideas.

Galvanized by Azariah's words, Asa undertakes sweeping reforms. From all Judah and Benjamin, as well as from newly annexed territory to the north which had formerly belonged to Ephraim (evidently from an unspecified northern campaign of Asa; see 2 Chr. 17:2), idols are rounded up and destroyed (2 Chr. 15:8)—even the Asherah image belonging to Asa's mother (15:16). Asa also undertakes repairs to the altar of burnt offering, thus becoming the first king since Solomon to work on the temple precincts (15:8). Finally, the king summons his people to a covenant renewal ceremony. In addition to all Judah and Benjamin, Asa invites "those from Ephraim, Manasseh, and Simeon who were residing as aliens with them, for great numbers had deserted to him from Israel when they saw that the LORD his God was with him" (15:9). While this verse might be understood to show an openness to the northern kingdom, note first that those invited were no longer northerners: they had left their own people "when they saw that the LORD his God was with [Asa]." Second, these former northerners are described as "aliens"; a term typically used for non-Israelites living in the land! In fact, the northern kingdom of Israel is here regarded as if it were a foreign country.

Asa's covenant renewal ceremony takes place in the third month of his fifteenth year (15:10). The ceremony may be connected with the Festival of Weeks, or Pentecost, which also takes place in the third month. Since Asa's covenant renewal ceremony is dated to his fifteenth year, the Chronicler probably imagines that Asa's reforms and repairs took about four years, after his decade of rest was interrupted by the war with Zerah. The huge sacrifice offered (seven hundred oxen and seven thousand sheep) is said to come "from the booty they had brought," suggesting to some scholars that his victory over Zerah was still fresh (15:11; so Elmslie 1916, 231). But this booty could have come from Asa's unspecified northern campaign (see 15:8; 17:2), which could also have been the source of the northern deserters in 15:9.

Asa's covenant is a curious combination of Chronistic and Deuteronomic concepts: "They entered into a covenant to seek the LORD, the God of their ancestors, with all their heart and with all their soul" (15:12). The expressions "seek the Lord" and "God of the ancestors" are, of course, typical of Chronicles. However, to love God, or seek God, or follow God's commandments "with all [one's] heart and with all [one's] soul" is typical Deuteronomic language (see, for example, Deut.

171

6:5; Josh. 22:5; 1 Kgs. 2:4). Of particular interest for understanding Asa's reform is Deuteronomy 4:29. After describing the exile that will result from Israel's idolatry (Deut. 4:25–28), Moses offers words of hope: "From there you will seek the LORD your God, and you will find him if you search after him with all your heart and soul" (Deut. 4:29). Asa's covenant, then, speaks to the situation of the Chronicler's community. They had been delivered out of exile, as Deuteronomy 4:29 promised; now, it behooved them, like Asa, to renew their dedication to the Lord.

Asa and his people take an oath to seek the Lord "with all their heart and with all their soul" (15:12). The Hebrew word *lebab*, or "heart," is used elsewhere to express entire commitment, just as we speak in English of giving something or someone our "wholehearted" support (see the discussion above on 1 Chr. 12:17 and 38). Hebrew *nephesh*, here translated "soul," usually means simply "life"; to seek God with all one's life would also mean entire commitment. In the Hebrew Bible, these two words, used together, always appear in the context of commitment to a covenant. Indeed, Asa and his people are so fervently and passionately committed, they declare that anyone who does *not* swear to seek the Lord is to be killed (15:13)!

The violent undercurrent of fanaticism in Asa's covenant, which calls for the slaughter of anyone, "young or old, man or woman," outside their committed group, is deeply disturbing—particularly in our day, which has seen so much violence motivated by religion. Certainly, unrestrained emotionalism has its dangers. Recognizing this, the apostle Paul urged that in worship "all things should be done decently and in order" (1 Cor. 14:40). However, it may be that the danger contemporary Western Christianity needs to fear more is that our faith should lose its passion and vision. The distinguished Southern writer Flannery O'Connor once said that she was a Catholic, "not like someone else would be a Baptist or Methodist but like someone else would be an atheist" (quoted by Wood 1994, 1076). Surely, our churches could use some of that passionate intensity, which in our time is more usually associated with extremists or unbelievers.

Asa's ceremony is a joyous, rollicking celebration, "with shouting, and with trumpets, and with horns" (15:14). The fervor and depth of the community's commitment is the cause of this celebration: "All Judah rejoiced over the oath; for they had sworn with all their heart, and had sought him with their whole desire, and he was found by them" (15:15). This verse of Chronicles inspired Philip Doddridge to compose his famous hymn, "O Happy Day, That Fixed My Choice" (*United Methodist Hymnal* 1989, no. 391), which celebrates the bliss of a life committed to the Lord:

It's done, the great transaction's done!
   I am my Lord's and he is mine;
He drew me and I followed on,
   charmed to confess the voice divine.
Now rest, my long-divided heart,
   fixed on this blissful center, rest.
Here have I found a nobler part;
   here heavenly pleasures fill my breast.

As in the service of worship following David's last prayer (1 Chr. 29:20–22), there is in Asa's service nothing of lugubriousness or long-faced sacrificial solemnity! One is reminded of Jesus' parable of the hidden treasure: "The kingdom of heaven is like treasure hidden in a field, which someone found and hid; then in his joy he goes and sells all that he has and buys that field" (Matt. 13:44). The committed life is a joyous life.

In 2 Chronicles 15:16, the Chronicler resumes use of 1 Kings (2 Chr. 15:16–19//1 Kgs. 15:13–15). Now, we learn that Asa's reforms were not completely successful, as "the high places were not taken out of Israel" (15:17). This could conflict with the Chronicler's earlier statements about Asa's reforms (14:3–5). Note, however, that earlier, it was in Judah that Asa succeeded in removing the high places; perhaps the Chronicler's point is that the northern kingdom of Israel with its high places remains outside Asa's purview (in contrast to the later reforms of Hezekiah and Josiah, which will at last include the northern sites; see 31:1; 34:6–7). Indeed, Israel's threatening presence to the north will emerge in the latter part of Asa's reign as the cause of his downfall. Still, the Chronicler credits Asa with the best intentions (15:17) and records his acts of personal and filial piety (15:18). The Lord responds to Asa's faithfulness by blessing his land with rest (15:15); indeed, for the next twenty years, Judah is free from war (15:19).

In Asa's thirty-sixth year, Baasha of Israel attacks from the north (2 Chr. 16:1–6//1 Kgs. 15:16–22). Indeed, Baasha's forces advance to within ten miles of Jerusalem, and begin to establish a fortified stronghold at Ramah. Asa responds to this threat by calling upon Ben-hadad of Damascus for help. Asa's request that Ben-hadad's kingdom (Aram, or Syria, to the north of Israel) intervene is based on an appeal to a treaty between Jerusalem and Damascus, perhaps dating back to Solomon (16:3); however, Asa also sweetens the deal by sending Ben-hadad "silver and gold from the treasures of the house of the LORD and the king's house" (16:2). Asa's diplomacy is successful: Ben-hadad attacks Israel's northern border, forcing Baasha to withdraw from Ramah. Asa's forces then occupy Ramah, and using the materials Baasha had left behind, fortify Geba and Mizpah as Judean strongholds (16:6).

173

While the Chronicler places the conflict over Ramah in Asa's thirty-sixth year, the Deuteronomistic History claims that Baasha died in Asa's twenty-sixth year (1 Kgs. 16:8). Indeed, it may well be that the unspecified northern campaign implied in 15:8–11 *was* the conflict with Baasha, and that the Chronicler has shifted his account of the conflict to the later part of Asa's reign while leaving these earlier mentions intact. Attempts to resolve the issue historically (for example, by suggesting that the "thirty-fifth year" is dated from the division of the kingdoms; so Williamson 1982, 256–58) fail to appreciate the Chronicler's literary and theological purpose. In the final form of the narrative in Chronicles, Asa's reign is divided into two parts: a period of faithfulness, resulting in blessing, and a period of faithlessness, resulting in curse. Each part is associated with a prophet, and a military campaign: Azariah addresses Asa following his victory in the south over Zerah; Hanani speaks in response to Asa's handling of Baasha. For the first thirty-five years of his reign, Asa had proven the truth of Azariah's words: "If you seek [God], he will be found by you" (15:2). But now, in his last six years, Asa's reign will prove the other side of that message: "if you abandon him, he will abandon you."

For the Chronicler, Asa's solution to the threat posed by Baasha is not a clever bit of diplomatic maneuvering, but an act of faithlessness. The oracle of Hanani the seer reveals God's judgment on Asa (16:7–9). God's intention, according to Chronicles, had been to give Asa victory, not only over Israel, but over Aram as well! The God who had given Asa victory over Zerah's overwhelming force would have been ready and willing to support him once again, "[f]or the eyes of the LORD range throughout the entire earth, to strengthen those whose heart is true to him" (16:9; a quote from Zech. 4:10).

When I was a child, I remember singing a terrifying hymn with the refrain, "Watching you, watching you, every day mind the course you pursue; / Watching you, watching you, there's an all-seeing eye watching you" (*Best Loved Songs and Hymns* 1961, no. 192). God's omnipresence can seem oppressive (see Ps. 139:7–12)! In Chronicles, however, God's all-seeing eye is a source of strength and confidence. Similarly, Jesus speaks of the Father's attentiveness even to the fall of a sparrow (Matt. 10:29). Whatever the situation, wherever we are, God knows, and can be trusted to give strength and deliverance. However, Asa did not trust the Lord, and so missed his chance at victory; further, the Lord declares, "from now on you will have wars" (2 Chr. 16:9). For the Chronicler, the constant conflict between the north and Judah during Asa's reign described in Kings (1 Kgs. 15:16) came about as a result of Asa's faithlessness.

Asa's broken faith with God manifests itself in broken faith with his people. He puts Hanani in stocks, and treats his own people with cruelty (16:10). Asa's cruel treatment of his people may be a reference to the forced labor used to build his northern fortifications (16:6); in Chronicles, native Israelites have not been used as forced laborers before this. In the end, Asa suffers personally for his faithlessness: his feet become severely diseased. Yet, even then, the king does not turn to the Lord, but relies in vain on doctors (16:12). So, after a life of faithfulness and blessing, Asa turns from the Lord, and dies. The Chronicler records elaborate funeral arrangements for Asa: "They laid him on a bier that had been filled with various kinds of spices prepared by the perfumer's art; and they made a very great fire in his honor" (16:14). He is buried in a rock-hewn tomb among his ancestors, in the city of David. The honor paid to Asa in his death suggests that he was loved and respected; evidently, the faithlessness of his last six years did not completely outweigh the faithfulness of his first thirty-five. Still, he stands as an object lesson of the central message of Chronicles: faithfulness leads to blessing, faithlessness to curse.

17:1—21:10
Jehoshaphat (//1 Kgs. 15:24b; 22:1–36, 41–50a)

The reign of Jehoshaphat begins with an account of his northern defenses. To guard against the threat that his father had faced, Jehoshaphat "strengthened himself against Israel" (17:1). This barrier against the north is theological as well as military. Jehoshaphat "walked in the earlier ways of his father"—that is, as Asa had walked for his first thirty-five years (17:3). Specifically, this means that he rejected the Baals, "but sought the God of his father and walked in his commandments, *and not according to the ways of Israel* " (17:4, emphasis added). For this reason, the Lord gives Jehoshaphat security and wealth. Jehoshaphat responds to the Lord's blessing by undertaking reforms like those of his father (17:6; compare 14:3–5).

Jehoshaphat's reforms involve not only the elimination of outlying shrines, but also a vigorous program of religious education (17:7–9). Significantly, this program involves not only priests (two: Elishama and Jehoram; recall the importance of teaching priests in Azariah's oracle, 15:3), but also nine Levites and five lay people from Jehoshaphat's official administration. The presence of laity on Jehoshaphat's commission

175

suggests that this list comes from a source, rather than being a creation of the Chronicler's, since the Chronicler's History stresses the teaching role of Levites and priests (35:3; Neh. 8:7–8; so Myers 1965, 99). These sixteen are sent throughout Judah to teach, "having the book of the law of the Lord with them" (2 Chr. 17:9): evidently, the Torah. Similarly, later in the Chronicler's History, Ezra the scribe will be sent "to make inquiries about Judah and Jerusalem according the the law of your God, which is in your hand" (Ezra 7:14). Once more, the importance of written Scripture to the Chronicler is apparent.

Jehoshaphat's faithful adherence to the word of the Lord has consequences, not only within his kingdom, but beyond his borders: "The fear of the LORD fell on all the kingdoms around Judah, and they did not make war against Jehoshaphat" (17:10). His neighbors to the south and west, Philistia and the Arab tribes, pour their wealth into Judah as tribute (17:11), making Jehoshaphat the first Davidic king since Solomon to receive the obeisance of a foreign power (compare 9:22–28). Jehoshaphat's security is further ensured by an army of 1,160,000 troops, quartered in fortified cities all over Judah (17:14–19). The number of Jehoshaphat's troops is certainly exaggerated. However, it helps the Chronicler make a point about God's faithfulness to Judah, and to David's line. The loss of the northern tribes has not resulted in the weakening of Judah. Quite to the contrary, the number of troops controlled by Judah's kings has increased steadily, from Rehoboam's 180,000 to Abijah's 400,000 to Asa's 580,000 to, now, Jehoshaphat's 1,160,000. Judah's faithful kings have gone from strength to strength, and from victory to victory.

The list of Jehoshaphat's military commanders, like the list of sixteen persons commissioned to teach the law, is likely derived from an old Judean source. Among these commanders, Chronicles lists "Amasiah son of Zichri, a volunteer for the service of the LORD" (17:16). Like the presence of laity in Jehoshaphat's teaching commission, Amasiah's leadership role suggests something important about Jehoshaphat's regime. That laity and civilians would want to serve speaks well for the fervor and enthusiasm Jehoshaphat's reforms brought to Judah. That such persons should be *permitted* to serve speaks strongly for the openness of Jehoshaphat's administration.

Like his father Asa, Jehoshaphat in his downfall is linked to the northern kingdom. However, while Asa had fallen from faith by conflict with the north, Jehoshaphat's fall involves an alliance with Israel. In Chronicles, Jehoshaphat has no need to enter into this alliance. God has already demonstrated that, as long as Jehoshaphat is faithful, his kingdom will be secure. Evidently, as in the case of Rehoboam, Jehoshaphat's wealth and security lulled him into faithlessness (18:1; compare 12:1). The alliance between the two kingdoms is sealed by the marriage of Ahab's daughter Athaliah to Jehoshaphat's son Jehoram, a marriage that will have dreadful repercussions for Judah (2 Kgs. 8:18, 26; see also 2 Kgs. 11:1–20//2 Chr. 22:10—23:21). Whereas before, Jehoshaphat had "strengthened himself against Israel" (17:1), now he joins in feasting and celebration with his northern neighbor (18:2). Indeed, when Ahab asks Jehoshaphat's support in his war with Aram to reclaim Ramoth-gilead, Jehoshaphat replies, "I am with you, my people are your people. We will be with you in the war" (2 Chr 18:3//1 Kgs. 22:4).

The account of Ahab and Jehoshaphat's joint campaign against Aram "is the only time in Chronicles that a lengthy text from 1 or 2 Kings dealing with a northern king is included" (Klein 1993, 668; see 2 Chr. 18:3–34//1 Kgs. 22:4–40), and therefore is deserving of close scrutiny. It is, however, the exception that proves the rule. The Chronicler does not use this account to inform the reader about the doings of the northern kingdom. Rather, the story of Jehoshaphat and Ahab illustrates how even good kings like Jehoshaphat could fall into faithlessness, by placing their trust in foreign alliances rather than in the Lord. Of course, for the community of the Chronicler, Jehoshaphat's misplaced trust in political alliances foreshadowed the disastrous reigns of Jehoiakim and Zedekiah, whose trust in alliances with Egypt and other kingdoms led them to rebel against Babylon, with fatal consequences for Judah and Jerusalem. Positively, this story also illustrates the Lord's faithfulness, and willingness to deliver when true repentance is offered.

Jehoshaphat asks Ahab to seek a word from the Lord before going to battle. While commendable, this request is too little too late. Jehoshaphat has already committed himself and his troops to Ahab's Aramean campaign; whatever the answer might be, he cannot back out now. When Ahab obligingly trots out four hundred court prophets, who all agree in predicting victory, Jehoshaphat skeptically asks if there is "no other prophet of the LORD here of whom we may inquire" (18:6). Ahab summons Micaiah son of Imlah, though he warns Jehoshaphat that Micaiah "never prophesies anything favorable about me, but only disaster" (18:7).

Meanwhile, another prophet, Zedekiah son of Chenaanah, performs a prophetic sign act. Wielding horns of iron, he declares, "Thus says the LORD: With these you shall gore the Arameans until they are destroyed" (18:10). Zedekiah's symbolic prophecy is not that different from sign acts performed by other prophets, such as Hosea's marriage to a prostitute (Hos. 1:2–9), Jeremiah's yoke (Jer. 27:1–15), or Ezekiel's toy siege of Jerusalem (Ezek. 4:1–3). Such sign acts are more than mere object lessons. The prophet is imitating the acts of God, and so participating in what God is bringing about. Zedekiah's sign act, then, would have been understood as enacting the victory that God would give to Ahab. The imagery of the horns of iron may have been suggested by the bull imagery of the northern Israelite shrines (see 11:15).

Now, Micaiah comes on the scene. At first, his message apes that of the four hundred. But when Ahab, either sensing that Micaiah is holding back or stung by the prophet's sarcasm, insists on the truth, Micaiah tells it: "I saw all Israel scattered on the mountains, like sheep without a shepherd; and the LORD said, 'These have no master; let each one go home in peace' " (18:16). The image of the king as a shepherd, and the people as his flock, was common in the ancient Near East. It is often found in the Hebrew Bible (for example, Ezek. 34:1–31 and Ps. 23), and stands behind the New Testament use of this image (for example, Luke 15:3–7 and John 10:1–18). Micaiah inverts this comforting image of strength, however. He describes the people of Israel in chaos, bereft of their leader—like sheep *without* a shepherd (an image used to great effect in Matt. 9:35–38). Ahab will die at Ramoth-gilead.

Of course, this poses a difficult question. When prophets disagree, how is one to know which one to heed? Micaiah declares that Ahab will be killed in battle; Zedekiah, that he will return victorious. Both Micaiah and Zedekiah claim to be prophets. Both speak in the name of the Lord. Indeed, Micaiah does not deny that Zedekiah's words, and those of the four hundred court prophets, are inspired by a spirit from God. However, he describes a vision of the heavenly court, where the Lord, who wishes to destroy Ahab, asks for a spirit to go and entice the king into fighting at Ramoth-gilead (18:18–22). It is this lying spirit that speaks through Zedekiah and his fellows; in fact, however, "the LORD has decreed disaster for you" (18:22).

Zedekiah is furious. Slapping Micaiah's face, he demands, "Which way did the spirit of the LORD pass from me to speak to you?" (18:23). Zedekiah sincerely believes in his own prophecy, and in its supernatural origin. Who then are Ahab and Jehoshaphat to believe? Deuteronomy 18:21–22 uses accurate prediction as the test of true prophecy. But in practice, this test would have been difficult to apply, since the truth of any prediction can only be known by hindsight. By this standard, one could not tell in advance whether a prophetic word was true or false. Time would prove Micaiah's prediction to be accurate. But Ahab, naturally, believes Zedekiah's promises of victory—and marches off to die.

178

We live in a complex, pluralistic society, surrounded by multiple, conflicted messages and messengers. For us, spiritual discernment is more important, and yet also more difficult, than it has ever been. 1 John 4:1 advises, "Beloved, do not believe every spirit, but try the spirits to see whether they are from God." All spirituality is not equal, however sincere or well-intentioned. There is definitely such a thing as bad faith, which deceives rather than enlightens, hurts rather than heals. For the early Christian teacher whose voice we hear in 1 John, the test of truth in spiritual discernment is a matter of both content and of intention: "every spirit that confesses that Jesus Christ has come in the flesh is from God" (1 John 4:2). Faithfulness to Christ, and to the love and purpose of God manifested in Christ (see 1 John 4:7–8), is the evidence of spiritual truth.

But, discerning "Christlikeness" is no simple task. Our personal, subjective spiritual experience cannot be ignored. However, as the example of Zedekiah illustrates, sincerity and passion are no guarantees of truth; one can be sincerely wrong! Likewise, in our Western technological society, the successes of reason may prompt us to think that the scientific method is the final arbiter of truth. However, science has been so successful largely because of the modesty of its aims. Science serves admirably as the means for discerning how the objective world works. However, science does not, and indeed cannot, answer questions of meaning and purpose. Like experience, reason is an essential part of our spiritual discernment; after all, truth must be intelligible. However, the realm of the spirit exceeds the grasp of human reason.

In their quest for truth and understanding, Christians appeal to Scripture and tradition as checks and balances on the vagaries of individual experience and the limitations of human reason. Intriguingly, these are the final arbiters of truth for the Chronicler as well. As we have seen, Chronicles consistently stresses the importance of the word of God, manifest in prophetic word and in sacred text. Further, the Chronicler understands the Lord as the "God of the ancestors"; the experience of God in Israel's past has surpassing relevance for the Chronicler's own community. Sincere people of faith will still disagree, of course. However, the foundational word of God in the whole of Scripture, and the continuity of the experience of the people of God through the ages, enable us to find common ground, despite our disagreements.

Ahab proceeds with his planned assault on Ramoth-gilead, ordering Micaiah imprisoned until his return. Micaiah declares, "If you return in peace, the LORD has not spoken by me" (18:27). Perhaps sobered by this grim send-off, Ahab decides on a stratagem for surviving the battle: "The king of Israel said to Jehoshaphat, 'I will disguise myself and go into battle, but you wear your robes.'" (18:29). Clearly, Ahab is not interested in the welfare of his ally! Following orders, Jehoshaphat goes into battle as Ahab's decoy. Ahab's caution proves warranted, for the king of Aram has instructed his troops to seek out the king of Israel; further, his decoy strategy appears successful, as the Syrian charioteers, taking Jehoshaphat for Ahab, come at him in force (18:30–31).

Now that his alliance with Ahab is about to get him killed, Jehoshaphat comes to his senses. As he should have done from the beginning, Jehoshaphat calls upon the Lord for help—and he is delivered. God causes the charioteers to recognize that Jehoshaphat is not the king of Israel, and they wheel off to look for Ahab (18:31). This divine rescue is so much in keeping with the Chronicler's purpose that one is tempted to find here an expansion of the account in 1 Kings (note that the MT of 1 Kgs. 22:32 makes no mention of the Lord's help); however, the best old LXX texts also mention the Lord helping Jehoshaphat, so it is probable that here, as throughout this chapter, the Chronicler is faithful to his source (so Klein 1974, 50).

Meanwhile, Ahab's attempt to elude God's judgment has proven fruitless. Entirely by accident, an arrow strikes Ahab through a gap in his armor, and he is mortally wounded. Just as Micaiah had said he would, Ahab dies at Ramoth-gilead (18:33–34).

Jehoshaphat has learned his lesson: he cannot rely upon political alliances for his security, but must rely wholly on the Lord. However, as is typical of Chronicles, this message is driven home by a prophetic pronouncement. Once Jehoshaphat returns to his palace in Jerusalem, he is approached by Jehu, the son of Hanani the seer (19:1). Evidently, this is the same Hanani who had pronounced the Lord's judgment on Jehoshaphat's father Asa when Asa forsook the Lord and placed his faith in political alliances (16:7–9). Now, Hanani's son bears the same message to Asa's son: "Should you help the wicked and love those who hate the LORD? Because of this, wrath has gone out against you from the LORD" (19:2). Evidently, the divine wrath was averted from Jehoshaphat because of his reforms (19:3); it would, however, strike at his heirs. Jehoshaphat's son, grandson, and daughter-in-law will all die unmourned and rejected, without a memorial among the descendants of David (chaps. 21—23).

Unlike his father Asa, who had ordered Hanani put in stocks, Jehoshaphat takes the message of Jehu, Hanani's son, to heart. Throughout his whole kingdom, from Beer-sheba to the south to "the hill country of Ephraim" on his northern border, Jehoshaphat "brought them back to the LORD, the God of their ancestors" (2 Chr. 19:4). By installing a system of Levitical judges, under priestly oversight, throughout the land of Judah, Jehoshaphat made it possible for his people to understand and live by the law (2 Chr. 19:5–11). In doing this, Jehoshaphat was revitalizing the system of Levitical judges established, according to Chronicles, by David himself (see 1 Chr. 23:4; 26:29–32). As the shift from trial by village and tribal elders to a complex judicial system administered by royal officials certainly took place in Israel during the monarchy, the Chronicler may well have found this system of judicial officials in an authentic, Judean source (Bright 1981, 251).

Jehoshaphat exhorts his judges, "Consider what you are doing, for you judge not on behalf of human beings but on the LORD's behalf; he is with you in giving judgment" (19:6). Therefore, the judges must take care to rule fairly and impartially and refuse all bribes. Indeed, they are held responsible for ensuring that the people know and follow the law, "so that they may not incur guilt before the LORD." Should the judges fail in this responsibility, the guilt of the people will fall on their heads (19:10).

Those who know the word of the Lord must share what they know. The Lord warned the prophet Ezekiel, "If I say to the wicked, 'You shall surely die,' and you give them no warning, or speak to warn the wicked from their wicked way, in order to save their life, those wicked persons shall die for their iniquity; but their blood I will require at your hand" (Ezek. 3:18). This same, awesome responsibility is expressed in Matthew 16:19, where the church is entrusted with the keys of the kingdom of heaven: "whatever you bind on earth will be bound in heaven, and whatever you loose on earth will be loosed in heaven" (see also Matt. 18:18). Should we fail in our responsibility to share the gospel, and sit on the keys with which we have been entrusted, the church ends with us. As the apostle Paul wrote, "But how are they to call on one in whom they have not believed? And how are they to believe in one of whom they have never heard? And how are they to hear without someone to proclaim him?" (Rom. 10:14). Like Jehoshaphat's judges, we who have received the word of the Lord bear the responsibility of sharing that word in our communities.

Jehoshaphat, unlike his father, has learned to place his faith in the Lord alone. This newly restored faith is put to the test by an attack from the south and east. It is unclear what nations take part in this assault. Second Chronicles 20:1 identifies Jehoshaphat's assailants as "the Moabites and Ammonites, and with them some of the Meunites," the latter group likely coming from Meon, a settlement near Hebron in the southern reaches of Jehoshaphat's kingdom. (Later, Uzziah will also have trouble with these people; see 2 Chr. 26:7.) But, in 20:2, Jehoshaphat is told, "A great multitude is coming against you from Edom, from beyond the sea [that is, the Dead Sea]," and in 20:10, the enemies are identified as "the people of Ammon, Moab, and Mount Seir," the latter being a clear reference to Edom (see the discussion of 1 Chr. 1:38–42, above). Edom, Moab, and Ammon were three minor kingdoms bordering on ancient Israel: Ammon just across the Jordan to the east, Moab to the southeast, across the Dead Sea, and Edom to the far southeast. All had a complex relationship with Israel and Judah, being sometimes vassals,

181

sometimes allies, and sometimes enemies. According to Deuteronomy 23:3–6, Ammonites and Moabites living in the land, "[e]ven to the tenth generation" were barred from the worshiping congregation, while Edomites could be included after three generations among the people Israel (Deut. 23:8).

The complex relationships among these kingdoms make it probable that Jehoshaphat did have some conflict with Ammon, Moab, and Edom (note the reference to "the acts of Jehoshaphat, and his power that he showed, and how he waged war" in 1 Kgs. 22:45). However, the Chronicler's account of Jehoshaphat's wars is theology, not military history. In response to this invasion of his kingdom, Jehoshaphat does just what he should do: "he set himself to seek the LORD, and proclaimed a fast throughout all Judah" (20:3). The people respond to Jehoshaphat's call by streaming into Jerusalem to pray before the temple.

Jehoshaphat leads the assembly in a prayer that begins by proclaiming the Lord's sovereignty over all the peoples of the earth (20:6). God's dominion over the nations was demonstrated in ancient days when the Lord expelled the peoples that had formerly inhabited Palestine, and gave the land to Israel in accordance with the ancient promise to Abraham (20:7). This memory will prove particularly significant later in the prayer. But first, Jehoshaphat recalls the construction of Solomon's temple, and particularly Solomon's prayer: "If disaster comes upon us, the sword, judgment, or pestilence, or famine, we will stand before this house, and before you, for your name is in this house, and cry to you in our distress, and you will hear and save" (20:9; a neat, concise summary of 2 Chr. 6:3–42). In keeping with God's promises at the temple's dedication, Jehoshaphat and his people assemble at the temple in a time of national emergency, to call upon the Lord.

Having earlier mentioned God's destruction of the people in the land, Jehoshaphat now cites God's gracious forbearance toward Ammon, Moab, and Edom, who had been spared in the days of the conquest (20:10; see Num. 21—25). But now, "they reward us by coming to drive us out of your possession that you have given us to inherit" (20:11). Jehoshaphat, acknowledging his helplessness, gives the entire matter over to the Lord—which is exactly what he ought to do, from the Chronicler's perspective.

As was promised, the Lord responds to Jehoshaphat's prayer. The answer comes in dramatic fashion, in the sight of all Judah, men, women, and children alike. The spirit of the Lord comes upon "Jahaziel son of Zechariah, . . . a Levite of the sons of Asaph" (20:14; for the prophetic role of Asaph, see 1 Chr. 25:2), who declares: "Listen, all Judah and inhabitants of Jerusalem, and King Jehoshaphat: Thus says the LORD to you: 'Do not fear or be dismayed at this great multitude; for the battle is not yours but God's" (20:15). Jehoshaphat is told where the armies will assemble, so that his forces can march to meet them. However, he is not to fight them; rather, the Lord says, "take your position, stand still, and see the victory of the LORD on your behalf, O Judah and Jerusalem" (20:17). This is a clear allusion to Exodus 14:13, where Moses instructs the Israelites at the Red Sea, "Do not be afraid, stand firm, and see the deliverance that the LORD will accomplish for you today" (note that the same Hebrew word is translated "victory" in 20:17, and "deliverance" in Exod. 14:13). Just as God had fought for Israel against Egypt at the Red Sea (see Exod. 14:14, 25), so God will fight now against Ammon, Moab, and Edom. To this good news, the people respond with worship, praise, and song, led by the Levitical singers (20:18–19).

The advance of Jehoshaphat's host is more a liturgical procession than a military maneuver. Jehoshaphat exhorts the people, "Listen to me, O Judah and inhabitants of Jerusalem! Believe in the LORD your God and you will be established; believe his prophets" (20:20). It is intriguing that here, belief in the Lord is linked to belief in the prophetic word. This exalted view of prophecy is reminiscent of Amos 3:7: "Surely the Lord GOD does nothing, without revealing his secret to his servants the prophets." In Chronicles, it is through Scripture and through the prophets that God's will is made known: indeed, as the Chronicler ascribes his authoritative sources to prophetic authors, the authority of text and prophet may be seen as one and the same. Before the army marches a specially appointed choir, singing the song of God's faithfulness to the worshiping congregation of Israel: "Give thanks to the LORD, for his steadfast love endures forever" (20:21; see the discussion of this refrain in 2 Chr. 5:13, above).

Meanwhile, the Lord has prompted a division among Judah's attackers. Ammon and Moab turn first on Edom, and then upon one another. By the time Jehoshaphat and his people arrive, they find no one left to fight—only a battlefield filled with corpses. Once more, the implied allusion is to the Red Sea, where, after the Lord's single-handed victory over Pharaoh, "Israel saw the Egyptians dead on the seashore" (Exod. 14:30). Jehoshaphat and the people of Judah "found livestock in great numbers, goods, clothing, and precious things, which they took for themselves until they could carry no more" (20:25). This plundering of the dead calls to mind the account of God's eschatological victory over Gog in Ezekiel 39, after which Israel "will despoil those who despoiled them, and plunder those who plundered them" (Ezek. 39:10).

After three days, when the dead armies have been thoroughly despoiled, the people assemble at the Valley of Beracah (which sounds like the Hebrew word for "blessing"), to bless the Lord and prepare for their return to Jerusalem. Like the march against Judah's enemies, the

183

journey back home is a festal procession; the people return to the Jerusalem temple rejoicing, "with harps and lyres and trumpets" (20:28). News of the Lord's victory spreads throughout the region; as a result, once again "[t]he fear of God came on all the kingdoms of the countries" (20:29; compare 17:10), and Jehoshaphat was once more left in peace. Jehoshaphat's security is assured, not by his military might or by foreign alliances, but by faith in the Lord demonstrated through acts of piety.

For the concluding summary of Jehoshaphat's reign, the Chronicler resumes his use of Kings (20:31–37//1 Kgs. 22:41–49). Jehoshaphat receives a good grade for his twenty-five years of service: "He walked in the way of his father Asa and did not turn aside from it, doing what was right in the sight of the LORD" (20:32//1 Kgs. 22:43). Little wonder that he is buried with honor, in the city of David (21:1). The Chronicler's only reservation about Jehoshaphat's reign is that the high places were not removed, so that the people were not yet entirely committed to the Lord (20:33//1 Kgs. 22:43; however, see 2 Chr. 17:6). The prophetic source claimed for the life of Jehoshaphat is "the Annals of Jehu son of Hanani, which are recorded in the Book of the Kings of Israel" (20:34). Intriguingly, "Israel" is here substituted for "Judah" in 1 Kings 22:45, suggesting that Jehoshaphat was the true king, not of Judah alone, but of all Israel (see also 2 Chr. 21:2). Jehu, of course, was the prophet who chastised Jehoshaphat for his northern alliance.

Indeed, the story of Jehoshaphat ends with a postscript condemning another alliance with the northern kingdom: a maritime trade project out of Ezion-geber, in cooperation with Ahaziah of Israel. The Chronicler's source also mentions this enterprise, and its failure (see 1 Kgs. 22:47–49). However, in Chronicles the project fails because it is based on a foreign alliance, as the prophetic witness reveals: "Eliezer son of Dodavahu of Mareshah prophesied against Jehoshaphat, saying, 'Because you have joined with Ahaziah, the LORD will destroy what you have made.' And the ships were wrecked and were not able to go to Tarshish" (20:37). The moral of Jehoshaphat's story, then, is, "Avoid foreign alliances. Put your trust entirely in the Lord."

21:1b–20
Jehoram (//1 Kgs. 22:50b; 2 Kgs. 8:17–24)

The reigns of Jehoram, Ahaziah, and Athaliah (2 Chr. 21:1—23:21) constitute a single story arc in Chronicles, in which the grim consequences of Jehoshaphat's alliance with Ahab are spun out (a similar position is held by Johnstone 1998, 121–22). In sharp contrast to Abijah, Asa, and Jehoshaphat, these three monarchs are absolutely condemned by the Chronicler. All follow the ways of Israel, and do evil. In their reigns, Judah is led into idolatry, and so into decline. All three, as a result, die shameful deaths, and are denied a burial place among the sons of David—indeed, not until Jotham dies will a king of Judah once more be buried in the tombs of the Davidic kings. Finally, for none of these three does the Chronicler provide a statement of his sources, even when such a listing is provided in Kings (see 2 Kgs. 8:23). Chronicles denies that there is any memorial, in monument or in text, for any of these among David's faithful descendants. The Chronicler's dismissive words regarding Jehoram could as easily apply to all three: "He departed with no one's regret" (21:20).

Jehoram's reign begins in blood. Chronicles records the names of Jehoram's younger brothers, whom Jehoshaphat had honored with rich gifts and control over fortified cities throughout Judah (21:2–3). But Jehoram, evidently seeing his siblings as a threat to his own power, has his brothers put to death as soon as he has become established on the throne. He also murders certain "officials of Israel." Doubtless these are not northern officials, but members of the Judean bureaucracy loyal to Jehoshaphat's other sons; note that Jehoshaphat himself is called "the king of Israel" in the MT of 21:2 (the NRSV has chosen to follow some texts of the LXX, as well as the Syriac and the Vulgate, and read "Judah" here; however, the more difficult reading of the MT is probably the original text).

At this point, Chronicles resumes its use of the narrative in Kings (2 Kgs. 8:17–22//2 Chr. 21:5–10). Jehoram's wickedness, already evident in his treatment of his own brothers, now finds an explanation. In direct contrast to his father Jehoshaphat, who "walked in [God's] commandments, and not according to the ways of Israel" (2 Chr. 17:4), Jehoram "walked in the way of the kings of Israel, as the house of Ahab had done; for the daughter of Ahab was his wife." (21:6). Jehoram's downfall is his marriage to Athaliah, arranged by Jehoshaphat and Ahab to seal their ill-fated alliance (see 2 Chr. 18:1).

Still, despite the wickedness of Jehoram and Athaliah, God's faithfulness to David's house remained intact, "because of the covenant that he had made with David" (2 Chr. 21:7; see 1 Chr. 17:1–15; 2 Chr. 13:5). God's promise to David is expressed poetically as "a lamp to him and to his descendants forever" (2 Chr. 21:7//2 Kgs. 8:19). The reference is to 1 Kings 11:36, where, despite the loss of the northern tribes in Jeroboam's revolt, David's descendant is promised "one tribe [clearly,

185

Judah], so that my servant David may always have a lamp before me in Jerusalem." One is reminded also of 2 Samuel 21:17, where David's heroes swear to their leader, "You shall not go out to battle any longer, so that you do not quench the lamp of Israel." There, David's friends act to protect their king, and so safeguard his line; here, it is God who acts (or rather, refrains from acting in judgment) in order to preserve the light of hope and promise that David's line represents. In Chronicles, a parallel may also be implied to the lamps in the temple, whose maintenance by the priests was "a statute forever throughout your generations" (Lev. 24:1–4; see also 2 Chr. 13:11). Once more, the covenants of David and Aaron are intertwined.

Jehoram's breach of faith cannot negate God's promise regarding David's house; it does, however, have direct consequences for Jehoram's reign. Edom rebels against Jehoram, as it had earlier rebelled against Jehoshaphat (see 2 Chr. 20:2, 10); this time, however, the rebellion succeeds. Edom, joined in revolt by Libnah, would never again be subject to Judah (21:10; but see 25:11–20). According to the Chronicler, this took place "because he had forsaken the LORD, the God of his ancestors" (21:10). Just as security had come to Jehoshaphat through faithfulness and obedience to the divine word, insecurity and rebellion strike Jehoram because of faithlessness and disobedience.

The full scope of Jehoram's faithlessness, and its consequences, is expressed in 2 Chronicles 21:11–20 (material unique to Chronicles). While both Asa and Jehoshaphat were praised for removing the high places of Judah, Jehoram "made high places in the hill country of Judah, and led the inhabitants of Jerusalem into unfaithfulness, and made Judah go astray." For this final rebellion against God, there are consequences not only for the southern kingdom, but for Jehoram personally. These consequences are spelled out in a message from the prophet Elijah (21:12–15).

Elijah has not been mentioned in the text of Chronicles to this point; he was, after all, a prophet of Israel, not of Judah. However, as the great prophetic foe of the northern king Ahab, his wife Jezebel, and their family (see 1 Kgs. 16:29—19:21; 21:1–29; 2 Kgs. 1:1–18), it is certainly appropriate that Elijah should rebuke Ahab's son-in-law. Elijah's prophetic word is expressed in writing, as a letter. Historically, written prophecy did not emerge until the eighth century, with the prophets Amos and Hosea in the north, joined by Micah and Isaiah in the south. But in Chronicles, where the word of God is encountered in written Scripture, even the words of the old prophet Elijah are expressed as a text. Like the prophecy of Azariah (15:2–7), the letter of Elijah was composed by the Chronicler. However, Elijah's condemnation of Jehoram, Ahab's son-in-law, presupposes knowledge of that prophet's opposition to Ahab's family; once more, the Chronicler assumes that his audience has read Kings.

Elijah's letter condemns Jehoram for "walking in the way of the kings of Israel" (21:13; compare 21:6), particularly his father-in-law Ahab, and for the murder of his brothers. Because of this, the Lord declares, a great plague will come upon Jehoram's people, his family, and his possessions, while he himself will die of a loathsome and painful disease of the bowels (21:14–15). The plague, it develops, is Philistia and Arabia: nations that had been loyal to Jehoshaphat (17:11), but now turn violently upon the kingdom of his son. Jehoram's treasures are stolen, and his wives and sons (save Athaliah and the youngest son, Jehoahaz) are kidnapped. Such a raid is historically plausible, particularly in the wake of Edom's successful revolt. The capture of Jehoram's family does not require the capture of Jerusalem; his wives and sons may have been living in the outlying regions (so Myers 1965, 122). In Chronicles, this story serves a dual purpose. First, the Philistine and Arab invasion demonstrates conclusively the Lord's judgment upon Judah, as well as upon Jehoram. That the culprits were nations who had formerly been friendly to Jehoram's father Jehoshaphat intensifies the contrast between righteous Jehoshaphat and sinful Jehoram. Further, the reference to Ethiopia in 21:16 calls to mind Zerah's assault during Asa's reign, turned aside because of Asa's faithfulness; now, Jehoram's faithlessness has resulted in a successful southern assault on Judah. Second, the story of the loss of Jehoram's wives and sons explains how it was that Jehoram's youngest son was able to succeed his father to the throne, as the Chronicler's source in Kings makes clear (2 Kgs. 8:25; note that 2 Chr. 22:1 states that Jehoram's older sons were killed by Arab troops in an assault on Jehoram's camp).

Jehoram's final illness is described in gory detail (2 Chr. 21:18–19). Christian readers may be reminded of the grisly deaths of Judas and Herod Agrippa in Acts, which are likewise meted out for egregious acts of impiety (Acts 1:16–20 and 12:20–23). Jehoram's humiliation does not end with his painful death, however. In Chronicles, he is expressly denied the honors that had been paid to his ancestors, specifically the funeral fire (2 Chr. 21:19; compare especially 16:14). Indeed, the Chronicler even denies Jehoram a burial plot among the other kings of David's line; while his grave is in the city of David, he is expressly not buried "in the tombs of the kings" (21:20; compare 2 Kgs. 8:24). It is a fitting end for a wicked king.

22:1–9
Ahaziah (//2 Kgs. 8:25—10:14)

Sadly, the evil consequences of Jehoshaphat's ill-fated northern alliance do not end with Jehoram's death. As Jehoram's only surviving son, Ahaziah takes the throne. The names "Jehoahaz" (21:17) and "Ahaziah" are alternate versions of the same name, both meaning "the Lord has grasped." The use of both names in Chronicles suggests that the Chronicler is referring to multiple sources, as do the alternate accounts of how Ahaziah came to the throne (compare 21:16–17 with 22:1) and the inconsistency regarding Ahaziah's age: if, as 21:20 says, Jehoram died at forty, his youngest son could scarcely have been forty-two when his reign began (compare 2 Kgs. 8:26, which says that Ahaziah was twenty-two).

Like his father Jehoram, Ahaziah followed the ways of the north, specifically the ways of Ahab—after all, his mother was Athaliah, Ahab's daughter, and his advisors were the counselors of Ahab's son Jehoram, king of Israel (22:3–4). As an ally of Jehoram, Ahaziah goes to war with Israel against Aram, and following the battle visits the wounded king in Jezreel (22:5–6). According to 22:7, Ahaziah's visit at precisely this time is God's doing, since it puts the king of Judah directly into the path of Jehu's purge. Ahaziah, who had followed the way of Ahab, is to be destroyed together with all of Ahab's line.

The Chronicler condenses the story of Jehu's purge into three brief, pithy verses (22:7–9; compare 2 Kgs. 9:1—10:14). The account in Chronicles, though sharply abridged, substantially agrees with the account in Kings. In both, Jehu has been "anointed to destroy the house of Ahab" (22:7; see 2 Kgs. 9:1–13). Likewise in both, Ahaziah and Jehoram ride out to meet Jehu, not knowing his grim purpose (22:7//2 Kgs. 9:21). Finally, in both accounts, Jehu kills "the officials of Judah and the sons of Ahaziah's brothers, who attended Ahaziah," as well as Ahaziah himself (22:8; compare 2 Kgs. 10:12–14). However, the Chronicler departs substantially from his source with regard to Ahaziah's death and burial. In Kings, Ahaziah is mortally wounded while fleeing Jehu; following his death in Megiddo, his officers take Ahaziah's body back to Jerusalem for burial "with his ancestors in the city of David" (9:27–28). But in Chronicles, Ahaziah is hiding from Jehu in Samaria. He is deliberately sought out, brought before Jehu, and executed. For the sake of his grandfather Jehoshaphat, "who sought the LORD with all his heart"

(22:9), Jehu gives Ahaziah the honor of a decent burial. However, like his father before him, he is denied a tomb among the sons of David. Because Ahaziah and Jehoram followed the ways of Israel, and "did what was evil in the sight of the LORD" (22:4), they are given no memorial among the faithful kings of Judah.

22:10—23:21
Athaliah, and Jehoiada's Coup (//2 Kgs. 11:1–20)

The death of Ahaziah creates a crisis of succession in Judah, as "the house of Ahaziah had no one able to rule the kingdom" (22:9). Into this power vacuum steps Athaliah, wife of Jehoram, mother of Ahaziah, and daughter of Ahab—Judah's first, and only, ruling queen. To consolidate her position, Athaliah sets out to eliminate everyone with a legitimate claim to the throne. Only Joash, infant son of Ahaziah, survives the slaughter, thanks to the courage of his aunt Jehoshabeath, who entrusts the child to her husband, Jehoiada the priest. So, Joash grows up in the confines of the temple, while for six years Athaliah rules what is by rights his kingdom (22:10–12//2 Kgs. 11:1–3).

According to 2 Chronicles 23:1, when Joash turned seven, "Jehoiada took courage," and began preparing for rebellion. The Hebrew word translated "took courage" in the NRSV is the same term used to describe the consolidation of power by Solomon (2 Chr. 1:1) and Jehoshaphat (2 Chr. 17:1) at the beginning of their reigns. Clearly, the child Joash cannot act. It is up to his foster father Jehoiada the priest to do what Joash would do, were he of age.

The Chronicler lists the names of the military commanders who took part in Jehoiada's coup, evidently drawing once more on special Judean royalist sources either inaccessible to or ignored by the Deuteronomists. In Kings, the coup is restricted, realistically, to the military. However, the Chronicler's idea of kingship, and of the prerogatives of priests and Levites, requires a different view. In Chronicles, the military commanders are sent throughout Judah, to gather together the Levites and the elders of the clans and summon them to the house of God in Jerusalem. So it is "the whole assembly" that makes covenant to acknowledge Joash as king (2 Chr. 23:3), just as all Israel had acclaimed David (1 Chr. 11:1). Joash's right to the throne is grounded in God's promises to David (2 Chr. 23:3; see 1 Chr. 17:10b–14), a right the assembly freely acknowledges. Indeed, not since David's time have

189

the people made a covenant with their king (see 1 Chr. 11:3). The reign of Joash promises a fresh start, a new dawn after the darkness of Jehoram, Ahaziah, and Athaliah (sadly, this promise is only partially fulfilled; see 2 Chr. 24:1–27).

Having gained the assent of the assembly, Jehoiada proceeds with his plot to overthrow Athaliah. His plan is a clever one. Joash, recall, has been hidden for six years in the temple precincts. The coup is set for the changing of the guard on the sabbath, when the temple courts will be thronged with worshipers (23:5) and numerous troops will be in motion to and from their stations surrounding the temple and the palace. Taking advantage of the confusion, the commanders are to see to it that none of their troops actually go off duty, greatly increasing the size of the guard (23:8). Then, some troops are to slip into the temple and surround the child king. So, when Joash comes out of the temple, he will have a ready-made defense force strong enough to hold off any attacks until he has been officially crowned, in the sight of the congregation.

The necessity for the Levites' participation in the coup now becomes clear. The Chronicler assumes that the guards posted around the temple precincts are Levites (so Childs 1979, 648–49; see 1 Chr. 15:18, 23–24; 26:1–19). The purpose of this Levitical guard is stated in 23:6: "Do not let anyone enter the house of the LORD except the priests and ministering Levites; they may enter, for they are holy, but all the other people shall observe the instructions of the LORD" (for the responsibility of the Levites to regulate access to the sanctuary, see also Num. 3:7–8; 8:19). Since only priests and Levites were normally permitted to enter the temple precincts, the troops guarding Joash must also be Levites (2 Chr. 23:7). This warlike, martial role is in keeping with old ideas of Levitical service in the Torah (see Exod. 32:25–29; Deut. 10:18). The captains of the Levitical troops are armed with "the spears and the large and small shields that had been King David's" (2 Chr. 23:9): evidently, a reference to votive offerings of weapons taken in battle (so Japhet 1993, 833; see, for example, 1 Chr. 18:7; 26:26). Whether such weapons would actually have been usable or not is beside the point. Just so, when David began his rebellion against Saul, he was armed with the sword of his old adversary Goliath, taken from its place of honor in the temple at Nob and given to him by the priest Ahimelech (1 Sam. 21:8–9). Joash's supporters, once more, hark back to the glories of David in their support of David's descendant.

Jehoiada's plan succeeds. Surrounded by well-armed Levites, Joash is brought out before the people and crowned as king. Faithfully following his source in Kings, the Chronicler briefly describes the rites of coronation: Jehoiada and his sons crown Joash, anoint him with oil, and give him the *'edûth* (translated "covenant" in the NRSV; see 23:11//2 Kgs. 11:12). The crown is self-explanatory; however, some comment about the other elements of Joash's coronation is in order.

In the Hebrew Bible, people and things are anointed with oil as a sign of commissioning to special service (for example, Exod. 30:26–30; Isa. 45:1), or of special honor (for example, Ps. 23:5). The title "anointed one," or "messiah," can be used for the high priest (Lev. 4:3, 5, 16; 6:22), and rarely, for the community (see the discussion of 1 Chr. 16:22//Ps. 105:15, above). Preeminently, however, the king is the anointed one, set aside for honor and for service as God's particular representative (see, for example, Ps. 2).

In the early Christian community, Jesus came to be understood as the inheritor of the honor and service invested in David's line. The title "Christ," given to Jesus by the early church, derives from the Greek word *chrisma*, meaning oil or unguent: something that one smears on. *Christos*, then, would mean "one smeared," presumably with oil: a literal rendering of the Hebrew *meshiah* ("messiah"). "Jesus Christ" is more than a name. It is a confession, perhaps the earliest confession of the Christian community—the confession that in Jesus, the hopes and dreams invested in David's line have found fulfillment.

Of course, it is also a confession that transforms, indeed subverts, expectations. In debate with the Pharisees (who believed in a literal future messiah), Jesus asserts that Messiah is *not* the "Son of David"— or, at any rate, that Messiah is more than that (Matt. 22:42–45). In Mark's Gospel, what it means to be the Christ is understood, not in terms of kingship, but in terms of humble service (Mark 10:45), and ultimately, of suffering and death: only when Jesus is dead on the cross does a human being at last confess, "Truly this man was God's son!" (Mark 15:39). It does not do, then, to claim in triumphalist fashion that the New Testament supersedes the Old. The Christian confession that Jesus is the Christ emerges out of the ancient faith of Israel. However, it does not invalidate that faith (see Matt. 5:17–18 and Rom. 9—11, especially 11:26–29).

The Hebrew term *'edûth* is something of a puzzle. The NRSV translation "covenant" seems to imagine a legal document confirming the covenant between Joash and the assembly, by which he was acknowledged as Judah's ruler (see 2 Chr. 23:3). The JPSV renders *'edûth* as "insignia," apparently imagining some symbol of kingship. However, elsewhere in the Hebrew Bible, the term typically refers to the Ten Commandments (for example, Exod. 31:18; 34:29). Perhaps, in connection with the coronation of a king, *'edûth* refers to the copy of the law that, according to Deuteronomy, was to be given to the king (Deut.

191

17:18–20). The king was to study and live by this law, so that he could govern justly and lead his people by example. We have already seen how far short of this ideal Israel's kings could fall. However, in comparison with our contemporary cynicism about public service, that the ideal was upheld at all is remarkable.

The people respond to Joash's coronation enthusiastically, and acclaim him as their king. Only now, upon hearing their cheers from her palace (significantly, the queen is not at the temple on the sabbath), does Athaliah realize that something unusual is going on. Running to the temple, she sees "the king standing by his pillar at the entrance" (2 Chr. 23:13): apparently, one of the free-standing bronze pillars, either Jachin or Boaz, beside which the king was customarily crowned (2 Kgs. 11:14; for the association of the king with the pillar, see also 2 Kgs. 23:3//2 Chr. 34:31, and possibly Judg. 9:6). Athaliah hears the cheering of the crowds and the blowing of the trumpets, led by the Levitical singers and musicians. Her cries of "Treason! Treason!" fall on deaf ears; Jehoiada orders Athaliah, and any who wish to follow her, put to the sword (2 Chr. 23:13–15).

Once more, Jehoiada makes a covenant, "between himself and all the people and the king that they should be the LORD's people" (23:16; see 15:12, where Asa and his people make a similar covenant). The explicit inclusion of Jehoiada as a party to the covenant underlines once more the connection between priest and king in Chronicles. The consequence of this covenant is a thorough reformation of the religious life of Judah. Negatively, the Baal temple (evidently built by Athaliah) is destroyed, Baal's priest Mattan is executed, and every vestige of the Baal cult is eliminated (23:17). Positively, the neglected service of the temple of the Lord is reactivated; priests (to take charge of the sacrifices), Levitical singers and musicians, and gatekeepers are all put in place, in accordance with the commands of David and with the Torah of Moses (23:18–19; compare 2 Kgs. 11:18b). Religiously as well as politically, the reign of Joash promises to be a new beginning.

Like his source in Kings, the Chronicler has little to say about Athaliah, apart from her merciless seizure of the throne and her execution following Jehoiada's coup. Some contemporary interpreters find here evidence of virulent sexism in Chronicles and Kings. To be sure, the thought of a woman in the royal palace would have been galling to the Chronicler (see the above discussion of 2 Chr. 8:11, where Solomon builds a separate house for his Egyptian wife). However, the rejection of Athaliah in both Chronicles and Kings, to the point of virtually ignoring the six years of her reign, has more to do with her religion and her lineage than her gender. Athaliah's construction of a temple to Baal, together with her absence from the temple on the sabbath, indicates

192

that she worshiped Baal rather than the Lord, like her mother Jezebel (see also 2 Chr. 24:7). Further, God had promised rulership in Jerusalem to David's descendants. Clearly, Athaliah could make no claim to being in David's line; indeed, she was only able to seize the throne after slaughtering all legitimate claimants—with the exception, of course, of Joash.

The motif of the threatened child and its marvelous rescue is common in world folklore; in Scripture, it features prominently in the stories of Moses (Exod. 2:1–10) and Jesus (Matt. 2:13–23). This could throw doubt on the historical accuracy of the story of Joash, or at least, on the legitimacy of his descent. One could ask how Joash could have escaped Athaliah's notice during her slaughter of Ahaziah's heirs, or how likely it is that he could have survived so long undetected. However, Chronicles faithfully records the account of Joash's survival found in Kings. The Chronicler obviously assumes its veracity, and we have no compelling evidence that falsifies this report. Such questions, moreover, are quite beside the point. The story of Jehoiada's coup is a thrilling affirmation of God's faithfulness. The Lord, who had promised to preserve David's line forever, will not let "the lamp of Israel" go out (see 2 Sam. 21:17; 2 Chr. 21:7).

24:1–27
Joash (//2 Kgs. 11:21—12:21)

Like the reign of Asa, the reign of Joash falls into two parts in Chronicles: a time of faithfulness, while Jehoiada was still alive (compare 2 Chr. 24:2 with 2 Kgs. 12:2), and a time of unfaithfulness, after the old priest dies. Just as it was Jehoiada who ousted Athaliah and brought Joash to the throne, in Chronicles it is Jehoiada who truly rules during the early part of Joash's reign, first doubtless as regent, later as Joash's closest advisor. God's blessing upon Joash during this time is shown, as is typical in Chronicles, through the birth of children (2 Chr. 24:3; see, for example, 1 Chr. 14:3–7; 2 Chr. 11:18–23). Once Jehoiada is dead, however, Joash falls into apostasy and becomes a murderer. Significantly Joash, like his father, grandfather, and grandmother, is not buried among the descendants of David (2 Chr. 24:25; compare 2 Kgs. 12:21); Jehoiada, however, is (2 Chr. 24:16).

193

The first independent, kingly act of Joash described by the Chronicler is his decision to restore the temple, which had suffered from neglect and from outright theft throughout the reign of Athaliah, "that wicked woman" (2 Chr. 24:7). Joash turns to the Torah for what should be done. Exodus 30:12–16 and 38:25–26 stipulate that a regular contribution be taken from the people for the support of the shrine (see also Neh. 10:32–33, where Nehemiah uses this tax to fund the temple services). Joash orders that this tax, which apparently had not been assessed for some time, be taken from the people to fund the temple repairs. However, the ordered repairs are not made. The Chronicler rejects the explanation of his source, that the priests were embezzling the money for their own use (2 Kgs. 12:7). In Chronicles, the problem lay rather in the collection process: due to a lack of zeal on the part of the Levites, the gathering of the money for the repairs went slowly (2 Chr. 24:5–6).

Joash solves the problem by setting up a way for the people to give to the temple directly, rather than having their required contribution collected from them. A box is placed outside the temple gate, where the people can drop in the offering "that Moses the servant of God laid on Israel in the wilderness" (24:9). Evidently, the custom of placing offerings for temple upkeep into a box outside the temple gate reflects the practice of the second temple; note that in 2 Kings 12:9 the box is placed by the altar in the temple forecourt, so that the priests must still collect the offerings and bring them to the box. The practice described in Chronicles apparently continued into the time of Jesus (see the story of Jesus and the widow's offering, Mark 12:41–44//Luke 21:1–4).

A recently published ostracon—that is, a pottery fragment with writing on it—supports the historicity of Joash's collection (Bordreuil, Israel, and Pardee 1998, 3–7; see also Horn and McCarter 1999, 153–54). The inscription states that three silver shekels were given to Zechariah for "the house of the Lord," as commanded by "King Ashyahu"—likely an alternate form of Joash (recall that Ahaziah could also be called "Jehoahaz"; see 2 Chr. 21:17). This pottery fragment is remarkable, not only for the support it gives to an event in the life of Joash, but because it represents the oldest extrabiblical evidence for the temple in Jerusalem.

Joash's idea catches on; the people give freely and abundantly. The money is brought to Jehoiada and Joash, who together distribute it to the work, as needed—a collaboration of priest and king that doubtless, for the Chronicler, reflects the way things ought to be managed (24:12, 14; for other examples of this dual leadership in the postexilic period, see Hag. 1:1; 2:1–5; Zech. 3:1–10; 4:1–14). The generous offerings of the people pay, not only for the necessary repairs, but for more beyond: vessels of gold and silver are prepared for use in the temple rituals.

In Chronicles, whenever the people are given the opportunity to give and to serve, they respond with enthusiasm. This poses a challenge to congregations in our day. Are we as generous with our time, gifts, and talents? I suspect that our communities seem stale, static, and tired in comparison, either unwilling or unable to do or to give. Every pastor has heard the same excuse, over and over, like a mantra: "I am too busy. Between my job and my family, I just don't have any time or energy left for the church." So, we ask and expect little, of ourselves or our churches. But perhaps the real problem is not that we are too busy, but that we are not busy enough—or rather, that we are busy about the wrong sorts of things. In Charles Dickens's marvelous novella *A Christmas Carol*, when the ghost of Jacob Marley bewails his wasted life, Scrooge says, "But you were always a good man of business, Jacob."

> "Business!" cried the Ghost, wringing his hands again. "Mankind was my business. The common welfare was my business; charity, mercy, forebearance, and benevolence were, all, my business. The dealings of my trade were but a drop of water in the comprehensive ocean of my business!" (Dickens 1976, 21)

As we involve our churches directly and personally in real ministry, we will discover resources previously unguessed and untapped. Perhaps if we ask much and expect much, our people, like the community of Chronicles, will respond with enthusiasm, beyond our expectations.

Jehoiada, like David, dies "full of days" (2 Chr. 24:15; compare 1 Chr. 29:28), after a rich and long life. Chronicles tells us that he lived to be one hundred and thirty, longer than either Moses or Aaron; this long lifespan is surely intended to demonstrate God's blessing on Jehoiada (see Myers 1965, 136, 138). That he was honored by the people of Judah as well is shown by his burial among Jerusalem's past kings, in the royal cemetery called "the city of David." As long as Jehoiada lived, the Chronicler tells us, the people, clergy, and king of Judah remained faithful; they "offered burnt offerings in the house of the Lord regularly" (24:14). Sadly, this portends a breakdown in piety and worship following the old priest's death.

Without Jehoiada, Joash loses his moral and spiritual direction. Other advisors now have the king's ear, and their advice proves ruinous for Judah and its king. Once more, the temple is neglected; indeed, it is abandoned in favor of idol worship (2 Chr. 24:18). The word of God is not lacking; prophets rise up to speak against Judah's corruption. However, the divine word is not heeded—a deadly decision in the world of Chronicles. Disaster, the reader knows, must be just ahead.

195

One such prophet is Jehoiada's son, Zechariah. Like David's officer Amasai, the priest Zechariah is possessed by the spirit (see the discussion of 1 Chr. 12:18, above). His message, though, is reminiscent of the message of Shemaiah to Rehoboam: "Thus says God: Why do you transgress the commandments of the LORD, so that you cannot prosper? Because you have forsaken the LORD, he has also forsaken you" (2 Chr. 24:20; compare 12:5). Zechariah's prophecy may also allude to the prophecy of Haggai, who told his postexilic community that, until they devoted themselves to God's temple, they could not prosper (see Hag. 1:2–11).

Joash and his people are warned, in no uncertain terms, that their abandonment of the temple and refusal to heed the divine word will result in judgment. However, rather than hearing the message, they turn on the messenger. At Joash's command, Zechariah is stoned to death in the temple forecourt, an act that will be remembered as an egregious example of cruelty and injustice (2 Chr. 24:21; see Matt. 23:35//Luke 11:51). The scene of the crime is nearly as horrifying as the crime itself. Death was a major source of uncleanness in ancient Israel: unburied carcasses of humans or animals, carnivorous birds and animals or scavengers that live off of death, even mourners and the period of mourning itself all were ritually unclean. When stoning is commanded in the law (ironically, this penalty is normally reserved for crimes against God, such as blasphemy or idolatry), the sentence is to be carried out outside of the town, where it will not bring defilement upon the community (see, for example, Lev. 24:14; Num. 15:35; Deut. 17:5). That Joash orders Zechariah stoned to death in the sacred temple precincts shows his contempt, not only for the son of the man to whom Joash owed his very life, but also for the temple itself. Zechariah's last words are a cry for God to see and avenge, not only Zechariah's innocent death, but the willful defilement of God's shrine.

God's vengeance comes through an invasion from Aram, or Syria. Twice, Judah had invaded Aram in ill-fated alliances with the northern kingdom of Israel (see 2 Chr. 18:3–34; 22:5–6). Now, Aram strikes back. Just as God had given success to Abijah and Asa when they were outnumbered in battle, because they trusted in the Lord, so now, "[a]lthough the army of Aram had come with few men, the LORD delivered into their hand a very great army, because they had abandoned the LORD" (2 Chr. 24:24). Joash, who was seriously wounded in the battle, is murdered in his bed by conspirators. Because of his complicity in the murder of Zechariah, "they did not bury him in the tombs of the kings," although his body is buried within the city of David (2 Chr. 24:25; contrast 2 Kgs. 12:21).

196

The invasion of Judah by Aram is very likely historical. In 2 Kings 12:17, the leader of this invasion is identified as Hazael (842–806 B.C.). A strong king and able general, Hazael stood off the Assyrians under Shalmanesar III, and after their withdrawal from the region turned his attention to the south, annexing the kingdom of Israel and extending his territory down the Mediterranean coast as far as Gath (2 Kgs. 12:17; see Bright 1981, 254–55). However, 2 Kings 12:18 records that Hazael withdrew from Judah when Joash paid him a huge tribute, and does not mention a battle.

The Chronicler says that he has based his history of Joash on "the Commentary [Hebrew *midrash*] on the Book of the Kings" (2 Chr. 24:27). This could mean that Chronicles draws here upon a source other than our 2 Kings, perhaps indeed on an alternate version of this narrative. To be sure, as we have seen, there are numerous differences in the two accounts. Kings says nothing of the death of Jehoiada, the apostasy of Joash following Jehoiada's death, or of the murder of Zechariah, and the account of Joash's temple repairs in Chronicles differs strikingly from that in Kings. On the other hand, most of the differences can best be explained as reflecting the Chronicler's own interests and perspectives, without requiring us to postulate any source other than Kings. The Chronicler may have known from his own Judean sources that Joash's complicity in Zechariah's death motivated the conspiracy against Joash (note that while 2 Kgs. 12:20–21 describes Joash's assassination and names the conspirators, it says nothing of their motivation). However, it seems best to understand Chronicles here as substantially a retelling of the Joash story in Kings.

25:1–28
Amaziah (//2 Kgs. 14:2–13, 15–20)

Amaziah's reign turns out much like the reign of his father Joash (see 2 Kgs. 14:3). In the Chronicler's account, an early faithful period, in which Amaziah experiences success in battle (2 Chr. 25:1–13) is followed by a later faithless period, in which he suffers defeat; indeed, like his father, Amaziah is assassinated by conspirators (2 Chr. 25:14–28). This division is the outward expression of Amaziah's inner uncertainty, for he "did what was right in the sight of the LORD, yet not with a true heart" (2 Chr. 25:2). Apart from this passage, the expression rendered "true heart" in the NRSV (also translated "whole heart," "full intent," or "single mind") appears many times in Chronicles. For example, those who came to David at Hebron did so "with full intent to make David king" (1 Chr. 12:38). David's advice and prayer for his son Solomon was that he be single-mindedly devoted to the Lord (1 Chr. 28:9) and to the Lord's commandments (1 Chr. 29:19). In David's final days, the people who contributed to the building and the service of the temple were praised, "for with single mind they had offered freely to the LORD" (1 Chr. 29:9). Jehoshaphat urged his judges to act "in the fear of the LORD, in faithfulness, and with your whole heart" (2 Chr. 19:9). This dedication was sadly lacking in Amaziah. Like Rehoboam, who "did evil, for he did not set his heart to seek the LORD" (2 Chr. 12:14), Amaziah was not committed to the Lord's service, and so succumbed to the temptations of arrogance and the worship of alien gods.

Still, Amaziah's reign begins well. His first kingly act is to try and execute the assassins who had murdered his father. However, he does not pursue vengeance upon the families of these men, because the Torah decrees, "The parents shall not be put to death for the children, or the children be put to death for the parents; but all shall be put to death for their own sins" (2 Chr. 25:4//2 Kgs. 14:6; quoted from Deut. 24:16). At the beginning of his reign, then, Amaziah is obedient to the word of the Lord in Scripture.

Amaziah is also obedient, at first, to the prophetic word. In 25:5–10, the king begins preparations for war with Edom. Judah and Benjamin are able to field an army 300,000 strong. The contrast to the 1,160,000 troops in Jehoshaphat's army shows the depredations wrought by the reigns of four disastrous rulers. To strengthen his forces, Amaziah hires a hundred thousand Ephraimite mercenaries for a hundred talents of silver. However, a nameless man of God warns the king against any alliance with the north, even with northern mercenaries, "for the LORD is not with Israel—all these Ephraimites" (25:7). Instead, Amaziah is urged to go alone, trusting in the Lord, "for God has power to help or to overthrow" (2 Chr. 25:8; see also 1 Chr. 29:12; 2 Chr. 14:11). With the man of God's assurances that the booty from victory over Edom will more than make up for his lost investment, Amaziah writes off the hundred talents of silver, and tells the Ephraimites to go home.

Sure enough, after heeding the prophetic word, Amaziah wins a stunning and total victory: ten thousand Edomites are killed in battle (25:11//2 Kgs. 14:7), and another ten thousand prisoners of war are executed, hurled to their deaths from atop Sela, the rocky peak which was the center of the Edomite homeland (25:12). Amaziah's victory is diminished, however, by the depredations of the scorned Ephraimite mercenaries. Robbed of their opportunity to gain booty in battle, and unwilling to settle for the silver they had already been paid, these soldiers of fortune make up their loss by raiding Judah's northern towns, "from Samaria to Beth-horon" (25:13)—an action that corroborates the prophet's distrust.

The messiness of this incident makes it unlikely that the Chronicler has invented it. Surely, a story composed to support the idea that heeding the prophetic word brings victory would have been better and more effectively told without reference to Amaziah's cruel treatment of his prisoners, or to the despoiling of northern Judah by the spurned Ephraimite mercenaries. Rather, the Chronicler is making use of his own Judean sources to fill out the scant references in Kings to Amaziah's Edomite victory.

Sadly, this victory carries within it the seeds of Amaziah's downfall. Amaziah brings back to Jerusalem the gods of Seir. In the ancient world, the idols of a conquered people were often carried off into captivity, to symbolize their defeat by the conqueror's gods (see, for example, the narrative of the ark's capture by the Philistines in 1 Sam. 4:1—7:2). Sometimes, however, the gods of a vanquished people became incorporated into the religion of the victors: as, for example, when the mythology of the conquered Greeks displaced and transformed the traditional religion of the victorious Romans. Perhaps for this reason, the Torah commands that divine images taken in battle are to be destroyed, not taken as trophies (Deut. 7:5; 12:3; for David's obedience to this command, see 1 Chr. 14:12). Amaziah, evidently enamored by aspects of Edomite religion, begins making sacrifices to the Edomite gods. Again, a prophet sent from God comes to turn the king from a disastrous course. This time, however, Amaziah does not listen; the prophet is ordered to be still or die (25:16). The reader, of course, knows what this means: Amaziah is doomed.

For the story of Amaziah's fall, the Chronicler resumes use of 2 Kings (2 Chr. 25:17–28//2 Kgs. 14:8–13, 15–20). Emboldened by his victory over Edom, Amaziah makes threatening overtures toward Israel. Joash, the king of Israel, responds with a parable: the lowly thornbush demanded a marriage alliance with the lofty cedar, but was instead trampled by a passing animal (25:18). The point of the parable is clear; as succinctly stated in Proverbs 16:18, "Pride goes before destruction, and a haughty spirit before a fall." Amaziah is overreaching himself, and will be swatted down if he persists.

The use of parables by Jesus in the New Testament is of course well known. However, the reader may be less familiar with the parables of the Hebrew Bible, where these pointed, pithy stories are often used to puncture inflated egos. Recall, for example, Nathan's parable of the poor man's lamb, which causes David to incriminate himself (2 Sam. 12:1–15). Particularly relevant to Amaziah's situation, however, is the parable of Jotham, related to the lords of Shechem when Abimelech son of Gideon aspired to kingship over them (Judg. 9:7–15). In this story, a lowly bramble aspires to kingship over the trees of the forest; as in the parable of Joash, the hearer is meant to scoff at the briar's ludicrous brashness.

199

Not surprisingly, Amaziah's aggressive posturing is not discouraged by this humiliating parable; instead, he is stung into entering a war for which he is ill prepared. The Chronicler, however, asserts that this "was God's doing, in order to hand them over, because they had sought the gods of Edom" (25:20). As is the Chronicler's wont, historical or political motivation gives way to divine action, whether in reward or in punishment. Amaziah is utterly defeated: he is himself taken captive, and Joash's troops ravage all Judah. The walls of Jerusalem itself are breached, the temple is looted, and hostages are taken: including Obed-edom (evidently a member of the Levitical family of gatekeepers descended from David's Obed-edom; see 1 Chr. 26:4–5), who was in charge of the temple treasures (2 Chr. 25:24). In short, Joash's assault serves as a foreshadowing of the destruction and exile to be brought by Babylon. Like that eventual devastation, the conquest of Jerusalem by Joash comes about because of Judah's faithlessness: specifically, because Amaziah worships idols and rejects the divine word.

Amaziah's punishment strikes not only at his kingdom, but at his own life. Although he lives on for fifteen years after the death of his Israelite conqueror, they are years spent in flight: a conspiracy in Jerusalem forces him to flee to Lachish. The motivation for such a conspiracy is not difficult to imagine, after the consequences of Amaziah's catastrophic war with Israel. However, Chronicles connects this conspiracy, not to Amaziah's failed military adventures, but to his idolatry and rejection of the word of God (25:27). Eventually, Amaziah is hunted down and killed by assassins, just as his father had been. Then, his body is brought back to Jerusalem and "buried with his ancestors" (25:28). Note, however, that while the NRSV reads "city of David" for the place of Amaziah's burial (following the LXX and 2 Kgs. 14:20), the MT has "city of Judah": an old name for Jerusalem (found, for example, in the Babylonian Chronicle from the eighth century B.C.). This suggests that, in the Chronicler's view, Amaziah was buried in Jerusalem, but not in the royal cemetery (so Japhet 1993, 872). Like every king of Judah since Jehoram, Amaziah is denied burial among Judah's faithful kings.

26:1–23
Uzziah (//2 Kgs. 15:1–7)

Apart from the length of his reign (fifty-two years) and the statement that he was a leper, 2 Kings has little to say about Uzziah (usually called Azariah in Kings). Nearly all of the account in Chronicles, then, is drawn from the Chronicler's own Judean sources. These fit, however, with what we can deduce about the time from archaeological evidence, and from extrabiblical sources.

The first half of the eighth century B.C. was marked by a power vacuum in the ancient Near East. The great military power of the day, the Assyrian Empire, was occupied with internal affairs, or with enemies far from Palestine. Syria, to the north, had been broken by an Assyrian invasion in 796 B.C. and had not recovered. This gave the kingdoms of Israel and Judah space and time to grow and prosper. Although the Chronicler does not record the prosperity of the northern kingdom under Uzziah's contemporary Jeroboam II, his success was a major reason for the successes of Uzziah in the south. Apparently in alliance with the north, and freed from worries about Assyria, Uzziah was able to extend his borders as far south as the port of Eloth (also called Elath) on the Gulf of Aqaba, and so presumably to reactivate the trade with Africa that had brought such wealth to Solomon (26:2). Meanwhile, the borders of Jeroboam II of Israel extended as far north as Lebo-hamath (2 Kgs. 14:25). Between them, these eighth-century rulers controlled territory equivalent to that held by Solomon in the glory days of the united monarchy.

In the Chronicler's account, Uzziah wins victory after victory. To the west, he campaigns successfully against the Philistines, regaining control of the coastal trade routes (2 Chr. 26:6). To the south, Uzziah is victorious against the Arab kingdoms, the people of Gur-baal (otherwise unknown) and the Meunites (26:7; see also 20:1). Indeed, the Meunites pay tribute to Uzziah (reading "Meunites" for "Ammonites" in 26:8, with the LXX and in light of 27:5), and are evidently incorporated into Judah: note that, in the lists of returnees from exile in Ezra 2:50//Nehemiah 7:52, the "Meunim" are listed among the temple servants (Horn and McCarter 1999, 325).

However, Uzziah's victories do not come at the expense of his people. Chapter 26:9–15 describes a secure, prosperous kingdom. Uzziah supports agriculture on a large scale, providing cisterns for water and armed watchtowers for protection, "for he loved the soil" (26:10). He reorganizes and revitalizes the military for Judah's defense, raising an army 307,500 strong (26:11–14). Uzziah refortifies Jerusalem, rebuilding and strengthening walls left breached and in ruins by Joash's invasion (26:9; see 25:23). Further, he erects special "inventions" (as translated by Williamson 1982, 337) on Jerusalem's towers and at the corners of its walls, "for shooting arrows and large stones" (26:15). The NRSV translates this obscure Hebrew term as "machines": presumably

201

catapults or ballistae. Indeed, based on this interpretation, some have suggested a very late date for Chronicles, since the earliest known use of catapults was in the third century B.C. (so Welten 1973, 111–14). However, the famous relief of the Assyrian siege at Lachish illustrates the use of raised, fortified platforms on the city walls for archers and, presumably, for the hurling of stones onto the heads of besieging troops; these are probably the "inventions" of Uzziah to which the Chronicler makes reference (see Shea 1999, 42–43; Pritchard 1969, 129–31, figs. 371–73).

In Chronicles, the successes of Uzziah at home and in the field are attributed to Uzziah's faithfulness; particularly, to the influence of an otherwise unknown advisor named Zechariah, "who instructed him in the fear of God" (26:5). As long as Zechariah lived, Uzziah "set himself to seek God": that is, he was dedicated to right worship in the temple (on the significance of "seeking God" in Chronicles, see for example 2 Chr. 7:14; 14:4; 15:4). During these days, God prospered Uzziah; "he was marvelously helped until he became strong" (25:15).

Unfortunately, like Rehoboam (2 Chr. 12:1–2), Uzziah lets his strength and prosperity lead him to pride and destruction (26:16–21). Uzziah usurps the authority of the priests and enters the temple himself, to make an offering of incense. For this reason, the Chronicler tells us, Uzziah is stricken with leprosy. He is forced to live apart, in a house separate from the palace, and Uzziah's son Jotham rules in his stead as regent until the king dies. Even after his death, Uzziah's disease marks him: he is buried "near his ancestors in the burial field that belonged to the kings," but not in the city of David itself, "for they said, 'He is leprous'" (26:23; compare 2 Kgs. 15:7). The Chronicler's claims about Uzziah's burial find some support in a plaque preserved in the Russian Orthodox convent on the Mount of Olives. The plaque, dating to the Herodian period but of unknown provenance, bears an Aramaic inscription reading, "To this place we have brought the bones of Uzziah, king of Judah—do not open!" Evidently Uzziah *was* buried outside the royal cemetery and, centuries later, some kind souls reburied his bones within it.

The Chronicler identifies the prophet Isaiah son of Amoz as a source for Uzziah's life (26:22). Although the superscription to the book of Isaiah claims that the prophet was active "in the days of Uzziah, Jotham, Ahaz, and Hezekiah" (Isa. 1:1), the narratives and datable oracles of the eighth-century Judean prophet belong primarily to the reigns of Ahaz and Hezekiah. This follows from the prophet's call vision, which we are told came to him "[i]n the year that King Uzziah died" (Isa. 6:1). In short, the Chronicler has not learned about Uzziah from our book of Isaiah. Rather, we find here, once again, the Chronicler's assumption, first, that prophets write books (with Isaiah being the first example of a prophet cited by the Chronicler from whom we actually

202

have a book in hand), and second, that the sources he cites concerning Judah's kings are of prophetic authorship.

Uzziah's tragic story reflects a disagreement between the king and the priesthood over the powers and prerogatives of kingship. Such conflicts were nearly as old as Israel. On the one hand, kingship clearly had sacred significance in ancient Israel. In Psalm 2:7, the king on his coronation day declares,

> I will tell of the decree of the LORD:
> He said to me, "You are my son;
>   today I have begotten you.

Indeed, in Psalm 45:6, the psalmist, addressing the king, says, "Your throne, O God, endures forever and ever." Little wonder, then, that kings could play a significant role in Israel's worship, even acting as priests: consider the examples of David (2 Sam. 6:17), Solomon (1 Kgs. 8:62–64), Jeroboam (1 Kgs. 13:1; significantly he, like Uzziah in 2 Chr. 26, is offering incense), and Ahaz (2 Kgs. 16:12–13).

On the other hand, nowhere in the Torah is a role for the king in Israel's liturgy spelled out. Indeed, the list of kingly duties in Deuteronomy 17:14–20 gives the king no priestly rights or privileges; these are expressly restricted to the Levitical priests, "for God has chosen Levi out of all your tribes, to stand and minister in the name of the LORD, him and his sons for all time" (Deut. 18:5). In 1 Samuel 13:2–15, when Saul takes it upon himself to offer sacrifices at Gilgal, Samuel declares, "You have done foolishly; you have not kept the commandment of the LORD your God, which he commanded you. . . . [N]ow your kingdom will not continue" (1 Sam. 13:13–14). Certainly in Chronicles, as we have seen, sacrifice is everywhere restricted to the priests of Aaron's line. So, when Chronicles describes the consecration of David's tent-shrine and of Solomon's temple, proper cult personnel are clearly in evidence, to counter the suggestion that even these greatest of Israel's kings took it upon themselves to act as priests (see 1 Chr. 15:11—16:6; 2 Chr. 7:1–7). In Chronicles, then, it follows that a king claiming priestly authority could expect to be punished.

Uzziah's punishment, being stricken on his forehead with leprosy, calls for examination. In the Bible, "leprosy" does not refer to what we today call leprosy, or Hanson's disease. Hanson's disease is an affliction of the nervous system that affects the ability to feel pressure or pain. As a result, the patient with Hanson's disease often suffers terrible accidental disfigurement. Biblically, "leprosy" is a catchall term for a host of disfiguring skin diseases, involving some kind of discoloration of or discharge from the skin. In the priestly worldview, leprosy was ritually defiling. The priests were charged therefore with diagnosing leprosy

(Lev. 13:2; Deut. 24:8). Any spot or discoloration that grew and spread, whether on a person, an animal, or even a garment, leather bag, or plastered wall, could be identified as leprous, and therefore unclean (see Lev. 13—14). When a person was diagnosed with leprosy, he or she was barred from contact with others until the leprosy was gone (Lev. 13:45–46). Only after an examination by the priests confirming that the leprosy was gone, and the performance of certain cleansing rituals, could the person be reintegrated into the community (Lev. 14:1–32; see also Mark 1:44).

This raises grim questions concerning the Uzziah narrative. Since only the priests could identify leprosy, and only they could declare a leper cured, the diagnosis of leprosy would have been a powerful tool for social control—and a weapon for choking dissent. Uzziah's "leprosy" brought an effective end to what the Chronicler acknowledges was a very successful reign, and stymied any attempt on Uzziah's part to accrue to himself, or to his office, priestly rights and privileges. The priests win, as of course they must.

Naturally, the Chronicler does not view the matter this cynically; he is convinced that Uzziah's leprosy was a real, and deserved, consequence of spiritual arrogance. Several features of Uzziah's story in Chronicles resonate with other texts. The priestly act Uzziah was attempting to perform, the offering of incense, is also ascribed to the heretical kings Jeroboam (1 Kgs. 13:1) and Ahaz (2 Chr. 28:3). Note, too, that the attempt to burn incense before the Lord was the undoing of Korah and his Levitical followers in the priestly story of Korah's rebellion (Num. 16:3–11, 35). Similarly, Uzziah's punishment is reminiscent of that meted out to Miriam, when she aspired to Moses' office (Num. 12:10–15). In Chronicles, Uzziah becomes, like Asa, Joash, and Amaziah before him, an example of a king who is blessed so long as he is faithful, but who falls to the curse once he becomes faithless.

27:1–9

Jotham (//2 Kgs. 15:33–38)

Jotham is the first king since Abijah whose report in Chronicles is uniformly positive. As the account in Kings also presents Jotham as a pious king, the Chronicler is largely faithful to his source, though with some Chronistic flourishes. So, to the statement, "He did what was right in the sight of the LORD, just as his father Uzziah had done" (2 Kgs. 15:34), 2 Chronicles 27:2 adds, "only he did not invade the temple of the LORD"—a reminder of the proud act that, in the Chronicler's view, resulted in Uzziah being stricken with leprosy. Jotham, then, is like his father, but without his father's failings. Unfortunately, the people do not follow the example of their king; they remain morally and spiritually corrupt (27:2). The corruption of the past six rulers, it seems, has taken its toll.

The record of Jotham's accomplishments is largely unique to Chronicles. With his source, the Chronicler recalls Jotham's repairs to the temple gate (27:3//2 Kgs. 15:35)—an act of particular significance in Chronicles, where righteous kings carry out temple repairs and reforms. However, in Chronicles, Jotham also establishes fortified strongholds throughout Judah's hill country, and continues his father's work refortifying Jerusalem, adding in particular to "the wall of Ophel," on the southern ridge of the temple mount (Elmslie 1916, 291). But his military actions are not merely defensive. Jotham defeats the Ammonites and forces them to pay a rich tribute in silver and grain (27:5).

The reason for this success is of course clear to the reader, but 27:6 makes it explicit: "So Jotham became strong because he ordered his ways before the LORD his God." Unlike the last three kings, who started out well but could not stay the course (see 25:2), Jotham is disciplined and committed. Specifically, he is committed to continually placing his decisions and actions before the Lord, to ensure that what he wills and does is in keeping with God's will for his life. For us as for Jotham, this is not a once-for-all decision, but a daily struggle. That is why we need the support of the community of faith, and the discipline of continual prayer and reflection upon the Scriptures. No less a teacher than the apostle Paul described his lifestyle as continual preparation and training, like an athlete preparing for the games, "so that after proclaiming to others I myself should not be disqualified" (1 Cor. 9:27). We, like Jotham, must be prepared to order our ways and stay the course if we wish to be God's people. As Jesus sternly warns, "No one who puts a hand to the plow and looks back is fit for the kingdom of God" (Luke 9:62). Beginning is good. Continuing is better. Finishing is best.

Strangely absent from the account of Jotham's life in Chronicles is any mention of Pekah and Rezin's assault upon Judah (compare 2 Kgs. 15:37). Pekah (737–732 B.C.) was king of Israel, having taken the throne from Pekahiah—probably with the assistance of Rezin, king of Syria in Damascus. Pekah and Rezin, together with the leaders of other minor kingdoms in Syria-Palestine, attempted to form an alliance against Assyria. Tiglath-pilesar III (745–727 B.C.), leader of the rejuvenated Assyrian empire, had designs on Palestine and the Mediterranean coast. Judah wisely attempted to stay out of the matter. This prompted Pekah and Rezin to take action to force Judah's hand, through what is generally called the Syro-Ephraimite War. The invasion of Pekah and Rezin, their siege of Jerusalem, and Judah's decision to become a voluntary vassal of Assyria in exchange for deliverance and protection, all took place during the reign of Jotham's successor, Ahaz. However, the account in 2 Kings dates the beginning of Pekah and Rezin's assault to the reign of Jotham.

It is possible that the Chronicler ignores the Syro-Ephraimite onslaught because it complicates his desire to depict Jotham as a righteous king, successful in all his undertakings. However, the Chronicler is not averse to complexity in his portrayals. Abijah's short life, for example, is not presented as a judgment from God, and Amaziah's right action with regard to dismissing the Ephraimite mercenaries does not protect Judah from the vengeance of these scorned warriors. In Chronicles, bad things do happen to good people! Another possibility is that the Chronicler does not mention the assaults of Pekah and Rezin during the reign of Jotham because he did not believe that there had been any. The dating of the various actions leading up to the Syro-Ephraimite War is a complex problem. However, it is certainly arguable that the alliance did not begin making threatening overtures toward Jerusalem until 733 B.C., during the reign of Ahaz. Otherwise, one might wonder why Ahaz waited so long before asking for help, or why the Assyrians took so long to respond (Donner 1977, 430). Perhaps the Chronicler, with his demonstrated access to Judean royal sources, was able to date the beginnings of the Syro-Ephraimite War more accurately than the Deuteronomistic History does.

The final demonstration of Jotham's faithfulness to the end is the Chronicler's report concerning his burial: "Jotham slept with his ancestors, and they buried him in the city of David" (27:9). Jotham is the first king since Jehoshaphat to be buried in the royal cemetery, the city of David, among the tombs of his ancestors. It is an honor befitting a king whose life, particularly when contrasted with his predecessors, is a model of faithfulness. Sadly, however, the corruption of the nation has already gone deep; Jotham's successor will revert to the old, faithless ways.

28:1–27
Ahaz (//2 Kgs. 16:1–20)

The story of Ahaz in Chronicles follows the basic framework of the account in Kings, particularly in the beginning and at the end. However, the insertion of material unique to the Chronicler, and his retelling of the material taken from Kings, results in a completely new narrative. The reader is reminded, once again, that the Chronicler is not interested in history so much as *story*. By retelling the story, Chronicles reclaims the flow of Israel's ancient narrative, recalling that what made them a people was not politics, but liturgy. It is in their worship that the people become God's people, and so become, and remain, Israel. Faithfulness to God and to the divine word, demonstrated in right worship, leads to blessing; refusal to hear and obey, shown in false worship, leads inexorably to curse.

The negative side of this equation is seldom expressed as strongly in Chronicles as in the account of Ahaz's reign. From Kings, the Chronicler derives a picture of Ahaz as the stereotypical bad king, who "did not do what was right in the sight of the LORD, as his ancestor David had done, but he walked in the ways of the kings of Israel" (28:1–2//2 Kgs. 16:2–3). Ahaz, we are told, took part in abominable rites of child sacrifice: he "made his sons pass through fire," and, the Chronicler adds, burned incense (so Japhet 1993, 894; the NRSV reads "made offerings") in the valley of the son of Hinnom (28:3). This valley outside of Jerusalem, part of the ancient boundary between Judah and Benjamin, had an evil association with idolatrous practices, and particularly with human sacrifice (see 33:6; Jer. 7:31–32); its name in Hebrew, Gehenna, became another word for hell (for example, Matt. 5:22; Mark 9:43, Jas. 3:6). For Ahaz to offer incense (the same Hebrew word is used in 28:3 and in 26:16, where Uzziah's sacrilegious act is described) in this evil place confirms that he is not merely a passive participant in obscene rites, but an active leader. So also, the Chronicler tells us, Ahaz "even made cast images for the Baals" (28:2): like Jeroboam, Ahaz manufactures divine images for his people to worship (so Williamson 1982, 344). Divine retribution, the reader knows, is sure to follow.

The account of the Syro-Ephraimite War in Chronicles differs substantially from the presentation in 2 Kings 16:5–9 and Isaiah 7:1—8:15. While elsewhere in Scripture, Pekah and Rezin are described as allies working in concert, in Chronicles their attacks are treated separately. Further, rather than focusing on the siege of Jerusalem as do Isaiah and Kings, Chronicles describes the widespread destruction and terrible casualties the war brought to greater Judah. It appears probable that the Chronicler is relying here, at least in part, on old Judean sources: note the specific account of how one Ephraimite champion, Zichri, "killed the king's son Maaseiah, Azrikam the commander of the palace, and Elkanah the next in authority to the king" (28:7). The numbers in Chronicles are, of course, exaggerated—the armies of Israel kill

120,000 Judeans in a single day (28:6), and take 200,000 prisoners (28:8). However, a protracted and costly war must have preceded the siege described in Isaiah and Kings (see, for example, Isa. 3:1—4:1). By focusing on the victories of Pekah and Rezin rather than on their failed siege of Jerusalem, Chronicles shows that though Jerusalem did not fall, Ahaz was in no sense a victor. Further, by treating the allies separately, the Chronicler is able to address in greater depth the disturbing spectacle of Ephraimites, who by rights should be subjects of David's descendant, not only waging war against Ahaz, but winning.

Once more, as in the days of Amaziah, people from Judah are taken into exile (28:5, 8; see also 2 Chr. 25:23–24). Of those captured by the Syrians (28:5), nothing more is said. However, the mass exile of 200,000 on their way to Samaria is halted by the prophecy of Oded. While the reason for Judah's bitter defeat has already been made clear (28:6), Oded begins by repeating the point; Israel had been victorious "[b]ecause the LORD, the God of your ancestors, was angry with Judah" (28:9). But even so, the savagery of Israel in victory had been extreme: "you have killed them in a rage that has reached up to heaven" (28:9; recall the enormous number of casualties). Oded declares that this carnage is enough, without the added shame of enslaving the survivors. Israel itself, after all, has no claim to righteousness, and also stands in danger of suffering from the divine wrath (28:10–11). Four chiefs of Ephraim agree with Oded, and stand up to the returning warriors: "You shall not bring the captives in here, for you propose to bring on us guilt against the LORD in addition to our present sins and guilt. For our guilt is already great, and there is fierce wrath against Israel" (28:13). In the face of this testimony, the Ephraimites use the booty they had taken in battle to feed, clothe, and care for the exiles, and then return them to their fellow Judeans at Jericho (28:15).

What are we to make of this extraordinary reversal? Those who hold that Chronicles is favorable to the north find here confirmation of this idea. With this action by Ephraim, south and north have apparently changed places: the north is repentant and righteous, the south rebellious and sinful (so Williamson 1982, 343–44). "Whatever our perspective on this story," one could well argue, "it is clear that the northerners are an organic part of the people of Israel" (so Japhet 1993, 903).

However, the prophecy of Oded is an accusation ("what have you except sins against the LORD your God?" 28:10), and the words of the Ephraimite chiefs are an admission of guilt. Indeed, 28:2 states that Ahaz "walked in the ways of the kings of Israel." The sin of Ahaz is precisely the sin of the north: namely, the sin of faithlessness to the divine word, manifested in false worship. The northerners, for all their kindness to the exiles, are nowhere said to repent of this sin; indeed they *cannot* repent

208

of this sin and remain a separate nation, estranged from Judah and its temple. To be sure, under Ahaz, Judah has sunk deeper into darkness. But that does not mean that Israel has come into the light.

The story of the returned exiles is meant, not to redeem the northern kingdom, but to shame the community of the faithful. Even these northern sinners, who freely acknowledge their sin, can act in accordance with the righteous dictates of God. True, they act out of self-interest, to avoid divine wrath. But nonetheless, they do good. Christian readers may be reminded of Jesus' parable of the good Samaritan (Luke 10:25–37), which indeed may have been inspired by this passage in Chronicles (so Allen 1999, 601). There as here, expectations are confounded. Goodness turns up in unexpected places, shaming those who should themselves have been the examples of righteousness.

The leadership role played by the chiefs of Ephraim could show that by this time, the northern monarchy had already fallen (so Williamson 1982, 347). However, the fact that the four chiefs are named suggests that the Chronicler is drawing upon a source. The most likely time for a list of northern officials being included into the Judean sources accessible to the Chronicler would be the reign of Hezekiah, when some northern refugees came south and were reincorporated into a united Israel. Quite probably, then, the Chronicler is using material from Hezekiah's time, out of its proper chronological sequence, to foreshadow the imminent fall of the northern kingdom.

Ahaz appeals to Assyria for help, and so voluntarily surrenders the independence of his kingdom. In Chronicles, however, the appeal is prompted, not only by the Syro-Ephraimite alliance, but by other problems as well: specifically, by invasions from Edom (note that the Edomites, like the Syrians, take away captives) and Philistia (28:17–18). This is likely an accurate reflection of Judah's situation. Philistia was an often-rebellious Assyrian vassal, on the edge of Assyria's sphere of influence; indeed, in 734 B.C., Tiglath-pilesar had engaged in a campaign against Philistia (Donner 1977, 425). Philistia may have assaulted Israel to forward the aims of the Syro-Ephraimite alliance against Assyria, as well as to grab territory for itself from a weakened neighbor.

Assyria comes, but not as a deliverer. Rather than going up against Damascus (as in 2 Kgs. 16:9), Tiglath-pilneser (the Chronicler's way of rendering the name of the Assyrian monarch; see also 1 Chr. 5:6, 26) goes up against Ahaz. So, despite emptying his treasury, bankrupting his nobles, and even robbing the house of the Lord to pay tribute, Ahaz finds no deliverance. This account of the reign of Ahaz as the beginning of Assyrian oppression is doubtless a reflection of hindsight.

The cause of all these disasters, of course, is the sin of Ahaz, "for he had behaved without restraint in Judah and had been faithless to the

209

LORD" (28:19). However, far from being turned to the Lord by these disasters, Ahaz "shut up the doors of the house of the LORD and made himself altars in every corner of Jerusalem" (28:24). In an ultimate demonstration of faithlessness, Ahaz rejects the Lord utterly. Rather than making temple repairs, like such predecessors as Joash or Asa, Ahaz actually vandalizes the temple for metals that he can use to pay the Assyrian tribute (28:24).

Having rejected the Lord, Ahaz turns instead to the gods of Damascus (28:23). The closest thing to this blasphemy in the Chronicler's source is 2 Kings 16:10–16. There, a new altar design is brought back from Damascus by Ahaz when he goes to swear fealty to Assyria. When the altar is completed, it is set up in the place of the old bronze altar, and Ahaz himself offers sacrifices to consecrate it. None of this is mentioned in Chronicles, but the account of Ahaz's worship of the gods of Damascus clearly is aimed at this action. For the Chronicler, the design for the temple and all its accoutrements had been revealed directly to David. A new altar, particularly one based on a foreign pattern, would represent false worship as surely as the erection of an idol. Like Uzziah, Ahaz attempts to act as priest: but to false gods. So, also like Uzziah— and indeed, like every king since Jehoshaphat except for righteous Jotham—Ahaz is not buried with his ancestors (28:27).

Why is the Chronicler so overwhelmingly negative about Ahaz? One reason may be that Ahaz provides an opportunity for the Chronicler to expound upon his central theological themes. Like the prophet Ezekiel, the Chronicler emphasizes divine justice and personal responsibility (so Japhet 1993, 45). Indeed, the sequence of kings from Jotham to Ahaz to Hezekiah could serve as a pageant, acting out the themes of Ezekiel 18:1–32. The righteousness of Jotham could not deliver his son Ahaz from the consequences of Ahaz's sin. Nor, however, will the sins of Ahaz condemn his own son to a life of sinfulness. Indeed, Hezekiah will become one of the great reforming kings in Judah's history. With Ezekiel, the Chronicler can affirm of the Lord, "the life of the parent as well as the life of the child is mine; it is only the person who sins that shall die" (Ezek. 18:4).

Of course, another clear reason for the unstinting condemnation of Ahaz is that he was the first king to succumb to a foreign power, and he did so willingly, without resistance. Ahaz stands as a grim example of the foolishness of foreign alliances. Such alliances are condemned in the reigns of others as well, particularly Jehoshaphat. Yet Jehoshaphat is not utterly condemned, and Ahaz is. The difference is that Jehoshaphat saw the light, and was able to break free. Ahaz remains unrepentant, and entangles Judah in a web from which it will never again escape.

29:1—32:33

Hezekiah
*(//2 Kgs. 18:1–6, 13–37; 19:14–19, 35–37; 20:1–3,
12–21//Isa. 36:1–22; 37:14–20, 36–38; 38:1–3;
39:1–8)*

By far, the majority of the material in the four chapters of Chronicles pertaining to Hezekiah is unique to the Chronicler. Even the name of this great reformer is different in Chronicles: while the son of Ahaz is called "Hezekiah" (Hebrew *Ḥizqiyyah*) in Kings, in Chronicles he is far more often called "Yeḥizqiyyahu," a more fulsome form of the name. The use of the name "Hezekiah" in English translations of Chronicles (for example, in both the NRSV and the JPSV) is a bow to a very old translator's convention; the LXX likewise uses Hezekiah (Greek *Ezekias*) in both Kings and Chronicles.

Into a framework derived from his source in Kings, the Chronicler has inserted four major units: 29:3–36, concerning the Levitical purification of the temple following Ahaz's death; 30:1–27, the description of Hezekiah's great Passover; 31:2–19, a description of the divisions of priests and Levites in Hezekiah's time; and 32:2–6 and 27–30, an account of the military and economic expansions carried out by Hezekiah. Much of this material derives from old Judean sources, and is in many cases historically accurate. The effect of these insertions is to invert the priorities of Kings, which emphasizes Hezekiah's struggles with Sennacherib over his religious reforms (Myers 1965, 188). In Chronicles, Hezekiah is the reformer par excellence, comparable in his accomplishments to David and Solomon (29:2; 30:26). For while David communicated the plan for the temple and its liturgy, and Solomon implemented the plans of his father, it was Hezekiah who reinstituted the liturgy of David, and rededicated the temple of Solomon, following the apostasy of Ahaz. Further, with his reforms centering worship on Jerusalem and his overtures to the survivors of the northern kingdom, Hezekiah recalls the glories of the united monarchy.

The account of Hezekiah's reign begins, in Chronicles as in its source, with praise: "He did what was right in the sight of the LORD, just as his ancestor David had done" (29:2//2 Kgs. 18:3). Statements comparing the kings of Judah with David are fairly common in Kings (for positive examples, see 1 Kgs. 3:3; 15:11; and 2 Kgs. 14:3; negative examples include 1 Kgs. 11:33; 14:8; and 15:3). However, only three of these comparisons are picked up by the Chronicler. Ahaz, as we have seen, is condemned because he "did not do what was right in the sight

211

of the LORD his God, as his ancestor David had done" (2 Kgs. 16:2//2 Chr. 28:1). Note that this is just the opposite of what is said concerning Ahaz's son Hezekiah. Both Hezekiah (2 Kgs. 18:3//2 Chr. 29:2) and Josiah (2 Kgs. 22:2//2 Chr. 34:2–3) follow David's example, and are praised. In this way, the Chronicler emphasizes the faithfulness of the two great reforming kings, and particularly singles out Hezekiah by contrast with his father.

Hezekiah's first act as king is to open the temple gates Ahaz had closed (2 Chr. 29:3; see 28:24). The importance of the temple gates as symbols of access to the Lord's presence can be seen particularly in Ezekiel 40—42, where a significant portion of the description and measurement of Ezekiel's visionary temple is devoted to the gates, and in Psalm 24:7 and 9 (the reader may be familiar with Handel's powerful, stirring setting of these words in his oratorio *Messiah*):

> Lift up your heads, O gates!
> and be lifted up, O ancient doors!
> that the King of glory may come in.

To say that the gates are opened is to say that the Lord is at home, and accessible. Similarly, in Revelation 3:8, the faithful Philadelphian church is told by the victorious Christ, "I have set before you an open door," while the faithless Laodiceans are separated from Christ by a closed door, at which the Lord stands, knocking (Rev. 3:20). Ahaz had closed the doors of the temple, and so closed his heart to God's presence and purpose. But Hezekiah, in contrast, has opened the doors, and declares his intention to seek and serve the Lord.

In 29:5–11, Hezekiah calls upon the Levites to purify the defiled temple. The Hebrew word used for the temple's defilement, *niddah* (translated by the NRSV as "filth"), is most frequently found in the Priestly material of the Torah and in Ezekiel, with reference to ritual uncleanness. The term appears only twice in the Chronicler's History, in 29:5 and in Ezra 9:11. There, Ezra bemoans the uncleanness and defilement of the peoples surrounding Judah, into which he fears the people of God are being absorbed by intermarriage. In Ezra as here, it is idolatry in particular that is the subject of concern.

Hezekiah ascribes the defilement and corruption of the temple generally to "our ancestors"; Ahaz is not mentioned (but see 29:19). Still, it was clearly Ahaz who not only defiled the temple with idolatry but, even more seriously, actually shut up the temple, putting a halt to the liturgy practiced continuously since David's time (29:6–7; see 28:24). Hezekiah describes the trouble, bloodshed, and captivity to which Judah has been subject as the consequence of these actions: "Our fathers have fallen by the sword and our sons and our daughters and our wives are in captivity for this" (29:9). These words address not only the historical situation of Hezekiah, but the much more recent past of the Chronicler's own community as well. Indeed, 29:8, which describes Judah and Jerusalem as "an object of horror, of astonishment, and of hissing," quotes from Jeremiah 29:18, with reference to Jerusalem following the Babylonian conquest.

In response to his community's need, Hezekiah calls for a new covenant with the Lord (29:10), just as Asa (15:12) and Jehoiada (23:16) had done before him. However, as no covenant ceremony is described, it may be better in this case to understand Hezekiah's words as a call to the Levites for a renewed and total commitment to the Lord (Japhet 1993, 919). The responsibilities of the offices of priest and Levite are spelled out once more: "the LORD has chosen you to stand in his presence to minister to him, and to be his ministers and make offerings to him" (29:11). Intriguingly, Hezekiah addresses the priests and Levites familiarly as "my sons" (2 Chr. 29:11): the only place in the Hebrew Bible where such an address is used (Japhet 1993, 919). Once more, king and priest are joined in the Chronicler's narrative.

In 29:12–15, the fourteen Levites taking part in Hezekiah's restoration are named, by clan. Two are descended from each of seven Levitical families, the number seven doubtless being chosen because of its sacral significance. Three of the seven are the familiar Levitical clans, descended from Levi's three sons Kohath, Merari, and Gershon. Another three of the families are the descendants of David's three Levitical singers, Asaph, Heman, and Jeduthun. The seventh Levitical clan, Elizaphan, was also mentioned in connection with David's successful attempt to bring the ark into Jerusalem (1 Chr. 15:8; note that there, a different list of six Levitical clans is given). The clan list thus links Hezekiah's temple restoration to David's establishment of the Jerusalem shrine, and underlines once more the essential role of the temple musicians in Jerusalem's liturgy.

The priests and Levites consecrate themselves for their task, and then begin "as the king had commanded, by the words of the LORD" (29:15). Like David, Hezekiah functions as a prophet (see 1 Chr. 28:11–19; 2 Chr. 8:14; 29:25). While priests and Levites work together on the cleansing of the temple, a clear division of labor is followed. The priests cleanse the temple, particularly the "inner part": that is, the most holy place, which the Levites are forbidden to enter (compare Lev. 10:18, where the same term for the holy place is used; so Williamson 1982, 355). The Levites then carry the unclean things (presumably idols and the accoutrements of their worship) to the valley of Kidron, as had been done in the temple purification under Asa (2 Chr. 15:16). Second Kings 23:4, 6, 12 mentions this use of the valley of Kidron in connection with Josiah's reforms, though curiously this is not mentioned in Chronicles.

The cleansing of the temple, which takes sixteen days to complete, begins on the first day of the first month (29:17). Offerings are made "for the kingdom and for the sanctuary and for Judah" (29:21). In the Law of the Temple in Ezekiel 40—48, the first day of the first month marks the beginning of a week of sacrifices to atone for the temple, as well as for the people (Ezek. 45:18–20). The ritual in Ezekiel and in 2 Chronicles 29 is reminiscent of the Day of Atonement, although Leviticus 23:26–32 places this rite on the tenth day of the seventh month. The ritual for the Day of Atonement in Leviticus 16:1–28 calls for sin offerings similar to those described in 2 Chronicles 29:20–24, though the number of animals is different (one bull, two rams, and one goat, with a second goat for Azazel, in Leviticus, as compared to seven bulls, rams, lambs, and goats in Chronicles). Note that, in both Leviticus and Chronicles, the goat is intended to atone for the sins of the people (Lev. 16:15; 2 Chr. 29:23–24). That the ark with its "mercy seat" is not mentioned in Chronicles or Ezekiel may suggest that what is described here is the rite of atonement as practiced in the second temple, which of course had no ark.

Another parallel to Hezekiah's temple cleansing and rededication is the dedication of the altar in Numbers 7:87–88, which also featured a sin offering of bulls, rams, lambs, and goats, though again in different numbers (twelve each, followed by a huge number of offerings of well-being). Similarly, the dedication of the second temple would involve "one hundred bulls, two hundred rams, four hundred lambs, and as a sin offering for all Israel, twelve male goats, according to the number of the tribes of Israel" (Ezra 6:17; see also Ezra 8:35). Essentially, in resuming the temple liturgy, Hezekiah is beginning anew, with a renewed dedication of altar and shrine and a cleansing, not only of the temple, but of the community.

The sin offering that in 2 Chronicles 29:21 is said to be offered for Judah is in 29:24 said to be for "all Israel." Elsewhere in Chronicles, as we have seen, the expression "all Israel" is sometimes used for all of the twelve tribes, sometimes, following convention, for the northern kingdom alone, and sometimes, as seems the case here, for Judah alone. Some make a sharp distinction between the use of "Israel" in Chronicles, where "Israel" is held to be inclusive, referring to both south and north, and in Ezra–Nehemiah, where the term is allegedly exclusive, applying to Judah and Benjamin alone. From Hezekiah onward, once the northern kingdom had ceased to be, it is argued that "all Israel" in Chronicles always includes the northern tribes (Williamson 1977, 126–30). If this is so, then the king's command in 29:24 must be meant to correct the narrower intention of the priests: the sacrifice is not for Judah alone, but for the northern tribes as well (Williamson 1982, 357). However, all of the actions of the priests are performed at the king's command—indeed the king is understood to be a prophet, voicing the word of the Lord (29:15, 20–21). Nothing in 29:21 suggests a misunderstanding, let alone an act of disobedience. We do best, then, to see "Judah" in 29:21 and "all Israel" in 29:24 as synonymous terms, referring to the faithful southern kingdom. Later, in chapter 30, northerners will once more be included in faithful Israel—but only those northerners who respond to Hezekiah's invitation, and even they are included only because the king prays for them (30:18–20).

Following the statement of the sacrifices offered and their associated ritual in 29:20–24, Chronicles turns to the description of the service itself (29:25–30). Hezekiah's service of atonement and rededication includes the music of the Levitical singers, "according to the commandment of David and of Gad the king's seer and of the prophet Nathan, for the commandment was from the LORD through his prophets" (29:25). Several features of this remarkable statement bear consideration. Once more, a clear connection is established between music and prophecy (see 1 Chr. 25:1–5). Further, the word of the Lord commanding the installation of the Levitical musicians is attributed, not to David alone, but also to Gad and Nathan, emphasizing the authority of the prophetic word (see also 20:20). Finally, David is expressly included, with Nathan and Gad, among the Lord's prophets. This is important for the Chronicler, who holds that the temple plan, its personnel, and its liturgy were all revealed to David by the Lord, so that David, like Moses, is a prophet. As we have seen, Hezekiah the descendant of David is also a prophet. When he commands the Levites and priests to cleanse and atone for the temple and the community, Hezekiah does not speak on his own authority, but is a channel for the divine word.

The sin offerings are followed by freewill offerings of the people (29:31–36). The offerings of the people are of two types: thank offerings (Hebrew *todah*) and burnt offerings (Hebrew *'olah*). The thank offering was one form of the offering of well-being, or peace offering (Hebrew *shelem*; see Lev. 7:12–15). In this sacrifice, a portion was burned on the altar, a portion was given to the priests for their use (in 29:33, these are referred to as "consecrated offerings"; see Lev. 22:3, 6–7, 12), and the remainder was returned to the worshiper, to be consumed in a feast. As might be expected, the offering of well-being was offered on occasions

215

of celebration; the thank offering, in particular, was offered in thankfulness for God's blessing or deliverance (see Pss. 66:13–15; 116:17–19). The burnt offering, on the other hand, involved incinerating the entire animal on the altar. Only the hide was not consumed, but was given to the priests for their use (Lev. 1). This sacrifice, then, truly *was* a sacrifice—the worshiper got nothing material back; in economic terms, it represented a total loss. Burnt offerings were made for a variety of reasons: as a plea for forgiveness, as the fulfillment of a vow, or as a demonstration of grateful praise. Here in Chronicles, the motivation for these voluntary offerings is gratitude at the Lord's forgiveness. Certainly, we as well should respond to God's love and deliverance with thankfulness and praise.

Once more, the response of the people exceeds all expectations (see 2 Chr. 24:11–14). So many thank offerings and burnt offerings are brought forward that the available priests are swamped, and Levites must be pressed into service to assist them in skinning the burnt offerings. The Levites, indeed, are praised for being "more conscientious than the priests in sanctifying themselves" (29:34). However, this is not, as it is sometimes read, a condemnation of the priests. The sacral personnel of the temple are faced with an emergency situation. This spontaneous, mass demonstration of piety has taken everyone by surprise, "for the thing had come about suddenly" (29:36). The Chronicler recognizes the *possibility* of Levites serving in a limited priestly role, when necessary, indicating once more the conciliatory attitude toward the Levites and the old Levitical traditions in Chronicles. However, the Levites still do not offer sacrifices, a task restricted to the priests in Chronicles, and even their involvement in skinning the burnt offerings represents a concession to an extraordinary situation, not a fundamental change in status.

With the temple cleansed and restored, Hezekiah turns his attention to reunification and reform. In 2 Chronicles 30:1, "all Israel and Judah," explicitly including Ephraim and Manasseh, is summoned to Jerusalem for Passover. Ordinarily, Passover would have taken place on the fourteenth day of the first month (Num. 9:1–3). However, it could not be celebrated at the regular time, "because the priests had not sanctified themselves in sufficient number, nor had the people assembled in Jerusalem" (2 Chr. 30:3). The Torah permits a worshiper to celebrate Passover one month late, if he or she is unclean through contact with a corpse or is traveling, and so cannot observe the feast at the regular time (Num. 9:9–11). Here, however, this provision is extended to the entire nation.

The reasons given for the delay of the Passover make two intriguing assumptions. First, it is assumed that a huge crowd will gather, requiring unusual numbers of priests to be consecrated and ready to

216

offer the sacrifices. As the crisis prompted by the huge response to Hezekiah's service of atonement had shown, too few priests had been prepared to serve in the first month—and that service had involved only the people of Judah. The "great numbers" anticipated for Hezekiah's Passover are to come "from Beer-sheba to Dan" (30:5), an old formula for the territory of all Israel (see, for example, Judg. 20:1; 2 Sam. 3:10; 24:2//1 Chr. 21:2; 1 Kgs. 4:25). Hezekiah's Passover will involve not only Judah, but also, as we will see, the remnants of the northern kingdom.

Second, it is assumed that the Passover is to be celebrated in Jerusalem. According to Deuteronomy 16:5–6, the Passover sacrifice could only be offered in Jerusalem. Certainly, in second-temple times, this was the preferred practice (see, for example, Luke 2:41; John 2:13; 11:55). However, in Exodus 12:1–28, it is assumed that the rite is celebrated in individual households. Many scholars have proposed that the Deuteronomic law requiring the Passover to be observed in Jerusalem comes from the time of Josiah, as part of his policies centralizing worship in Jerusalem. The reforms of Josiah, after all, sound much like the book of Deuteronomy. Indeed, 2 Kings 22:3—23:25 describes a scroll found in the temple in 622 B.C., which so impressed Josiah that he reordered his kingdom in line with its teachings. Most interpreters believe that this book was some form of Deuteronomy, which is therefore frequently dated to Josiah's time (see the discussion of the reign of Josiah, below).

However, great changes taking place during his reign would likely have made Hezekiah particularly interested in uniting all the remnants of Israel around the central shrine. In the fourth year of Hezekiah's reign, calamity struck the northern kingdom (2 Kgs. 18:9–12). A final, abortive attempt at revolt by Israel's last king, Hoshea (732–724 B.C.), prompted the Assyrian Shalmanesar V (727–722 B.C.) to annihilate the northern kingdom. The capital, Samaria, fell to a lengthy siege in 722 B.C., and Israel ceased to be. Shalmanesar's successor, Sargon II (722–705 B.C.), deported huge chunks of the population, resettling the land with refugees from elsewhere in his empire. These scattered Israelites vanished from history, becoming the fabled "lost tribes" of Israel. But not even the Assyrian military machine could kill and deport everyone! Portions of the original population remained, hidden in the hills, or trickling southward into Judah as refugees. Surely, Hezekiah would have been interested in reaching out to this remnant of the northern tribes, and in reclaiming the territory lost to David's house by Jeroboam's revolt—particularly, as the attention of Assyria was focused elsewhere, due to revolts in other parts of the empire.

217

That Hezekiah indeed *was* interested is shown by the name he gave to his son and successor: Manasseh, after the ancestor of the second-largest northern tribe (note that the former northern kingdom could be referred to as "Ephraim and Manasseh"; see 2 Chr. 30:1, 10; 31:1). Consider, too, the claim in 2 Kings 22:3—23:25 that the scroll inspiring Josiah's reforms was found in the temple. If indeed the core of the Deuteronomic legislation dates to the time of Hezekiah, this could well have been the case: a law book assembled in the time of Hezekiah's reform, hidden away in the temple and forgotten through the reigns of Manasseh and Amon, could have been rediscovered in Josiah's reign. Finally, note that chapter 30 abounds in irregularities: the delayed date of the Passover, the participation of people who were not ritually clean, and finally the spontaneous extension of the feast for an additional week. Surely, if the Chronicler were inventing the account of Hezekiah's Passover, he would have taken care to make his account more typical, and less difficult (Williamson 1982, 362–64). In short, the Chronicler's description of Hezekiah's Passover, uniting north and south at the one shrine in Jerusalem, likely draws upon an old Judean source, and may represent an authentic memory of Israel's past.

The Chronicler does not ascribe this openness to the north to the king alone. The decision to invite the northern tribes is made by "the king and all the assembly" (30:4), while the letters issuing the invitation come "from the king and his officials" (30:6). Like his ancestor Jehoshaphat, Hezekiah demonstrates a democratic flair in his rule (so Japhet 1993, 941; see the discussion above of 2 Chr. 17:7–9, 16). The participation of the people in Hezekiah's decisions is another witness to the extent of the community's repentance (see 29:31–36). The people, rededicated to the Lord, eagerly follow where their king leads.

Hezekiah's letter of invitation (2 Chr. 30:6–9) primarily addresses the survivors of the former northern kingdom, "who have escaped from the hand of the kings of Assyria" (30:6). These are urged to reject the sin of their ancestors, "who were faithless to the LORD" (30:7). The term rendered "faithless" in the NRSV (Hebrew *ma'al*) is in 1 Chronicles 5:25 rendered "transgressed"; in each case, it is this faithlessness to the Lord that led to the north's downfall. The character of this faithlessness is made clear by its solution: "return to the LORD"—that is, "come to his sanctuary, which he has sanctified forever" (1 Chr. 30:6, 8–9). By repudiating the temple and its liturgy, the northern tribes had repudiated the Lord (see 13:8–12). Now, by returning to the temple and worshiping the Lord in truth, they will exchange their faithlessness for faithfulness, and once more experience the blessings of the Lord's presence. Indeed, even their exiled kindred will return (30:9).

218   Hezekiah's letter is another masterpiece of the Chronicler. While, as we have seen, the letter in its literary and historical context addresses the remnant of the northern kingdom, it is sent "throughout all Israel *and Judah*" (2 Chr. 30:6, emphasis added; compare 30:10): that is, it also

addresses the Judean community of the Chronicler. In Chronicles, the fall of Jerusalem and the exile of Judah would come, just as the fall of Israel had, because of faithlessness (1 Chr. 9:1; 2 Chr. 36:14; see Johnstone 1998, 96–97). Hezekiah's letter, then, speaks to the situation of the community after the exile as well as to that of the northern remnant. The central theme of this letter is return and repentance; the Hebrew word *shûb* (rendered "turn" and "return" in the English text) recurs again and again. The Chronicler's community had experienced the truth of God's promise of return from exile. But now they, like Hezekiah's community, need to respond to God's faithfulness with faithfulness, by returning to the temple and its ancient liturgy.

The letter of Hezekiah is modeled after Zechariah 1:2–4, which also addresses the postexilic community (so Williamson 1982, 367–68). There as here, the theme is return and repentance: "Return to me, says the LORD of hosts, and I will return to you, says the LORD of hosts" (Zech. 1:3). Note, too, that in both passages, the sins of the ancestors are to be repudiated (compare 30:8 and Zech. 1:4), so that the wrath of the Lord, directed against the ancestors, might not fall upon their descendants as well (30:8; Zech. 1:2). Once more, the Chronicler finds God's word for his own community in the words of Scripture, specifically in the prophetic word.

Sadly, Hezekiah's invitation is rejected by many in the north, who laugh at and scorn his messengers (30:10). The reader may be reminded of Jesus' parable of the wedding feast (Matt. 22:1–14; compare Luke 14:15–24), where the messengers are also scorned and ill-treated. However, as in Jesus' parable, the failure of those invited to respond does not mean that the feast is not held, or that it is a failure. Some, "from Asher, Manasseh, and Zebulun," do humble themselves and come to the feast (on the importance of humbling oneself, see the discussion on 7:14, above). In Judah, meanwhile, the response is once more overwhelming. The people respond with "one heart": that is, in unity, dedication, and singleness of purpose (2 Chr. 30:12; see 1 Chr. 12:38, where those who come to make David king are likewise said to be of "one heart"). In the end, as had been anticipated, it is "a very large assembly" that gathers in Jerusalem for the feast (2 Chr. 30:13).

In 2 Chronicles 30:13 and 21, the festival the assembly had gathered to celebrate is called "the festival of unleavened bread" rather than the Passover. These two festivals are closely linked in most biblical references (for example, Exod. 12:1–20; Lev. 23:4–8; Mark 14:1); indeed, Passover and the Feast of Unleavened Bread are at times combined (Deut. 16:1–8; Ezek. 45:21–24), and by New Testament times, could be explicitly identified with one another (Luke 22:1). However, they appear to have separate origins: note that the Book of the Covenant

219

(Exod. 20:22—23:33), likely the oldest law collection in the Hebrew Bible, includes the Feast of Unleavened Bread among the three pilgrim feasts, but does not mention Passover (Exod. 23:15; see also Exod. 34:18, 22–23 and 2 Chr. 8:12). If the combination of Passover and Unleavened Bread took place in connection with the centralization of worship in Jerusalem (as Deut. 16:1–8 suggests), then the Chronicler may describe here an innovation going back to Hezekiah. Alternatively, Hezekiah's feast may originally have been the Feast of Unleavened Bread, and the combination of the two in this narrative may be the work of the Chronicler, reflecting the practice of his own community (so Williamson 1982, 363–65).

The worshipers who have assembled in Jerusalem at their king's invitation extend the cleansing of the temple that Hezekiah had ordered to Jerusalem itself. The altars in Jerusalem, particularly the incense altars, are carried off and cast into the Wadi Kidron—to which, recall, the unclean items removed from the temple had also been taken (30:14; for the improper offering of incense, see 26:16 and 28:3). This act, carried out by the people, not the priests and Levites, provides further indication of the community's rededication to the Lord.

With the city as well as the temple cleansed, the festival begins on time, on the fourteenth day of the second month (see Num. 9:9–11). The priests and Levites, shamed by their failure to be prepared in the first month as well as by the example of the laity, have sanctified themselves in sufficient numbers, and stand ready to serve (30:15). They conduct themselves "according to the law of Moses the man of God" (30:16); as elsewhere in Chronicles, Scripture provides direction for right worship.

It is fortunate that the priests and Levites *are* ready, for a great number of those attending are ritually unclean, and so cannot kill their own sacrifices; the Levites must do this for them (30:17; for the killing of the sacrifice by Levites, see also Ezra 6:20; Ezek. 44:11). Nothing is said of the reasons for their defilement; however, since many of those said to be defiled come from the north (30:18), we may find here competing ideas about what constitutes ritual purity, or about the requirements for the observance of Passover. From the Chronicler's perspective, however, this means that "they ate the passover otherwise than as prescribed" (30:18)—that is, in violation of God's word in Scripture (see 30:5). But rather than barring these persons from participation, Hezekiah prays for them: "The good LORD pardon all who set their hearts to seek God, the LORD the God of their ancestors, even though not in accordance with the sanctuary's rules of cleanness" (30:18–19). The Lord hears the king's prayer, and the community is healed (30:20; compare 7:14).

220

Hezekiah's prayer, and the Lord's favorable response, strike a blow against rigid legalism. Clearly, it is more important to set one's heart to seek God than it is to be in a state of scrupulous ritual purity. Similarly, Micah asks, "[W]hat does the LORD require of you but to do justice, and to love kindness, and to walk humbly with your God?" (Mic. 6:8). In his teaching, Jesus as well placed "the weightier matters of the law: justice and mercy and faith" above ritual law (Matt. 23:23). So, for Jesus, meeting human need by healing on the sabbath was more important than strict adherence to the regulations of the rabbis (so, for example, Mark 3:1–6).

Particularly instructive in this regard is Paul's treatment of the question of eating food offered to idols, an issue which divided the early church. According to Acts 15:20, abstaining "from things polluted by idols" was part of that bare minimum of Jewish law which all believers, Jew and Gentile alike, were bound to follow. Similarly, the John of Revelation held that those who ate food sacrificed to idols separated themselves from Christ (Rev. 2:14, 20). Other Christians, however, reasoned that since there was only one true God, the idols were mere statues; food sacrificed to them was no different than any other kind of food (see 1 Cor. 8:1–6). Paul refused to settle the matter legalistically, either way. He argued that the food itself was not the issue; what really mattered was sensitivity to one another in the body of Christ. If the faith of "weaker" Christians is threatened when they see other believers eating food sacrificed to idols, then the "stronger" Christians need to abstain (1 Cor. 8:7–13).

Today, the church is divided by other questions and controversies. Yet, we still are tempted to appeal to legalism, whether in our reading of Scripture or in our application of community standards, to resolve our differences—even though such an appeal rarely resolves anything. We need to remember that Scripture itself rejects this narrow, rigid standard. How much better, like Hezekiah, to trust in God's grace to cover our lack of scrupulosity, and to recall that devotion to the Lord is our first, and highest, calling.

The seven days of the feast go by in praise and rejoicing (30:21–22). Hezekiah praises the Levites in particular (perhaps the Levitical musicians) for their skill and leadership. But then, the assembly doesn't want to stop: they agree to continue for another seven days! Hezekiah and his officials provide the animals for the sacrifices and sacred meals that continue for another week, and the priests ensure that there are a sufficient number of sanctified personnel to offer the sacrifices of the assembly (30:24; for the responsibility of the secular leadership to provide for the temple, see also 31:3).

The list of participants in this joyous celebration is a testimony to inclusivity: the whole assembly of Judah, the priests and Levites, the whole assembly of Israel, and resident aliens from both north and south take part (30:25). No wonder the Chronicler enthuses that "since the time of Solomon son of King David of Israel there had been nothing like this in Jerusalem" (30:26). Hezekiah's Passover has become a reunion of the formerly divided monarchy—a return, in however small a measure, to the days before Jeroboam's revolt. The service concludes with a benediction pronounced by the Levitical priests (not, as the NRSV reads, "the priests and the Levites"; for the priestly responsibility for the benediction, see 1 Chr. 23:13; Num. 6:22–27). The words of the priests are heard in God's "holy dwelling in heaven" (30:27)—wording reminiscent of Solomon's temple dedication prayer (see 6:21).

The departing worshipers, still filled with zeal from their celebration before the Lord, extend the cleansing of Jerusalem into the entire land (31:1). The text here refers back to the account of Hezekiah's reforms in Kings (2 Kgs. 18:4), save that in Chronicles the people, rather than the king "broke down the pillars, hewed down the sacred poles, and pulled down the high places and the altars." All Israel is purged, north and south alike; only then do the people return to their homes. However, for those who have taken part in Hezekiah's Passover, nothing could ever be the same again. They are no longer a divided people, north against south. Worshiping together, they have become once more one Israel, united by one faith and one purpose. Plainly, right worship and right action are inseparably joined in Hezekiah's reform. Indeed, it is right worship that empowers and inspires right action.

Hezekiah's reforms continue with the restoration of the divisions of the priests and Levites and of the regular liturgy, as established by David (see 1 Chr. 23:2—26:32). The liturgy is a shared responsibility of the priests, who are responsible for the sacrifices, and the Levites, whose calling is "to minister in the gates of the camp of the LORD and to give thanks and praise" (31:2). The expression "the camp of the Lord" calls to mind the days of the wilderness wandering, when the Levites, who were responsible for guarding the tabernacle, had camped surrounding it (Num. 1:53). Similarly, in 1 Chronicles 9:19, the Levitical gatekeepers are "in charge of the work of the service, guardians of the thresholds of the tent, as their ancestors had been in charge of the camp of the LORD, guardians of the entrance." "The camp of the LORD," then, is a poetic expression for the temple complex.

The sacrificial animals for the regular liturgy are provided by Hezekiah himself (31:3). Solomon too had provided for the day-to-day liturgy of the temple (8:12–13). Apparently, this is a reflection of Persian-period practice, in the Chronicler's own time. In an Aramaic doc-

222

ument preserved in Ezra 6:6–12, the Persian ruler Darius issues a proclamation which makes the state's support for the Jerusalem temple explicit. First, he directs that the costs for rebuilding the temple be paid from the royal treasury: in particular, from the tribute of the province of Abar-Naharah, in which Jerusalem was located (Ezra 6:8). Then, Darius further stipulates that whatever might be required for the temple service is to be provided daily by the province, so that sacrifices can be offered and prayers made "for the life of the king and his children" (Ezra 6:9–10).

The support of the Persian state for the Jerusalem temple is not remarkable. A votive inscription found on a statue dedicated to the Egyptian priest Udhahoresne gives testimony to Darius's support for temples in Egypt as well. Udjahoresne was a high official in the temple of Neith (an Egyptian goddess, mother to Ra, the sun god) and the House of Life, an institution dedicated to medicine and the healing arts as well as to the god Osiris. Of Darius, the Udjahoresne inscription declares, "His majesty had commanded to give them every good thing, in order that they might carry out all their crafts. I supplied them with everything useful to them, with all their equipment that was on record, as they had been before" (Lichtheim 1980, 40).

The commissioning of Udjahoresne by Darius brings to mind the commission of Ezra under Artaxerxes. Here, too, a religious official, empowered by Persia but with roots among the native populace, is sent to order the religious life of a people, with the Persian state footing the bill. Like Darius, Artaxerxes I directed that the treasurers of the province were to provide whatever the law required for the temple, although unlike Darius, Artaxerxes set explicit limits upon this generosity (Ezra 7:21–23)! A similar pattern is found in the Law of the Temple in Ezekiel 40—48. There, the expenses of the sacrificial liturgy are defrayed by the government, from the considerable estates of the prince and from the taxes collected from the province (45:13–17). In short, Chronicles appears accurately to reflect the state-supported temple of the Chronicler's day.

However, while provisions for the sacrifices come from the king, the livelihood of the priests and the maintenance of the shrine depend upon the generosity of the people (see the discussion of 1 Chr. 6:54–81, above). Like Joash before him, Hezekiah calls upon the people "to give the portion due to the priests and the Levites" (31:4; see the discussion of 24:4–10, above). In the following verses, "the people of Israel" (here, presumably, northerners living at some distance from the temple) give abundantly from the produce of their fields, while "people of Israel and Judah living in the cities of Judah" (southerners and northern refugees

223

living in the south, much closer to Jerusalem) bring in animals from their flocks and herds. However, in 31:4, the command is given only to the people of Jerusalem. This may reflect the situation in the period after the exile, when "Judah" consisted of little more than the city and its immediate surroundings. Then, as Malachi 3:8–10 shows, there was considerable resistance to paying this tithe (so Klein 1993, 688). However, in Chronicles the people give so extravagantly that heaps of goods are piled in the temple precincts! When Hezekiah asks about these heaps, the chief priest Azariah explains, "Since they began to bring the contributions into the house of the LORD, we have had enough to eat and have plenty to spare; for the LORD has blessed his people, so that we have this great supply left over" (31:10).

The principle that God shows generosity to the generous is found throughout Scripture. Malachi challenged his own parsimonious community in the Lord's name: "Bring the full tithe into the storehouse, so that there may be food in my house, and thus put me to the test, says the LORD of hosts; see if I will not open the windows of heaven for you and pour down for you an overflowing blessing" (Mal. 3:10). So, Jesus urged his followers to "give, and it will be given to you. A good measure, pressed down, shaken together, running over, will be put into your lap; for the measure you give will be the measure you get back" (Luke 6:38; see also 2 Cor. 9:6) It is important, however, that this principle not be misunderstood: it is no mystical get-rich-quick scheme! To be sure, those who practice lifestyles of giving will tell you that God has blessed them with happiness and fulfillment. But, as Paul observes, we are given the blessings we receive in order that we might be able to give even more (2 Cor. 9:8). After all, the universe is the Lord's; our giving is in truth only a giving *back* (see 1 Chr. 29:14). In Chronicles, as the people give generously, they find themselves generously blessed, so that they may in turn give all the more.

To provide a place to put all this abundance, Hezekiah has storerooms built in the temple complex (2 Chr. 31:11; see 1 Kgs. 6:5–6; Ezek. 41:5–11). Then, to handle the administration of this wealth, he appoints Levitical administrators, just as David had done (2 Chr. 31:11–15a; see also 1 Chr. 26:20–28). Hezekiah gives to Kore, keeper of the eastern gate, the responsibility "to apportion the contribution reserved for the LORD and the most holy offerings" among the families of the priests and Levites (for the administrative responsibilities of the gatekeepers, see 1 Chr. 9:28–29). A portion is given to all males over three years old, both to those enrolled by divisions (that is, the Levites) and those enrolled by genealogy (that is, the priests; 2 Chr. 31:15b–19). Those younger than three years are excluded because they are still nursing, and cannot eat a portion of the offerings. That the Levites are enrolled "by divisions" means that they are grouped according to the service that they perform (see 1 Chr. 23:4–5; for Levitical service beginning at age twenty, see the discussion of 1 Chr. 23:24, 27, above). The priests, on the other hand, are grouped by families (2 Chr. 31:17; see 1 Chr. 24:1–19).

In 31:20–21, the Chronicler resumes his use of the narrative in Kings (compare 2 Kgs. 18:3, 5–6). Hezekiah, we are told, was faithful to the Lord, and observed the Torah; further, he sought the Lord "with all his heart." God, therefore, blessed Hezekiah; as the Chronicler simply states, "he prospered" (31:21; so also 32:30). The requirements for prosperity are made very clear in Chronicles. David tells his son Solomon that he will prosper if he observes the Torah (1 Chr. 22:13). Correspondingly, the prophet Zechariah asks King Joash, "Why do you transgress the commandments of the LORD, so that you cannot prosper?" (2 Chr. 24:20). The Chronicler says of only two kings that they prospered: Solomon (1 Chr. 29:23) and Hezekiah.

The faithfulness of Hezekiah is put to the test by the invasion of Sennacherib (32:1–23//2 Kgs. 18:13–37; 19:14–19, 35–37//Isa. 36:1–22; 37:14–20, 36–38). The Chronicler's source for the account of the Assyrian invasion is 2 Kings, which has also been used by the editors of the book of Isaiah. However, this account, which in Kings makes up the bulk of the Hezekiah narrative, is in Chronicles condensed and abridged—just as the account of Hezekiah's reforms, the subject of only a few verses in Kings, makes up the bulk of the narrative in Chronicles. The Chronicler does not describe Hezekiah's revolt (compare 2 Kgs. 18:7–8), so that Sennacherib's invasion seems to come out of nowhere. The detailed preparations the king has made for the defense of Jerusalem, however, reveal that Hezekiah had been getting ready for some time (32:3–8).

Hezekiah timed his revolt carefully, striking upon the death of Sargon II. Evidently, Hezekiah banked on Sargon's successor being preoccupied for some time after his accession with internal affairs and revolts closer to home, giving Judah time to strengthen its defenses. Hezekiah's overtures to the northern survivors made it possible for him to present a strong, unified front at home. Further, we learn from Kings and Isaiah that Hezekiah had also established alliances with other powers in the region, particularly with Egypt (2 Kgs. 18:21//Isa. 36:6; Isa. 30:1–17). Chronicles does not mention these alliances—little wonder, given the Chronicler's attitude toward foreign entanglements.

However, the Chronicler does describe Hezekiah's defensive preparations. In addition to fortifying Jerusalem itself with an additional outer wall and strengthening the Millo (evidently, an earth-filled, stepped terrace structure, part of Jerusalem's defenses; for the building

225

of the Millo by David, see 1 Chr. 11:8), the king also organizes and arms his citizens, and appoints officers to lead them. In particular, the Chronicler describes Hezekiah's actions with regard to Jerusalem's water supply. The primary water source for Jerusalem was the Gihon spring, which fed a small stream called Shiloah, in the Kidron Valley (1 Kgs. 1:33; 2 Chr. 32:30; 33:14; Isa. 8:5–8). To conceal this vulnerable spot from the Assyrians, and to make its water inaccessible to them, Hezekiah stops up the spring, diverting its waters so that they can be collected by means of a tunnel dug out from within the walls of the city (32:30). Hezekiah's tunnel, and evidence of his outer wall, have been found by archaeologists, confirming the accuracy of the Chronicler's sources at this point (see Horn and McCarter 1999, 182).

Like Asa before him (14:6–7), Hezekiah is well-prepared to defend his kingdom. However, also like Asa, Hezekiah puts his trust in the Lord, rather than his own strength (32:7–8; see 14:11). In neither case is this a contradiction. Both kings are aware that all things come from God, including their own capabilities. Hence, the preparations of Asa and Hezekiah reflect, not a lack of trust, but a faithful response to God. Asa and Hezekiah realize that victory belongs to God, and is awarded as God sees fit. However, their preparations become, in part, the means by which God brings victory. To paraphrase Louis Pasteur, perhaps grace, like chance, favors the prepared mind.

The new king of Assyria, Sennacherib (705–681 B.C.), wastes no time in responding to Hezekiah's revolt. From Assyrian annals, as well as from Kings, we learn of his victories throughout Palestine, which decimate Judah (Horn and McCarter 1999, 178–80; 2 Kgs. 18:13). Chronicles, however, says only that Sennacherib "invaded Judah and encamped against the fortified cities, thinking to win them for himself" (32:1). Whatever Sennacherib may have thought, Chronicles implies, the final victory would belong to the Lord.

Sennacherib sends messengers to Hezekiah from Lachish, calling for his surrender (32:9–15//2 Kgs. 18:19–35//Isa. 36:1–20). Although neither Kings nor Chronicles describes the fall of Lachish, both assume that this former Judean stronghold was the headquarters for the Assyrian army in Judah. An impressively detailed relief from the walls of Sennacherib's palace at Nineveh depicts the conquest of Lachish, from the mounting of the siege to the parade of the captives (see Shea 1999, 42–43; Pritchard 1969, 129–31, figs. 371–73).

In Chronicles as in Kings, the message of Sennacherib is actually directed, not at Hezekiah, but at the people of Jerusalem (note that both emphasize the messengers' use of Hebrew, the language of the people, rather than Aramaic, the language of international diplomacy;

see 32:18; 2 Kgs. 18:26–28//Isa. 36:11–13). It is a propaganda piece, intended to break the morale of the city's defenders. However, as edited by the Chronicler, Sennacherib's message primarily serves to cast the Assyrian invasion as a religious conflict.

First, Sennacherib declares that the Lord will not help Hezekiah, because Hezekiah has removed the Lord's high places and altars, ordering that sacrifices be offered in Jerusalem alone (32:12//2 Kgs. 18:22//Isa. 36:7). In its historical context, this is a marvelously nuanced challenge, aimed at dividing the community on a controversial point; presumably, there were many in Israel who did feel threatened and disenfranchised by Hezekiah's centralization policies. But in Chronicles, the people themselves had purged first Jerusalem, and then the land north and south, of all high places and altars (30:14; 31:1); here, there is no division for the Assyrians to exploit. Sennacherib's words only demonstrate his total incomprehension of the ways of the Lord, and the faith of Israel.

Next, Sennacherib turns to Assyria's successful history as an imperial power: "Who among all the gods of those nations that my ancestors utterly destroyed was able to save his people from my hand, that your God should be able to save you from my hand?" (32:14//2 Kgs. 18:33–35//Isa. 36:18–20). Here again, the larger context of Chronicles gives the lie to Sennacherib's proud speech. Three times in the Chronicler's History so far, during the reigns of the good kings Abijah (13:3–20), Asa (14:9–15), and Jehoshaphat (20:1–30), massive foreign invasions have been thwarted by the Lord. The reader of Chronicles knows full well, then, that Sennacherib too will fail. Further, the experience of the Chronicler's own community of returned exiles told them that God could triumph over a great power to deliver God's people. The Chronicler contemptuously points up the fatal error of Sennacherib's messengers: "They spoke of the God of Jerusalem as if he were like the gods of the peoples of the earth, which are the work of human hands" (32:19).

The outcome of Sennacherib's siege of Jerusalem is clear: according to both the biblical witness and the Assyrian annals, the siege was withdrawn, and the city did not fall. The explanation for this startling conclusion, however, is anything but clear. The account in 2 Kings preserves possibly three alternate traditions. In 2 Kings 18:13–16, Hezekiah meekly surrenders to save his city, emptying his treasury and stripping the gold from the temple doors to pay the tribute demanded by Sennacherib. The annals of Sennacherib likewise claim that Hezekiah, shut up in his city "like a bird in a cage," had been forced to pay tribute (Horn and McCarter 1999, 180). In 2 Kings 19:6–7 (//Isaiah 37:6–7), a distraught Hezekiah is assured by a word of the Lord from the prophet Isaiah that Sennacherib "shall hear a rumor and return to his own land; I will cause him to fall by the sword in his own land," a prediction that is fulfilled in 2 Kings 19:36–37//Isaiah 37:37–38. Here again, partial confirmation comes from Assyrian sources: Sennacherib was assassinated by his sons, though not until 681 B.C. Finally, 2 Kings 19:35//Isaiah 37:36 declares that "the angel of the LORD set out and struck down one hundred eighty-five thousand in the camp of the Assyrians"—referring, perhaps, to a plague in the Assyrian siege camp which forced them to withdraw.

So, why didn't the Assyrians press on with their siege? Perhaps the best historical explanation is that they didn't have to. With the revolt effectively surpressed, and Hezekiah paying tribute, there was no pressing need for Sennacherib to take Jerusalem—particularly as Hezekiah's preparations made the city a very hard nut to crack (Horn and McCarter 1999, 183). However, the fact that the greatest military power of the day had withdrawn without conquering Jerusalem was remembered as a testimony to God's miraculous preservation of God's own city. In Chronicles, which sharply condenses its source, the prayers of faithful Hezekiah and the prophet Isaiah prompt the Lord to send an angel to destroy the Assyrian army. Like Abijah, Asa, and Jehoshaphat, Hezekiah is delivered from the invader by the Lord: indeed, in Chronicles the invasion of Sennacherib becomes, curiously, an affirmation of the Lord's blessing upon Hezekiah (Williamson 1982, 378). Nothing is said in Chronicles of Hezekiah paying tribute to Assyria. Indeed, like Jehoshaphat and Solomon before him, Hezekiah receives gifts from foreign powers, and is "exalted in the sight of all nations from that time onward" (32:23).

The Chronicler's account of Hezekiah's illness (32:24) and of the visit of the Babylonian envoys (32:25–26, 31) is even more sharply edited than his version of Sennacherib's invasion. Indeed, the Chronicler's version is so pared down that it cannot be understood without reference to the source in Kings (2 Kgs. 20:1–21//Isa. 38:1—39:8). Only the barest facts about Hezekiah's illness are recorded: Hezekiah became ill, he prayed, the Lord answered him with a sign. The Chronicler assumes that his readers know the story of the miraculous sign of the shadow on the sundial moving backwards, and of Hezekiah's healing. He does not retell this story, perhaps because he mistrusts it as a wonder tale, or perhaps because it unnecessarily detracts from his central focus on Hezekiah as a king blessed for his religious reforms. In its present sharply truncated form, this incident contrasts favorably with the account of Asa, also stricken by illness late in his reign, who turned to physicians rather than, as Hezekiah does, to prayer (see 16:12).

The Chronicler's account of the Merodach-baladan incident is even more cryptic. Because of his pride, Hezekiah was subject to God's wrath, but because he humbled himself, it did not strike during his reign. The Chronicler assumes that the reader will catch the reference to the visit of the envoys from Merodach-baladan, ruler of Babylon, to whom Hezekiah had pridefully shown all the riches of his kingdom. Isaiah, when he hears of this, declares that Babylon will one day return, to loot the treasuries of the king and the temple and to carry the people into exile. The Chronicler puts the best possible face on Hezekiah's selfish response: "Why not, if there will be peace and security in my days?" (2 Kgs. 20:19; compare Isa. 39:8). The delay of the wrath of God to future generations recalls the similar story of Jehoshaphat, whose repentance and reforms diverted the wrath due to him for his foreign alliances onto the reigns of his wicked descendants (see the discussion of 19:2–3).

Perhaps the Chronicler chooses not to retell the story of the Babylonian envoys because it assigns at least partial blame for the exile to Hezekiah. This would needlessly complicate the Chronicler's narrative, in which Hezekiah is praised as the reformer par excellence, and the exile is brought about by Judah's faithlessness. Chronicles does, however, make one final reference to the visit, in response to the record of Hezekiah's great wealth (32:31). In keeping with the Chronicler's usual disinterest in politics, no human motivation for the visit is given. Instead, the Babylonian envoys are said to have been a test from God. Sadly Hezekiah, like David, falls prey to the temptations of pride (see 1 Chr. 21:1–27); however, God is merciful and forgiving, and still gives Hezekiah peace and security all his days.

The description of Hezekiah's economic expansion in 32:27–30 serves in its context in the Chronicler's History to confirm God's blessing upon the faithful reformer. However, this description evidently derives from an authentic old Judean source. Archaeological evidence suggests that a tremendous economic expansion did take place in the time of Hezekiah. Particularly important is the wide distribution of the *lmlk* jars (clay jars for oil or wine, stamped with the words "[belonging] to the king" and dating to the reign of Hezekiah), and of clay seals stamped with the royal insignia of Hezekiah (see the table in Vaughn 1999, 166). Indeed, Hezekiah's own personal seal has come to light, providing a fascinating personal connection with this ancient king (Horn and McCarter 1999, 177). In short, Hezekiah really did establish "storehouses . . . for the yield of grain, wine, and oil" throughout Judah, and he really "provided cities for himself," just as Chronicles claims.

229

The Chronicler ascribes his source for Hezekiah's reign to the prophet Isaiah: scarcely surprising, given the role played by Isaiah in

Hezekiah's story (32:32; compare 2 Kgs. 20:20). Like the other good kings of Judah, he is buried in the royal cemetery, and honored by all.

33:1–20
Manasseh (//2 Kgs. 21:1–10, 17–18)

Manasseh reigned longer (fifty-five years) than any other king in Judah's history. Yet, despite being blessed with health, peace, and stability, he was far from a model of righteousness. In both Chronicles and Kings, Manasseh's reign represents a serious slide backward from the reforms of Hezekiah. Indeed, not since the days before Israel's entry into Canaan had such idolatry been seen in the land (33:2//2 Kgs. 21:2). Manasseh reverses the reforms of his father, rebuilding the high places the people had demolished in Hezekiah's time (33:3; see 31:1), and returning to the temple and its courts the altars that Hezekiah's temple restoration had removed (33:4–5; see 29:16–17).

The deities worshiped by Manasseh are old Canaanite gods and goddesses: specifically the fertility deities Baal and Asherah, and the "hosts of heaven" (gods associated with the sun, moon, and stars, especially the zodiac; see Deut 4:19; 17:3). Note that in the NRSV of 2 Chronicles 33:3 (//2 Kings 21:3), the Hebrew word *'asherah* is rendered as "sacred pole" (see also 31:1). These poles, called by the name of the goddess, were evidently cult objects used in her worship; their use was absolutely forbidden in the Torah (Exod. 34:13; Deut. 7:5; 12:3). In Chronicles we read that Manasseh "erected altars to the *Baals*" and "made sacred *poles*" (33:3, emphasis added), while in 2 Kings 21:3, the singular is used. The Chronicler's use of the plural intensifies Manasseh's idolatry. It also reflects a feature of Canaanite religion, wherein a deity could be identified with its manifestations in various places: as, for example, the Baal of Peor (Num. 25:3), or "Baal-zebub, the god of Ekron" (2 Kgs. 1:2–3).

Like Ahaz, Manasseh participates in the obscene rites of child sacrifice practiced "in the valley of the son of Hinnom" (33:6; see the discussion of 28:3, above). He also "practiced soothsaying and augury and sorcery, and dealt with mediums and with wizards": supernatural sources of knowledge forbidden to the people of Israel (see Deut. 18:9–12, where, as in 33:6, child sacrifice and the practice of divination are linked). In Chronicles, such actions specifically recall King Saul, who also consulted a medium and "died for his unfaithfulness" (1 Chr. 10:13–14).

Twice, in 2 Chronicles 33:4 and 7–8, Manasseh is condemned for acting contrary to the word of the Lord. Neither text seems to refer to any specific text of Scripture; rather, both are summaries of the Deuteronomic theology regarding God's election of Jerusalem (see Deut. 12:2–7; 1 Kgs. 8:29). However, the reader is reminded that this election is not irrevocable. God's name will remain in Jerusalem, and God's people will remain in the land of promise, only if "they will be careful to do all that I have commanded them, all the law, the statutes, and the ordinances given through Moses" (33:8//2 Kgs. 21:8). Manasseh's actions threaten the very foundations of Israel's existence, particularly as he does not act alone, but is followed by "Judah and the inhabitants of Jerusalem" (33:9). Just as the influence of the good king Hezekiah had reformed all Israel, the influence of wicked Manasseh corrupts his people as well.

For the first nine verses of chapter 33, the story of Manasseh in Chronicles closely follows its source in Kings, with few significant changes. But then, the two accounts sharply diverge. The reasons for this divergence lie in the theological purposes of the Deuteronomist on the one hand, and of the Chronicler on the other.

The Deuteronomistic History interprets Israel's past in terms of the covenant blessings and curses of Deuteronomy: when Israel is obedient to the commandments of the Lord, the nation is blessed; when the commandments are violated, the nation is cursed. Serious problems, then, were raised by the death of the good king Josiah, and the subsequent decline and fall of Judah. How, after Josiah's righteous reforms, could everything have gone so wrong? The final form of the Deuteronomistic History explains this collapse by reference to the reign of Manasseh (so Cross 1973, 285–86). So wicked was this king, and so corrupt did the nation become under his influence, that God determined that Jerusalem must be destroyed in consequence (2 Kgs. 21:10–15, 23:26–27). The righteousness of Josiah could only delay this outpouring of divine wrath (see 2 Kgs. 22:14–20).

The Chronicler, on the other hand, operates under different theological presuppositions. In his view, the exile was not due to the actions of any particular king, but to the faithlessness of all Judah (36:14–17; see also 1 Chr. 9:1). Therefore, Chronicles can adopt a more balanced view toward Manasseh. While the account in 2 Kings has nothing substantive to say about Manasseh's fifty-five years on the throne, Chronicles recalls the king's public works, drawing once more on old Judean sources that are almost certainly accurate (33:14).

The Chronicler's bent for individual responsibility is given specific application in Manasseh's reign. The prophetic word, which in 2 Kings 21:10 is the declaration of Judah's fate, is in 33:10 a warning from the

Lord, which Manasseh and his people did not heed. As a result, the Assyrians "took Manasseh captive with hooks" (a better translation of the Hebrew than the NRSV "took Manasseh captive in manacles"; cf. Amos 4:2), and the king himself went into exile. Only when he humbled himself and repented did God permit Manasseh to return to Jerusalem. The chastened king became a reformer like his father (33:15–16). But he could not undo all the evil that he had done: the high places remained, and sacrifices to the Lord continued to be offered outside of the temple in Jerusalem (33:17).

What are we to make of this curious account? We might speculate that the exile and repentance of Manasseh were required in the story-world of Chronicles to make sense of Manasseh's long, peaceful reign. How could such a wicked king have escaped the consequences of his wickedness? In Chronicles, of course, he doesn't. Manasseh acted faithlessly, and suffered the consequences of his faithlessness; only when he repented was he restored. On the other hand, we do not elsewhere find the Chronicler creating stories out of whole cloth. While he is often selective and creative in the use of his sources, the Chronicler is faithful to his traditions, even when their implications are disturbing. So, for example, the tragic early death of the good king Abijah is not explained away by some conjectured apostasy. While the way that Chronicles relates the story of Manasseh is highly colored by the Chronicler's theology, the basic elements of that story, Manasseh's exile and his return, may derive from an authentic old tradition.

Manasseh is mentioned in seventh-century Assyrian inscriptions as a loyal vassal who contributed as required to support the long Assyrian campaign against Egypt (see the translations of Oppenheim 1969, 291, 294). However, that may have changed after 652 B.C., when Shamash-shum-ukin, ruler of Babylon and brother to the Assyrian king Assurbanipal (669–626 B.C), launched his revolt. The revolt spread quickly, supported in particular by the Arab tribes, and though Babylon was pacified by 648 B.C., the empire never recovered. Perhaps Manasseh, too, supported Shamash-shum-ukin's revolt—or was suspected of doing so by his Assyrian overlords. The treatment of Manasseh described in 33:11–13 is in keeping with the actions of Assurbanipal toward other vassals of questionable loyalty. Both Necho of Egypt and the Arab leader Uate' were captured, brought before the king, and then, when sufficiently intimidated, returned to their homelands to rule once more (Horn and McCarter 1999, 332–33, n. 160). The actions of Manasseh described in 33:14—further construction on the walls of Jerusalem and the placement of military commanders in the fortified cities of Judah—could be the actions of a king preparing for revolt (so Horn and

232

McCarter 1999, 188). However, as Assurbanipal returned Manasseh to power rather than executing him, it is more likely Manasseh's military preparations were the acts of a loyal Assyrian vassal, preparing to stand as a buffer against future Egyptian aggression (so Bright 1981, 314).

Of course, even if Manasseh's exile and return were historical events with political causes, Chronicles does not present them in that way. The Chronicler, disinterested as always in political motivations, sees both Manasseh's exile and his return as acts of God, prompted by Manasseh's sin and repentance. Manasseh serves as a compelling illustration of the extraordinary grace of God, offered freely to penitents whatever their offenses—and a firm rebuttal to those who would see a firm divide between "Old" Testament *law* and "New" Testament *grace*. In fact, the grace of God is the living heart of the whole of Scripture. The forgiveness of sins in Jesus' ministry (for example, Mark 2:5; Luke 7:40–50) builds on the foundation laid in the Hebrew Bible regarding the character of God, who loves and forgives (for example, 2 Chr. 7:14; Neh. 9:17). Indeed, the life of Paul, persecutor of the church turned apostle, forms an intriguing parallel to the Chronicler's life of Manasseh (see 1 Cor. 15:9–10). The Chronicler would be in perfect agreement with 1 John 1:9: "If we confess our sins, he who is faithful and just will forgive us our sins and cleanse us from all unrighteousness."

The sources given for the life of Manasseh in Chronicles are "the Annals of the Kings of Israel" and "the records of the seers" (33:18–19; compare 2 Kgs. 21:17); once more, the Chronicler's sources are ascribed to prophetic authorship. These records are said to have included Manasseh's prayer of repentance, but the prayer is not found in Chronicles. An anonymous Greek-speaking Jew in the first century B.C., feeling this lack, composed the apocryphal Prayer of Manasseh, a heartfelt penitential prayer. But despite Manasseh's repentance, Chronicles agrees with its source that the king was buried at his residence, not in the royal cemetery (33:20//2 Kgs. 21:18).

33:21–25
Amon (//2 Kgs. 21:19–24)

The account of Amon's reign in Chronicles substantially follows the account in Kings. The Chronicler presents Amon as a virtual clone of his father, with one exception: Amon "did not humble himself before the LORD, as his father Manasseh had humbled himself, but this Amon incurred more and more guilt" (33:23).

In Chronicles as in Kings, Amon dies by assassination. Neither text provides a motivation for this act. However, as Assyrian power was on the wane, it is perhaps most likely that Amon was killed in an anti-Assyrian coup (Bright 1981, 316). His assassins, however, are caught and executed, and power passes to "the people of the land" (33:25): evidently, a group of landed nobles who place Josiah, a boy only eight years old, on the throne. Probably, until Josiah reaches maturity, these same persons administer the kingdom.

Now, once more, the text of Chronicles departs from its source: 2 Kings 21:25–26 mentions the source for Amon's life, in the Annals of the Kings of Judah, and describes his burial alongside his father, in the gardens of Uzza. Chronicles lacks this information. As 2 Kings 21:24 and 26 end with the same words in Hebrew, it is possible that the eye of a scribe skipped over these last two verses. However, as we saw in the cases of Jehoram, Ahaziah, and Athaliah (chaps. 21—23), the omission of a source reference and of proper burial arrangements are marks of condemnation in Chronicles. Most probably, then, the Chronicler ignores the last two verses of his source, implying that Amon does not deserve a memorial, in tomb or in text (so Japhet 1993, 1014).

34:1—35:27
Josiah (//2 Kgs. 22:1—23:30//1 Esd. 1:1–33)

In Chronicles as in Kings, Josiah is a righteous reformer. However, in the Deuteronomistic History, Josiah is *the* righteous reformer, the only king (including David!) to escape any condemnation. Indeed, Josiah is the only person in Scripture who "turned to the LORD with all his heart, with all his soul, and with all his might" (2 Kgs. 23:25; see Deut. 6:5). It seems probable, then, that the first edition of the Deuteronomistic History reached its climax in Josiah's reign (Cross 1973, 283–85). In the Chronicler's History, on the other hand, it is Hezekiah who is *the* righteous reformer. Josiah is significant as the last of the reformers, the last good king, and the last king to be spared the penalty of exile; however, he otherwise stands as one among others. This different attitude results in a different presentation. Although, as will be seen, the account of Josiah's reign in Chronicles is based substantially on the account in Kings, that text is expanded and reordered to fit the Chronicler's unique perspective.

Chronicles begins, as does Kings, by affirming the righteousness of Josiah, who "did what was right in the sight of the LORD, and walked in all the way of his father David" (34:2//2 Kgs. 22:2; for the significance of this comparison, see the discussion of 29:2 above). But then, the Chronicler stays with the young Josiah for a while longer (much as Luke stays with the child Jesus; see Luke 2). At the age of sixteen, "Josiah began to seek the God of his ancestor David" (34:3). Even as an adolescent, Josiah is conspicuously interested in the worship of the Lord, and in the temple. No wonder Josiah begins his reforms in his twelfth year (34:3)—that is, as soon as he turns twenty and assumes full authority as king (so Williamson 1982, 398; on twenty as the age of majority, see 1 Chr. 23:24, 27; 27:23; 2 Chr. 31:17).

This, clearly, is quite a departure from the Chronicler's source! In 2 Kings, Josiah's reforms begin in his eighteenth year, following the discovery of the book of the law in the temple (2 Kgs. 23:1–23). To be sure, the book of the law was found in the temple because Josiah had instituted temple repairs (2 Kgs. 22:3–8), showing that even in the Deuteronomistic History some acts of reform precede the king's eighteenth year (so Klein 1993, 693). However, the description of Josiah's reforms in Chronicles is based on the account in 2 Kings 23:1–20: the Chronicler has no source for Josiah's reform apart from Kings. Further, more is involved here than a question of chronology. In the Deuteronomistic History, the book of the law (probably, as we have seen, an early form of the book of Deuteronomy) prompts and structures Josiah's reforms. But in Chronicles, the book is found *because of* Josiah's reforms: its discovery is "a reward for faithfulness" on the part of Josiah (Williamson 1982, 401). By rearranging and judiciously editing his source, the Chronicler has produced a substantially different view of Josiah, his reforms, and his law book.

In Chronicles, Josiah's reforms parallel the reforms of Hezekiah, in both form and content (so Myers 1965, 205), save that Josiah does not need to cleanse the temple at the outset—Manasseh has already done this (33:15–16; however, see 34:8). The reform begins in Jerusalem and Judah, with the removal of the high places, altars, and sacred poles. These Josiah not merely disassembles, but destroys, grinding them to powder. He also puts to death the priests and worshipers of these illicit shrines (34:4–5; compare 2 Kgs. 23:6, 14–16). Then, the reform moves north, to "the towns of Manasseh, Ephraim, and Simeon, and as far as Naphtali" (34:6). Like Hezekiah, Josiah includes the north in his reforms. However, while Hezekiah could only invite the northerners to participate, Josiah carries his reform to them, going himself deep into the territory of the former northern kingdom, and establishing his authority over it. By the time Josiah returns to his capital, all Israel has been purged (34:7).

Historically, Josiah was able to reassert control over the north because of the rapid dissolution of the Assyrian empire. An alliance of

235

Nabopolassar of Babylon and Cyaxeres of Media began taking apart the remnants of the empire in 616 B.C.; by 612 B.C. Ninevah, the capital of the Assyrian empire, had fallen (see the prophecies of Nahum, which date to this time). Long before this, however, the western part of the empire would have been left to fend for itself. Josiah was free to assert his independence, and to reunite David's divided kingdom once more. The Chronicler, however, is more interested in religious reform than political reunification. Under Josiah, the one faith of ancient Israel, centered on the temple of Solomon and the liturgy of David, has become once more the one faith of *all* Israel, north and south alike.

Now, in 34:8, we come to Josiah's eighteenth year (//2 Kgs. 22:3). The account of Josiah's temple repairs is drawn from Kings, with minor additions. The mention of "Maaseiah the governor of the city, and Joah son of Joahaz, the recorder" assisting Shaphan in organizing the repairs was more than likely a part of the Chronicler's source text; he would have no compelling reason to insert, or invent, such a minor detail. On the other hand, the note that the "keepers of the threshold" who collect the money for the temple repairs are Levites reflects the role played by the Levites elsewhere in Chronicles (see especially 24:4–7). The Levites also play an active role in the repairs themselves, serving as supervisors, administrators, and even (as those who enjoy background music while they work will be interested to hear) as musical accompanists (34:12–13)!

Just as in Hezekiah's day, contributions for the temple come from all Israel, north and south (33:9; see 31:4–6). Chronicles specifies the nature of Josiah's temple repairs, and the reason that they are necessary: they are "for the buildings that the kings of Judah had let go to ruin" (33:11). The plural "buildings" suggests that it was not only the temple proper, but the entire complex that was in need of repair (compare 1 Chr. 29:4, where the MT has plural "houses"). The "kings of Judah" who had let the temple fall into disrepair could be Manasseh and Amon, calling into question Manasseh's alleged temple restoration; note, too, that 34:8 says that the repairs began after Josiah "had purged the land *and the house,*" suggesting that Josiah may have carried out temple reforms like Hezekiah's after all. On the other hand, Hezekiah in his reform had blamed his ancestors generally for the temple defilement carried out by Ahaz specifically (29:6–7); certainly the plural does not in Hezekiah's case include his righteous grandfather Jotham (see chap. 27). Perhaps nothing more is meant than that the temple structure has been long neglected; apart from Hezekiah's work on the gates (29:3), no repairs have been made to the temple since Joash was king (24:12–13).

Even before the repairs have begun, as the money is being collected, Hilkiah the priest discovers the book of the law, and through Josiah's secretary Shaphan brings its contents to the attention of the king (34:14–18; compare 2 Kgs. 22:8–10). In the Chronicler's History, where the revelation of God's will comes through the written word of Scripture, this discovery is particularly significant, as is its timing. Josiah has demonstrated his faithfulness to God since his youth, by earnestly seeking God in worship, by cleansing all Israel of illicit shrines and re-establishing the centrality of Jerusalem, and by undertaking repairs and renovations of the temple complex. Now, God rewards Josiah by revealing to him God's word. Once more, the central theme of Chronicles is made plain: "If you seek him, he will be found by you; but if you forsake him, he will abandon you forever" (1 Chr. 28:9). Josiah, who has spent his whole young life seeking, has found God, revealed in God's word.

However, finding God can be a disturbing experience! When the prophet Isaiah saw the Lord in his call vision, he also experienced a profound sense of his own defilement (Isa. 6:5). Simon Peter, discovering that the rabbi Jesus was indeed divine, cried out, "Go away from me, Lord, for I am a sinful man!" (Luke 5:8). So also, Josiah finds himself and his kingdom (which in Chronicles consists explicitly of "those who are left in Israel and in Judah") judged and condemned in the words of this law, so that he tears his robes in mourning and despair (34:19–21//2 Kgs. 22:11–13). If indeed Josiah's law book was a form of Deuteronomy, Josiah's despair may have been prompted by the truly horrifying covenant curses in Deuteronomy 28:15–68.

The king directs his staff to "inquire of the LORD": that is, to get prophetic confirmation that this book is indeed divine word (34:21; see 18:4). They send the scroll to the prophet Huldah, wife of Shallum (34:22//2 Kgs. 22:14; other female prophets are Moses' sister Miriam [Exod. 15:20] and the judge Deborah [Judg. 4:4]). Huldah's prophecy (2 Chr. 34:23–28//2 Kgs. 22:15–20) confirms that the scroll is indeed divine word, and that the curses it describes will indeed come upon the land and its inhabitants, just as Josiah had feared. However, because Josiah has humbled himself, he will not see this evil; indeed, the Lord declares, "I will gather you to your ancestors and you shall be gathered to your grave in peace" (34:28//2 Kgs. 22:20). Unfortunately, this final word to Josiah is not fulfilled; Josiah in fact dies tragically, in battle (35:24). Still, for the Chronicler, it is in the words of prophets like Huldah that the word of God is encountered. Hence, although the Chronicler knows that this word did not come true, he preserves it 237 nonetheless—just as the editors of the Deuteronomistic History had.

The phenomenon of unfulfilled prophecy may be disturbing to

many readers. However, examples are not difficult to find. In Ezekiel 26:1–7, the prophet declares that Nebuchadnezzar will lay waste to Tyre; then, in a later-dated prophecy, Ezekiel states that, since Nebuchadnezzar had been unable to conquer Tyre, the Lord would give him Egypt instead (Ezek. 29:17–20). In Jonah 3:4, the prophet confidently delivers his message: "Forty days more, and Ninevah shall be overthrown!" However, when the people of Ninevah repent, God changes God's mind, and the city is preserved. Consider, too, the repeated assertion in Revelation that the end of the world will come soon (1:1–3; 22:12, 20). Clearly, the prophets were not infallible fortune tellers, given perfect visions of a fixed, immutable future. Prophecy, time, and divine providence are all more complex than that! We cannot approach the Bible as a magic book, which simply and infallibly answers all our questions about life and the future. The study and application of Scripture calls for prayer, hard work, and struggle. However, there is no work so deeply satisfying, or so much worth doing! For as Chronicles continually reminds us, if we seek God, we will *find* God.

In Chronicles as in Kings, Huldah's prophecy prompts Josiah to call for a ceremony of covenant renewal (34:29–33//2 Kgs. 23:1–3), a call that, again, parallels Hezekiah's reform (see 29:10). In 34:29–32, Josiah meets with all Judah and Jerusalem to renew their covenant with the Lord, just as in 2 Kings 23:1–3. Intriguingly, 34:30 reads "the priests and the Levites," where 2 Kings 23:2 has "the priests, the prophets." This may merely be a slip of the pen; after all, the pairing "priests and Levites" is common, and is of particular significance to the Chronicler. On the other hand, it may be a deliberate shift, reflecting either a prophetic role for the Levites (see 1 Chr. 25:1–5), or the displacement of prophets in the postexilic community by Levitical scribes and teachers, such as Ezra. Benjamin is added in 34:32, in keeping with the special role Benjamin plays in the entire Chronicler's History (see the discussion of 1 Chr. 7:6–12, above). The Chronicler also adds another verse, which extends the covenant to all Israel (34:33). Negatively, this verse states that the abominations were removed from the entire land. The Hebrew word rendered "abominations" in the NRSV is used in 33:2 for the idolatrous worship practiced by Manasseh, in imitation of the nations who had inhabited the land before Israel. Later in the Chronicler's History, in Ezra 9:1 and 11, the same word is used for the corrupt worship practices of the nations, which prompt Ezra to ban intermarriage. Josiah's reforms, then, rooted idolatry out of all Israel. Positively, 34:33 declares that Josiah "made all who were in Israel worship the LORD their God." This unity of faith would continue throughout Josiah's reign.

Now, Josiah celebrates a great Passover feast, just as Hezekiah had following his reforms (35:1–19//1 Esd. 1:1–22//2 Kgs. 23:21–23; compare 2 Chr. 30:1–27). The account in Chronicles is framed by references to 2 Kings (2 Chr. 35:1//2 Kgs. 23:21; 2 Chr. 35:18–19//2 Kgs. 23:22–23), but is unique in content. The Chronicler emphasizes that the procedures followed in Josiah's Passover are taken from the Torah (35:6, 12). While Hezekiah had been forced by circumstances to delay his Passover until the second month, Josiah's is held at the proper time (35:1; see 30:2–3): perhaps in part because Josiah encourages the priests, so that they are ready in sufficient numbers (35:2; see 29:34; 30:3). It is also held at the proper place, "in Jerusalem" (35:1//1 Esd. 1:1, compare 2 Kgs. 23:23), and with the proper personnel (35:2–6). Unlike Hezekiah's Passover, which was atypical in so many ways, the Chronicler aims to present Josiah's Passover as a model celebration.

Before the feast begins, Josiah gives a special charge to the Levites. He reminds them that they are no longer responsible for the physical portage of the ark and the tabernacle: the temple is in place, and the ark is at rest within it. From now on, their task is to serve in the liturgy of the temple (35:3; see 1 Chr. 23:24–32). Several features of Josiah's charge to the Levites are of particular interest. First, the Levites are identified as the teachers of all Israel (35:3). Teaching is a responsibility entrusted to the Levites throughout the Chronicler's History (see 17:7–9; Neh. 8:7–8). Second, the duties of the Levites are said to be spelled out in "the written directions of King David of Israel and the written directions of his son Solomon" (35:4). The importance of David and Solomon as founding figures of Israel's worship is here again stressed. That their directives are written down underlines the importance of text as the means by which God's word is expressed in Chronicles. The importance of Scripture is shown also in 35:6, which directs that the Levites are in everything to act "according to the word of the LORD by Moses." Finally, Josiah directs that the Levites are to be responsible for killing the Passover lamb. In Hezekiah's Passover as well, the Levites killed the Passover lamb; but there, this was necessary because many had come to the feast in a state of ritual impurity, and could not perform the act themselves (30:17). In Josiah's Passover, however, the slaughter of the Passover lamb has become a permanent Levitical responsibility (35:6, 11). Therefore, a particular division of Levites is given responsibility for each of the "ancestral houses of your kindred the people" (35:5)—that is, the laity (so Japhet 1993, 1049). Apparently, Levitical slaughter of the sacrifices was the practice in the Chronicler's own community (see also Ezra 6:20; Ezek. 44:11). Again as in Hezekiah's reforms, the animals for the sacrifices are provided by the king and his officials (35:7–9; see the discussion of 31:3, above).

239

Chapter 35:10–15 describes the actual celebration, with the proper roles and places for the priests and the Levites carefully prescribed. The

Levites slaughter and skin the animals, the priests offer the sacrifices to the Lord, and then the Levites prepare the peoples' portions and distribute them to the crowds. Note that the skinning of the Passover lambs (35:11) is distinct from the emergency service provided by the Levites in 29:34, where the Levites were skinning the burnt offerings. The Levitical musicians also participate in the Passover (35:15). However, the gatekeepers remain at their posts; their portions are prepared and brought to them by other Levites (35:15).

The preparation of the Passover meal provides an intriguing example of the Chronicler's exegetical methods. Exodus 12:9 directs that the Passover must not be boiled (Hebrew *bashal*) in water, but is rather to be roasted in fire. Deuteronomy 16:7, on the other hand, directs that the Passover *is* to be boiled (again, *bashal*). Confronted with these conflicting authoritative traditions from the Torah, the Chronicler refused to choose one or the other, but rather preserved them both "by an artificial, exegetical harmonization" (Fishbane 1985, 134). The MT of 35:13a reads literally, "Then they boiled [*bashal*] the Passover in fire according to the ordinance." While literally nonsensical, this curious statement enables the Chronicler to maintain his claim that Josiah's Passover was carried out in obedience to the whole Torah.

Following the Passover, the Feast of Unleavened Bread is observed for seven days—as in the case of Hezekiah's Passover, the two feasts are linked (35:17; see the discussion of 30:13, above). Chapter 35:18 states, "No passover like it had been kept in Israel since the days of the prophet Samuel" (compare 2 Kgs. 23:22). In view of the numerous parallels to Hezekiah's Passover, this may seem a surprising statement. However, Hezekiah's Passover was marred by numerous irregularities. As presented by the Chronicler, Josiah's Passover was celebrated precisely as it should have been. Further, the reference back to Samuel plays a part in the structure of the entire Chronicler's History. Hezekiah's Passover was said to be like nothing since the days of Solomon (30:26). Later, in Nehemiah 8:17, the Festival of Booths celebrated following the reading of Ezra's law is said to be like nothing since the days of Joshua. These three great feasts, which punctuate the Chronicler's History, look progressively further and further back into Israel's traditions, to the days and deeds of progressively more ancient heroes (Blenkinsopp 1988, 54). For the Chronicler, the present must build upon the foundation laid in Israel's past, in the ancient tradition—which is why he has written this book.

240

Now, we come to the tragic conclusion of Josiah's story. In order to understand the circumstances of Josiah's death, we need to know something of the political players in this drama. As we have seen, the collapse of Assyria had made Josiah's independence, and his reassertion of control over the north, possible. But even with the fall of Ninevah in 612 B.C., a remnant of the old empire clung to life in Haran. Unexpectedly, Assyria was propped up in its final hours by Egypt, a bitter Assyrian rival in the days of Manasseh. However, after the Assyrians invaded Egypt and sacked Thebes, the two enemies declared a peace in 665 B.C. The Saite Dynasty, which unified Egypt and sponsored a cultural renaissance, was founded by an Assyrian protégé, Psammetichus I (664–610 B.C.). By the end of his reign, Psammetichus was in control of much of the Mediterranean coast, with Philistia under his thumb. His successor, Necho II (610–595 B.C.), remained an Assyrian ally as long as there was an Assyria to support. So, when in 610 B.C. the last Assyrian king was forced to abandon Haran as well, Necho marched north to his aid.

Josiah intercepted Necho's army at the plains of Megiddo (35:22//2 Kgs. 23:29). His reasons for such a quixotic act are unclear. Perhaps Josiah feared that even a small Assyrian resurgence would mean the end of his independence. In Chronicles, Necho tries to dissuade the Judean king. The Pharaoh declares that God has sent him to the support of Assyria. He warns Josiah, "Cease opposing God, who is with me, so that he will not destroy you" (35:21). As it turns out, Necho's words actually do come "from the mouth of God" (35:22; compare 1 Esd. 1:28, where the warning is said to be from the prophet Jeremiah). Just as God had addressed David through the warrior Amasai (1 Chr. 12:18), and Joash through the priest Zechariah (2 Chr. 24:20), God speaks to Josiah through the Pharaoh. Josiah, however, ignores this prophetic word, and so disaster overtakes him.

In Chronicles, Josiah's end is very like the end of the wicked king Ahab, who also went to war in defiance of a prophetic warning (see 18:16). Like Ahab, Josiah goes into battle in disguise (compare 35:22 and 18:29; note that 1 Esdras lacks this). But Josiah's disguise proves as useless as Ahab's had been; like the old Israelite king, he is found by the enemy archers, and is mortally wounded (compare 35:23 and 18:33–34; 1 Esd. 1:29 says only that "the commanders came down against King Josiah"). Even the words spoken by the dying kings are alike (compare 35:23 and 18:33; note that the same Hebrew word, meaning "I am wounded," appears in both contexts). Perhaps the most tragic aspect of Josiah's sad story is that this righteous, reforming king should end up just like the wicked apostate Ahab. The moral for the Chronicler's community is plain: if they reject the word of God, they too will be swept away, despite their former righteousness. 241

Like his great grandfather Hezekiah, Josiah is buried in the royal cemetery, among his ancestors (35:24). He is mourned by all; indeed, the prophet Jeremiah composes a lament for the fallen king, though Chronicles does not include it (35:25). Ominously, Josiah's mourners do not include representatives of the northern tribes. With Josiah's death, the hopes for the reunification of David's kingdom die as well. However, the Chronicler's source for the righteous king's reign is, once more, "the Book of the Kings of Israel and Judah" (35:27; compare 2 Kgs. 23:28), so perhaps the dream is not dead, but merely deferred. Chronicles ends this account with an affirmation of Josiah's obedience to the Torah, which for the Chronicler is as fine an obituary as anyone could ask (35:26; compare 2 Kgs. 23:25, and the far more fulsome accolade in 1 Esd. 1:33).

36:1–21
The Decline and Fall of Judah

Josiah was the last independent king of Judah. From now on, Judah would be under the domination of one or another foreign power: first the Egyptians, then the Babylonians, then, in the Chronicler's own day, the Persians. The cause of this political decline and fall, in the Chronicler's view, was Judah's far more serious *spiritual* decline and fall, from the renewed faithfulness of all Israel in Josiah's reign (see 34:33) to persistent and universal faithlessness under Zedekiah (36:14–16). The final chapter of Chronicles swiftly summarizes the reigns of the last four kings of Judah, who presided over this spiritual collapse. The Chronicler's source is 2 Kings, although the events described there are condensed and differently interpreted.

Jehoahaz (36:1–4)
(//2 Kgs. 23:30–35//1 Esd. 1:34–38)

With the early, unexpected death of Josiah, the people of the land once more step forward, and name Josiah's youngest son Jehoahaz king in his father's place (see 1 Chr. 3:15). That the youngest son should be made king is unusual, but not without precedent. Solomon and Abijah were both youngest sons, named as heirs by their fathers; presumably, in naming Jehoahaz, the people of the land were carrying out Josiah's wishes. However, this choice is not permitted to stand. Within three months of Jehoahaz's accession, Necho, whose troops now occupy Palestine, deposes Jehoahaz and deports him to Egypt (36:4//2 Kgs.

23:34). The Pharaoh lays a heavy tribute on Judah, and appoints a new king of his own choosing: Jehoahaz' older brother Jehoiakim. Judah is now an Egyptian vassal.

Chronicles lacks the stereotypical negative judgment of Jehoahaz found in Kings (see 2 Kgs. 23:32). No mention is made of Jehoahaz's burial place, or of sources for his reign, but this information is lacking in 2 Kings as well (though 2 Kgs. 23:34 does record that Jehoahaz died in Egypt), and so its absence probably should not be read as a negative evaluation in this case. To the Chronicler, Jehoahaz is a nonentity, neither good nor evil, his reign too brief to make any impact either way. However, he does establish a pattern that will prevail through the rest of Chronicles: like Jehoahaz, and indeed like Judah itself, every king after Josiah will go into exile.

Jehoiakim (36:5–8)
(//2 Kgs. 23:36—24:7//1 Esd. 1:39–42)

The account of Jehoiakim's reign in Chronicles is so sharply abridged as to be cryptic. Nothing is said about Jehoiakim's shift of loyalties from Egypt to Babylon (2 Kgs. 24:1), doubtless prompted by the Babylonian defeat of the Egyptian army at Carchemish and Hamath, forcing the Egyptians to withdraw from Palestine (Horn and McCarter 1999, 193; see 2 Kgs. 24:7). Nor does the Chronicler record Jehoiakim's rebellion against Nebuchadnezzar (605–562 B.C.), which brought on the first siege of Jerusalem, leading ultimately to the first exile (2 Kgs. 24:1–2, 10–16). These gaps are not surprising, however; the Chronicler, as we have seen, is not interested in political motivations for events. In Chronicles, the Babylonian invasion comes about because of Jehoiakim's sin (36:5//2 Kgs. 23:37; 36:8//2 Kgs. 24:5).

Nor, in Chronicles, does Jehoiakim escape the consequences of his sin. While 2 Kings does not say so explicitly, it is presupposed that Jehoiakim died in the siege of Jerusalem, leaving it to his son Jehoiachin to surrender the city and save it from destruction. But in Chronicles, Jehoiakim is taken into exile, together with some of the sacred temple vessels (36:6–7). The exile of Jehoiakim is strongly reminiscent of the exile of Manasseh (33:11–13). However, we have no reason for thinking that the Chronicler is making use of any source apart from Kings here (although 36:6–7 is probably itself the source for the exile of Jehoiakim in Dan. 1:1–2). While 2 Kings 24:6 states that Jehoiakim "slept with his ancestors," it does not say explicitly that he died in Jerusalem, or that he was buried there. The Chronicler has drawn his own conclusions. As we have seen, in Chronicles *all* of Judah's last four kings go into exile.

243

Jehoiachin (36:9–10)
(//2 Kgs. 24:8–17//1 Esd. 1:43–46)

The reign of Jehoiachin as well is sharply condensed in Chronicles. The statement in 2 Chronicles 36:9 that Jehoiachin became king at the age of eight is a scribal error; note that the LXX and 1 Esdras 1:43 both have "eighteen," following 2 Kings 24:8. Further, the Chronicler's statement, "He did what was evil in the sight of the LORD" (36:9//2 Kgs. 24:9), would hardly be possible if Jehoiachin was too young to be accountable for his actions. Jehoiachin, like his father, is taken into exile in Babylon, along with still more sacred vessels. The Chronicler does not mention the large body of persons exiled along with Jehoiachin, probably in order to keep his story simple and straightforward: Jehoiachin is exiled for his own wickedness; later, the people will be exiled for theirs. Neither Kings nor Chronicles mention sources for Jehoiachin's reign, or his burial place. In Kings, this may be because Jehoiachin had not yet died at the time the Deuteronomistic History was completed (see 25:27–30), and because his reign was so short that no official entry was written for him in the Annals of the Kings of Judah (as was also the case for Jehoahaz).

Zedekiah and the Fall of Jerusalem (36:11–21)
(//2 Kgs. 24:18—25:21//1 Esd. 1:46b–58)

Just as Pharaoh Necho had installed Jehoiakim on the throne in Jerusalem, Nebuchadnezzar installs Jehoiachin's brother, Zedekiah (for the relationship between Zedekiah and Jehoiachin, see the discussion of 1 Chr. 3:16, above). Chronicles alludes in its account of Zedekiah not only to 2 Kings, but also to Jeremiah, noting that Zedekiah ignored this prophet, "who spoke from the mouth of the LORD" (36:12). The specific reference appears to be to Jeremiah 27, where the prophet declares in the Lord's name, "Bring your necks under the yoke of the king of Babylon, and serve him and his people, and live" (Jer. 27:12). Zedekiah, however, refuses to humble himself, and so brings upon himself suffering and exile. The prophet Ezekiel also condemns Zedekiah as a covenant breaker: "Because he despised the oath and broke the covenant, because he gave his hand and yet did all these things, he shall not escape" (Ezek. 17:18).

Zedekiah's rebellion against Babylon is, more seriously, a rebellion against God, and an act of impiety. Oaths of fealty in the ancient world were sworn in the name of the gods, who were called upon as witnesses and guarantors of the covenant between the king and his vassals. Neb-

244

uchadnezzar had made Zedekiah "swear by God" (36:13). By breaking this covenant and rebelling against Babylon, Zedekiah has sworn falsely in the Lord's name, and brought condemnation upon himself.

But Zedekiah is not alone in his faithlessness. Priests and people alike "were exceedingly unfaithful" (36:14). Chapter 36:15–16 reads like a summary of Judah's sorry history. Like Manasseh, they have worshiped abominations, and polluted the temple. Like Asa, Joash, and even Josiah, they have repeatedly rejected the prophetic word, and so rejected God. In the end, there is no recourse but destruction and exile.

Chapter 36:17–19 rapidly summarizes the account of exile and destruction in 2 Kings. The people are slain, the temple is destroyed, the walls and palaces of Jerusalem are toppled and burned. However, a note of hope is found in 36:20–21. The exile will not be forever. The survivors of Jerusalem's destruction will be the slaves of Babylon "until the establishment of the kingdom of Persia" (36:20). The Chronicler, of course, knows that the exile had ended when Cyrus the Great of Persia conquered Babylon in 537 B.C., and issued his edict setting the exiles free. The mention of the Persians also serves as a flash forward, to the Chronicler's own time.

The duration of the exile is explained by reference to the prophet Jeremiah, who had declared that the exile would last seventy years (Jer. 25:11–12; 29:10). However, the seventy-year period itself is further explained by reference to Torah. According to Leviticus 25:1–7, the land is to be given a sabbath every seventh year. Nothing is to be planted, nor is any formal harvest to take place; "there shall be a sabbath of complete rest for the land, a sabbath for the LORD" (Lev. 25:4). Following the seventh sabbatical year, the fields are to be left fallow for an additional year, the year of jubilee (Lev. 25:8–12). The sabbatical years could be regarded as good agricultural practice: letting fields lie fallow allows the soil to replenish itself. However, Leviticus does not regard this as a practical matter, but a spiritual one. The land is the Lord's; by setting apart a time when no one can use the land for personal profit, the law emphasizes this divine ownership.

In Leviticus 26:14–33, the consequences for violating God's commandments, particularly regarding the land's sabbaths, are presented in an escalating scale. The ultimate penalty is devastation and exile; "Then the land shall enjoy its sabbath years as long as it lies desolate, while you are in the land of your enemies; then the land shall rest, and enjoy its sabbath years" (Lev. 26:34). Second Chronicles 36:21 understands the years of exile in just this way. The notion that the exile was a punishment for sabbath-breaking is expressed as well in the prophecies of

Jeremiah (see Jer. 17:19–27) and Ezekiel (for example, Ezek. 20:1–32). To this, however, Chronicles and Leviticus add an element of rehabilitation. After seventy sabbatical years, the land would once more be healed and holy. Israel would be able to begin again.

36:22–23

Postscript: the Edict of Cyrus
(//Ezra 1:1–3)

The final verses of Chronicles are taken, virtually word for word, from the opening verses of Ezra. This, added to the absence of these verses in 1 Esdras, strongly suggests that 36:22–23 was not originally a part of Chronicles, but has been added to emphasize the connection between Chronicles and Ezra–Nehemiah (see the discussion of this point in the Introduction). The words are taken from the edict of Cyrus, permitting the exiles to return and rebuild the temple.

Ending on these words, Chronicles has come full circle. The temple, built by Solomon in accordance with David's design, had been destroyed—brought to nothing by the faithlessness of God's people. But now, the temple is to be rebuilt; the ancient liturgy is to be celebrated once more. The fate of this temple, the Chronicler implies, is in the hands of his community. The invitation has been issued: "Whoever is among you of all his people, may the LORD his God be with him! Let him go up" (36:23). It is left to the reader to respond.

BIBLIOGRAPHY

For Further Study

Ackroyd, Peter R. Chronicles, the First and Second Books of the. Pages 163–65 in *Harper's Bible Dictionary*. Edited by Paul J. Achtemeier. San Francisco: Harper and Row, 1985.

Allen, Leslie. 1 and 2 Chronicles. Pages 299–659 in *The New Interpreter's Bible*, vol. 3. Edited by Leander E. Keck. Nashville: Abingdon, 1999.

Braun, Roddy. 1 Chronicles and 2 Chronicles. Pages 342–71 in *Harper's Bible Commentary*. Edited by James L. Mays. San Francisco: Harper and Row, 1988.

Elmslie, W. A. L. *The Books of Chronicles*. The Cambridge Bible for Schools and Colleges. Cambridge: Cambridge University Press, 1916.

Japhet, Sara. *I & II Chronicles*. The Old Testament Library. Louisville, Ky.: Westminster/John Knox, 1993.

———. Chronicles, Book of. Pages 517–34 in vol. 5 of *Encyclopaedia Judaica* 5. Jerusalem: Keter, 1971.

Johnstone, William. *1 and 2 Chronicles,* vol 5. Journal for the Study of the Old Testament Supplements 253 and 254. Sheffield: Sheffield Academic Press, 1997.

Klein, Ralph W. Chronicles, Book of 1–2. Pages 992–1002 in vol. 1 of *Anchor Bible Dictionary*. Edited by David Noel Freedman. New York: Doubleday, 1992.

———. Introduction and Notes to 1 and 2 Chronicles. Pages 605–98 in *HarperCollins Study Bible*. Edited by Wayne Meeks. San Francisco: HarperCollins, 1993.

Myers, Jacob M. *I and II Chronicles*. Anchor Bible 12 and 13. Garden City, N.Y.: Doubleday, 1965.

Selman, Martin J. *1 and 2 Chronicles: An Introduction and Commentary,* 2 vols. Leicester, England: Inter-Varsity Press, 1994.

Williamson, H. G. M. *1 and 2 Chronicles*. New Century Bible Commentary. Grand Rapids: Eerdmans; London: Marshall, Morgan, & Scott, 1982.

Literature Cited

Ackroyd, Peter R. 1985. Chronicles, the First and Second Books of the. Pp. 163–65 in *Harper's Bible Dictionary*. Edited by Paul J. Achtemeier. San Francisco: Harper & Row.

Albright, William F. 1920. The Babylonian Temple-tower and the Altar of Burnt-Offering, *Journal of Biblical Literature* [*JBL*] 1:140–41.

Alexander, Philip. 1988. Retelling the Old Testament, in *It Is Written: Scripture Citing Scripture: Essays in Honour of Barnabas Lindars, SSF.* Ed. by D. A. Carson and H. G. M. Williamson. Cambridge: Cambridge University Press.

Allen, Leslie. 1999. 1 and 2 Chronicles, in *The New Interpreter's Bible,* vol. 3. Ed. by Leander E. Keck. Nashville: Abingdon.

Best Loved Songs and Hymns. 1961. Ed. by Ruth W. Shelton. Dayton, Tenn.: R. E. Winsett.

Bickerman, Elias. 1962. *From Ezra to the Last of the Maccabees: Foundations of Post-Biblical Judaism.* New York: Shocken.

Blenkinsopp, Joseph. 1988. *Ezra–Nehemiah.* Old Testament Library. Philadelphia: Westminster Press.

Boraas, Roger. 1985. Seba, Sabeans, in *Harper's Bible Dictionary.*

Bordreuil, Pierre, Felix Israel, and Dennis Pardee. 1998. King's Command and Widow's Plea: Two New Hebrew Ostraca of the Biblical Period, in *Near Eastern Archaeology* 61.

Boyce, Mary. 1984. Persian Religion in the Achemenid Age, in *Introduction: The Persian Period.* Vol. 1 of *The Cambridge History of Judaism.* Ed. by W. D. Davies and Louis Finkelstein. Cambridge: Cambridge University Press.

Braun, Roddy. 1988. 1 Chronicles *and* 2 Chronicles, in *Harper's Bible Commentary.* Ed. by James L. Mays. San Francisco: Harper and Row.

Bright, John. 1981. *History of Israel,* 3d ed. Philadelphia: Westminster.

Childs, Brevard. 1979. *Introduction to the Old Testament as Scripture.* Philadelphia: Fortress.

Cody, Aelred. 1969. *A History of Old Testament Priesthood.* Vol. 35 of Analecta Biblica. Rome: Pontifical Biblical Institute.

Cross, Frank Moore, Jr. 1998. Kinship and Covenant in Ancient Israel, in *From Epic to Canon: History and Literature in Ancient Israel.* Baltimore: Johns Hopkins University Press.

———. 1975. A Reconstruction of the Judean Restoration. *Interpretation* [*Int.*] 29.

———. 1973a. The Priestly Houses of Early Israel, in *Canaanite Myth and Hebrew Epic: Essays in the History of the Religion of Israel.* Cambridge, Mass.: Harvard University Press.

———. 1973b. The Themes of the Book of Kings and the Structure of the Deuteronomistic History, in *Canaanite Myth and Hebrew Epic.* Cambridge, Mass.: Harvard University Press.

deVries, Simon. 1988. Moses and David as Cult Founders in Chronicles, in *JBL* 107.

Dickens, Charles. 1976 [1843]. *A Christmas Carol.* In *A Charles Dickens Christmas.* New York: Oxford University Press.

Dillard, Annie. 1984. *Holy the Firm.* New York: Harper.

Donner, Herbert. 1977. The Separate States of Israel and Judah, in *Israelite and Judean History.* Ed. by John H. Hayes and J. Maxwell Miller. London: SCM Press.

Elmslie, W. A. L. 1916. *The Books of Chronicles.* The Cambridge Bible for Schools and Colleges. Cambridge: Cambridge University Press.

Finkelstein, J. J., trans. 1969. The Laws of Ur-Nammu, in *Ancient Near Eastern Texts Relating to the Old Testament [ANET].* Ed. by James B. Pritchard. Princeton: Princeton University Press.

Fishbane, Michael. 1985. *Biblical Interpretation in Ancient Israel.* Oxford: Clarendon Press.

Freedman, David Noel. 1961. The Chronicler's Purpose, in *Catholic Biblical Quarterly [CBQ]* 23.

Friedman, Richard Elliot. 1987. *Who Wrote the Bible?* New York: Harper and Row.

Gelston, Anthony. 1996. The End of Chronicles, in *Scandinavian Journal of the Old Testament* 10:53–60.

Hanson, Paul. 1975. *The Dawn of Apocalyptic.* Philadelphia: Fortress.

Hendel, Ronald S. 1996. The Date of the Siloam Inscription: A Rejoinder to Rogerson and Davies, in *Biblical Archaeology* 58.

Herdner, A., ed. 1963. *Corpus des Tablettes en Cunéiformes alphabétiques.* Paris: Imprimerie Nationale.

Hoglund, Kenneth G. 1997. The Chronicler as Historian: A Comparativist Perspective, in *The Chronicler as Historian.* Journal for the Study of the Old Testament Supplement [JSOTS] 238. Ed. by M. Patrick Graham, Kenneth G. Hoglund, and Steven L. McKenzie. Sheffield: Sheffield Academic Press.

Horn, Siegfried, and P. Kyle McCarter. 1999. The Divided Monarchy: The Kingdoms of Israel and Judah, in *Ancient Israel,* revised and expanded edition. Ed. by Hershel Shanks. Washington, D.C.: Biblical Archaeology Society.

Jacobsen, Thorkild. 1987. *The Harps That Once . . . Sumerian Poetry in Translation.* New Haven and London: Yale University Press.

Japhet, Sara. 1993. *I & II Chronicles.* The Old Testament Library. Louisville, Ky.: Westminster/John Knox.

Johnstone, William. 1998. *Chronicles and Exodus: An Analogy and its Application,* JSOTS 275. Sheffield: Sheffield Academic Press.

249

Klein, Ralph W. 1974. *Textual Criticism and the Old Testament: From the Septuagint to Qumran*. Philadelphia: Fortress.

———. 1992. Book of 1–2 Chronicles, in *Anchor Bible Dictionary*, vol. 1. Ed. by Noel Freedman. New York: Doubleday.

———. 1993. Introduction and Notes to 1 and 2 Chronicles, in *Harper-Collins Study Bible*. Ed. by Wayne Meeks. San Francisco: Harper-Collins.

Knauf, Ernst Azel. 1992. Seir, in *Anchor Bible Dictionary*, vol. 5.

Knoppers, Gary. 1999. Hierodules, Priests, or Janitors? The Levites in Chronicles and the History of the Israelite Priesthood, in *JBL* 118.

Lichtheim, Miriam. 1980. *The Late Period*. Vol. 3 in *Ancient Egyptian Literature*. Berkeley: University of California Press.

Lipinski, E. 1978. North Semitic Texts, in *Near Eastern Religious Texts Relating to the Old Testament*. Ed. by Walter Beyerlin. Translated by John Bowden. Philadelphia: Westminster.

Mays, James Luther. 1994. *Psalms*. Interpretation series. Louisville, Ky.: John Knox Press.

McBride, S. Dean, Jr. 1973. Jeremiah and the 'Men of Anatot,' a paper presented to the Colloquium for Old Testament Research at the Colgate-Rochester Divinity School. (August 23.)

Meyers, Carol and Eric. 1993. *Zechariah 9—14*. Anchor Bible Series, vol. 25C. Garden City, N.Y.: Doubleday.

Meyers, Carol. 1992. Jachin and Boaz, in *Anchor Bible Dictionary*, vol. 3.

Milgrom, Jacob. 1970. *Studies in Levitical Terminology, I: The Encroacher and the Levite; The Term 'Aboda*. University of California Publications, Near Eastern Studies 14. Berkeley: University of California Press.

Mosis, Rudolf. 1973. *Untersuchungen zur Theologie des chronistischen Geschichtswerkes*. Freiburg.

Myers, Jacob M. 1965. *I and II Chronicles*. Volumes 12 and 13 of Anchor Bible Series. Garden City, N.Y.: Doubleday.

Na'aman, Nadar. 1986. Hezekiah's Fortified Cities and the LMLK Stamp, *Bulletin of the American Schools of Oriental Research* 261.

Oppenheim, A. Leo, trans. 1969. Babylonian and Assyrian Historical Texts, in *Ancient Near Eastern Texts Relating to the Old Testament*, 3d ed. (ANET). Ed. by James B. Pritchard. Princeton: Princeton University Press.

Otto, Rudolph. 1958 [1936]. *The Idea of the Holy*. Trans. by John W. Harvey. New York: Oxford University Press.

Pritchard, James B., ed. 1969. *The Ancient Near East in Pictures Relating to the Old Testament (ANEP)*. Princeton: Princeton University Press.

Rosenthal, Franz, trans. Canaanite and Aramaic Inscriptions, in *ANET.*

Rowley, Harold H. 1939. Zadok and Nehushtan, in *JBL* 58.

Schniedewind, William M. 1995. *The Word of God in Transition: From Prophet to Exegete in the Second Temple Period.* JSOTS 197.

Shanks, Hershel. 1999. Biran at Ninety, *Biblical Archaeology Review* 25.

Shea, William H. 1999. Jerusalem Under Siege: Did Sennacherib Attack Twice? in *Biblical Archaeology Review* 25.

Smith, Mark. 1992. Rephaim, in the *Anchor Bible Dictionary*, vol. 5.

Stinespring, W. F. 1992. Temple, Jerusalem, in *The Interpreter's Dictionary of the Bible,* vol. 4. Ed. by George Arthur Buttrick. Nashville: Abingdon Press.

Tarr, Herbert. 1987. Chronicles, in *Congregation: Contemporary Jewish Writers Read the Jewish Bible.* Ed. by David Rosenberg. San Diego: Harcourt Brace Jovanovich.

Throntveit, Mark. 1992. *Ezra-Nehemiah.* Interpretation series. Louisville, Ky.: John Knox Press.

———. Linguistic Analysis and the Question of Authorship in Chronicles, Ezra and Nehemiah, *Vetus Testamentum* 32.

Tuell, Steven. 1992. *The Law of the Temple in Ezekiel 40—48.* Harvard Semitic Monographs 49.

United Methodist Hymnal. 1989. Nashville: United Methodist Publishing House.

van der Kooij, Arie. 1991. On the Ending of the Book of 1 Esdras, in *VII Congress of the International Organization for Septuagint and Cognate Studies, Leuven, 1989.* Ed. by C. E. Cox. Atlanta: Scholars Press.

Vaughan, Andrew G. 1999. *Theology, History, and Archaeology in the Chronicler's Account of Hezekiah.* Archaeology and Biblical Studies, vol. 4. Atlanta: Scholars Press.

Wellhausen, Julius. 1885. *Prolegomena to the History of Ancient Israel.* Reprint, New York: Meridian Books, 1957. Edinburgh: Black.

Welten, Peter. 1985. *Geschichte und Geschichtsdarstellung in den Chronikbüchern,* in Wissenschaftliche Monographien zum Alten und Neuen Testament, vol. 42. Neukirchen: Neukirchener Verlag.

Williamson, H. G. M. 1996. The Problem with First Esdras, in *After the Exile: Essays in Honour of Rex Mason.* Edited by John Barton and David J. Reimer. Macon, Ga.: Mercer University Press.

———. 1982. *1 and 2 Chronicles.* The New Century Bible Commentary Series, Grand Rapids: Eerdmans; London: Marshall, Morgan, & Scott.

———. 1977. *Israel in the Books of Chronicles.* Cambridge: Cambridge University Press.

Wood, Ralph. 1994, November 16. Flannery O'Connor's Racial Morals and Manners, in *The Christian Century* 111.

Wright, John W. 1998. The Founding Father: The Structure of the Chronicler's David Narrative, in *JBL* 117.

Yadin, Yigael. 1983. *The Temple Scroll,* Volume 1: Introduction. Jerusalem: Israel Exploration Society.

Zunz, Leopold. 1892. Dibre hajamim oder die Bücher der Chronik, in *Die gottesdienstlichen Vorträge der Juden, historisch entwickelt.* Frankfurt: J. Kauffmann.